D1519047

Re(con)figuring Psychoanalysis

Re(con)figuring Psychoanalysis

Critical Juxtapositions of the Philosophical, the Sociohistorical and the Political

Edited by

Aydan Gülerce
Boğaziçi University, Turkey

First published 2012 by
PALGRAVE MACMILLAN

Palgrave Macmillan in the UK is an imprint of Macmillan Publishers Limited,
registered in England, company number 785998, of Houndmills, Basingstoke,
Hampshire RG21 6XS.

Palgrave Macmillan in the US is a division of St Martin's Press LLC,
175 Fifth Avenue, New York, NY 10010.

Palgrave Macmillan is the global academic imprint of the above companies
and has companies and representatives throughout the world.

Palgrave® and Macmillan® are registered trademarks in the United States,
the United Kingdom, Europe and other countries.

ISBN 978–0–230–29375–5

This book is printed on paper suitable for recycling and made from fully
managed and sustained forest sources. Logging, pulping and manufacturing
processes are expected to conform to the environmental regulations of the
country of origin.

A catalogue record for this book is available from the British Library.

A catalog record for this book is available from the Library of Congress.

10   9   8   7   6   5   4   3   2   1
21 20 19 18 17 16 15 14 13 12

Printed and bound in the United States of America
by Edwards Brothers Malloy, Inc.

to:
all infants of all times
for:
reminding us about the '   '

Contents

List of Illustrations

Preface

Following the Lacanian return to Freud and the feminist return to Kleinian object-relations theory, psychoanalysis has been fascinating and refashioning scholars in social, political, cultural, literary and film studies fields over the past several decades. However, it has continued to be underutilized, if not rejected, across Americanized and asociocultural psychological circles, for various reasons including the fundamental differences that outweigh their common interests such as subjectivity. Notwithstanding the mainstream majority, and against the biologizing, interiorizing and individualizing tendencies of its own tradition, revitalization of psychoanalysis has been gradually increasing among the psychoanalytically informed and critically minded psychologists. This book offers recent insights on and challenges to some leading figures in psychoanalysis by those scholars who do not doubt the relevance of psychoanalysis to today's world focused as they are on the *feminist, philosophical, critical, discursive* and *psychosocial* fields of academic psychology.

As for the background and the legitimate question of representation of this collection, the volume can be viewed as an 'end product' of a pending/continuously revisioned project. Previously, my fantasies and attempts – to bring dialogically together, first, some 'insiders' to psychoanalysis with political, social and cultural theorists who are inspired by post-Freudians, and then, international psychoanalysts from various continents to reflect on psychoanalysis from their own geopolitical and cultural 'locations' at a time of its rapid globalization – were only partially realized. Thus, it seemed to me not only more realistic this time to gather psychoanalytic theoreticians and/or practitioners who are affiliated with the International Society for Theoretical Psychology, but even more interesting to facilitate some conversations on how they see themselves in relation to the notion of 'psychoanalysis as sociohistorical and political critique' while still aiming at a transdisciplinary readership. Therefore, I am grateful to all the participants who responded to my invitation to critically (re)visit some conceptual and/or controversial sites of sociopolitical significance within the broad psychodynamic (meta)paradigm with particular reference to its liberatory potentials for different subjectivities and contexts.

Some aspects of this volume merit further comments. I believe the authors share a (non-territorial) concern not with psychoanalysis' 'seduction' of other fields, but perhaps with its inept 'uses' such as superficial appropriations of its theory of subjectivity (without thorough appreciation of the complexities in its full account), the psychopathologization of societies/communities and so forth. That puts the contributors in an understandably difficult (knowledge-practice) position as the 'insiders', particularly in the current hybrid intellectual culture of genre-mixing which is 'allergic' to any disciplinary 'expertise' or 'authority'. Of equal interest to the authors is what psychoanalysis has been bringing 'home' from those cross-(sub)disciplinary dialogues 'outside' the clinic. So the book implicitly attempts a small step towards the main challenge that is envisaged: How do psychologists/psychoanalysts themselves critically interpret/transfer not only the knowledge of the individual to the societal and the political within the same discourse, but also translate psychoanalysis' own deep/latent/subtextual content (say, libidinal economy) to the surface/manifest/textual level of some other *language games* of collective action (say, political economy) without losing its 'core meanings', 'rigour', 'sex appeal' and 'mystery'? That, to me at least, seems an unavoidable task for psychoanalysis' own dialogical moves, intelligible and legitimate turns for fair-plays out in the 'open' intellectual space and transdisciplinary praxis.

I would like to thank Palgrave Macmillan for the realization of this publication, in particular Monica Kendall for her meticulous copy-editing work, and Begüm Özdemir for her clerical assistance whenever I needed it.

Aydan Gülerce
Boğaziçi University
Istanbul, Turkey

Notes on Contributors

Lisa Baraitser is a feminist writer, a psychotherapist and Senior Lecturer in Psychosocial Studies at Birkbeck College, University of London, UK. She is the author of *Maternal Encounters: The Ethics of Interruption* (2009), and founder of MaMSIE (Mapping Maternal Subjectivities, Identities and Ethics).

Peter Branney is Senior Research Fellow in the Centre for Men's Health, Leeds Metropolitan University, UK. He is particularly interested in critically exploring contemporary issues around gender and health while developing and evaluating appropriate methods of enquiry.

Stephen Frosh is Pro-Vice-Master, Head of the Department of Psychosocial Studies and Professor of Psychology at Birkbeck College, University of London, UK. He is the author of many books and papers on psychosocial studies and on psychoanalysis, including *Hate and the Jewish Science: Anti-Semitism, Nazism and Psychoanalysis* (Palgrave, 2005), *For and Against Psychoanalysis* (2006), *After Words* (Palgrave, 2002), *The Politics of Psychoanalysis* (Palgrave, 1999) and *Psychoanalysis Outside the Clinic* (Palgrave, 2010).

Abe Geldhof, MSc, is a clinical psychologist. He is preparing a PhD at the Department of Psychoanalysis and Clinical Consulting at Ghent University, Belgium, on Lacan's theory concerning the status of *jouissance* in psychosis, and also works in private practice.

Brendan Gough is Chair in Social Psychology at Nottingham Trent University, UK. He has published various papers on gender identities and relations which draw upon discursive and psychoanalytic concepts, including areas such as sexism, homophobia and men's health. Brendan is co-editor of *Qualitative Research & Psychology* and *Social Psychology & Personality Compass* (Critical Psychology Section), and is co-author of *Critical Social Psychology* (with M. McFadden, 2001), *Reflexivity in Qualitative Research* (with L. Finlay, 2003) and *Masculinity and Men's Health* (with S. Robertson, 2009).

Aydan Gülerce is Professor of Clinical Psychology at Boğaziçi University in Istanbul, Turkey. She has published in various areas including metatheory, critical psychology, psychoanalysis, discourse analysis, cultural psychology, individual and social change, family assessment and therapy, (inter)subjectivity and transdisciplinarity. She is the founding editor of *Social Practice/Psychological Theory*, and is on the editorial boards of *International Journal of Idiographic Science, Journal of Multicultural Discourses* and *Culture & Psychology*.

Grahame Hayes lives in Durban and retired from the University of KwaZulu-Natal, Durban, South Africa at the end of 2011. He is a founding, and current managing, editor of the journal *PINS* (*Psychology in Society*). He is interested in the social application of psychoanalytic ideas and has published in this area.

Derek Hook is a Lecturer in Psychosocial Studies at Birkbeck College, London, UK, and a visiting Associate Professor in Psychology at the University of the Witwatersrand, Johannesburg, South Africa. He is the author of *Foucault, Psychology and the Analytics of Power* (Palgrave, 2007) and of *Critical Psychology of the Postcolonial* (2011). He is also a founding editor of the journal *Subjectivity* (Palgrave).

Shannon D. Kelly, LPC, is a psychotherapist, practising in community mental health in Georgia, USA. She has given presentations and published articles in the areas of Lacanian psychoanalysis, clinical ethics, addiction treatment and gender studies.

Anna Madill is Reader in the Institute of Psychological Sciences at the University of Leeds, UK. She is co-founder and current Chair of the British Psychological Society Qualitative Methods in Psychology Section, is Associate Editor of the *British Journal of Clinical Psychology*, and is on the editorial boards of the *British Journal of Social Psychology* and the journal *Qualitative Research in Psychology*.

Kareen Ror Malone is Professor of Psychology at the University of West Georgia, USA. She is Associate Editor of *Theory & Psychology* and has co-edited three volumes of Lacanian psychoanalysis. She is the author of numerous chapters, articles, reviews in the areas of Lacanian psychoanalysis, gender, race and science, feminism and the epistemology of psychology, cognitive psychology and subjectivity.

Mandy Morgan is Associate Professor in Critical Psychology and Head of the School of Psychology at Massey University in Aotearoa/New Zealand. She has particular interests in theoretical debates concerning the relationships between feminism, poststructuralism and psychology, and has published in a variety of places, including the journal *Theory & Psychology*.

Calum Neill is a Lecturer in Critical Psychology at the School of Health & Social Sciences at Edinburgh Napier University, Scotland. His research interest includes intersubjectivity, political subjectivity, Lacanian discourse analysis and Lacan's ethics. He is on the editorial boards of the *International Journal of Žižek Studies* and the *Annual Review of Critical Psychology* and is author of *Lacanian Ethics and the Assumption of Subjectivity* (Palgrave, 2011).

Bert Olivier is Professor of Philosophy at the Nelson Mandela Metropolitan University in Port Elizabeth, South Africa. He has published widely in the philosophy of culture, of art and architecture, of cinema, music and literature, as well as the philosophy of science, epistemology, psychoanalytic, social, media and discourse-theory.

Narcisa Paredes-Canilao is Professor of Philosophy at the University of the Philippines Baguio. Her teaching and research interests are feminism, epistemology of the sciences and the social sciences, and discourse with special focus on metaphors and their foundational role in knowledge.

Ian Parker is Professor of Psychology in the Discourse Unit at Manchester Metropolitan University, UK, where he is also managing editor of *Annual Review of Critical Psychology*. He has published extensively, and his books include *Psychoanalytic Culture: Psychoanalytic Discourse in Western Society* (1997) and *Slavoj Žižek: A Critical Introduction* (2004).

Stijn Vanheule is Associate Professor of Clinical Psychology in the Department of Psychoanalysis and Clinical Consulting at Ghent University, Belgium. He is the author of *The Subject of Psychosis: A Lacanian Perspective* (Palgrave 2011), and multiple papers in the areas of Lacanian and Freudian psychoanalysis, psychoanalytic research into psychopathology, psychoanalytically informed clinical psychodiagnostics, and the methodological fields of qualitative and small sample research.

List of Abbreviations

SE   *The Standard Edition of the Complete Psychological Works of Sigmund Freud*, trans. from German under the general editorship of James Strachey, in collaboration with Anna Freud, assisted by Alix Strachey and Alan Tyson, 24 vols (1953–74). London: Hogarth Press and the Institute of Psycho-Analysis.

Entrance: Contemporary Conditions of (Im)possibility and a Revisionary Meaning Context of Psychoanalysis

Aydan Gülerce

It is highly likely that the broad and charged title of this book, *Re(con)figuring Psychoanalysis: Critical Juxtapositions of the Philosophical, the Sociohistorical and the Political*, will lead your imagination to an infinite intellectual space that its content certainly is not able to explore, to visit or even to articulate, just as it presents me with ample possibilities at the moment, while I search for an opening line. If I have not found one and have not begun already, I think, I am about to opt for a collage of some (motion) pictures of humanity in its current appearances in the real world, which one can easily gather by simply turning to everyday life, to multivariant channels of mass media and to social networks worldwide. On the one hand, we are faced with wars and the industrialization of war; brutal killings, terrorism, violence against 'identified' groups based on their gender, age, race, religion, nation, ethnicity and various other differences/preferences; extreme poverty and the deep gap between the rich and the poor; the destruction of nature, global warming and other environmental issues, including nuclear threat; serious hunger, hygiene and epidemic health problems; new forms of imperialism and global capitalism; economic crisis and unemployment; population growth, unregulated urbanization and migration; the exploitation of children and the disabled; unequal access to literacy, to education, to knowledge and to other cultural sources; exclusion and all sorts of oppression and discrimination against the 'different'; distrust in modern medicine; dissolution of familial/social relations and psychological isolation; anxieties about loss of meaning and human(ist) values concerning love, intimacy, privacy, security, honesty, loyalty, responsibility and morality; social injustice and corruption; fundamental religious and neo-fascist movements; and so on. On the other, what we see

1

are extreme affluence, scientific and technological advancements; rapid (re)production and circulation of excessive information; computerized technology and communication; increased mobility; flexible and multiple opportunities in many domains of life; social networks of solidarity for a more humane world; public resistance against oppressive governance; anti-imperialist and anti-autocratic 'Third World' revolutionary movements; and various celebratory discursive practices of social justice, democracy, human rights, feminism, children's rights, 'identity' rights, freedom of speech, diversity, inclusion, empowerment, institutional reforms, global health, a sustainable planet, world peace, love, faith and so on. The confusion between new potentials and optimistic opportunities for some societies, communities, groups and individuals, and yet disruption, suffering and pessimism for many others, is considerably high.

If we pause for a moment and listen to the remarks on what these issues are all about, the (still) picture gets more complicated and even ironic: One's 'global' is 'local' to another, one's 'abject' is 'free agent' to another, one's 'anxiety' is 'harmony' to another, one's 'uncertainty' is 'security' to another, one's 'democracy' is 'hypocrisy' to another, one's 'liberation' is 'oppression' to another, one's 'new' is 'old' to another, one's 'wealth' is 'poverty' to another, one's 'science' is 'common sense' to another, one's 'knowledge' is 'ignorance' to another, one's 'symmetry' is 'asymmetry' to another, one's 'metaphor' is a 'thing-itself' to another, one's 'depth' is 'surface' to another, one's 'irrational' is 'rational' to another, and many more controversions. In the meantime, sceptics and affirmatives are now divided on new arguments for contemporary (Western[1]) culture and thought, as they cannot decide easily whether our times point at 'late modernity' (Harvey, 1989; Jameson, 1984), 'risk society' (Beck, 1992; Giddens, 1991) or 'postmodernity' (Baudrillard, 1988; Lyotard, 1984), which indicates various ruptures, such as the 'end of history' (Fukuyama, 1989), 'end of ideology' (Bell, 1960), 'death of the subject' (Althusser, 1969; Derrida, 1976), 'end of scientific Truth' (Feyerabend, 1975) and so forth.

Perhaps, nothing but a *borderline paradox* (without any pathological connotations whatsoever) can best describe the current picture of global community. I here am simultaneously referring to both our global sociohistorical life conditions and the hegemonic knowledge-practices that have been *worlding* (in Heidegger's sense) the collective intellectual space. I risk to use this saturated, or empty, and yet generic term of 'borderline' in order to signify not only the wide spectrum of paradoxes which puzzle the concerned and reflective intellectuals in respect to many crucial topics, such as truth, justice, equality, reality, knowledge, representation, science, accuracy, legitimacy, belief, ideology, rationality, modernity, society, global capitalist order, technology, autonomy, self, subjectivity, identity, authenticity, meaning, culture, diversity, integrity, sanity, change and so forth, to name only a few. But also to the entrapment that almost all peoples experience at gut level themselves, directly or vicariously, as *participant observers* of our times. They are both the recipients and co(re)producers of many contradictory messages which oscillate between dramatic extremes, perhaps more than ever before.

Nonetheless, and from a macro *postglocal*[2] perspective, there is something tragically ironic about our times that also calls for the use of 'borderline' as a metaphor and for this particular interpretation: It is understandable perhaps that one side of the geopolitical border on the Shakespearean theatre of the world, that is the 'noble' and early industrialized, 'developed' 'New World', the so-called Western(ized) modernity, narrates this ambiguity as an 'acute state' or a 'passing phase', judged by its own criteria and worldview. Let us call that, if you will, a *borderline crisis* and a 'temporary' *regress*. Whereas for the other(ed) side, the 'primitive' and 'premodern', 'underdeveloped' 'Old World', this *double-binding* (in Batesonian sense) positioning has been experienced as almost a 'chronic condition' of 'speechlessness' and 'learned helplessness' for quite some time. The so-called traditional Rest, in other words, has been in a *borderline arrest*, on the way towards *progress*. Put in a philosophical, sociohistorical, political-economical and cultural-technological context, therefore, the asymmetry (of power and other kinds) between the two (split) worlds has been magnified since the Enlightenment, and as the Industrial Revolution, French Revolution, modernity, capitalism, sexual revolution, Fordism and, more recently, the information revolution, and so forth, that all have emerged in and have disseminated from the Western Judeo-Christian soils.

We can say, perhaps, that other than their industrial/economic effects, the visible and tangible 'technologies of computerized connection', indeed, serve(d) a mobilizing function in the wake of postmodernity, just as the railroad (as the visible and tangible technology of the time) has served modernity's building sovereign nation-state as one cohesive unity and made a fundamental change in mentality towards (presumed) self-sameness.[3] The rapid circulation of virtual images and excessive information, and the international/domestic migration of actual peoples are creating a similar rupturing effect. With one exception this time, however, that the grand narratives of modernity, such as progress, linear and teleological development, unidirectional dissemination 'from one centre to the periphery' with the utopia of *global village* failed: The earth proved not to be a giant closed 'container' with a substance that could be homogenized (read: the 'deficient part', the Old World peoples could be tamed, civilized, modernized, liberated, developed, capitalized, universalized and so on). Rather, as the globe shrank further each day, the *far distant* or the *invisible* human difference which was kept 'out of sight, out of mind' became very *near by*, as near as one's self, and became so *visible*. On the other hand, a paradigmatic shift (in the Kuhnian sense) in mentality, for instance, towards relativity and relationally interdependent complexity, took place much earlier in theoretical physics and in other 'hard disciplines'. However, its reflections on, realizations by, social thought, and its translations to common sense (including that of 'intellectuals'), have been posing new challenges that urgently press for more apt epistemologies-ontologies-hermeneutics-aesthetics-ethics-political praxis of *difference* and *otherness* than the available ones in global circulation.

Since many problematic presumptions of (Western) modernist thought have already been scrutinized by various critiques under the umbrella term of postmodernism, something exciting has also been happening in the intellectual world of *power/knowledge* (in the Foucauldian sense) that the avant-garde is now 'willing' to leave the positivist field of domination and the artificially induced 'borders' between the identified/split/polarized categories of Western scientism. And yet, that search itself, understandably, has been constrained by the enduring characteristics of Western thought and knowledge-practice habits which are also saturated with all the 'usual suspects' of the Judeo-Christian fantasy of saviour, Cartesian worldview, Western capitalism and the English language. Notwithstanding, our *ecliptic* times offer a good opportunity for *levelling* within an *intermediate borderspace* and for *rapprochement* towards *dialogic reflexivity*. This seems to be the best time to reinterpret, to filter, to repair, to restore, to reshuffle, to subvert and to replace whatever we might have survived, or invent a new 'humanness'. It is about time to connect diverse knowledge towards further *perspectivalism* and to act for more humane lives on a sustainable planet.

Besides the geopolitical cartography, therefore, the metaphor of 'borderline' also points to the fact that most academics nowadays are seemingly 'preoccupied' with crossing various thick or permeable 'borders' in the mental maps of modern disciplinary knowledge-practices, including non-science and sociopolitical praxis. It seems, to me at least, however, that the great variety, complexity and interconnectivity of those *glocal* individual/collective *symptoms* (e.g. Lacan, 1953; Sontag, 1978; Žižek, 1999) which were described at the beginning, including *la belle indifférence* and *alienation* before the global destruction, can be neither described, understood, interpreted nor changed in terms of these new pastiche-like hybrid fields of study, not to mention modern positivist science and its rationalist social, cultural and political theories (Gülerce, 2009). Although grand narratives of universalist and generalist discourses such as humanism, liberalism and Marxism have been objected to by postmodernist and poststructuralist critics (who promoted the particular, local and specific instead), still, something is seriously missing or wrong, for the 'same' mistakes are repeated in our times: Just as utopian modernism could not prevent the exploitation of the 'others' in the name of 'liberation', fragmentary postmodernism excludes the 'different' in the name of 'inclusion'.

As seeking ways 'out'/'forward' calls for novel understandings and praxis, no better conceptual resource than ('good old') psychoanalysis seems readily available to the 'secularized' contemporary (Westernized) thought. Besides, psychoanalysis rapidly travelled from Europe first to North and South America. Then, it diffused transnationally through its American, British, Spanish and French appropriations and languages to the rest of the world (e.g. Damousi and Plotkin, 2009; Parker and Gülerce, 2008). Thus, there must have been enormous accumulated transcultural reflections to feed back to psychoanalysis other than its 'nationalist' or 'essentialist' *indigenization* practices.

Furthermore, with its *as if* character and overarching intellectual interests, psychoanalysis resides between many borders that have been emblematic of the dichotomic Cartesian mind and (Western) modernity's scientific, social, cultural, political and economic order. Obviously, psychoanalysis has always inspired many modern disciplines and philosophy, most famously feminism and European Marxism, with its theory of personhood. More recently (particularly after Lacan's return to Freud via poststructuralism, and feminists' emphasis on Kleinian intersubjectivity and otherness), it has been revitalized and refashioned by contemporary feminist theory, political theory, social theory, cultural theory, literary theory, art and film critiques, and so on, with a particular interest in subjecthood. It is hard to say, however, that the perils and transformative potentials of psychoanalysis have been fully explored and have been revised in regard to the inclusively *glocal* human thought, imagination, experience, social practice, dialogical reflexivity, ethics of responsibility and international political praxis.

It is not only that psychoanalysis is paradoxical by definition. Psychoanalysis also historically and simultaneously contains traditional, romanticist, modernist and (now called) postmodernist components and tensions as its 'built-in character'. Indeed, using Toynbee's (1963) historical demarcations of Western civilization and his early use of the term 'post-Modern age' with an early start (1875 onwards), psychoanalysis has emerged in the very era of, and has evolved in response to, the dramatic rupture from the previous age of the 'Modern'. In other words, when this desire for a 'radical break-up' with the dominant modes of thought, established social norms and stable ways of life of European society (marked by the ethos of Enlightenment, the bourgeoisie, capitalism, social stability, rationalism, certain(ty) metanarratives, truth claims and so on) led to a *crisis in society and knowledge* with an intense anxiety of uncertainty, ambiguity, chaos, incoherence, fragmentation and disorder, psychoanalysis 'helped' with the (invention of unconscious) creation of distance from otherness and space for self-sameness (classical psychoanalysis), with (cognitive/ego) 'adaptation' (the Americanized version) and by making the (affective/phantasmic) 'transition' smooth (the British School) in the past century.

Toynbee's universalistic and cyclical philosophy of history, just as Nietzsche's (1967) sociocultural nihilism, predicted a historical process of *regression* and erosion of moral values as a catastrophe for the established order, institutions and forms of modernity. As is known, postmodernity and postmodernism became rather household terms to signify the social and cultural conditions, and the philosophical and intellectual movements, that became more apparent in the West in the 1950s and have accelerated and spread worldwide since then. If our time, irrespectful of its periodization and name, or an 'as yet nameless era' (Drucker, 1957) if you like, is frequently described as ambiguous, and, hence, anxiety-producing for its promising/threatening features, and represents the 'unleashing of will, instinct, and impulse' (Bell, 1976), then, can a psychoanalytic 'way of thinking' and its revised theorizing of construction of personhood serve as convenient tools (once again) to 'cope' with the current *global crisis* and overcome the paradox which binds all parties involved, not only the 'victimized', as if there is 'no exit'? This book brings together some 'realistically optimistic' authors whose responses to this question, perhaps, can be reduced to a category of a 'conditional yes'.

The response is positive if one particularly joins Bauman (1991, p. 272) in his interpretation of postmodernity that (Western) 'modernity is coming of age: modernity looking at itself at a distance rather than from inside, . . . psychoanalysing itself, discovering the intentions it never before spelled out, finding them mutually cancelling and incongruous'. One of the 'intentions' of modernity, as it has been crystallized by the critics by now, was to constitute a particular form (capitalist) of social order, for instance, that manages to reconstruct and control the irrational forces of nature in the interest of rationally satisfying human needs. Psychoanalysis, as one of the earliest (romanticist) critiques of modernity, sided with human irrationality, and it (partially) belonged to the humanities. However, since psychoanalysis was deeply embedded also in modernist mentality, it utilized its 'instrumental rationality' (in the Habermasian sense) and provided the much needed formula of the workings of the modern (rational) human mind, and it has (totally) identified itself with the natural sciences and the prevailing ideology. Therefore, like anything paradoxical, psychoanalysis has been reproducing the very categories and ruling principles of even what it wished to criticize by its theoretical discourse and clinical practice.

To conclude, let us return to Bauman's remark on postmodernity. He adds that it 'is modernity coming to terms with its own impossibility; a self-monitoring modernity, one that consciously discards what it was once unconsciously doing' (1991, p. 272). If we see psychoanalysis playing an important role in this process, then, we now can phrase some of the (rhetorical) questions at work in *Re(con)figuring Psychoanalysis*: *Critical Juxtapositions of the Philosophical, the Sociohistorical and the Political*: How well does psychoanalysis, as a child of Judeo-Christianity and (Western) modernity, confront, swallow and redefine its own metaphysical, religious, predeterminist, essentialist, Eurocentric, universalist, colonialist, imperialist, capitalist, masculinist, gendered, patriarchal, familial, normativist, conservative, conformist, elitist, individualist, and various other biases and constraints of the 'past' era that have been put under scrutiny? How is it coming to terms with its own 'impossibility', not necessarily as a 'science' (e.g. Crews, 1975; Grünbaum, 1984; Popper, 1963) nowadays perhaps, but as a (dying and impossible) profession (e.g. Castoriadis, 1987; Freud, 1937; Zaretsky, 2004)? Can it 're-call' and 're-form' its old/new products that have been un/knowingly and transnationally exported to many other disciplines and to common sense for more than a century? Can psychoanalytically informed scholars consciously repair what psychoanalysis has been un/consciously doing and 'lacking'? How can it (re)install a political agency for liberation and emancipation, for instance, that its 'apolitically political' and 'atheistically religious' discourse has been suppressing over the past century? In what other ways than 'expert guided excursions to the dark continent' of the other (which frequently referred to female sexuality) and 'lifting up repression' can psycho-analysis transform the mass culture, society and politics in the new era? In what other ways than sexuation and sexual difference can it conceptualize multiplicity of human difference and likeness without a fixed hierarchical developmental order? Is 'auto-analysis' of psychoanalysis (in isolation), or self-reflexivity of 'autonomous' Western Self/thought/civilization/culture (as in Cartesian meditations) possible? If not, whose Self/thought/civilization/culture/language/episteme would be given the privilege of being the 'analyst'? How can it re(con)figure itself and its self for *rapprochement* with its others and other 'selves' by attuning to the others in its self, if unable to find itself in the others? How can it further transform itself intentionally towards a reflective cultural *habitus* (Bourdieu, 1999) of *reconstructive discoursive practices* and *dialogically relational ethics of acceptance* across numerous artificially invented cognitive-affective borders through a broad array of philosophical, sociohistorical, cultural and political dialogues? How is it possible to imagine something novel for psychoanalysis (to use it before and after its own change) as a critical hermeneutic sphere for reflective transformations?

Notes

1. I am aware of the fact that every use of the problematic term 'Western' (which has been saturated, or has gained many meanings, to the extent that the term does not mean 'anything' any more) reproduces this very confusion. However, until the transformation is made to the 'new thinking' this seems necessary/inevitable. New thinking cross-cuts all those categories of the old thinking which has made false dichotomies and polarizations. Thus, once the shift/change is achieved, it is expected that there will be no need to use this term.
2. *Glocalization* refers, in Robertson's (1995) coinage of the term, to simultaneity of the processes of globalization and localization.
3. See, for example, *Middlemarch*. George Eliot gives an excellent account of social change via the invention of the steam engine and of the railroads spreading all over England through the character of the businessman Caleb Garth and others.

References

Althusser, L. (1969). *For Marx*, trans. B. Brewster. London: Verso.
Baudrillard, J. (1988). *Jean Baudrillard: Selected Writings*, ed. M. Poster. Cambridge: Polity.
Bauman, Z. (1991). *Intimations of Postmodernity*. London: Routledge.

Beck, U. (1992). *Risk Society: Towards a New Modernity*. London: Sage.
Bell, D. (1960). *The End of Ideology: On the Exhaustion of Political Ideas in the Fifties*. Glencoe, IL: Free Press.
Bell, D. (1976). *The Cultural Contradictions of Capitalism*. New York: Basic Books.
Bourdieu, P. (1999). *The Logic of Practice*. Stanford University Press.
Castoriadis, C. (1987). *The Imaginary Institution of Society*. Cambridge, MA: MIT Press.
Crews, F. C. (1975). *Out of My System: Psychoanalysis, Ideology, and Critical Method*. Oxford University Press.
Damousi, J. and Plotkin, M. B. (2009). *The Transnational Unconscious: Essays in the History of Psychoanalysis and Transnationalism*. London: Palgrave Macmillan.
Derrida, J. (1976). *Of Grammatology*. Baltimore, MD: The Johns Hopkins University Press.
Drucker, P. F. (1957). *The Landmarks of Tomorrow*. New York: Harper & Row.
Feyerabend, P. (1975). *Against Method: Outline of an Anarchistic Theory of Knowledge*. London: New Left.
Freud, S. (1937). *Analysis Terminable and Interminable, SE*, vol. 23, pp. 216–53.
Fukuyama, F. (1989). The end of history? *The National Interest*, 16, 3–18.
Giddens, A. (1984). *The Constitution of Society: Outline of the Theory of Structuration*. Cambridge: Polity.
Giddens, A. (1991). *Modernity and Self-identity: Self and Society in the Late Modern Age*. Cambridge: Polity.
Grünbaum, A. (1984). *The Foundations of Psychoanalysis: A Philosophical Critique*. Berkeley: University of California Press.
Gülerce, A. (2009). Transdisciplinarity and transnationalization (in (theoretical) psychology): Blurring or redefining boundaries and identities (or else)? In T. Teo (ed.), *Varieties of Theoretical Psychology*. Ontario: Captus Press, pp. 113–24.
Harvey, D. (1989). *The Coalition of Postmodernity*. London: Blackwell.
Jameson, F. (1984). Postmodernism, or the cultural logic of late capitalism. *New Left Review*, 146, 53–93.
Lacan. J. (1953/2002). *Écrits: A Selection*, trans. B. Fink. New York: W. W. Norton.
Lyotard, J.-F. (1984). *The Postmodern Condition: A Report on Knowledge*, trans. G. Bennington and B. Massumi. Minneapolis: University of Minnesota Press.
Nietzsche, F. (1967). *The Will to Power*. New York: Random.
Parker, I. and Gülerce, A. (eds) (2008). Psychoanalysis: Cultural origins and practices. *Special Issue. Theory & Psychology*, 18, 2.
Popper, K. (1963). *Conjectures and Refutations*. London: Routledge & Kegan Paul.
Robertson, R. (1995). *Globalization: Social Theory and Global Culture*. London: Sage.
Sontag, S. (1978). *Illness as Metaphor*. New York: Farrar, Straus & Giroux.
Toynbee, A. (1963). *A Study of History*. Oxford University Press.
Zaretsky, E. (2004). *Secrets of the Soul: A Social and Cultural History of Psychoanalysis*. New York: Vintage.
Žižek, S. (1999). *The Ticklish Subject: The Absent Centre of Political Ontology*. London: Verso.

Invitation: Revisioning Psychoanalysis (The Un/limited Un/conscious)

Aydan Gülerce

Taking seriously psychoanalysis, human suffering, open hatred and widespread violence, but also human 'rights'/'capacity' for love, joy and creative imagination, the contributors to this volume believe that psychoanalysis 'still' has a great deal to offer. For they do not doubt the importance and relevance of psychoanalysis to the contemporary culture and society at large. They diverge, or partially converge, however, in their own primary concerns, reservations, reasons, conditions of possibility and the internal/external intertextuality engaged in their discussions, regarding these and many other unstated and inarticulable questions of this book.

To state explicitly at the outset, and despite the academic genre which calls for a 'predetermined' structure and divisions of unity/coherence, the essays are deliberately not grouped around some common threads, themes, 'schools' of psychoanalysis, theorists, geographies, for instance, or some other criteria, albeit one could connect and cluster them, *a posteriori*, in multiple possible ways. Neither are they presented in any serious order for a reason that dovetails the plurality of 'identity claims' and of meaning centres/peripheries in contemporary psychoanalysis and its infinite areas of 'application' and/or revision, particularly if a radical subversion is at stake. Each contribution brings to the fore some important and interconnected issues that make psychoanalysis relevant to our lives, and engages in current theoretical debates and discussions around those. The authors explicitly/implicitly explore future (im)possibilities of psychoanalysis, and offer their own critiques, versions, and fantasies, of a re-visioned psychoanalysis.

What follows, therefore, is only an 'extended invitation' to your own dialogues with the refreshing works in this 'collection'. Each piece is displayed in a separate gallery, so to speak, which can be visited in any order as they all connect with one another. Also, some brief grounding, contextualizing and reframing trains of thought accompany my brief introductions to the chapters. Rather than a systematic/justified attempt at curation to channel your thoughts and imagination, however, these might be seen, if you will, as some reminiscences from the 'permanent collection' and pieces from the 'previous exhibits' on the 'connecting hallways' (just like the ones in the 'foyer'). In the worst-case scenario, they might be heard as the 'free associations', which are not 'free' (Grünbaum, 2002), and the prompting murmurs, which might not 'survive', of the overwhelmed analysand on the couch and the analyst.

The end of Freud? (or, The cult-ivated un/conscious)

In 'In memory of Sigmund Freud', W. H. Auden (1939) wrote:

> if often he was wrong and, at times, absurd,
>   to us he is no more a person
> now but a whole climate of opinion
>
> under whom we conduct our different lives

Although Freud died on 23 September 1939, for 'cigar *is* cigar' when it comes to chin cancer, he already had begun to haunt many minds long before then. Actually, since the very inception of psychoanalysis, both his personal life and his ideas have been subject to strong accusations. The controversy and criticisms of various sorts in different time periods and contexts, known as 'Freud bashing', 'Freud wars', 'Freud assault', 'killing Freud' and so on (e.g. Cioffi, 1974, 1998; Crews, 1975, 1995, 1999; Forrester, 1977; Grünbaum, 2002; Kramer, 2009; Masson, 1992; Popper, 1963; Sulloway, 1979; Webster, 1996), but also the enormous idealization which his work has attracted as a 'way of protecting personal life itself' (Zaretsky, 2004), have continued until this day. Thus various unanswered questions, like the one that appeared in the cover story of the famous issue (November 1993) of *Time*, 'Is Freud Dead?', remain curious, and are rebottled every now and then. Perhaps, it still 'will take a long time before we lose our subservience to psychoanalysis', as Wittgenstein phrased it (Bouveresse, 1995).

Undoubtedly, psychoanalysis has provided a language for defining characteristics of the modern human condition and mental functioning. This strong language soon became a crucial part of various sectors (i.e. health, education, child care) of the *psy-complex* (Foucault,

1980a; Ingleby, 1985; Rose, 1990). Freud (1920) himself stated that psychoanalysis was a 'far-fetched speculation'. In other words, however 'scientific' he claimed psychoanalysis was, he 'knew' deep down that its fundamental concepts of personhood were *hypothetical constructs*, that they were not *natural* and *universal* entities. It must be obvious to us by now that psychoanalytical 'truth' is not *historical*, but *narrative* (e.g. Spence, 1982). Thus, if those constructs 'work', it is not because they are 'true', but because they are constructed to fit and are custom-made. Better, in Parker's (1997, p. 6) words, they are 'structured into Western culture'. Cultural phenomena, of course, include much wider apparatus than the academic knowledge/professional practices of the *psy-network*. In effect, and particularly in Europe, the impact of psycho-analysis on social sciences, humanities and art has been significant even during Freud's lifetime. That is another way of saying that Freud's inten-tional engagements in literature, arts and 'high culture' through the works of 'creative artists' (i.e. Wilhelm Jensen, Leonardo, Michelangelo, Shakespeare), as well as the 'psychopathology of everyday life', sup-ported his arguments, 'validated' his 'scientific' concepts and undoubt-edly helped with the diffusion of psychoanalytic language into general culture. Thus, European civilization as 'Freud's (*symbolic, residential*) culture', and psychoanalysis as 'Freud's (*imaginary, diasporic*) culture', mutually and 'socially' co-constructed each other over the past century.

In 'Freud's Culture' (Chapter 1), Ian Parker offers a critical overview of Freud's discussions of culture by paying particular attention to the leads of psychoanalysis as sociocultural critique, and by highlighting some of his telling conceptions as they appear in direct quotes from Freud. Parker traces Freud's early and increasing awareness of culture which, for him, does not only inhabit a particular language, in both narrow linguistic and broad discursive senses of the term, but also inhabits all other constitutive components of psychoanalytic knowledge-practice to work as a 'talking cure'. Thus, Parker first stresses how important it was for Freud that the analysts must be 'well at home' in subjects such as 'the history of civilization, mythology, the psychology of religion and the science of literature', and points at the German scientific culture of his time with its sharp divide between the natural and the human sciences. He then takes up a significant issue that Freud did not refer to group psychology as the application of an individual analysis to a small group, as it has been frequently understood. Rather Freud was interested in collective activity and was questioning the binary opposition between the individual and the social. Parker also provides succinct outlines of Freud's views on mythological structure which un/consciously operates as a 'schema', on worldviews, and on political ideologies and religion. Having 'translated'/reread the famous title of Freud's book *Civilization and its Discontents* as 'the uneasiness inherent in culture', Parker contours Freud's distinctions between civilization and culture, and the reversible relations between the individual pathology and the communal pathology. He then accentuates Freud's suggested task of analysis being to broaden up the 'field of perception' of the 'I' as a clinical practice, yet at the same time locating that 'I' in culture as a cultural practice. Parker concludes with Freud's own foresights regarding the progress of psychoanalysis and how it becomes a constructive part of culture, blended with Parker's own reflections.

History: repeated, mourned, forgotten, forgiven, or else? (or, The institutional/ized un/conscious)

Psychoanalysis quickly became a mass phenomenon in the United States (albeit in the form of 'self-improvement') soon after Freud's talk at Clark University in 1909 (Zaretsky, 2004), whereas it remained marginalized in Europe until the end of World War II. An important reason for this delay is frequently connected to the racist/anti-Semitic climate in *fin-de-siècle* Vienna (e.g. Bettelheim, 1990; Gay, 1988; Schorske, 1980). Since the formation of the analytic circle in 1902, as a matter of fact, all of Freud's early associates were exclusively Jewish until Freud's correspondence with Jung in 1906. It was already widely understood, even back then, not only that psychoanalysis was a 'Jewish thing', but that it also owed its insights to a singular ('pervert') genius. These were of significant concern to Freud himself in those years (and later as well, for he was very ambitiously engaged in the expansion of psychoanalysis until his last day) in terms of the future of psychoanalysis. Thus, meetings with two young men made 1907 a happy year for Freud. The first one was with Max Eitingon (a Russian-born medical student); Freud described his conversations with him to Ernest Jones as the 'first training analysis' (Jones, 1955), although the fact that Bleuler sent Eitingon to Vienna instead of him made the second young man, Carl G. Jung, quite jealous and upset. However, Freud was even more delighted to meet Jung in Amsterdam, during the First International Congress of Psychiatry and Neurology. That is not only because Jung had already 'converted Bleuler' to a new science of psychology, and had innovated the *word-association* test which echoed and expanded Freud's technique of *free association*, but he was a Christian, 'the son of a Swiss-Protestant clergyman, no less'. By the first analytic congress in Salzburg in 1908,

Freud had already fancied Jung as his successor, 'the crown prince' of psychoanalysis. However, 'the fact that analysis was poised between an institutional integration that would destroy its unique contribution and a marginality that could destroy its effectiveness came to the fore at the Nurnberg Congress' (Zaretsky, 2004, p. 88). Jung became the first president of the International Association of Psychoanalysis, Adler was appointed as the head of the Vienna branch, and so on. So even though Freud had realized 'his incredible daydream' (Gay, 1988, p. 207) at last, the 'wishful fantasy' did not last long for the new/old 'nightmares' (re)appeared, and the *real* traumas followed one after the other.

Exactly 60 years before its question of whether Freud was dead, *Time* magazine had Adolf Hitler's picture on its cover with the story of 'GERMANY: National Revolution!' and of the anti-Semitism that became government policy. In fact, that same month in Germany, all organizations (from universities to the press and professional groups) were brought under the Nazi 'coordination', *Gleichschaltung*, and their Jewish members 'joined the exodus' as 'Hitler's gift' to the countries which took them. The 'spectacular burning of books' included the works of Freud, Melanie Klein, Anna Freud, Bronislaw Malinowski and Erich Fromm. Five years later, Freud took the Orient Express to Paris on 4 June 1938 and the next day he travelled to London with his close friends/doctors. As soon as the group arrived at the house which Ernest Jones had rented, after he had driven them from Victoria Station, Freud stepped out into the garden with a view over Regent's Park, 'threw up his arms and said, "Heil Hitler!"' (Maddox, 2006, p. 235). This, of course, was not one of the indicators that Hannah Arendt (1961/2006), the well-known German-born Jewish American political philosopher (who left Nazi Germany and Heidegger in 1933), had in mind when she remarked in her interrelational analysis of (Nazi) totalitarianism: European Jews 'ultimately sold themselves'.

In 'The Re-enactment of Denial' (Chapter 2), Stephen Frosh reflects on the two biennial IPA Congresses that were held in Germany (in Hamburg in 1985, and in Berlin in 2007) after World War II, and powerfully analyses the resonance between the events at the two meetings as they demonstrate the very title of his essay. Frosh first applies Cohen's typology of denial to German psychoanalysts' 'refusal' to come to terms with their past, namely their taking part in the Third Reich and active engagement with Nazis. As these *literal, interpretive* and *justificatory* forms of denial leave out the subject's 'defensive work to keep at bay something that is, unconsciously, already known', Frosh brings in this psychoanalytic emphasis in the form of *fending-off* as the fourth type.

He also stresses (through Seu) the collective, 'social' aspects of denial, 'at the "microsocial" level of groups and institutions... as well as by large sections of a society'. Frosh gives a critical account of the Hamburg Congress to show how all these four types were seen at work, and how the conference theme of 'identification and its vicissitudes' revolved around the betrayal of its Jewish 'father'. Thus he reframes the 'identification question' by making references to the papers which understood the meaning of this first post-war meeting on German soil: How to come to terms with a Nazi father, or to say 'our Hitler'. Again, despite the 'promising' scholarly work and other events that took place, including a new generation of psychoanalysts, in the following 22 years, and the avowed goals which were explicitly signified by its title, 'Remembering, Repeating, and Working Through', the 2007 Berlin Congress gave evidence, as Frosh states, 'of a continuing uncertainty or even reprise, a repressed, perhaps, and a threatening return'. This is vividly illustrated by his retelling (via Erlich et al., 1990) of a special group event, 'Being in Berlin', which is especially 'designed' to encourage 'working through': the 'container' transforms first into 'a cattle car', then a gas chamber in the stuffy congress room, then into a 'non-existing, "fabricated" room' in a foyer space, thus turning the entire experience into an 'enforced nomadism' and giving full proof that anti-Semitism remains unresolved and that psychoanalysis is haunted by its 'Jewishness'. Frosh concludes that just like the Germans' unworked-through Nazi past, psychoanalysis needs to come to terms with its own, what he calls, 'Jewish complex', and that, in both cases, analysis seems/is 'interminable, indeed'.

Uni/multi/trans-versality of the psyche (or, The indigenously oceanic un/conscious)

The 'new science' of psychoanalysis emerged and developed, in a sense, in response to the 'medicalization' of Jewishness and 'racist biologization' of science and medicine in *fin-de-siècle* Vienna. Gilman (1993, p. 10), for instance, analysed Freud's strategic devices 'to adumbrate within the rhetoric of psychoanalysis all the charges against the Jewish race by carefully framing them into the universal attributes of a human being'. One of the earliest disputes in psychoanalysis that took place between Freud and Jung was not because of the latter's anti-Semitism (as openly expressed later) or different religion, but of their different understandings of religion, and different approaches to the inherently racial human psyche and culture. While Jung's Christian/Aryan identity had vital importance to Freud in avoiding the charge of psychoanalysis as a 'Jewish science' (e.g. Frosh, 2005), Freud's Judeo/Jewish identity, 'racial memory' and emphasis on ('essentialistically Jewish') sexuality served Jung to distance himself to create his own conceptual system. Jung (1933) transmuted those phylogenetic aspects of Freud's (*indigenous*) psychoanalysis into the *universal archetype*, as soon as he realized that he could not 'psychoanalyse and cure' Freud's own, and the collective 'Jewish neurosis' of the time. Jung's analytic psychology rejected positivism, scientism and Darwinism, by turning to other ancient mythologies, then Greek, mystic and Eastern worldviews, and to a *philosophy of nature*. These ideas (including Jensen's *Gradiva*) were introduced to Freud, an 'atheist', by Jung, as he was convinced that their relevance and usefulness would provide additional 'empirical evidence worldwide' for psychoanalysis. Freud's grounding the libido in biology, and his preference for 'secular' science and Darwinism were because of his refusal of mysticism, religion and spirituality. As he clearly expressed in *Totem and Taboo*, Freud (1913, p. 1) was interested in 'contemporary, but primitive' people, for 'we can recognize in their psychic life a well-preserved picture of an earlier stage of our own development'.

Freud, 'the Moses of psychoanalysis', supposedly wanted to avoid the individualism/particularism of Christianity by presuming the universality of the structure of the Oedipus myth. Also, Freud's mythology started 'History' with Sophocles' (495–405 BC) *Oedipus Rex* and (the idealized and adored) Greek civilization by omitting/repressing the entire pre-Oedipal (presumably maternal and spiritual) period of Minoan-Mycenaean ('Western') civilization. Obviously, there have been ('non-Western') other histories, other mythologies, other worldviews, and other civilizations in other geographical and meaning centres which all pre-dated Western thought and civilization (which frequently failed on others' 'civility tests'). Historical documents also indicate that the central psychoanalytic notions of the unconscious mind and dream work date back to the Sumerians in 2500 BC (e.g. Ellenberger, 1970). That is why, being better informed in cultural anthropology than Freud, Jung placed the human soul, where the psychic history of humanity lived, in an intermediate realm between modern psychology/psychiatry and religion. Jung seriously questioned the secular conflict (of the sixteenth century) and formulated his *depth psychology* as a reconciliation of the conflictual separation between the truths of natural sciences, myth and of religion. Unlike the anthropological influence of Malinowski (*functionalist*) on Freud, his *collective unconscious* (as a supplement to the *immediate/personal unconscious*) was inspired by Bastian's (*relativist* Boas' mentor) anti-Darwinist *psychic unity of mankind* and *primordial thoughts*, and resembled Levy-Bruhl's use of *collective representations.* Clearly, both Freud and Jung, just as psychoanalysis in general, conformed to the determinist, teleological, universalist, racist/colonialist and individualist presumptions of the progression, emancipation and salvation narratives of Judeo-Christianity and modernity, far from seeking a possibility for an 'exit' from its hegemonic and missionary discourse.

More recently, the 'archetypal psychology' (Hilman, 1972) is developed as *polytheistic psychology* which recognizes the myriad myths and fantasies, only one of which is the skin-bound, self-contained and autonomous Western ego (e.g. Sampson, 1989). Thus, the problematic aspects of sociality and collectivity, which psychoanalysis prescribed as ('cure') as/what it described ('disease'), are further scrutinized by the philosophically, politically, psychoanalytically informed social critique such as Deleuze and Guattari's (1983) *Anti-Oedipus*, and Castoriadis' (1987) *social imaginary.* Added to those are the nationalist and/or anti-colonialist *indigenous psychology* movements that emerged, and were advocated by Western(ized) scholars, in countries such as India, Korea, Mexico, Japan, the Philippines, Taiwan and so forth, and spread around the 'Third World' (e.g. Damousi and Plotkin, 2009; Heelas and Lock, 1981; Kakar, 1978; Lawson et al., 2007).

In '*Sa loob ang kulo*: Speaking the Unconscious in the Transformations of a Filipino Proverb' (Chapter 3) Narcisa Paredes-Canilao brings together these critical voices in an illustrative discussion of a concept of the unconscious, *kulo* (the boiling), that may have been originally enunciated by an old Filipino proverb, *Ang taong walang kibo, nasa loob ang kulo* (A quiet person has anger boiling inside), and continues to be invoked in today's shortened expression, *Sa loob ang kulo.* Paredes-Canilao first charts the inception and subsequent development of the concept *kulo* (the boiling), in both its semiotic and its sociohistorical manifestations, from pre-colonial times to globalization, and how it makes sense within the traditional Filipino worldview. She then demonstrates how the syntax, logical grammar and topological qualities of *kulo's* enunciations all cooperate in supporting its identification as a concept of the indeterminate unconscious. Paredes-Canilao discusses how *kulo* resonates well with metaphors in Western psychoanalysis that are meant to signal a more dynamic rethinking of the unconscious, in terms of drives or desire. In her conclusion, she articulates some suggestions borne out by the study on what a metaphorics/metaphorology of the unconscious might contribute to the reformations of psychoanalysis.

Knowledge/science of/as *das Ding* and *die Sache* (or, The gendered un/conscious)

Myths, metonyms and metaphors of nature continuously served as the earliest and most powerful signs of (social) construction of order over the world (see Verene, 1981; Vico 1725/1948). These 'primitive' beliefs were then turned into and 'ruled' organized religions, philosophical reasonings and science. Knowledge and science-making have always been joint human productions/social constructions, albeit the awareness of *sociology of, social construction of, archaeologies of and genealogies of knowledge* (e.g. Berger and Luckman, 1966; Foucault, 1969; Kuhn, 1970; Manheim, 1936; Scheler, 1980) came in later. Needless to mention perhaps, even in its most 'fluid', 'softened', 'liquid' or 'flexible' forms, those myths and metaphors (i.e. object, material, power, force, machination, mechanism, absence/presence, etc.) spoke and reified (*naturalized, physicalized* and *psychologized*) a masculinist unconscious in commonsense knowledge, science, language and body politics. Science itself was equated with the masculine (self, subject), and nature with the feminine (other, object), to begin with. In terms of 'psychoanalysis of knowledge', not surprisingly, therefore, science (civilization) uses manipulation as a method; is obsessed with instrumentation, with quantification, with the 'hardness', 'visibility' and 'tangibility' of technology; is oriented towards power/capital with a fantasy to explore, to conquer, to discover and to control; aims at the explosive discharge of energy, mass (re)production and so forth.

Actually, psychoanalysis used all the forms of metaphors which Averill (1990) sorted out in the psychological sciences that point to its 'mixed scientific-gender identity'. Although Freud aspired towards *Humanwissenschaften* and kept his interest in *Geisteswissenschaften* in the 'closet', he 'openly' identified with *Naturwissenschaften*. Indeed, his *Project for Scientific Psychology* attempted a theory of mental functioning along the 'hard scientific' lines of the legendary Helmholtz School, which is described as 'materialistic', 'physicalist physiological' and 'rigorously mechanistic' (Gay, 1988; Leader, 2000). Freud, like his 'contemporary' conservative Darwinian (read evolutionist, racist, sexist and developmentalist) psychologists 'essentialized' sex exactly as it is spelled out in Darwin's (1871) *The Descent of Man*. Darwin identified the female intellect with the 'lower races', described it as passionate, intuitive and 'imitative' and placed it in opposition to the male 'energy' and 'inventive genius'.

Freud's masculinist, intrusive, patronizing and colonialist approach to the 'dark continent' of female sexuality was criticized by early feminist female psychoanalysts who 'knew' at least 'what women did not want': Karen Horney (1922) objected to male-centric (Oedipal) psychoanalysis, which is developed by, for and about men. She reframed *penis envy* as a metaphor of resentment to narcissistic male power. Yet, she (as Jones, and Deutsch) biologized femininity as an innate disposition that was created in *nature*. Whereas for Freud, men and women (both bisexual at birth) are made in *culture*, despite his unfortunate claim that 'anatomy is destiny' (which could be read not in terms of 'contradiction', but of the conceptual differences between sexuation, sexuality and gender, albeit they are frequently conflated in psychoanalytic theory and discourse).

Thirty-two years after her joint seminar with Horney (in Leader, 2000), Melanie Klein (1957) offered a matricentric version of (pre-Oedipal) psychic development to stress the significance of the role of the female body (the womb even prior to the breast) and of the infant's attachment to the mother in the structuration of psychic (object-relational/intra-intersubjective) experience. The second wave of feminism further objected to Freud by arguing that 'the riddle of the nature of femininity' (Freud, 1933, p. 113) or female sexuality is not a repressed version of male sexuality, and that the libido itself is defined as masculine force (e.g. Millett, 1971), whereas Klein received more credit from a group of contemporary feminists who followed Juliet Mitchell's (1974) seminal work *Psychoanalysis and Feminism*. They returned to Freud/Klein/Lacan with an emphasis on the double-sidedness of (inter)subjectivity (e.g. Benjamin, 1988; Chodorow, 1978, 1979, 1999; Dinnerstein, 1976; Irigaray, 1985; Kristeva, 2001; Mitchell, 1988; Sayers, 1987; Segal, 1999). However, primary feminist concern has been with *sexuation* or *ontology* of the female and with *gender-identity politics*.

With an *epistemological* focus, Keller (1984) offered an object-relational analysis of the systematic psychic and institutional masculine dominance of the natural sciences and pointed to the problematic equation of women with gender, and the psychodynamics of that social construction. As she questioned, 'Is sex to gender as nature is to science?', her subject towards understanding the 'science-gender system' was 'not women *per se*, or even women and science: it was the making of men, women, and science, or, more precisely, how the making of men and women has affected the making of science' (p. 4). Harding (1986) also extended her approach to the sex-gender system to *The Science Question in Feminism*. The 'postmodern turn' further pressed (psychoanalytically informed) feminist scholars to uncover the political power of academe and its normative knowledge claims with the supposed *God's eye view* (Haraway, 1991). The main argument has been against the presumed neutrality and objectivity assertions that what might be applicable to only certain men, culture, race and class are 'universal'. They criticized the Enlightenment ideals including autonomous and self-legislating self, and *instrumentalist reason* (Habermas, 1987; Horkheimer and Adorno, 1979), that were re-enacted in masculinist constructions and praxis of modernity. Some feminists tried to 'locate the cause' of women's oppression, some acknowledged other silenced voices (such as race and class) that women were not the only ones categorically left out, some argued for a 'politics of recognition' which embraces multiple liberatory possibilities for women against essential(izing) criteria of identification and for conscious negotiation, and so forth (e.g. Benhabib, 1984; Benjamin, 1998; Butler, 1990; Flax, 1990; Fraser and Honneth, 2003; Haraway, 1991; Harding, 1991).

In 'Beyond Objectivity to Extimité: Feminist Epistemology and Psychoanalysis' (Chapter 4) Kareen Ror Malone and Shannon D. Kelly first examine how the issue of objectivity is 'deconstructed' in feminist science studies through Lacanian lenses. They criticize that although there has been a certain invasion of psychoanalytically informed object relations in science studies (e.g. Keller, 1984) and science education, such work has not yet made the epistemological forays that have been attempted by those who interrogate the very foundations of science in their feminist critiques such as Haraway or Longino. The authors introduce Lacanian psychoanalytic ideas through Jacques-Alain Miller's elaboration of extimité serving as the basis. They further bring these epistemological questions to bear on the practice of science, minding that materiality is often deflected through instrumentation and that many informal practices of science entail a relation to a subjective factor that remains within the material world. Insofar as women and persons of colour serve as images or even fetishes in terms of a particular white fantasy of alterity, this remainder implicates both the progress of diversifying science and the new paradigms through which people are thinking of science practices.

The authorship in psychoanalysis (or, The singular un/conscious)

For Foucault (1969, p. 149) 'the notion of "author" constitutes the privileged moment of individualization in the history of ideas, knowledge, literature, philosophy and the sciences'. He differentiates the 'founders of discursivity' as a third category of authors from the ones in literature and science. Freud and Marx illustrate this type, for they provide a paradigm, a set of images, metaphors, concepts, terms and language to organize thought and experience.

To expand a type of discursivity, such as psychoanalysis as founded by Freud, is not to give it formal generality that it would not have permitted at the outset, but rather to open it to a certain number of applications... In other words, unlike the founding of a science, the initiation of a discursive practice does not participate in its later transformations... On the other hand, re-examining Freud's texts modifies psychoanalysis itself, just as a re-examination of Marx's would modify Marxism. (pp. 156–7)

Wittgenstein (1948) commented that Freud's work died with him, for no one can do psychoanalysis in the way he did. Indeed, Freud (1914, p. 7) himself once claimed that 'no one can know better than I do what psychoanalysis is, how it differs from other ways of investigating the life of the mind, and precisely what could be called psychoanalysis and what would better be described by some other name'.

Lacan, on the other hand, was very critical of American ego psychology for not understanding Freud, and he considered himself Freudian (not Lacanian), remaining 'loyal' to the authorship of Freud. Excluding many personal attacks that centred around his narcissism and womanizing, however, some still criticized him for distorting Freud (e.g. Bowie, 1991; Green, 2002) on various other specific grounds. They ranged from reducing psychoanalysis to semiotics (e.g. Bruner, 1986) to reducing it to 'zero' (e.g. Roudinesco, 1997) because of his 'cutting up of the timing' of an analytic session (Lacan, 1953). While some feminists were highly critical of his 'phallocentrism' (e.g. Irigaray, 1985; Rose, 1986), some made better uses of it for feminist theory and politics (e.g. Butler, 1993; Gallop, 1985; Grotz, 1990).

Undoubtedly, Lacan stimulated an extensive rethinking of Freudian concepts and has been extremely provocative and productive in his reconceptualizion of psychoanalysis. He returned to it as a 'talking cure', based on the spoken words and the language of analysis, and turned away from its biologism. In order to do this, he followed the structural linguistics of Ferdinand de Saussure and Roman Jakobson for both of whom language was a system of signifiers. In this system, the 'speaking subject', more accurately, the pronoun 'I', actually does not refer to a 'subject' but an 'object' of that system for the language (relations between the signifiers). Thus the subject does not use and construct a language to make meaning; rather the structure of the language uses and constructs the subject. The subject, the agency of language, was in the Freudian *lapsus, condensation of jokes, interpretations of dreams* and so on, for 'the unconscious is structured like language'.

Lacan's theory of subjectivity that is determined by the symbolic order is explored in detail by Stijn Vanheule and Abe Geldhof in their essay entitled 'Knotted Subjectivity: On Lacan's Use of Knot Theory in Building a Non-universal Theory of the Subject' (Chapter 5). The authors provide a review of Lacan's conceptualization of the subject by paying particular attention to the shifts in his ideas and to the replacement of his concepts, including the Name-of-the-Father and object *a*. They explain how Lacan made use of the mathematical knot theory after the 1970s and examine how it enabled him to put forward a singularly organizing principle for subjectivity. For an illustration, they then turn to Lacan's discussion of James Joyce's life and work, for his ego and writing style had the status of a sinthome that innovatively refers to a singular knotting of the Real, the Symbolic and the Imaginary. In the last section of their chapter, Vanheule and Geldhof introduce David Nebreda, a photographer, and his unique work, 'photographic doubles', which they interpret as inventions to fulfil the function of a sinthome that provides 'a platform for the articulation of the subject, and for the extraction of an object *a*'.

Relational love and responsible care for the other (or, The ethical un/conscious)

As for Lacan, drawing conceptual distinctions between consciousness and the subject, but also between *le Moi* (the ego) and *le Soi* (the self), has crucial importance for Levinasian ethics of the other. For Levinas (1996), the ethical subject is not a conscious subject. Thus he criticizes the reduction of subjectivity to consciousness, which dominates modern philosophy. His subject, what he calls *psychismic*, is the subject of the trace, of the past, of the anarchic, and so forth, that escapes representation, presence and memory. Although in his view consciousness is the effect of traumatic affect, for his conceptualization of trauma, consciousness and the unconscious, and hence, ethics, is different from Freud. Levinas (1996, p. 83) refuses psychoanalysis:

The unconscious, in its clandestinity, rehearses the game played out in consciousness, namely, the search for meaning and truth as the search for the self. While this opening onto the self is certainly occluded and repressed, psychoanalysis still manages to break through and restore self-consciousness.

He also objects to Husserlian phenomenology and Heidegger's definition of life, and for Levinas (1969) life is love of life of the pre-conscious sentient subject of *jouissance*. The ethical 'subject' is the subject of pre-reflective sensibility who is vulnerable towards the other. That is why, for Levinas (1996), the possibility for the ethical relation to the other necessitates a certain affective and structural disposition towards otherness.

In a similar vein, and unlike Freud's universal and abstract consider-ations of morality, and Kant, in virtue of humanness, Klein's *super-ego* meant ethical responsibilities to actual people, and relational obliga-tions to particular communities. Klein (1932) made no clear distinction between ego and super-ego. She thought splitting was 'the first step in the formation of instinctual inhibitions and of the super-ego which may be the same thing as primal repression' (p. 127). While for Freud the internal world is dominated by the problem of authority, for Klein, therefore, it was dominated by obligations to particular communities (as in Adler's *social interest*).

On the philosophical side, while Derrida (1999) reads Levinasian ethics as a welcoming of the other, as 'an immense treatise of hospi-tality', he is actually questioning the mediations, or 'silence', between politics and ethics. He is most concerned that the primacy of an ethics of responsibility dangerously leaves open the political sphere, partic-ularly if 'the political invention' (p. 144) and 'the "peace process", the process of political peace' (p. 197) are executed in the name of the other. Derrida's response is not an ontological foundationalism, transcenden-talism or empty universalism. The indeterminacy of the deduction from ethics into politics entails that political action must respond to the singularity of the context, and thus the infinite deconstruction is an eth-ical demand. It goes without saying that, for Derrida, political decisions should not be driven procedurally from a pre-given notion of justice or a moral code as in Habermas and other modernist universalists, but must be singular, which does not mean arbitrary.

The ethics of psychoanalysis, for Lacan (1959–60/1992), entails a relation to the reality of the human condition which is 'the tragic sense of life', similar to Freud. In 'Beyond Identification: The (Im)possibility of Loving thy Neighbour' (Chapter 6), Calum Neill examines Freud's refusal of the directive to 'love one's neighbour' (in *Civilization and its Discontents*). He contrasts this with Kierkegaard's advocation of non-preferential love to expose the possibility of an ethical approach to the other beyond misrecognition and objectification. He suggests a potential approach which he develops through a critical reading of a key moment in Husserl's *Cartesian Meditations* where he advocates the analogical grasping of the other. Against Husserl, Neill posits the encounter with the other as an encounter with the infinite or inaccessible, that which cannot be reduced to comprehension. This, he shows, allows a conception of the subject as necessarily constituted in relation to the other in a manner that foregrounds the very assumption of a subjective position. Such a stance entails a thinking of ethics with, but not reducible to, politics; a social engagement which entails a responsibility for the other, a responsibility which does not allow the reduction of the other to a generalization but, rather, necessitates responding to the other as singular and unique.

Politics of a/sexuality (or, The un/lustful un/conscious)

Ethics and morality made their first entry into psychoanalysis through the 'wide open door' of human sexuality. An evolutionary account of the human race has been given as a history of human sexuality by Krafft-Ebing's (1886/1902) classic *Psychopathia Sexualis* where, on the 'progressive' line of evolution from 'primitive' sexuality to modern Christian liberalism as the most 'advanced' form, sexual attitudes of Judaism form an earlier stage. Thus, various Jewish attributes of sexuality, such as masturbation, homosexuality, incestuous inbreeding, perversity, disease, sexual excess, degeneration and so on, have been understood as the inherent nature of the Jewish race and fixation on that early stage. Freud redefined all these sexual(ized) categories in terms of 'degeneration of civilization' for the entire human population. For instance, he not only discussed syphilis as the illness that historically characterizes this trauma of civilization, but also coined the term 'syphilophobia', which is passed from one generation to the next (1905, p. 236). As is known, for Freud human civilization depended partly on the control of natural forces, and partly on the restrictions of human sexual and aggressive instincts, which were as powerful as natural forces, and indeed were conceptualized as natural/biological urges. Freud differentiated infantile sexuality from mature adult sexuality on the basis of the pleasure of satisfaction being before ('fore-pleasure') or after ('end-pleasure') the 'sexual act', though the latter originated in the former. Thus, as the polymorphous infantile sexuality matures, the infantile fantasies and sexual desires, perverse and otherwise, mature via negotiations with social norms of civilization and persist. If they are not experienced overtly, then they are repressed and expressed in terms of symptoms, dreams, art and so forth.

Freud was criticized for there is no *natural* sexuality, nor *natural* stages of sexual fantasy, as sexuality is negotiated with parents, who are themselves unconscious agents of their social class, society and emotional economy (Poster, 1978). Laplanche and Pontalis (1972), who are Freudians themselves, also argued that sexuality comes to the subject from the *other*. Particularly through Americanized ego psychology (i.e. Anna Freud, Hartmann, Erikson, Kris), as Lacan (1956/1968, p. 7) criticized, psychoanalysis had given up 'the most living terms of its experience: the unconscious and sexuality', although they both rejected the biologism of Freudian instinct theory. Critical social theorists (e.g. Brown, 1959; Marcuse, 1955, 1964, 1968; Reich, 1951) cross-fertilized Freud's libidinal economy with Marx's critique of political economy that at best gave an account of social conditions of possibility for repression of desire. Put differently, while for Freud repression was a prerequisite for civilization, for them, liberating sexuality from repression was a necessary step in political resistance against capitalist exploitation. Nevertheless, these 'sexual radicals' fell short of any substantial challenge to the existing framework of Freud, as they relied on drive reduction in the interest of work ethics. At the end of the day, these modernist and masculinist conceptions of sexuality, be it at the level of the individual or the society, remained within the universalist, the patriarchal, the conservative, the negative and the biological zone. Hence, both psychoanalysis and early critical theory fell short of spelling out the delicate and socially constructed relations between *Eros* and economic production, between love and politics, between desire and consumption that were returned to later (e.g. Deleuze and Guattari, 1983; Žižek, 1989). Poststructural and postmodern theories turned away from 'depth models' of sexuality 'beyond appearances' (in Baudrillard's sense) towards politics of identity and of desire.

On the other hand, cultural differences in terms of gendered patterns of sexual performances, such as male timidity, female activity in initiation, and experiences of orgasm depending on female sexual and social autonomy that were provided by anthropological studies (e.g. Ford and Beach, 1952), prepared the ground for social constructionists to challenge both the biologization and universalization of sexuality which is culturally learned. *Sexual Conduct* by Gagnon and Simon (1973/2005) can be considered as the eye-opening classic sociological text, for it radically questioned the naturalist, the biologist and the essentialist view, and the concept of repression. They not only criticized the repressionist perspective as Foucault (1980b) did, but also offered a positive and productive conception of sociality and social construction of the sexual self and desire. Rather than positing sexuality as an innate and biologically determined drive in the realm of the id which is given under the control/repression of the civilized ego, and super-ego, they located it in everyday life activities as social product.

Not necessarily being interested in the evolution of the human sexual mind or body, but in the discourse (of sexuality), Foucault discussed the political economy of the sexual body in *History of Sexuality*. Because he argued for that within the complex interplay of power and discourse, the symbols are not referential to the symbolized, but are productive investments. Thus, Western preoccupation with sexuality discourse needs to be understood in those terms of the apparatus of knowledge and power focused on sex (namely, *hysterization of women's bodies, pedagogization of children's sex, socialization of procreative behaviour* and *psychiatrization of perverse pleasures*). Actually, 'what this discourse of sexuality was initially applied to wasn't sex, but the body, the sexual organs, pleasures, kinship relations, interpersonal relations' (Foucault, 1980b, p. 210). 'Sex', in brief, and again in his own words, 'was a means of access both to the life of the body and the life of the species' (Foucault, 1979, p. 146). One concludes with Foucault that sexuality became a significant target of social regulation and control, *bio-power*, in 'modern' society, and replaced the threat of death which organized 'premodern' society. Contra Lacan's universalistic and ahistorical readings of Freud, Foucault argues that the idea of law is constitutive of desire. Yet, it still situates power as essentially normative, prescriptive and negative, as it is interested in censorship and prohibition.

Just like most 'postmodern' phenomena that emerged after the 1980s, HIV/AIDS (the 'syphilis of our times') does not only challenge the linear and monolithic accounts of human history, but brings to the fore the primary dialectics of heterosexist psychoanalysis, of *Eros* and *Thanatos*, in the private/public management of human lives in our times. Grahame Hayes in 'Desire in the Time of AIDS' (Chapter 7) offers from South Africa an analysis of the psycho-politics of desire, which is described as being despoiled by high rates of AIDS deaths, HIV infection and its people's apparent resistance to adopting safe sexual practices. He first draws attention to the 'de-sexualization' in psychoanalytic theory, which is not primarily a social theory, and argues that it should be part of social theory via translations. Hayes also discusses the consequences of 'forgetting' desire in the theory in the given context, and various reasons for the lack of effectiveness of HIV/AIDS intervention programmes in changing 'high-risk' sexual behaviours. He suggests that one of the contributing factors is an overly 'rationalist' approach to the understanding of sexual practices and desire. Hayes engages in a constructive critique of Berger's article entitled 'Re-sexualising the Epidemic', and offers his own psychoanalytic reading of desire in an attempt to more accurately capture the complexities of the operations of sexual desire.

Illuminations of darkness (or, The racist/colonial un/conscious)

As mentioned earlier, Freud (1913, p. 1) presupposed an equation between infantile psychic life and the developmental/evolutionary stage of the 'savage', for he believed that 'a comparison of the psychology of primitive peoples as taught by social anthropology with the psychology of the neurotics as it has become known through psychoanalysis, will reveal numerous points of correspondence and throw light upon familiar facts of both sciences'. Sciences, on the other hand, for Althusser (1969), and art and technology, for Heidegger (1977), were social practices in that participants were brought to or concealed, marked as invisible to, the world. Appropriating Heidegger's notions of 'worlding' and 'being in time', Derrida (1998) argued that psychoanalysis, which is totally ignorant of most of the world, has been disseminating the *homo psychoanalyticus* to people through its 'ongoing worlding'. Spivak (1987) reinterprets the 'worlding' of the unsayable and places the initially violent process ('strife') of projection in the specific context of coloniality. Other psychoanalytically informed postcolonialist works such as Bhabha's (1994) 'How Newness Enters the World' and Said's (1994/2004) 'Two Visions in *Heart of Darkness*' also discussed the imperializing/colonializing Western self which served 'epistemological violence'.

Political-historical accounts of psychoanalysis usually take on racist violence in terms of Jewishness in the context of the National Socialism of Nazism, and the 'inferior' (circumcised/castrated) male body, that its projection onto the other has been unconcealed by feminist political analysis. For example, by converging Freud's metaphor of the 'dark continent' for female sexuality with the explorer Stanley's (1878) first use of the same metaphor for Africa, Khanna (2003, p. 6) gives a thorough account of psychoanalysis as a racist colonial discipline:

As a discipline, it formalized strategies to normalize a form of civilized being constituted through colonial political dynamics. In the space between the earth and the colonizing world of late-nineteenth and early-twentieth-century Europe, a national-colonial self was brought into existence, or perhaps more accurately, into unconcealment. And it situated itself, with fascination, in opposition to its repressed, concealed, and mysterious 'dark continents': colonial Africa, women, and the primitive.

At the same time, psychoanalysis provides a language to understand colonialism and to analyse decolonization as illustrated in various works, such as Fanon's (1961/1968, 1952/1967) *The Wretched of the Earth* and *Black Skin, White Masks*, Mannoni's (1950/1990) *Prospero and Caliban: The Psychology of Colonization*, Memmi's (1965) *The Colonizer and the Colonized*, Obeyesekere's (1990) *The Work of Culture*, Sachs' (1996) *Black Hamlet*, Sartre's (1948/1976) *Black Orpheus* and Kovel's (1984) *White Racism: A Psychohistory*.

Frantz Fanon, a Martinican psychologist who was also trained in medicine and psychiatry in France, was appointed to a hospital in Algeria by the French colonial administration prior to the Algerian War of Independence. He resigned later and joined the Algerian revolutionaries and freedom fighters. He analysed the striking effects of colonially derived violence and of war in the 'neuroses' of White (French) soldiers and their Black (Negro–Algerian) victims. In *The Wretched of the Earth*, Fanon (1961/1968) gave an account of the 'chain reaction of violence–counterviolence' once it had been initiated by the colonizer (the stranger other) that led him to being called the 'apostle of violence'. His theory of praxis spelled out how violence works on a day-to-day basis on the part of the colonized (the native), and counterviolence as a necessary step towards independence, national consciousness and culture, and towards putting an end to further violence.

In 'Fanon and Libidinal Economy' (Chapter 8), Derek Hook turns to Fanon's (1986) *Black Skin, White Masks* for a closer look at the cursory libidinal economy Fanon constructs in the interest of developing a political analytics of the *affective logic* of racism. Hook carefully (and accurately) approaches libidinal economy as a constitutive element, the 'glue', of a collectivity, through recourse to Freud's theory of mass/group identification. Hook draws out a variety of themes and perspectives in relation to Fanon's analysis of colonial racism. He focuses on Fanon's analysis of the irrationality of 'negrophobia', and brings to the fore the role of fantasy which functions as 'pre-emptive structuring' of both affect and ideas. Hook attends also to Fanon's notion of 'colonial gaze', a notion that represents the convergence of two of Fanon's central issues: 'the violence of de-subjectivizing racist objectification' (identification/counter-identification) and sexual anxiety (desire). In addition, Hook discusses how these intersecting issues of otherness and sexuality problematize each other as 'potentially more inclusive categories', and also (given the conditions of possibility within the colonial space) produce 'unexpected desire' which engenders new layers of anxiety such as 'latent homosexuality'. Hook makes further clarification regarding the relation of racism and sexuality by differentiating the obscene stuff of *jouissance* from mere sexuality. He describes two modalities that bring the civilized subject's own lack to the forefront: 'obscene enjoyment' (the attributed *jouissance* of the other), and 'phallic loss' (imagined castration of the imaginary attribute). By tackling Gilroy's analysis of 'post-imperial melancholia', Hook extends Fanon's theorization of libidinal economy, connecting it to the contrary imperatives of amnesia/denial (in respect of the colonial past) and affirmation (of self-affirming images of greatness) of British cultural identity in our times. Against reductive psychologism and the limitations of discourse analysis, Hook concludes that 'extra-discursive' factors – operations of affect that analyses of libidinal economy foreground – need to be taken into account as the bridge between discourse and identification.

Politics of violence as articulation (or, The il/literate un/conscious)

Historical dialectical analyses of violence, by Hegel in relation to feudalism during the French Revolution, by Marx and Engels in relation to capitalism during the working-class revolution, and by Fanon in relation to colonization during the post-World War II decolonization and anti-imperialist nationalisms, all showed that violence is a structure. Yet this structure mediates between the individual and the society and is contingent on the political sociohistorical context. More recent Marxist studies of decolonization analysed the political economy of coloniality and of neocolonialism, the depletion of natural resources, the need for decolonization as a precursor to the international revolution of workers (e.g. Young, 2001). Undoubtedly, the impact of colonial violence is multi-levelled, and analyses of decolonization cannot be complete without understanding the political economy of affect. 'Ontological insecurity' that Giddens (1984, p. 375) defined as the lack of 'confidence or trust that the natural and social worlds are as they appear to be, including the basic existential parameters of self and body, social action, and, ultimately, the reproduction of the structure of society is the *sense* of security provided by the routinization of daily life' describes well what the poor and underprivileged people in de/colonized societies experience.

In his essay, 'Violent Crime in Post-Apartheid South Africa' (Chapter 9), Bert Olivier argues that psychoanalysis offers important insights into the astonishing extent of, and brutality accompanying, violent crime in contemporary South Africa, a comprehension of which exceeds the limitations of other theoretical frameworks. He first draws attention to Rossouw's philosophical approach in this regard, distinguishing among three social spheres – the *religious*, the *political* and the *economic* – and considering their alternating position of historical dominance to address the question of violence. He, then, feels a need to expand Rossouw's work to accommodate the problem of agency in order to understand the 'causality' implicated in the epidemic of violence. For this purpose, Olivier adopts a Lacanian framework to be able to show that individual subjects can only be adequately understood as agents if the different registers in which their subjectivity is articulated – the imaginary, the symbolic and the real – are taken into account. In his Lacanian formulation, the violence sweeping through contemporary South Africa is a manifestation of the failure of the symbolic register. While people, Olivier posits, each considered as an ego, experience one another as distinct individuals ('neighbours') in the imaginary register, the ineffable ('real') 'thing' in every individual is activated, with far-reaching violent consequences at the collective level. That is because the universalizing mediating function of the symbolic (a condition for experiencing what is commonly human) is fragmented due to the 'traumatic *breakdown*' of interpersonal relations as a result of the excessive concentration of exclusive symbolic activity in the neoliberal economic sphere. According to Olivier, an inclusive symbolic order which all South Africans can share can only be created via comprehensive symbolic practice, and only along this avenue can the present slaughter be brought to an end.

Domestication of violence (or, The de/colonized un/conscious)

Despite the controversial discussions they raised, various pioneering sociohistorical studies (e.g. Ariès, 1965; Engels, 1942; Laslett, 1971; Shorter, 1975) in/directly brought to the attention of psychosocial analysis the transformations of the (Western) family from its premodern forms to (post)modern forms. As Poster (1978, p. xvii) criticized, 'historians and social scientists in general have gone astray by viewing the family as a unitary phenomenon which has undergone some type of linear transformation'. He argued instead that the history of the family gives evidence for discontinuous family structures. Poster differentiated four types of family forms (namely the *aristocratic family* of the sixteenth and seventeenth centuries, the *peasant family* of the sixteenth and seventeenth centuries, *the working-class family* of the early Industrial Revolution and the *bourgeois family* in the mid-nineteenth century) that carried different effects of historical context, class, sexuality and emotions. His analysis also concluded that the construction and transformation of these family structures indicate no correlation with any single variable, such as modernization, industrialization, patriarchy, capitalism, urbanism or empathy, as frequently assumed. Notwithstanding that, there are at least three points of generalization that we can draw from psychoanalytic, social and historical discussions on the family on which perhaps we can anticipate more agreements: (1) Freudian analysis based on the appropriation of the Oedipus myth to a particular type of bourgeois family in a particular historical conjuncture, its particular structure and fantasy life with suprahistorical assumptions had been disseminated via colonization and imperialization. (2) If homogeneous sociality, romantic love, permanent monogamous marriage, conjugal intimacy, separation between private and public domains, the domesticity, the increased value of children, maternity and child care, self-realization and individualism over collective solidarity, and so on, are some social markers of (Western) modernity, multiple marriages and partnerships, fragmented lives, fluidity of the boundaries between private and public, the increased sexual and economic liberation and equality demands of women, *plastic* and *autonomous sexuality* (Giddens, 1992), but also increased violence against women and children became markers of postmodern society. (3) Family violence is a political issue and changing political and historical contexts define its social control policies. Nonetheless, from very early on, both liberal (i.e. E. A. Ross, who first used the phrase *social control*, and T. Parsons) and leftist (i.e. Frankfurt School) critiques excluded gender analyses and maintained patriarchal and father-hegemonic family structures in their conceptualizations.

Thus, particularly from a functionalist/instrumentalist view of social engineering, the family kept its significance as a fundamental and necessary agent of transition and social control, and target of *discursive regimes of power* by the State in post/modern and de/colonized societies as in the domestication of violence. Smith (1999) describes de/colonization as a process of fragmentation which occurs at multiple sites and causes alienation of indigenous peoples through re-presentation, disordering, disruption, renaming and reclassification of their pre-colonial systems and worlds. Recently, *Postcolonial Disorders* (DelVecchio Good et al., 2008) offered a collection of ethnographic studies which engaged colonial, postcolonial and neocolonial aspects of 'social pathologies and subjective experience' in various societies, including Brazil, Haiti, Morocco, Congo, Indonesia, Vietnam and China. Despite the diversity and wide range of issues covered, it is commonly accepted that 'postcolonialism' referred to 'an era and historical legacy of violence and appropriation, carried into the present as traumatic memory, inherited institutional structures, and often unexamined assumptions' (p. 6). While individual or anonymous violence comes to the fore as an epidemic in some fragmented societies, in some others the family becomes the site. If comparative world statistics indicate South Africa as world famous in the former, Aotearoa/New Zealand comes first in the latter.

In 'The Violence of an Idealized Family: A Kleinian Psychoanalytic Reading of *Te Rito*' (Chapter 10), Peter Branney, Brendan Gough, Anna Madill and Mandy Morgan provide an analysis of a family violence policy in Aotearoa/New Zealand. They argue that the long history of violence between the Māori and Western inhabitants (descendants of the British colonizers known as Pākehā) continues to manifest in policy-making structures in Aotearoa/New Zealand. They describe various binary cultural separations between Pākehā and Māori that dominate a political and social life in Aotearoa/New Zealand in terms of Kleinian psychoanalytic concepts such as paranoid-schizoid position and splitting. Furthermore, the authors read the text of *Te Rito*, a contemporary domestic violence policy in Aotearoa/New Zealand that forms a model for some other countries, from within a Kleinian psychoanalytic framework.

Curvilinear motherhood (or, The time-less and the place-less un/conscious)

Althusser criticized psychoanalysis, including Lacan, for neglecting historical materialism on which, as he argued, the theory of the formations of family ideology (namely *the ideology of paternity-maternity-conjugality-infancy and their interactions*) must depend. The 'continuity' approaches to family history (with a unitary model) theorized a linear change, for instance, from village sociability to social isolation and privacy (Ariès, 1965), from pre-industrial forms to 'modern' forms (Shorter, 1975), from 'cold' and 'distant' familial relationships towards empathy (de Mause, 1975) and so forth. Evolutionists, on the other hand, argued that empirical evidence on the long evolution of the human species confirms the hormonal impulse towards mothering. In their view, women's place in society is restricted by motherhood. So the historical evidence for the low value given to motherhood by the elite, from the Renaissance to the nineteenth century, points to 'an extreme aberration in human history'. From a critical historical perspective, the internal relations of the early bourgeois family, in which psychoanalysis was historically embedded, provided a secluded micro-world; this privacy, however, depended on a capitalist economy. As Poster (1978, p. 171) stated:

> The hostile tone of competitive capitalism defined the family as a negative opposite, as a place of close, warm, emotive relations. The shop was now a place of reason and action and the home a place of feeling, with a segmented personality required to go from one to the other... Norms for family relations no longer were set in the context of community traditions... The cozy domestic nest of the bourgeois family forms, in addition, the structure without which one cannot analyze the emotional configuration of the modern psyche. It provides just that social context absent in Freud's thought.

Apparently, the bourgeois family generated new forms of love, authority, emotional structure and child-rearing methods, but also of the oppression of children and mother which was dependent upon the critical and ambivalent mechanisms of love and authority, that were sharply different from those of the earlier aristocrat and peasant families. For the past two centuries, Western society has imposed a particular family ideology of maternalism that restricted the opportunities for women to participate publicly in the economic and political world. Psychoanalysis certainly complied with this ideology which assigns women primary reproductive and domestic duties in all of its own historical phases. Together with the increased interest of the object-relations theorists in the pre-Oedipal development, modern maternity gained a new meaning and enormous significance in the past century.

As a good example to the conservative position of psychoanalysis, Winnicott's (1953) notion of *good-enough mother* theorized an idealized mother who responds sensitively and adapts to all her infant's needs and desires. Also, his concept of *holding environment* described the good-enough mother who provides a container which includes the infant. It enables the infant to maintain the illusion of fusion with, and omnipotent control over, the mother('s breast). Thus, the (instinctual and naturally attuned) mother as 'manager' was put in full charge of the formation of the infant's selfhood, while she remained 'invisible' herself as 'primary maternal preoccupation' demanded. The mother sustained the infant's illusory omnipotence by immediate gratifications, by giving her passive body – 'placing her breast where the infant is ready to create, and at the right moment' (Winnicott, 1953, p. 11) – under the infant's active manipulation and magical control, by knowing when to wean from the breast and so on.

Developments in late global capitalism, such as small factories giving way to large corporations, fuse the old factory-working class and the new 'white-collar proletariat' so that the typical bourgeois family pattern describes only a small group of people, not only in the Western industrialized societies, but internationally. The overwhelming majority of the entire world population does not control the global capital. Hence, a vast, heterogeneous group of workers has emerged and followed the bourgeois family pattern despite various differences that remain between the white-collar middle class and the blue-collar working class (Poster, 1978). Expectedly, therefore, the new sociohistorical context of the ideology of consumerism and of 'hyperreality' (Baudrillard, 1988) places new demands on families as units of rapid consumption, and particularly on mothers as more 'permissive' and less 'normative' producers of isolated workers by all means. In contrast to the women of the Freudian/Victorian bourgeoisie, who were considered 'asexual' and avoided public life, today Western(ized) women avoid maternal care and participate more in public life, demanding and claiming equality in all avenues, from sex to politics and business. Marriages and 'objects of love and desire' change in form and are consumed rapidly. Family members (both parents and children) increasingly seek or find closeness outside the home, including the virtual world. As the technologies of self of postmodernity and the market logic of neoliberalism continuously blur the binary boundaries of modernity, such as the 'private' and 'public', 'feminine' and 'masculine', 'mother' and 'father', 'reproduction' and 'production', and so on, how psychoanalysis will respond to the maternal of our times remains open.

In 'Maternal Publics: Time, Relationality and the Public Sphere' (Chapter 11), Lisa Baraitser starts with an image of the word MOTHER carved into an abandoned wall in the East End of London which she calls a 'maternal monument' and uses to offer a psychosocial reading of maternal publics. In so doing, she raises questions about contemporary forms of collectivity and the contradictory temporalities of late global capitalism through psychoanalytic articulations of the maternal and the matrixial. To think about what mothers 'make public', Baraitser takes up Wright's concepts of *public time* and *time without qualities*, and develops further towards an understanding of the disturbance that the maternal produces in the contradictory workings of late global capitalism. As Kristeva in 'Women's Time', Baraitser, too, argues that maternal time is neither cyclical nor monumental, but 'wasteful', which is described as 'the time of waiting for childhood to unfold'. This definition situates the maternal, paradoxically, along with queer, on the underside of what Edelman calls *reproductive*. Thus, for Baraitser, the notion of the public time of 'waiting', or time 'without qualities', gives way to the emergence of a novel account of maternal temporality, in spite of the maternal being totally qualified time.

Integrally transformative transformations (or, The relational and radically pluralist un/conscious)

So far, the valuable contributions that feminist female psychoanalysts made did not quite subvert psychoanalysis, let alone sociopolitical theory, or society and culture at large. Freud's early abandonment of seduction theory, which had significant political implications, was also one of the reasons for the split between Ferenczi (known as one of his most gifted pupils) and Freud. Ferenczi (1920) persisted with the significant role of actual parental neglect and trauma, and was also the first to note that a child could *act out* the unconscious conflicts of parents. His early recognition of the importance of *countertransference* in regards to the co-constructive relationship between the 'subject' (the analyst) and the subject matter/'object' (the analysand) of psychoanalytic knowledge-practice was another reason for strong disagreement. As is known, Freud (initially) was not willing to give up the analyst's authority in the one-sided identification of the (female) analysand/pupil with the idealized power figure. Furthermore, his position is embedded in a *process philosophy* of life as a flux and continual series of energy transformations. His ideas have been extremely influential and fertile via two of his female analysands who further developed both of his points, consecutively: Clara Thompson in the United States, and Melanie Klein in England.

It was quite early in theory building that both of Freud's 'daughters' shifted psychoanalytic (normal developmental) theory towards mother-infant theory. The major conflict between Melanie Klein and Anna Freud lay in the constitutive role of anxiety and in their views of 'subjectivity/reality'. For Anna Freud (1937), anxiety was 'objective', and the child needed an assurance that there was nothing to be scared of. She further developed the ego's defence mechanisms and methods other than *repression*, which had significant implications for treatment, assessment and diagnosis that centred on 'ego strength'. Hartmann (1958) took further interest in the ego's *adaptive functions* (Freud's short-lived notion of *ego instinct*) and *apparatus of primary autonomy*. If Winnicott described the ideal mother, Hartmann searched for the 'good enough/resilient infant to fit and survive' evolution, so to speak, that is defined as the 'process of progressive "internalization"' (p. 57) as well as *average expectable environment*. His work led *ego psychology*'s further development via Jacobson, Erikson, Kris, Mahler, Spitz and many others, and its domination in the United States eventually paved the way to identity politics.

For Klein, the infant had good 'reasons' to be anxious of, things such as its own primary rage (*death drive*) which she added to Freud's second theory of anxiety that constituted her major difference from Anna Freud at the time. Klein, who was Winnicott's analyst (and Abraham's analysand after Ferenczi), made a significant impact (albeit un/admittedly) on all the major 'schools' of psychoanalysis, including Freud himself. She also caught the attention of (leftist) social theorists who wanted to move the Frankfurt School forward by replacing Freud with her pre-Oedipal theory (e.g. Alford, 1989; Dinnerstein, 1976; Richards, 1984; Rustin, 1982). Klein further developed Fairbairn's (1941) idea of the 'object-seeking' infant who diverted from the 'satisfaction-seeking' infant of Freudian/classical *drive theory*. Her notion of 'object-directedness' later led to the developments of 'relational psychoanalysis' (e.g. Mitchell, 1988; Ogden, 1982; Stern, 1985). This also assigns some (shared) 'responsibility' to the infant in the construction of the personhood.

The radical twist towards relational epistemology and politics, however, was not brought out first by women scholars, nor was it imported from the 'soft studies', for the 'physics envy' has taken over the entire field of 'respectable' knowledge and scientific rigour: If one seeks a 'true' paradigmatic rupture in psychoanalytic knowledge-practice one can find it in Sullivan's 'dialogical' notion of *participant observer* (in keeping with Heisenberg's *uncertainty principle* and view of the 'language and reality' in physics) and *interpersonal theory* better than the so-called break between *drive theory* and *ego/object* (representational) *relations schools.* The latter two served in the same epistemological-ontological paradigm that they 'monologically' and 'unidirectionally' focused on the intrapsychic 'self-system' *in* the person and how it is *shaped by* constitutional drives and/or by autonomous ego (albeit those are socialized by others). Sullivan (1940) was the first to acknowledge that the self, human mind and activity did not reside 'inside' the person as 'things', but rather are exhibited as 'the relatively enduring pattern of recurrent interpersonal situations' (p. xi). This meant not only that the individual (as a bounded entity in isolation) could not be the proper 'unit of analysis', but also the key issues to look for, and the questions to ask, should concern relationships and interactions. Sullivan (1953) insisted that the *human mind is social with an interpersonal motivation for connections, and that anxiety is not instinctual, but rather is induced by anxious others in relations.* Most of his ideas were also compatible with Ferenczi's stress on the role of actual interactions in the formation of pathology, and with Fromm's humanistic appropriations of the Marxist notion of history and the existentialist approach to human experience. Thus, Thompson further 'integrated' all under the label of 'interpersonal psychoanalysis', also known as the 'culturalists' who explored the actual effects of language, and cultural, social and familial relations.

Sullivan's notion of 'interpersonal field' and other ideas were refashioned four decades later by Laing (1961), who showed how every relationship implies the definition of self as induced by the action of others, and of the other as induced by self. One could also put oneself into what he called a 'false position' and ultimately into an 'untenable position'. He took part in the anti-psychiatry movement in the 1960s, together with Foucault, Thomas Szasz, David Cooper, Franco Basaglia and others who questioned many fundamental assumptions of hegemonic psychiatric knowledge and praxis. All these revolutionary ideas from within psychoanalysis, together with the General Systems theory (von Bertalanffy, 1968) and particularly the 'double bind' communication theory (Bateson et al., 1956) in the sociopolitical context of the time, paved the way to the family therapy movement under the charismatic leadership of a number of psychoanalysts. As is known, family systems thinking signified a radical shift in the epistemology/aesthetics of change, focusing on the familial structure-system, relational and communication patterns. It is also frequently acknowledged that no communication can be defined or examined properly at the level it occurs without any reference to the metacommunicative levels of punctuation and context. Although, as Wilden (1972) rightfully criticized, it has not been the case in practice, for their concept of context is restricted to the 'manifest' context of the 'here and now', and it is culturally, ideologically ignorant of the sociohistorical context. However, unlike the majority, Laing has sought to connect family therapy with new left politics, with Far Eastern mysticism and with a validation of schizophrenic experience as a healing process. Drawing heavily on Sartre's philosophy and on existentialist thought in general, Laing has associated the practice of family therapy with a general radical social theory. Lacan, on the other hand, did not only translate Freudian self psychology to French structuralism, but also shifted the focus on (mother's, or infant's) body and phantasy to an emphasis on speech and symbolic order. His matheme was concerned with the institution of psychoanalysis' scientific credibility.

In the last essay of the volume (Chapter 12), 'Psychoanalysis and *Türban*: Self-castrating Objects, or Transformational-Transformative Subject-Objects of Historical Time-Soci(et)al Discourse-Political Imaginary Spheres?', Aydan Gülerce draws attention to many unexplored resources in psychoanalysis and their flexible and creative 'uses' from a pluralist perspective, but I can let her speak for herself: In the good company of other chapters which discuss in detail various problematics that contemporary psychoanalysis engages, I risk an overall reflective commentary by claiming for myself a voice that is 'neither insider, nor outsider'. Thus, having been cultivated continually inside-and-outside the hegemonic intellectual geographies, multiple *discursive practices, language games*, orders of social power, and political systems-and-structures that do not truly 'relate' to one another, I sketch possibilities for further modifications of revisionary psychoanalysis for radical subversions in theory and in society in light of some of my own past/ongoing work which have been (necessarily and singularly) 'translating/appropriating' psychoanalysis. In this essay, I point to the necessity of some transformations at all levels of (psychoanalytic) knowledge-practice towards that purpose. I suggest to expand the imaginary-symbolic-actual *transitional space* in/of psychoanalysis. While underlining the significance of transgenerational un/conscious and intersubjective dynamics, I highlight family as a crucial mediating 'unit of analysis' and the 'covert agent of political intervention' in linking intra-psychic phantasy and international politics. I then turn to the veil, a highly contested issue of our times, for not only that it reflects, at once, many dichotomic inventions and polarized significations of the *hegemonic* thought and praxis, including masculine/feminine, Self/Other, West/Rest, Judeo-Christian/Islam, modern/traditional, authority/submission, past/present, unconscious/conscious, autonomy/symbiosis, hierarchy/undifferentiation, private/public, individual/collective, secular/religious, body/soul, matter/spirit, object/subject, to name only a few. But also, and needless to mention perhaps, that habitual knowledge-practices, including psychoanalysis, mostly reflect/are embedded in the former side of these binaries that invite further reflections. As a case in point, I offer a conceptualization of the *türban*, a particular version of headscarf that emerged in the 1980s in Turkey, as an individual/collective, private/public and cognitive/affective 'transformational-transformative object-subject'. In so doing, I hope to invite further transformative thinking on both psychoanalytic and sociopolitical accounts of subjectivity and intersubjectivity as well as social practice in our times.

So, here is a very short conclusion to this very long invitation: By the time it ends, it is hoped that this 'exhibit' will leave you with novel questions, but also unlimited possibilities that might inspire new beginnings in your own knowledge/practices, perhaps, by using psychoanalysis creatively while attending to numerous juxtapositions of the philosophical and political issues tested against the current sociohistorical conditions.

References

Alford, C. F. (1989). *Melanie Klein and Critical Social Theory*. New Haven: Yale University Press.

Althusser, L. (1969). *For Marx*, trans. B. Brewster. London: Verso.

Arendt, H. (1961/2006). *Eichman and the Holocaust*. New York: Penguin.

Ariès, P. (1965). *Centuries of Childhood: A Social History of Family Life (L'Enfant et la vie familiale sous l'ancien régime)*, trans. R. Baldick. New York: Vintage Books.

Averill, J. R. (1990). Inner feelings, works of the flesh, the beast within, diseases of the mind, driving force, and putting on a show: Six metaphors of emotion and their theoretical extensions. In D. E. Leary (ed.), *Metaphors in the History of Psychology*. Cambridge University Press, pp. 104–32.

Bateson, G., Jackson, D., Haley, J. and Weakland, J. (1956). Toward a theory of schizophrenia. *Behavioral Science*, 1, 251–4.

Baudrillard, J. (1988). *Jean Baudrillard: Selected Writings*, ed. M. Poster. Cambridge: Polity Press.

Benhabib, S. (1984). Epistemologies and postmodernism. *New German Critique*, 33, 103–27.

Benjamin, J. (1988). *The Bonds of Love*. London: Virago.

40   *Invitation*

Benjamin, J. (1998). *Shadow of the Other: Intersubjectivity and Gender in Psychoanalysis*. London: Virago.

Berger, J. (2005). Re-sexualising the epidemic. *Development Update*, 5(3), 45–67.

Berger, P. and Luckman, T. (1966). *The Social Construction of Reality*. New York: Doubleday.

Bettelheim, B. (1990). *Freud's Vienna and Other Essays*. New York: Knopf.

Bhabha, H. K. (1994). How newness enters the world. In *The Location of Culture*. London and New York: Routledge.

Bouveresse, J. (1995). *Wittgenstein Reads Freud: The Myth of the Unconscious*, trans. C. Cosman. Princeton University Press.

Bowie, M. (1991). *Lacan*. Cambridge, MA: Harvard University Press.

Brown, N. O. (1959). *Life Against Death*. Middletown, CT: Wesleyan University Press.

Bruner, J. (1986). *Actual Minds, Possible Worlds*. Cambridge, MA: Harvard University Press.

Butler, J. (1990). *Gender Trouble: Feminism and the Subversion of Identity*. New York: Routledge.

Butler, J. (1993). *Bodies that Matter: On the Discursive Limits of 'Sex'*. New York: Routledge.

Castoriadis, C. (1987). *The Imaginary Institution of Society*. Cambridge, MA: MIT Press.

Chodorow, N. (1978). *The Reproduction of Mothering: Psychoanalysis and the Sociology of Gender*. Berkeley: University of California Press.

Chodorow, N. (1979). *Feminism and Psychoanalytic Theory*. New Haven: Yale University Press.

Chodorow, N. (1999). *Power of Feelings*. New Haven: Yale University Press.

Cioffi, F. (1974). Was Freud a liar? *Listener*, 91, 172–4.

Cioffi, F. (1998). *Freud and the Question of Pseudoscience*. Chicago: Open Court.

Crews, F. C. (1975). *Out of My System: Psychoanalysis, Ideology, and Critical Method*. Oxford University Press.

Crews, F. C. (1995). *The Memory Wars: Freud's Legacy in Dispute*. London: Granta.

Crews, F. C. (1999). *Unauthorized Freud: Doubters Confront a Legend*. New York: Penguin.

Damousi, J. and Plotkin, M. B. (eds) (2009). *The Transnational Unconscious: Essays in the History of Psychoanalysis and Transnationalism*. London: Palgrave Macmillan.

Darwin, C. (1871). *The Descent of Man, and Selection in Relation to Sex*. London: John Murray.

de Mause, L. (1975). *The New Psychohistory*. New York: Psychohistory Press.

Deleuze, G. and Guattari, F. (1983). *Anti-Oedipus*. Minneapolis: University of Minnesota Press.

DelVecchio Good, M.-J., Hyde, S. T., Pinto, S. and Good, B. J. (2008). *Postcolonial Disorders*. Berkeley: University of California Press.

Derrida, J. (1998). Geopsychoanalysis. In C. Lane (ed.), *The Psychoanalysis of Race*. New York: Columbia University Press.

Derrida, J. (1999). *Adieu to Levinas*, trans. P. Anne-Brault and M. Naas. Stanford University Press.

Dinnerstein, D. (1976). *The Mermaid and the Minotaur*. New York: Harper & Row.

Edelman, L. (2004). *No Future: Queer Theory and the Death Drive*. Durham, NC: Duke University Press.

Ellenberger, H. F. (1970). *The Discovery of the Unconscious: The History and Evolution of Dynamic Psychiatry.* New York: Basic Books.
Engels, F. (1942). *The Origin of the Family, Private Property and the State: In the Light of the Researches of Lewis H. Morgan.* New York: International Publishers.
Erlich, H. S., Erlich-Ginor, M. and Beland, H. (2009). Being in Berlin: A large group experience in the Berlin Congress. *International Journal of Psychoanalysis,* 90, 809–25.
Fairbairn, W. R. D. (1941/1952). A revised psychopathology of the psychoses and psychoneuroses. In *Psychoanalytic Studies of the Personality.* London: Routledge & Kegan Paul, pp. 28–58.
Fanon, F. (1952/1967). *Black Skin, White Masks,* trans. C. L. Markmann. New York: Grove.
Fanon, F. (1961/1968). *The Wretched of the Earth,* trans. C. Farrington. New York: Grove.
Fanon, F. (1986) *Black Skin, White Masks.* London: Pluto.
Ferenczi, S. (1920). *Further Contributions to the Theory and Technique of Psychoanalysis.* London: Hogarth Press.
Flax, J. (1990). *Thinking Fragments: Psychoanalysis, Feminism, and Postmodernism in the Contemporary West.* Berkeley: University of California Press.
Ford, C. S. and Beach, F. A. (1952). Patterns of sexual behavior. *American Anthropologist,* 54, 1, 75–6.
Forrester, J. (1977). *Dispatches from the Freud Wars: Psychoanalysis and its Passions.* Cambridge, MA: Harvard University Press.
Foucault, M. (1969). What is an author? In J. V. Harari (ed.), *Textual Strategies.* Ithaca, NY: Cornell University Press.
Foucault, M. (1979). *Discipline and Punish: The Birth of the Prison,* trans. A. Sheridan. New York: Vintage Books.
Foucault, M. (1980a). *Power/Knowledge.* New York: Pantheon Books.
Foucault, M. (1980b). *History of Sexuality.* New York: Vintage Books.
Fraser, N. and Honneth, A. (2003). *Redistribution or Recognition?: A Political-Philosophical Exchange.* London: Verso.
Freud, A. (1937). *The Ego and the Mechanisms of Defence.* London: Hogarth Press and the Institute of Psycho-Analysis.
Freud, S. (1905). *Three Essays on the Theory of Sexuality, SE,* vol. 7, pp. 125–245.
Freud, S. (1913). *Totem and Taboo, SE,* vol. 13, pp. 1–164.
Freud, S. (1914). *On the History of Psycho-analytic Movement, SE,* vol. 14, pp. 1–66.
Freud, S. (1920). *Beyond the Pleasure Principle, SE,* vol. 18, pp. 1–64.
Freud, S. (1933). *New Introductory Lectures on Psycho-Analysis, SE,* vol. 22, pp. 1–182.
Frosh, S. (2005). *Hate and the 'Jewish Science': Anti-Semitism, Nazism and Psychoanalysis.* London: Palgrave.
Gagnon, J. H. and Simon, W. (2005). *Sexual Conduct: The Social Sources of Human Sexuality,* 2nd edn. New Brunswick, NJ: Aldine.
Gallop, J. (1985). *Reading Lacan.* Ithaca, NY: Cornell University Press.
Gay, P. (1988). *Freud: A Life for our Time.* New York: W. W. Norton.
Giddens, A. (1984). *The Constitution of Society: Outline of the Theory of Structuration.* Cambridge: Polity Press.
Giddens, A. (1992). *The Transformation of Intimacy.* Cambridge: Polity Press.
Gilman, S. L. (1993). *The Case of Sigmund Freud: Medicine and Identity at the Fin de Siecle.* Baltimore, MD: The Johns Hopkins University Press.

Green, A. (2002). *The Chains of Eros*. London: Karnac Books.

Grotz, E. (1990). *Jacques Lacan: A Feminist Introduction*. London: Routledge.

Grünbaum, A. (2002). Critique of psychoanalysis. In E. Erwin (ed.), *The Freud Encyclopaedia*. London: Routledge.

Habermas, J. (1987). *Lectures on the Philosophical Discourse of Modernity*. Cambridge, MA: MIT Press.

Haraway, D. (1991). *Simians, Cyborgs and Women: The Reinvention of Nature*. New York: Routledge.

Harding, S. (1986). *The Science Question in Feminism*. Ithaca, NY: Cornell University Press.

Harding, S. (1991). *Whose Science? Whose Knowledge? Thinking from Women's Lives*. Ithaca, NY: Cornell University Press.

Hartmann, H. (1958). *Ego Psychology and the Problem of Adaptation*. New York: International Universities Press.

Heelas, P. and Lock, A. (eds) (1981). *Indigenous Psychologies: The Anthropology of the Self*. London: Academic Press.

Heidegger, M. (1977). The origin of the work of art. In D. F. Krell (ed.), *Basic Writings*. New York: Harper & Row, pp. 174–7.

Hilman, J. (1972). *The Myth of Analysis: Three Essays in Archetypal Psychology*. Evanston: Northwestern University Press.

Horney, K. (1922). *Feminine Psychology*. New York: W. W. Norton.

Horkheimer, M. and Adorno, T. (1972). *Dialectic of Enlightenment*. New York: Seabury.

Ingleby, D. (1985). Professionals and socializers: The 'psy-complex'. *Research in Law, Deviance and Control*, 7, 79–109.

Irigaray, L. (1985) *This Sex which is Not One*, trans. C. Porter with C. Burke. Ithaca, NY: Cornell University Press.

Jones, E. (1955). *The Life and Work of Sigmund Freud, vol. 2: Years of Maturity, 1901–1919*. London: Hogarth Press.

Jung, C. G. (1933). *Modern Man in Search of a Soul*. New York: Harvest.

Kakar, S. (1978). *The Inner World: A Psychoanalytic study of Childhood and Society in India*. Oxford University Press.

Keller, E. F. (1984). *Reflections on Gender and Science*. New Haven: Yale University Press.

Khanna, R. (2003). *Dark Continents: Postcolonialism and Psychoanalysis*. Durham, NC: Duke University Press.

Klein, M. (1932). *The Psycho-analysis of Children*. London: Hogarth Press.

Klein, M. (1957). Envy and gratitude. In *Envy and Gratitude and Other Works 1946–1963*. New York: Delta.

Kovel, J. (1984). *White Racism: A Psychohistory*. New York: Columbia University Press.

Krafft-Ebing, R. F. von (1886/1902). *Psychopathia Sexualis, with Especial Reference to Antipathic Sexual Instinct: A Medico-Legal Study*, ed. and trans. F. J. Rebman. New York: Rebman.

Kramer, P. D. (2009). *Freud: Inventor of the Modern Mind*. New York: Harper Perennial.

Kristeva, J. (2001). *Melanie Klein*. New York: Columbia University Press.

Kuhn, T. S. (1970). *The Structure of Scientific Revolutions*. University of Chicago Press.

Lacan. J. (1953/2002). *Écrits: A Selection*, trans. B. Fink. New York: W. W. Norton.

Lacan, J. (1956/1968). The function of speech and language in psychoanalysis. In *The Language of the Self: The Function of Language in Psychoanalysis*, trans. A. Wilden. Baltimore, MD: The Johns Hopkins University Press.

Lacan, J. (1959–60/1992). *The Seminar VII. Ethics of Psychoanalysis*, trans. D. Porter. London: Routledge.

Laing, R. D. (1961). *The Self and Others*. London: Tavistock Publications.

Laplanche, J. and Pontalis, J.-B. (1972). *The Language of Psychoanalysis*, trans. D. Nicholson-Smith. London: Hogarth Press.

Laslett, P. (1971). *The World We Have Lost*, rev. edn. London: Methuen.

Lawson, R. B., Graham, J. E. and Baker, K. M. (2007). *A History of Psychology: Globalization, Ideas, and Applications*. Upper Saddle River, NJ: Pearson.

Leader, D. (2000). *Freud's Footnotes*. London: Faber & Faber.

Levinas, E. (1969). *Totality and Infinity*, trans. A. Lingis. Pittsburgh: Duquesne University Press.

Levinas, E. (1996). Substitution, trans. P. Atterton, G. Noctor and S. Critchley, In A. Peperzak, S. Critchley and R. Bernasconi (eds), *Emmanuel Levinas: Basic Philosophical Writings*. Bloomington: Indiana University Press.

Maddox, B. (2006). *Freud's Wizard: Ernest Jones and the Transformation of Psychoanalysis*. London: John Murray.

Manheim, K. (1936). *Ideology and Utopia*. London: Routledge.

Mannoni, O. (1950/1990). *Prospero and Caliban: The Psychology of Colonization*. Ann Arbor, MI: Ann Arbor Paperbacks.

Marcuse, H. (1955/1961). *Eros and Civilization*. New York: Vintage Books.

Marcuse, H. (1964). *One-dimensional Man*. Boston: Beacon.

Marcuse, H. (1968). *Negations*. Boston: Beacon.

Masson, J. (1992). *The Assault on Truth: Freud's Suppression of the Seduction Theory*. New York: Harper Perennial.

Memmi, A. (1965). *The Colonizer and the Colonized*, trans. H. Greenfeld. Boston: Beacon.

Millett, K. (1971). *Sexual Politics*. London: Rupert Hart-Davis.

Mitchell. J. (1974). *Psychoanalysis and Feminism*. London: Allen Lane.

Mitchell, S. (1988). *Relational Concepts in Psychoanalysis: An Integration*. Cambridge, MA: Harvard University Press.

Obeyesekere, G. (1990). *The Work of Culture: Symbolic Transformation in Psychoanalysis and Anthropology*. University of Chicago Press.

Ogden, T. (1982). *Projective Identification as Psychotherapeutic Technique*. New York: Jason Aronson.

Parker, I. (1997). *Psychoanalytic Culture: Psychoanalytic Discourse in Western Society*. London: Sage.

Popper, K. (1963). *Conjectures and Refutations*. London: Routledge & Kegan Paul.

Poster, M. (1978). *Critical Theory of Family*. New York: Seabury.

Reich, W. (1951). *Orgone Accumulator: Its Medical and Scientific Use*. London: Rising Free.

Richards, B. (ed.) (1984). *Capitalism and Infancy: Essays on Psychoanalysis and Politics*. London: Free Association Books.

Rose, J. (1986). *Sexuality in the Field of Vision*. London: Verso.

Rose, N. (1990). *Governing the Soul: The Shaping of the Private Self*. London: Routledge.

Roudinesco, E. (1997). *Jacques Lacan*, trans. B. Bray. New York: Columbia University Press.

Rustin, M. (1982). A socialist consideration of Kleinian psychoanalysis. *New Left Review*, 131, 71–96.

Sachs, W. (1996). *Black Hamlet*. Baltimore, MD: The Johns Hopkins University Press.

Said, E. (1994/2004). Two visions in *Heart of Darkness*. In S. Regan (ed.), *The Nineteenth Century Novel: A Critical Reader*. London: Routledge.

Sampson, E. (1989). The challenge of social change for psychology: Globalisation and psychology's theory of the person. *American Psychologist*, 44(6), 918–25.

Sartre, J. P. (1948/1976). *Black Orpheus*, trans. S. W. Allen. Paris: Presence Africaine.

Sayers, J. (1987). Melanie Klein, psychoanalysis and feminism. *Feminist Review*, 25, 25–37.

Scheler, M. (1980). *Problems of a Sociology of Knowledge*, trans. Manfred S. Frings. London: Routledge & Kegan Paul.

Schorske, C. E. (1980). *Fin-de-siècle Vienna: Politics and Culture*. New York: Knopf.

Segal, L. (1999). *Why Feminism?* Cambridge: Polity Press.

Shorter, E. (1975). *The Making of the Modern Family*. New York: Basic Books.

Smith, L. T. (1999). *Decolonizing Methodologies: Research and Indigenous Peoples*. New York: Zed Books.

Spence, D. P. (1982). *Narrative Truth and Historical Truth: Meaning and Interpretation in Psychoanalysis*. New York: W. W. Norton.

Spivak, G. C. (1987). *In Other Worlds: Essays in Cultural Politics*. New York: Methuen.

Stanley, H. M. (1878). *Through the Dark Continent*. New York: Harper and Brothers.

Stern, D. (1985). *The Interpersonal World of the Infant*. New York: Basic Books.

Sullivan, H. S. (1940). *Conceptions of Modern Psychiatry*. New York: W. W. Norton.

Sullivan, H. S. (1953). *Interpersonal Theory of Psychiatry*. New York: W. W. Norton.

Sulloway, F. J. (1979). *Freud, Biologist of the Mind: Beyond the Psychoanalytic Legend*. New York: Basic Books.

Young, R. J. C. (2001). *Postcolonialism: A Historical Introduction*. Oxford: Blackwell.

Verene, D. P. (1981). *Vico's Science of Imagination*. Ithaca, NY: Cornell University Press.

Vico, G. (1725/1948). *The New Science*, trans. T. G. Bergin and M. H. Fisch. Ithaca, NY: Cornell University Press.

Von Bertalanffy, L. (1968). *General Systems Theory*. New York: George Braziller.

Webster, R. (1996). *Why Freud was Wrong: Sin, Science, and Psychoanalysis*. New York: Lightning Source.

Wilden, A. (1972). *System and Structure: Essays in Communication and Exchange*. London: Tavistock Publications.

Winnicott, D. W. (1953). Transitional objects and transitional phenomena. *International Journal of Psychoanalysis*, 34, 89–97.

Wittgenstein, L. (1948). *Philosophical Investigations*. Oxford: Blackwell.

Young, R. J. C. (2001). *Postcolonialism: An Historical Introduction*. Oxford: Blackwell.

Zaretsky, E. (2004). *Secrets of the Soul: A Social and Cultural History of Psychoanalysis*. New York: Vintage.

Žižek, S. (1989). *The Sublime Object of Ideology*. New York: Verso.

1
Freud's Culture

Ian Parker

Psychoanalysis is a talking cure that is always located in a particular kind of language, the language of the culture that the psychoanalyst needs to have an awareness of in order to practise. The cure requires that there be some sense that things are unconscious to us, pushed out of awareness and kept at bay because they disturb and threaten to undermine what we think makes us happy, and such things also circulate in culture. Freud homed in on what was most disturbing: sexuality as the most intimate core of who we are and around which we construct hosts of fantasies about how we might love others and find satisfaction in that love. However, one of the lessons of psychoanalysis is that what appears to be most 'intimate' is rooted in our relations with others.

In Freud's work there is a cluster of assumptions about the self, and there are complex culturally specific images put to work about what is inside and outside us, what forms of motivation are primary and how they push to the surface, and what speaking about ourselves might cover over or reveal. This chapter critically reviews Freud's discussions of culture, starting with his arguments for the importance of culture in analytic training, then focusing on his views of collective activity, conceptions of myth and worldviews, the role of politics, religion, connections with his account of civilization, and concluding with consequences that Freud saw for the progress of psychoanalysis itself and for psychoanalysis as part of culture.

Freud

One of the things we notice about Freud's work over the course of his lifetime is that there is a shift away from individual neurological questions to questions of culture. We can trace the arc of this shift from his earliest work on the aphasias as disorders of language use in which Freud was already starting to make some connections between neurological disorders and the nature of language itself. Then we find even at the birth of psychoanalysis there is a necessary separation between biology and culture which is evident in his observation in his visit to Paris in the 1880s that hysteria is not a disorder peculiar to women as traditional psychiatry had it. Psychoanalysis operated on a concept of the 'drive' which, as Freud pointed out, operated at the border of the physiological and the psychical. Mental pain was always infused by cultural processes. Towards the end of his life Freud was less optimistic about the prospects of addressing this pain through individual therapy, and saw psychoanalysis as an approach to understanding the cultural-historical nature of human beings.

There is, in addition, all the way through the early history of psychoanalysis, the history Freud was responsible for shaping through interventions in key debates, a connection between clinical, professional and institutional disputes, and these disputes often connect with political questions. One example is the intense debate over the 'free clinics' and the provision of psychoanalytic treatment to working-class patients who could not afford to pay for consultations with an analyst in private practice. In the debates with Carl Jung over anthropology and literature, Freud honed his skills in interpreting cultural phenomena, and those debates quickly become inflected with a political dimension, one which became salient when the Nazis took power, when psychoanalysis was banned, and when Jung chose to remain at the head of a psychotherapy organization based in Berlin. The debates with Wilhelm Reich over the connection between psychoanalytic change and political change stretched the conceptual terrain in the other direction, and it does again make clear that psychoanalysis was immersed in cultural-political activities.

These debates have implications for clinical practice, and Freud was clear that psychoanalytic attention to fantasies about abuse, for example, have to be located in the context of abusive family relationships. Against the caricature of psychoanalysis as refusing to acknowledge the reality of child sexual abuse, we find many references in his early writings to the reality of the conditions in which his analysands find themselves. The argument is not that these circumstances are unimportant, but that psychoanalysis has a particular focus on the domain of fantasy. The case descriptions Freud provides have then opened the way to a detailed exploration of the nature of the culture in which the analysand speaks of their distress.

We can see the crucial role of culture in psychoanalysis in Freud's discussions of collective activity, his conception of myth and his comments on the role of worldviews in psychoanalysis. He makes specific comments on politics, religion and civilization, and there are then consequences for how we might understand clinical work. We will begin by looking at what Freud had to say about culture in psychoanalytic training.

Training

In the mid-1920s Freud was embroiled in a series of sharp debates over the role of 'lay analysis', that is, psychoanalysis carried out by those who were not medically trained. Psychoanalysis in the United States was controlled by doctors who insisted that a medical training was a prerequisite for analytic training, and this was to have profound consequences for émigré analysts fleeing fascism in Europe. When they arrived in the USA, those who were not medically qualified were not able to practise, and even some of the psychoanalysts who were also doctors had to undergo retraining because their medical qualifications were not recognized. Even the title of Freud's key intervention in these debates is telling. The title 'The Question of Lay Analysis', from which the following quote is taken, was originally translated as 'The Problem of Lay Analysis', which made it seem as if he was arguing with the US medics rather than against them:

> If – which may sound fantastic to-day – one had to found a college of psycho-analysis, much would have to be taught in it which is also taught by the medical faculty: alongside of depth-psychology, which would always remain the principal subject, there would be an introduction to biology, as much as possible of the science of sexual life, and familiarity with the symptomatology of psychiatry. On the other hand, analytic instruction would include branches of knowledge which are remote from medicine and which the doctor does not come across in his practice: the history of civilization, mythology, the psychology of religion and the science of literature. Unless he is well at home in these subjects, an analyst can make nothing of a large amount of his material. (Freud, 1926, p. 246)

We see a characteristic quality of Freud's writing here which we must take seriously if we want to understand psychoanalysis itself, which is that there is a careful rhetorical positioning of his own standpoint against those he wants to persuade. We will see this again and again in the following extracts. Here we see him posing the possibility of a college that sounds 'fantastic' and in which all of the standard psychiatric topics would need to be taught. Then there is the twist, that unlike standard psychiatric training, psychoanalysis requires something more and so it is this something more, an attention to culture, that we are invited to see as the defining elements of an authentic psychoanalytic training.

We should note that in Freud's proposal for a college of psychoanalysis, he does not suggest that there should be a merging of psychiatry, psychology and cultural studies. Instead, he counterposes a knowledge of biological processes as the kind of thing one might gain in a medical faculty to branches of knowledge that include the history of civilization, mythology, religion and literature. His argument, that the analyst must be 'at home' in these subjects, also has to be understood in the context of quite a sharp divide in German-speaking culture between the realm of the natural sciences and the human sciences. There are then consequences for how we should understand collective processes, a topic he addressed about five years before, and to which we should turn now.

Masses

The title of Freud's 'Group Psychology and the Analysis of the Ego' is, once again, a little misleading, and is a translation of the German title that was more directly concerned with collective phenomena generally. The reference to 'group psychology' already makes it seem as if Freud is proposing an application or extension of individual analysis to a form of 'Group Analysis', and as if he is concerned here with small groups. In fact, Freud was referring to 'mass psychology', and signalled this in the original title of his book. We should also bear in mind that the phrase 'analysis of the ego' is also quite problematic, and Freud was using an everyday commonsensical term in German ('Ich') to refer to the 'I'. The reference to the 'ego' in the title of his book about mass psychology tends to shift attention away from his theme, which is the immersion of the 'I' in society, to a binary opposition between the individual and the social, an opposition that he was actually questioning:

> The contrast between individual psychology and social or group psychology, which at first glance may seem to be full of significance, loses a great deal of its sharpness when it is examined more closely. It is true that individual psychology is concerned with the individual

man and explores the paths by which he seeks to find satisfaction for his instinctual impulses; but only rarely and under certain exceptional conditions is individual psychology in a position to disregard the relations of this individual to others. In the individual's mental life someone else is invariably involved, as a model, as an object, as a helper, as an opponent; and so from the very first individual psychology, in this extended but entirely justifiable sense of the words, is at the same time social psychology as well. (Freud, 1921, p. 69)

Freud insists here on a relational view of what we might now call the 'subject', pointing out that in the individual's mental life 'someone else is invariably involved', and he then goes on to spell out some of the ways that this 'someone else' might be involved. These implications of 'the other' in the mental life of the subject are then explored in psychoanalytic theory and clinical practice. This formulation differentiates psychoanalysis from 'individual psychology', and so we can see that for Freud psychoanalysis is defined by virtue of its attention to the subject as something always already 'social'. The kind of individual that psychoanalysis is concerned with is one that should be understood through the optic of social psychology.

Freud also neatly turns around a standard view of 'mass psychology', which is the focus of his book, and argues that this kind of mass psychology is not, as is often commonly thought, 'pathological'. Freud's examples in the book include 'crowds', and this aspect is often played up by other writers who are suspicious of crowd behaviour and who looked to Freud to support their argument that there is something pathological about collective activity. However, Freud also spends as much time discussing social institutions like the church and the army, and his analysis also refers to parliamentary assemblies. Here we have a range of instances where the subject is in relation to others, and if there is any hint of something 'pathological' in Freud's discussion at this point it is when he refers to the individual, for he says that it is only in 'exceptional conditions' that we are able to disregard the relation of this individual to others.

Myth

Let us go back a few more years in Freud's writing, to one of his case studies – this is from his discussion of the famous case of the 'Wolf-Man' – and here we can see how Freud locates the 'Oedipus complex' in an even more complex view of what 'myth' is and how it operates in the individual subject. It is clear here that what we learn from myth is not merely something that is added on to what we know about individual development, but that myth is embedded in the history of the subject. Freud makes reference here to a notion that was current in biological theory and was also being utilized in cultural analysis at the time, which is that 'ontogeny recapitulates phylogeny', that is, that individual development repeats in miniature the development of the species of which the individual is a member. For example, the human foetus shows at very early stages in its development gill-like mechanisms that testify to the emergence of the human species from an evolutionary sequence that included aquatic creatures:

> the phylogenetically inherited schemata...like the categories of philosophy, are concerned with the business of 'placing' the impressions derived from actual experience. I am inclined to take the view that they are precipitates from the history of human civilization. The Oedipus complex, which comprises a child's relation to his parents, is one of them – is, in fact, the best known member of the class. Wherever experiences fail to fit in with the hereditary schema, they become remodelled in the imagination – a process which might very profitably be followed out in detail. It is precisely such cases that are calculated to convince us of the independent existence of the schema. We are often able to see the schema triumphing over the experience of the individual. (Freud, 1918, p. 119)

Problematic as the direct appeal to evolutionary development to explain the functioning of Oedipal structure in human childhood is, Freud's discussion here also presupposes a much more nuanced engagement with cultural and philosophical debates. The mythological structure here operates as a 'schema' that overrides what the individual subject may directly be aware of; Freud says we see 'the schema triumphing over the experience of the individual'. This account thus operates in two ways. On the one hand there is a literal appeal to evolutionary biological processes, and Freud does try to ground the Oedipus complex in events in the 'primal horde' in other writings. On the other hand, however, there is a metaphorical aspect of Freud's argument, and the lesson is that what an individual may report of their 'experience' will not be sufficient to account for the structures that condition who they are, beyond conscious awareness there is something unconscious about the human subject, and this something unconscious is the stuff of myth.

We should not overlook the other cultural reference which Freud alludes to, which is that of the 'categories of philosophy'. These 'categories' are the kinds of schema that the Western Enlightenment philosopher Immanuel Kant describes in his philosophical writings, writings which Freud adverts to in other places, when, for example, he describes the super-ego – that which is 'above-I' – as operating in much the same way as Kant describes the moral 'categorical imperative'. The 'categories' here show us another side to the argument that Freud is making, for alongside the biological evolutionary reference – 'phylogenetically inherited schemata' and suchlike – he is concerned here with the 'placing' of impressions, and if we take the reference to Kant seriously, this 'placing' is in a 'structure' rather than in a series of mythological contents. That is what Oedipus gives us, the description of a 'structure' of relations between infant, care-giver and another figure that intervenes between those first two, not a description of particular culturally specific contents, of babies, mummies and daddies.

Worldviews

In addition to his clinical case histories, theoretical papers and a wide range of studies devoted to literature, history and cultural analysis, Freud took pains to explain psychoanalysis to a wider audience, and his introductory lectures at different points in his career provide valuable insight into how he saw his work intersecting with other fields of study. In the early 1930s, for example, he addressed the hopes that psychoanalysts might have to have their work seen as 'scientific'. There were high stakes here, and we have already noted the division between 'natural sciences' and 'human sciences' in the German-speaking world. Freud does not opt directly for either side of the divide, and it is clear here that he does not see psychoanalysis as providing its own distinct *Weltanschauung* or view of the world:

> Psycho-analysis, in my opinion, is incapable of creating a *Weltanschauung*. It does not need one: it is a part of science and can adhere to the scientific *Weltanschauung*. This, however, scarcely deserves such a grandiloquent title, for it is not all-comprehensive, it is too incomplete and makes no claim to being self-contained and to the construction of systems. Scientific thought is still very young among human beings; there are too many of the great problems which it has not yet been able to solve. A *Weltanschauung* erected

upon science has, apart from its emphasis on the real external world, mainly negative traits, such as submission to the truth and rejection of illusions. (Freud, 1933, pp. 181–2)

There are important lessons here for those who treat psychoanalysis as an overall covering explanation for every aspect of human experience and then try to apply the approach to explain in psychoanalytic terms every other domain. Freud argues that rather than psychoanalysis developing as a worldview itself, the closest it will come to a worldview is when it operates within a general scientific worldview. However, even this 'worldview' is carefully defined in 'negative' terms, for instead of providing a positive vision of how things are or how things should be, this 'worldview', such as it is, is concerned with 'truth' and 'rejection of illusions'.

There is another problem with the notion of 'worldview' that Freud notes here, another reason why psychoanalysis should be wary of turning itself into a worldview or even participating in a kind of worldview that pretended to provide a complete and inclusive system of knowledge. The problem is that psychoanalysis is 'incomplete' and it makes no claim to provide a 'self-contained' system. We can read this note of caution as also expressing something of the nature of psychoanalytic exploration of contradiction and division. Psychoanalysis does not aim at complete explanation, at a totalizing system of knowledge, but at a relation between the subject and knowledge in which both sides of the equation are defined by their incompleteness.

Politics

Individual and cultural 'worldviews' are anathema to psychoanalysis, and we see this warning once again in Freud's comments on political ideologies. The particular danger arises, he argued, when an ideological system imagines that it is 'self-contained' and 'exclusive'. Freud was politically rather a liberal figure, and viewed with suspicion all grand schemes to change the world. Even so, many of the early psychoanalysts were involved in left or centre-left politics and Freud's comments must be understood against this background. His comment that an enclosed political system like the 'Russian Bolshevism' that he warns against here might turn out to bear an 'uncanny likeness' to what they pit themselves against, is not an argument against politics as such, but an argument against 'worldview' politics:

The newly achieved discovery of the far-reaching importance of economic relations brought with it a temptation not to leave alterations in them to historical development but to put them into effect oneself by revolutionary action. Theoretical Marxism, as realized in Russian Bolshevism, has acquired the energy and the self-contained and exclusive character of a *Weltanschauung*, but at the same time an uncanny likeness to what it is fighting against. Though originally a portion of science and built up, in its implementation upon science and technology, it has created a prohibition of thought which is just as ruthless as was that of religion in the past. (Freud, 1933, pp. 179–80)

One way of reading this passage is to see Freud inveighing against any attempt to change the world, to see his reference to alterations in 'economic relations' that follow a path of 'historical development' as changes that must be allowed to take their course and not be interfered with by 'revolutionary action'. At the time he was writing, however, there were exactly these kinds of debates occurring among Marxists, and these debates were over the extent to which 'revolutionary action' might substitute for broader political change. The debate concerned tactics and ethics rather than whether change as such should or should not be aimed for.

Likewise, Freud's reference to Marxism as having built itself upon science, as 'originally a portion of science' as he puts it, should be understood within contemporary debates on the left. There was widespread agreement that a politically progressive scientific worldview, of which Marxism saw itself as a part if not sometimes in the vanguard, would replace archaic regressive religious conceptions of the world. The danger Freud points to is that a closed totalitarian system of thought, which Marxism could itself degenerate into, would then become like a kind of religious system. One can see here echoes of critiques of the Soviet Union that were being developed among Marxists in the 1930s. One thing is clear here, though, and that is Freud's suspicion of religious ideology as such.

Religion

We now go back to one of Freud's early writings – the earliest we will examine here – in which he develops one of his first sustained critiques of religious belief systems. This argument is taken up later in his work at a time when religious mystification has become hitched directly to political debate in the form of fascism, and then we can see him attempt to ground theological notions in detailed historical study. At this early point Freud is arguing from the ground of a 'human science' that would comprehend the development of human civilization, and 'religiosity' would then be symptomatic of a regression at the level of culture and at the level of the individual:

> one might venture to regard obsessional neurosis as a pathological counterpart of the formation of a religion, and to describe that neurosis as an individual religiosity and religion as a universal obsessional neurosis. The most essential similarity would reside in the underlying renunciation of the activation of instincts that are constitutionally present; and the chief difference would lie in the nature of those instincts, which in the neurosis are exclusively sexual in their origin, while in religion, they spring from egoistic sources. A progressive renunciation of constitutional instincts, whose activation might afford the ego primary pleasure, appears to be one of the foundations of the development of human civilization. (Freud, 1907, p. 126)

The crucial connection Freud makes between the individual and the cultural is twofold here. First, we see a mirror-like 'counterpart' to the 'formation of a religion' being described, which is 'obsessional neurosis'. The formation of a religion is what occurs at the level of culture, and culture itself is for Freud, as we will see, one of the achievements of 'the development of human civilization'. The obsessional-neurotic counterpart to this process is the disorder that occurs at the level of the individual. This then gives us an opening to understand how 'obsessional neurosis' appears as a concomitant of a certain kind of civilization, and so the psychoanalyst is pitched into a series of debates about the nature of our culture today.

The second aspect of the connection between the individual and culture is in the way Freud describes the 'sexual' as operating at the level of the individual and ego as operating at the level of culture. There is an implicit contrast here that can only be grasped if we remember that the 'instincts' that Freud refers to here are actually 'drives' – the word Freud uses in the original German text is 'drive', not the German word which refers to hard-wired biological processes – and that 'egoistic' is a rather clumsy translation of what concerns the 'I'. There is a relation between the individual and the cultural here that Freud describes as occurring inside the subject. Our 'individual' as well as the obsessional-neurotic distress that afflicts them is always already cultural. This raises questions about the 'development of human civilization', and what Freud means by 'civilization' as something conceptually distinct from culture.

Civilization

Freud's well-known phrase 'Civilization and its Discontents', which is taken from the standard translated title of his book of that name, is often read as a diagnosis of the particular forms of Western culture in which psychoanalysis itself took root. It is the kind of civilization that makes us discontented, and that reading of the phrase has led to a rich tradition of political analysis using psychoanalysis. However, while there are certainly aspects of capitalist culture that produce alienation and distress for the individuals who live in it, Freud is actually making a deeper point about the nature of our relations with others. Civilization refers to the particular set of technical accomplishments that we use to define a society, but 'culture' is the underlying stuff of human relatedness that we need as a precondition of any civilization whatsoever. Culture is what the infant enters as they navigate the Oedipus complex as a basic structure of dependency and then autonomy for the individual, and the title of Freud's study is actually 'the uneasiness inherent in culture'. There is no civilization that is not marked by this 'uneasiness', this contradiction between what we desire and those with whom we try to fulfil it:

> In an individual neurosis we take as our starting-point the contrast that distinguishes the patient from his environment, which is assumed to be 'normal'. For a group all of whose members are affected by one and the same disorder no such background could exist; it would have to be found elsewhere. And as regards the therapeutic application of our knowledge, what would be the use of the most correct analysis of social neuroses, since no one possesses authority to impose such a therapy upon the group? But in spite of all these difficulties, we may expect that one day someone will venture to embark upon the pathology of cultural communities. (Freud, 1930, p. 144)

Again, there is a surprising reversal in Freud's account, a contrast with what we might first expect him to say about normality and abnormality. The 'starting-point' he opens this passage with sets up an opposition between the 'normal' environmental background and the 'disorder' that the individual expresses in the particular form of their distress. Notice that the normal environment and the abnormal 'individual neurosis' are set up here not as absolute properties but as defined in relation to one another.

Then there is the reversal, when Freud points out that one day it may be possible to understand and perhaps provide therapeutic solutions to 'the pathology of cultural communities'. In that case it would be necessary to assume that there was a point from which the analyst could provide the 'correct analysis', and so it would be the individual who was 'normal'. But, as Freud notes, if this were to be possible, then the analyst would not be operating as an individual disconnected from any community, for a 'background' of some kind 'would have to be found elsewhere'. The lesson we can draw from this is that there is no independent point outside culture from which we can give diagnoses of its pathology, and even if one were pushed to imagine such an independent point it would not take the form of an individual.

Analysis

This brings us to one of the most cited and contested phrases in Freud's description of the aims of psychoanalysis as a clinical practice, 'Where id was, there ego shall be.' Once again we should note that the term 'id' gives to the term Freud actually used a specific character that is not there in the original German, which is 'Es' or 'it'. The famous phrase is given a quite specific cultural context in the next clause, when Freud says 'It is the work of culture – not unlike the draining of the Zuider Zee.' Now, if we follow this metaphor of the 'draining' of the Zuider Zee we can appreciate that this work of analysis, a 'work of culture', involves a 'draining' of the 'it' rather than simply beating it back into the depths of the unconscious. And there is, of course, another aspect of this draining of the Zuider Zee, which is that the land is reclaimed from it so that it is as if we are able to live in the domain of the it rather than being overwhelmed by it. Rather than escaping the 'it', the work of analysis, then, could just as easily be seen as enabling us to inhabit the realm of it:

> certain mystical practices may succeed in upsetting the normal relations between the different regions of the mind, so that, for instance, perception may be able to grasp happenings in the depths of the ego and in the id which were otherwise inaccessible to it. It may be doubted, however, whether this road will lead us to the ultimate truths from which salvation is to be expected. Nevertheless it may be

admitted that the therapeutic efforts of psycho-analysis have chosen a similar line of approach. Its intention is, indeed, to strengthen the ego, to make it more independent of the super-ego, to widen its field of perception and enlarge its organization, so that it can appropriate fresh portions of the id. Where id was, there ego shall be. It is the work of culture – not unlike the draining of the Zuider Zee. (Freud, 1933, pp. 79–80)

Freud argues that we 'appropriate fresh portions' of what has otherwise been inaccessible to us, parts of our lives that have assumed an independent existence and driven us without our conscious assent. He does not argue that we make ourselves independent of those aspects of our existence that have an 'it'-like quality, but he does argue that we can be more independent of the super-ego. We are not being invited to retreat from that which is in us, but to take some distance from what is above us.

Freud is very careful here to limit the claims of psychoanalysis, not to make it seem as if psychoanalysis offers the kind of 'salvation' that 'mystical practices' in religious worldviews have promised in the past. Psychoanalysis does not provide a 'worldview', as we have already pointed out, and so it certainly does not promise 'salvation'. Freud sets up an intriguing contrast here between that road to salvation and ultimate truths and psychoanalysis, and so sets himself against the idea that this is the road that we should travel in order to 'grasp happenings in the depths of the ego and in the id which were otherwise inaccessible to it'. The task of psychoanalysis is indeed to widen the 'field of perception' of the 'I', but at the same time to locate that 'I' in culture. Psychoanalysis as a clinical practice is therefore simultaneously a cultural practice, a cultural achievement.

Freudian culture

Freud's work has itself turned into a powerful cultural practice, and so we should conclude with some reflections on what we have described and some consequences for the way we might understand the popularity of Freud today.

Every week in newspapers and magazines we find another exposé of Freud as a fraud, and then, in the advice columns and first-person accounts, we read of childhood trauma, repression, denial and the value of talking to someone else about your problems. Rather than treat psychoanalysis simply as a key to unlock the secrets of the subject, psychoanalytic theory should be treated here as a powerful framework because psychoanalytic knowledge helps structure culture.

Freud looked to the collective cultural resources that structure our sense of ourselves and those aspects of our lives that lie outside conscious awareness. Freud invites us to take seriously psychoanalysis as a historically constituted symbolic resource rather than something lying in a mysterious spiritual realm. Such cultural resources do not float beneath the individual unconscious of each of us, but operate as an unconscious cultural precondition for us to think of ourselves as individuals. A multiplicity of tacit understandings, unacknowledged assumptions and unintended consequences frame our lives as we encounter and manage relations with others.

There are many different psychoanalytic resources with competing vocabularies, and so we need to acknowledge that there is no one correct interpretation, or one correct psychoanalytic system for the wording of an interpretation. It is the nature of the unconscious, the unconscious produced for us in culture now, to be riven by contradictory meanings and the nature of contemporary consciousness is to tolerate these contradictions, and to smooth them over.

Psychoanalysis is a rational therapeutic enterprise, a theoretical framework in the human sciences to notice contradiction. We struggle, then, over the tension between different contradictory understandings. Each version of psychoanalysis has an appeal within specific cultural arenas, and it would be a mistake to propose one version as applicable to all. Different individuals may have recourse to different forms of psychoanalytic argument on different occasions to understand themselves. Even resistance or the attempt to repudiate a certain form of psychoanalysis may be voiced from within a discursive framework that is structured by other different competing psychoanalytic suppositions. For example, someone may declare that they do not like psychoanalysis because it does not take seriously what people say about the reasons they do things, but then the same person may employ the idea that there are things we know about ourselves that are outside immediate awareness.

Different forms of psychoanalysis that are prevalent within contemporary culture are thus collective phenomena, and these collective phenomena will then manifest themselves for each individual subject in the clinic in distinct idiosyncratic ways. The psychoanalyst needs to know something of the forms that psychoanalysis takes in culture, and what the individual brings from culture into the clinic. There is no one specific form of psychoanalysis in culture, rather a competing network of contradictory notions, and a clinician working within a particular theoretical framework will need to know something about the range of psychoanalytic notions that an individual will bring to therapy as their own theoretical frames of self-reference. This kind of psychoanalytic subjectivity is the site upon which psychoanalysis might work, for without such a historically constituted form of subjectivity there will be nothing to interpret, no sense for the analysand that there is something 'unconscious' that is other to themselves, and so nothing for the analyst to interpret.

It is easy to write off psychoanalytic therapy as self-indulgence, and many psychologists spend much energy proving that Freud was 'unscientific' or corrupt, but that is really beside the point. The reason why discussions of Freud and the Freudians seem so interminable and obsessive is that psychoanalysis is so deeply woven into the fabric of our culture. It is there in our gossip about other people's experiences and strange ideas and it is there in our gossip about others and ourselves.

References

Freud, S. (1907). *Obsessive Actions and Religious Practices, SE*, vol. 9.
Freud, S. (1914). *From the History of an Infantile Neurosis, SE*, vol. 17.
Freud, S. (1921). *Group Psychology and the Analysis of the Ego, SE*, vol. 18.
Freud, S. (1926). *The Question of Lay Analysis, SE*, vol. 20.
Freud, S. (1929). *Civilization and its Discontents, SE*, vol. 21.
Freud, S. (1933). *New Introductory Lectures on Psycho-analysis, SE*, vol. 22.

2
The Re-enactment of Denial

Stephen Frosh

States of congress and denial

In 2007, the International Psychoanalytic Association (IPA) held its biennial Congress in Berlin. Germany had been the site for several such Congresses in the early history of psychoanalysis and the previous Berlin Congress was the last one attended in person by Freud. However, since World War II and the shift of psychoanalysis' 'mother-tongue' from German to English, only one previous Congress had been held in Germany. This was the Hamburg Congress of 1985, devoted to the topic of 'Identification and its Vicissitudes' and fraught with the tensions of a return to the site of desolation not only of psychoanalysis, but of course also of European Jewry, to which the overwhelming majority of pre-war psychoanalysts had belonged. The complexity and intensity of the emotional situation of Hamburg was such that it was always likely to be the case that the Congress would be a disappointment, and this is basically how things turned out – though the actual terms of this disappointment repay careful consideration and have been the subject of much subsequent reminiscence, scholarship and speculation (Freedman, 1988; Frosh, 2005; Moses and Hrushovski-Moses, 1986). The 2007 Berlin Congress, a generation later, took as its theme 'Remembering, Repeating, and Working Through' and was explicitly set up to examine some of the issues that lingered from the Hamburg Congress – issues of coming-to-terms, of laying-to-rest, of moving on, if one can translate the title into its underlying wishful fantasy. This Congress seems to have received positive reviews throughout the psychoanalytic world, at least as evident in the materials published so far; yet there is evidence even in these public materials of a continuing uncertainty or even reprise, a repressed, perhaps, and a threatening return. Not surprisingly, this lingering sorrow is connected with issues of culpability and accommodation with Nazism, of the ethics of psychoanalysis and its integrity, and of the denial and even betrayal of history. It may also testify to the actual, empirical difficulty of converting the wish for reparation – for dealing with hurt and destructiveness – into actual reparative acts; that is, one tendency that is traced in the material to be presented here is for these Congresses to act as if past trauma has been dealt with, without anything actually changing or being 'worked through'. The sense of something not dealt with is also, however, reflective of a much more specific dynamic that was once core to psychoanalysis and may still be so, if the evidence of the Congress can be taken seriously: the relationship of psychoanalysis to its own Jewish origins, to its treatment of its Jewish membership, and to the existence of anti-Semitism in its own institutional body.

A number of preliminaries are necessary before examining these issues, and in particular thinking about the resonance between events at the 1985 and 2007 Congresses. The argument here is that there is a lot left over, that the 2007 meeting did not put paid to the unresolved issues from the Hamburg Congress 20 years earlier, but rather found new ways to dramatize them, as if what still lies there, in the crevices of some kind of institutional unconscious, remains active or is stirred to life whenever someone purports to deal with it. One might expect this from an immersion in psychoanalysis itself: trauma does not usually go away; it is rarely fully worked through, however much it is remembered and repeated; something always seems to undermine what appear to be the very best intentions. This does not, of course, mean that anyone is to blame, or at least not in any simple way. It is just a fact: it is easier to remain in a situation of denial than to grasp the thing itself, with all its thorns. 'Denial', here, is connected with Stan Cohen's (2001) typology, in which he distinguishes between 'literal', 'interpretive' and 'justificatory' denial. The first simply states, 'this did not happen', and is very powerful and widespread, but thankfully no longer very evident in psychoanalysts' reflections on the Nazis, even though it was the primary approach taken prior to the Hamburg Congress. That is, in the 30 or 40 years after the war, German psychoanalysis proceeded as if it had had no part in the Third Reich, as if there had been no appeasement of or collaboration with the Nazis, as if it had been simply another victim. The second form of denial identified by Cohen (2001), 'interpretive denial', accepts that something happened but reinterprets it. This form of denial can also be seen in the psychoanalytic armoury with respect to Nazism, for instance in comparisons between the psychoanalysts and the German psychotherapists of the time. These present the analysts as standing out for something more ethically sound, for example rescuing people from the 'euthanasia' programme by offering them treatment instead of allowing them to be taken away into extermination camps. Even Goggin and Goggin (2001), who align themselves with the argument that psychoanalysis was oppressed in Nazi Germany, reject this as a defence, commenting on how some of the leading psychoanalysts were sucked into support for extermination of 'uncured' homosexuals and 'incurable' forms of battle fatigue. Finally, Cohen's (2001) third category of 'justificatory denial' which acknowledges what went on but argues that it was necessary, has been evident in related arguments that the actions of the pre-war German psychoanalysts were motivated by an attempt to preserve psychoanalysis in whatever form was possible, and the later claims that Freud had supported the German analysts' actions, or even that the Jewish dominance of psychoanalysis did, in fact, need some rectifying.

It should be noted that the categorization offered by Cohen may miss some of the resonances of the *psychoanalytic* notion of denial as a kind of active 'fending-off' process in which the subject has to carry out a good deal of defensive work to keep at bay something that is, unconsciously, already known. As presented above (though not in Cohen's original), it also perhaps underemphasizes the way in which denial can be a collective, 'social' phenomenon, at the 'microsocial' level of groups and institutions (Seu, 2010) as well as by large sections of a society. As has become evident in recent work on recognition and acknowledgement, questions of responsibility, especially the responsibility for harm done to others, are crucial in developing modes of ethical relationality that resist violence and promote active engagement with others who may at one time or another be strangers, 'aliens' or victims. This material is too dense to allow exposition here (see Frosh, 2011a), but it points to the intense and disturbingly self-searching way with which such acknowledgement has to be achieved if denial of the psychoanalytic variety is to be overcome. This includes the denial perpetrated by psychoanalysts and by the institutions of psychoanalysis as well.

Identification and its vicissitudes, or contending with 'our Hitler'

There are now many places in which the history of German psychoanalysis' engagement with Nazism is dealt with in detail, including Cocks (1997), Brecht et al. (1985) and Frosh (2005). This work has shown clearly that the psychoanalysts followed a policy of 'appeasement' towards the Nazis, characterized by an attempt to distance psycho-analysis from its 'Jewish' elements; that this resulted very quickly in the cleansing from the German Psychoanalytic Society of its Jewish members; and that the non-Jewish analysts who thereafter consti-tuted the Society managed to maintain their activities throughout the period of the Third Reich. For many years, this history was largely hidden, as the psychoanalysts set about rebuilding their organization and their myths, specifically presenting themselves – like many other Germans – as always having been victims and possibly opponents of Nazism (Brecht, 1995). It was only at the first post-war Congress to take place in Germany, the Hamburg Congress of 1985, that the real history broke into consciousness. More than anything else, this was through an accompanying exhibition, recorded in Brecht et al. (1985), which revealed to the psychoanalysts in an 'undeniable' way, through docu-ments and photographs as well as an understated commentary, simply how far the collaboration with the Nazis had gone, and how impos-sible it would be to see this as anything other than a betrayal of the Jewish analysts, and of psychoanalysis itself. It is this heritage with which the 'returnees' to Germany for the two Congresses have had to contend.

Not everything that goes on in conferences relates closely to the main event; people have their personal and professional agendas and interests, and many of the papers that are given there could be given anywhere in the world. This was no less true of the Hamburg and Berlin IPA Congresses than of any other, but it is nevertheless the case that everything that happened in both places seems to have happened under the shadow of the 'return to Germany', and, hence, could not escape the issue of what it means to have a Nazi past. Norbert Freedman (1988), introducing a special issue of *Psychoanalysis and Contemporary Thought* charged with communicating the events of the Hamburg Congress to an American audience, argues that the official theme, 'Identification and its Vicissitudes', 'was hardly the dominant issue' (p. 198). For him, the question was rather identification and *mourning*; or rather, the failure of mourning and the action that might have been taken to deal with this failure:

> In a letter to Dieter Ohlmeier, president of the German Psychoanalytic Association, Martin Wangh complained that the real theme should have been 'Mourning and Reconstitution.' Only one out of the five days of the programme was devoted to this theme. Yet

implicitly, in corridors, dinner conversations, and parties, it was all-pervasive. A review of over 200 newspaper reports on the Congress in the German press indicated that Wangh was right. The main focus of the Congress dealt with the reexamination of the history of psychoanalysis during the Nazi period and the persistence of the psychological phenomena created by the Holocaust. (p. 198)

The relationship between 'Identification and its Vicissitudes' and the proposed alternative, 'Mourning and Reconstitution', may seem like a technical one, but it says quite a lot about the possibilities for what in the Berlin Congress became coded as 'working through', and what is here thought about in relation to denial. It is true that a great deal of the work in Hamburg on 'Identification' had little to do with the Nazi phenomenon, and that in many places its clinical focus served to *distance* psychoanalysis from its history through a focus on the 'vicissitudes' of clinical work. On the other hand, there is no particular reason to suppose that the change of terminology would have prevented the same distancing and denying mechanisms from operating, and the term 'identification' does at least hold within it a sense of *accusation* that may be missing from the phenomenology of mourning. Who is it who is identified with what, exactly?

In this regard, the Hamburg Congress got off to a good start. The Congress was opened by the Mayor of Hamburg, Klaus von Dohnyani, who gave a remarkably well-informed and direct presentation of the issues and feelings that were involved in holding the Congress on German soil. Von Dohnyani noted that the exhibition had revealed the equivalence between the actions of psychoanalysts during the Third Reich and those of other Germans, even those who might seem well intentioned. 'For fear of losing everything,' he said, 'bit by bit was sacrificed, every step being rational – and yet at the same time always in the wrong direction. Here a compromise concerning persons, there a compromise of principles, but always in the pretended interest of preserving the whole – which in the end was lost' (Opening Ceremony, 34th IPA Congress, 1986, p. 4). Von Dohnyani then asked whether psychoanalysis could 'help us not only to understand ourselves better, but also to be and act better'; his doubts on this subject were clear for all to see. And finally, looking the issue of acknowledging the past through identification straight in the face: 'Whoever says: our Bach and our Beethoven, must also say: our Hitler. This, too, will be one of your topics' (p. 4).

Actually, it was not. As described in detail elsewhere (Frosh, 2005), all three of Cohen's types of denial plus the fourth, psychoanalytic, one could be seen at work in the Congress. There was praise for the achievements of the German Psychoanalytic Association in recuperating German psychoanalysis after the war, and there was an account of psychoanalysis as one of the *victims* of Nazism, but there was little that examined the specificity of the German psychoanalysts' culpability. There were references later to the power of the emotional atmosphere of the Congress and claims that the effect of this was that by its end 'Our German colleagues were not only colleagues but very often friends' (Weinshel, 1986, p. 89), as if reconciliation and forgiveness had been wrought. However, it is clear from the accounts of others present that not everyone agreed. Rafael Moses and Rena Hrushovski-Moses (1986) spoke on behalf of many Jewish analysts when they expressed their unease and disappointment. 'We left Hamburg before the official farewell party,' they wrote (p. 175). 'We were feeling vaguely depressed. The general atmosphere was that something had been missed. The central issue of this Congress – that it was the first one to be held in Germany since the Second World War and since the Holocaust – had been very much in the air but had not been adequately dealt with.' They go on to describe a sequence of events during the Congress in which both German and non-German (including Jewish) analysts stepped back from actually confronting the feelings swirling below the surface, as if they did not want to risk blowing something fragile apart. In what might perhaps be seen as a common defensive move, the past was invoked precisely in order that it should not be fully faced. Moses and Hrushovski-Moses suggest that behind all this there was a complex of dynamic forces, including particularly a fear on the part of German analysts that they were going to be attacked, so that they and the organizers of the Congress worked hard to avoid confrontations, and a complementary sense amongst non-German analysts that they wanted to move on, 'that the Germans of today could not and should not be held responsible for what their parent generation had done; that peace must be made and the past put aside' (p. 179). The concern then became that the Congress should 'go well' rather than deal with the issues, the kind of thing that often happens – in the service of denial – both in individual psychoanalytic sessions and in organizations and meetings of all kinds.

In a paper on the Hamburg Congress, John Kafka (1988, p. 299) notes one particular mechanism of denial, which he terms 'the syndrome of "dedifferentiation of holocausts"' which 'can manifest itself by a shift of focus to other historical or current events, injustices, tragedies, and slaughters'. Kafka locates the formal description of the defensive functions of this 'dedifferentiation' in a paper by Vogt, who analysed

his own 'profound relief upon hearing that the Israeli army had not prevented the slaughters in the Palestinian camps [in Sabra and Shatilla].
This led him to a piece of self-analysis in which he discovered he felt
relieved that "they too" could be guilty. Through this path he arrived
at the shocking insight of his own feelings of "identification" with Nazi
guilt' (Kafka, 1988, p. 299). Moses and Hrushovski-Moses (1986) had
already mentioned something similar occurring at Hamburg in relation
to the running together of different experiences as all on a par with the
Shoah. Kafka (1988, p. 299) confirms this:

> Think of a comment about the living reality of anti-Arab discrim-
> ination and cruelty compared with the merely historical concern
> with the Holocaust, and a comment by a Japanese psychoanalyst
> that 'we Japanese are experts on holocaust because of Hiroshima and
> Nagasaki'. A competition of horrors obstructs the study of a particular
> event.

The point here is neither to question the reality of these other
instances of violent oppression and suffering nor to assert the absolute uniqueness of the Nazi Holocaust as a phenomenon qualitatively
different from all others, a claim that is historically and politically
contentious. It is rather to ask why such comments materialize in the
specific setting of a psychoanalytic Congress in *Germany*, in the light of
all that has gone before, all that has to be negotiated and dealt with.
Kafka notes a number of things that are relevant to this, including
what he calls the 'tension' that comes from wanting to be done with
the 'obsession' with the Shoah and with German guilt, to let them off
the hook and move on – an impulse which he recognizes as one of
avoidance. 'I have seen in myself,' he writes (p. 305), 'in German and
non-German colleagues, and despite the most serious efforts to "deal"
with the Holocaust, an impatience, a wish to move away from the topic.'
There may also be something else at work, connected to finding oneself
in what still amounts to an anti-Semitic society, or at least a society in
which anti-Semitism has not been eradicated.

It should be clear that no one is being accused of bad faith here: what
the material shows is a mode of thoughtfulness and hopefulness that
tries to engage with the sorrow as well as the anger produced by the
Hamburg Congress. As is commonly the case, everyone seems to have
worked towards the success of the Congress both in terms of its smooth
running and as an attempt to manage something of an encounter with
the Nazi past. The meaning of meeting on German soil was certainly not
ignored. Yet, it is equally clear that the overall feeling was of something

missed, a chance not taken, a coming-together that looked like an 'event' but was actually a ritual, which made it possible to claim that an important thing had happened as a way of contributing to a defensive process. The exact parallel is perhaps that of the ambivalent patient (which may mean, *every* patient to some extent) who turns up to psychoanalysis precisely in order to stay the same; that is, the mere act of turning up is mistaken for doing the work, or is even an excuse for not doing it ('I am going to analysis, so that's enough; I don't need to take any further responsibility'). The psychoanalytic community certainly turned up in Hamburg, and it was clearly challenged by the exhibition, by the mayor, by the exposure of Germans and Jews to one another, by the reminders in the external situation. There was also some movement forward, without a doubt; but not much, or at least not enough. What happened seems to have been that a little air was let into a stuffy room, enough to make it liveable in again, but not enough to clean it out; and then the window was once again shut. Nothing was grasped hold of, with the consequence that no resolution could be achieved, but the cancerous mistrust and disturbance of unacknowledged yet deeply felt emotions continued to fester. This is all to say, that 'identification' was indeed an element of the Hamburg Congress, but one that dodged the central question, nominated by Janine Chasseguet-Smirgel (1987, p. 437) as, *'What is one to do with a Nazi father?'*

Remembering, repeating and working through, or, not enough chairs to go round

A lot has happened since 1985, including a considerable amount of scholarly work on the relationship of the psychoanalysts to the Nazis, important shifts in the German psychoanalytic situation, a series of powerful 'group relations' events between German and Israeli Jewish psychoanalysts (Erlich et al., 2009a) and, by no means least, the replacement of one psychoanalytic generation by another, less implicated and hence freer to feel. So the coming-together of 3000 analysts in Berlin in 2007 might not have been expected to have the poignancy of the 1985 gathering: perhaps they might already have been at the point of 'working through'. In this regard, it is important to note that a lot of the Congress was not devoted to the history described here, but was an ordinary, high-quality, technical Congress with many and varied presentations, and a good deal of enjoyment. Even in relation to the recognition of the Nazi past, the main theme was relatively neutral: the effect of the *emigration* from Berlin on the dissemination of psychoanalysis, presented as a 'new question ... how psychoanalysis – and which psychoanalysis? – was transferred from Berlin to the new centres on both sides of the Atlantic' (Tönnesmann, 2008, p. 413).

This would indeed be a new question, though of course not completely divorced from the previous one, which would hover over it as a silent shadow: *why* did the 'transfer' have to take place? In a keynote address to the Congress, Werner Bohleber (2007) offered a subtle and open account of the history of collective remembrance in post-war Germany, tracing the difficulties and silences within and between the generations and seeking to understand the 'apologetic victim-consciousness that members of the perpetrating generation retroactively created for themselves' (p. 346) as well as the impact of this on their children. He eventually concluded, soberly, 'in many cases, clarification and reconstruction has only so far been possible in a very fragmentary way, since the parents' silence could not be broken or the children instigated the clarification too late rather than within their parents' lifetimes' (p. 348). At the end, Bohleber asserted that the new 'third generation' 'takes its own more independent view of the events and the family involvements' (p. 348). This may be the case, but how does it figure as an account of what happens when the past is resurrected in an unavoidable way, by bringing it back 'home'? Once again, much of the presentation is meticulous and of great value, but seems to fall short of full acknowledgement of the unconscious, or at least emotional, elements of the potential encounter between post-Shoah psychoanalysts and the city of Berlin.

There is plenty of evidence that Berlin 2007 was an emotional affair. 'I felt fear,' writes Paul Schwaber (2007, p. 15), 'at night in Berlin, unable to sleep, I found myself reliving the phases of my life, thinking of people long past and wondering why; finally I was aware of fantasizing myself a little child, terrified, and aware that my loving parents were powerless to protect me. It was a massively regressive fantasy, shaped by history, and emerging in the dark in terrifying consciousness.' Bob Pyles (2007, p. 14) writes similarly, 'Like most of our colleagues, it was with considerable foreboding that I anticipated attending the congress in Berlin.' In these and other short testimonies, one element of the Congress stands out as separate from the usual academic and clinical engagement: the large group with the theme 'Being in Berlin', run on the three consecutive days of the Congress by two Israeli analysts, Shmuel Erlich and Mira Erlich-Ginor, and a German, Hermann Beland. On the whole, this group event is recorded positively in the accounts given by people who participated. Georg Bruns, Chair of the Berlin Congress Programme Committee, writes that 'not only was the history remembered, but there was also an opportunity to experience the associated emotions, at least in part, through the daily meetings of the large "Being in Berlin" group' (Bruns, 2007, p. 3). Schwaber (2007, p. 15) describes 'People rising to speak, briefly but movingly, followed by thoughtful silences until someone else chose to speak. It was a comfort not to feel alone with those thoughts.' This 'comfort' may genuinely have been the experience of many members of the group, but it is also apparent from the report of the group leaders that a lot more was afoot.

Erlich et al. (2009b) provide their account in a paper in the *International Journal of Psychoanalysis*. The event, they write, was convened because the organizers of the conference thought that the 'numerous' panels and papers devoted to the heritage of Nazism 'would not be enough' to acknowledge 'the special meaning of a psychoanalytic congress in Berlin, the Nazi capital, which for many is still heavily linked with the burden of that era' (p. 810). So on each of the three mornings, alongside all the other academic and professional panels, the 'Being in Berlin' event took place as an experiential group drawing on the Tavistock group relations tradition (Armstrong et al., 2005), where the group simply meets without any particular guidance, but with a broadly defined task and the help of, in this case, three 'consultants'. The formal announcement of the event in the Congress papers included a specific acknowledgement of what the emotional effects of being back in Germany might be for psychoanalysts; and it offered the group sessions as 'an opportunity for all who may wish to pause to reflect on their experience and to express personal thoughts and feelings' (Erlich et al., 2009b, p. 811). The agenda was thus clearly stated: to find a 'container' for reflecting about 'personal thoughts and feelings' generated by the experience of being in Berlin. As an invitation this is always hard to refuse, and for psychoanalysts, traders both in feelings and in thoughts about them, it could be read as a very powerful inducement to a kind of affective performance, in which feelings might be noted in oneself and others, articulated and in this way thought about as transformed. What happened, however, was not only that such performances occurred, as one would expect, but also – and perhaps one would expect this too – that the institutional setting, the Congress itself, 'performed' too, or enacted something around the group that revealed its own powerful 'unconscious'. That is, the setting both encouraged the articulation of feeling and at the same time, in a classic enactment of ambivalence, blocked its resolution. This all happened around the administrative arrangements for the group, which in a profession that takes very seriously the conditions under which it practises (the regularity of time and space, in particular) is exactly where one might look for symptomatic behaviour. That is, because psychoanalysis gives priority to the safety of the 'setting' as a way of 'containing' the flow of unconscious processes, these processes push precisely at the seams of the setting in order to make themselves felt.

The key symptom of this kind was the difficulty the organizers had in timetabling the group appropriately, as if it always slipped out of mind. 'Although the event had been discussed and formulated long in advance,' Ehrlich et al. note (p. 813), 'it turned out that, while the time slot was indeed the same every day (something we insisted on), the same space could not be; we would have to "wander" or "relocate" ourselves to a different room each day.' These words, 'wander' and 'relocate' are clearly not neutral, but are chosen to resonate with the impact of Nazism itself, and with its effects on psychoanalysis: 'it is a new kind of diaspora', as Anna Freud famously commented in the 1930s (Steiner, 2000). But even this enforced nomadism did not fully encompass the degree of institutional acting-out that the Being in Berlin group produced, even before it had properly got going. Not being sure how many people would attend, and perhaps being too timid or insecure to make their presence significant in the Congress, the group conveners had accepted a relatively small room for the group. About 25 chairs were laid out, lecture style, facing the front despite the organizers' request for a circle; and when people started to arrive it rapidly became clear that the room would not be able to hold them all. What happened next – and one has to recall that these are psychoanalysts that one is reading about – is eerie in its recapitulative power, its genuine 'remembering, repeating' without necessarily working through:

> The behaviour was both frightening and troubling: while 60 or 70 people were quite uncomfortably squeezed into the room, there seemed to be twice as many outside the door trying to get in. A struggle developed between the people standing inside and those outside. There were feeble attempts by those standing in the doorway to explain that there was no more room, and the noise from the hall was quite disruptive to whatever was beginning to transpire inside. Finally, there was a decisive slamming shut of the door. Immediately, associations came up from the group of being 'squeezed into a cattle car' and the 'doors being shut as in the gas chambers'. (Erlich et al., 2009b, p. 814)

For the second day, the Congress organizers arranged a larger space. However, rather than the 'container' referred to in the announcement of the group event, this turned out to be 'a non-existing, "fabricated" room' (p. 814), a foyer space from which a number of doors led to other panels taking place at the same time – doors which 'had to be closed and guarded by specially hired personnel' to make sure there were no interruptions. Apparently for safety reasons, only 50 chairs were initially supplied. More chairs had to be gathered, people grabbed them 'sometimes violently' and someone was hurt, and 'the rapid, rhythmic metallic sound of chairs being dislodged from the carriers was constantly in the background and several people associated it to the sound of trains' (p. 814). Even on the third day, when over 250 chairs were provided and appropriately laid out, the space was overcrowded and overexcited, lending tremendous urgency and pressure to the occasion and to the group itself.

It is one thing to recognize the impact of these disruptions to the frame of analysis, and another to be sure of their source. Erlich et al. (2009b) are in no doubt about the former, and seem to see the pain involved as having been in some ways conducive to their task:

> The unfolding drama of the impossible space, the provision of chairs, the discomfort and seemingly unsuitable conditions – all expressed poignantly, in unspoken ways, essential aspects of what 'being in Berlin' evoked. Attempting to provide a space for feelings and associations evoked images in the participants of the slamming shut of boxcar doors and the sound and sensation of trains; angry wishes for the 'conductor' – the leader or Führer – to act more forcefully in order to establish order in the chaotic situation; aggressive shouts and objections directed at the congress photographer who tried to take pictures, and so on. These were readily available associations and recapitulations. They testify to the poignancy and aliveness of the associations, symbolizations and feelings about Nazi Germany and its atrocities. (pp. 814–15)

Anyone who has participated in such an experiential large group will know both how disturbing it can be, and how engaging, how deeply it can dramatize the push-me-pull-you sensations of being isolated and then sucked in, alienated and engulfed (Frosh, 2008). In Berlin, in this coming-together of psychoanalysts from around the world to a place from which psychoanalysis had been so brutally expelled and also corrupted, it is clear that the staging of the group event facilitated a kind

of encounter that might otherwise have been avoided, leaving its participants both exhilarated and exhausted. Erlich et al. (2009b, p. 819)
provide some testimonies: 'One participant, a former president of the
IPA, said when it was over, "This is the real thing! What we will do
[in the forthcoming panel] is dead compared to this. This was alive!"
As Georg Bruns put it: "I felt this group to be the emotional centre of the
congress".' What was *achieved* is less easy to say. In the actual content of
the group – what was said and thought about – a number of disturbing
themes arose. Erlich et al. (2009b, pp. 816ff) list these as German shame
and hope; identifying with Hitler; the voices of the dead; being faceless
and nameless; the absent voices; Jewish-Nazi mothers; longing for the
'Jewish' mother; impossible marriages and the monsters they produce;
envy of the Jews; longing for the missing parts; silence and letting others speak for oneself; the pain of the next generation. In particular, the
juxtaposition of idealizing and denigrating attitudes towards Jews was
evident, especially the latter: 'there was envy directed at the Jews, and
envious attacks on what was described as their monopolization of suffering and not leaving room for the suffering of others' (p. 820). An
example that Erlich et al. (p. 817) give brings this to life: 'A woman talks
about her parents who, as members of the Resistance, were active in
hiding and protecting Jews. Rather than being proud of them, she felt
angry at and envious of "the Jews" who received her parents' attention
and care instead of her. The Jews seem to have the exclusive privilege of
suffering and sorrow, and "the Others" in the group feel envy and want
a space for their own suffering.' They go on to note something else,
a disturbing yet not surprising thing, that has echoes of the Hamburg
Congress and echoes still further back, and that perhaps lies closer to
the source of the thing, the dynamic that produced this powerful, near-
psychotic event in the first place. 'One deepening irrational process
that we did witness,' they write (p. 820), 'was the in vivo occurrence
of what might be described as the development of anti-Semitism.' The
'Nazi beast', it seems, lurks pretty near the surface, and one cannot easily
shake it off, even 60 years after the end of the Third Reich. Psychoanalysis is a place for remembrance, but there is also plenty of repetition
going on; and even though 'working through' might have been the
theme, and might have been engendered in the heightened emotion
of the Congress and the group event that went on within it, it is clearly
not complete, and perhaps may never be so.

Why might this be? One can only speculate of course, but looking
back over what is a sorry tale, with its heroes but with its villains too,
and with more people lost along the way, it seems that there remains

something deeply unresolved about the encounter of psychoanalysis with its own 'Jewishness', which leads both to the re-enactment of anti-Semitism inside its ranks and to the impossibility of fully rooting it out. That is to say, the emergence of psychoanalysis from a specific nexus of Jewish history and identity still haunts the profession – it cannot escape an encounter with this 'Jewish heritage' and the fantasies to which this gives rise, including anti-Semitic fantasies, even a hundred years after the event. This keeps cropping up: one sees it in the way in which psychoanalysis retains its association with Jewishness even if it is no longer (if it ever were, since its very earliest days) actually dominated by Jews. For example, the seemingly overdetermined fascination with Jews can be seen in Slavoj Žižek's (2005) Lacanian claim 'that the position of the analyst is grounded in Judaism' (p. 152) and his associated link between psychoanalysis and 'the Jewish moneylender, a shadowy figure to whom all the big figures of society come to borrow money, pleading with him and telling him all their dirty secrets and passions' (2006, p. 305). The anti-Semitic resonance here is to be taken not as an indication of some personal aberration on Žižek's part, but rather as another way in which the 'Jewish complex' of psychoanalysis keeps seeping through (Frosh, 2011b). Broadly, what seems to happen is that the disturbance to convention that is psychoanalysis (its 'scandalous' aspect) is mirrored *within* psychoanalysis by the disturbance due to its Jewish origins; and perhaps that the violence with which these origins were repudiated during Nazi times is an embarrassing but nevertheless accurate expression of the feelings to which they give rise. Freud was not always keen on psychoanalysis as a 'Jewish science', even if Anna Freud later on claimed it as 'a title of honour' (Freud, 1978, p. 148); for European psychoanalysis more generally, rooted in a culture that continues to allow resurgences of anti-Semitism, the conscious 'honour' may at times be lightly worn, a transparent surface only partially repressing the discomfort that an identification with Jewishness can produce.

To summarize: in the light of 'Being in Berlin', it is perhaps reasonable to claim that all the powerful work that has gone on to confront the past of the psychoanalytic movement has not shifted something deep and disturbing. We are used to the idea that many institutions – and even nation-states – are founded on a traumatic event, or at least on a myth of trauma; in the case of psychoanalysis, this includes both its place as a 'Jewish science' in a hostile world, and as the site for a great betrayal of the 'father'. This father is Freud himself, of course, who increasingly despaired of Western tolerance and, faced with intensifying anti-Semitism, identified himself more and more strongly as a Jew. But it is also the Jewish analysts from whom contemporary psychoanalysts are descended, dragging their transferences along with them: the writers, the trainers, the leaders of institutes, those who were driven out of Europe, those who were disparaged, uprooted, disposed of. Is it too extreme to suggest that anti-Semitism is endemic to psychoanalysis precisely because of its genuinely Jewish past? That just as the Germans have to come to terms with having a 'Nazi father', so the psychoanalysts have to come to terms with having a 'Jewish' one, and that – in a European culture founded in large part on Christian anti-Semitism – this is just as difficult a thing to do? At the very least, it seems, some old forms of hatred are easily remembered and repeated, and their working through is as yet a long way off. Analysis interminable, indeed.

References

Armstrong, D., Lawrence, G. W. and Young, R. M. (2005). *Group Relations*. London: Process Press.

Bohleber, W. (2007). Remembrance, trauma and collective memory: The battle for memory in psychoanalysis. *International Journal of Psychoanalysis*, 88, 329–52.

Brecht, K. (1995). In the aftermath of Nazi-Germany: Alexander Mitscherlich and psychoanalysis – legend and legacy. *American Imago*, 52, 291–312.

Brecht, K., Friedrioch, V., Hermanns, L., Kaminer, I. and Juelcih, D. (eds) (1985). *'Here Life Goes on in a Most Peculiar Way': Psychoanalysis Before and After 1933*. Hamburg: Kellner Verlag/London: Goethe Institut.

Bruns, G. (2007). Remembering in Berlin IPA Berlin Congress. *International Psychoanalysis: News Magazine of the International Psychoanalytical Association*, 16, 3.

Chasseguet-Smirgel, J. (1987). 'Time's white hair we ruffle': Reflections on the Hamburg Congress. *International Review of Psycho-Analysis*, 14, 433–44.

Cocks, G. (1997). *Psychotherapy in the Third Reich*. Oxford University Press.

Cohen, S. (2001). *States of Denial: Knowing about Atrocities and Suffering*. Oxford: Polity.

Erlich, H. S., Erlich-Ginor, M. and Beland, H. (2009a). *Fed with Tears, Poisoned with Milk: Germans and Israelis, the Past in the Present*. Giessen: Psychosozial-Verlag.

Erlich, H. S., Erlich-Ginor, M. and Beland, H. (2009b). Being in Berlin: A large group experience in the Berlin Congress. *International Journal of Psychoanalysis*, 90, 809–25.

Freedman, N. (1988). The setting and the issues. *Psychoanalysis and Contemporary Thought*, 11, 197–212.

Freud, A. (1978). Inaugural lecture for the Sigmund Freud Chair at the Hebrew University, Jerusalem. *International Journal of Psycho-Analysis*, 59, 125–48.

Frosh, S. (2005). *Hate and the Jewish Science*. London: Palgrave.

Frosh, S. (2008). Desire, demand and psychotherapy: On large groups and neighbours. *Psychotherapy and Politics International*, 6, 185–97.

Frosh, S. (2011a). The relational ethics of conflict and identity. *Psychoanalysis, Culture and Society*, 16, 225–43.

Frosh, S. (2011b). Psychoanalysis, antisemitism and the miser. *New Formations*, 72, 94–106.

Goggin, J. and Goggin, E. (2001). *Death of a 'Jewish Science': Psychoanalysis in the Third Reich*. West Lafayette: Purdue University Press.

Kafka, J. S. (1988). On reestablishing contact. *Psychoanalysis and Contemporary Thought*, 11, 299–308.

Moses, R. and Hrushovski-Moses, R. (1986). A form of group denial at the Hamburg Congress. *International Review of Psycho-Analysis*, 13, 175–80.

Opening Ceremony, 34th IPA Congress (1986). *International Journal of Psychoanalysis*, 67, 2–4.

Pyles, R. (2007). Remembering, repeating, and working through – the IPA in Berlin. *The American Psychoanalyst*, 41, 14.

Schwaber, P. (2007). On being in Berlin. *The American Psychoanalyst*, 41, 15.

Seu, I. (2010). Doing denial: Audiences' reactions to human rights appeals. *Discourse and Society*, 21, 438–57.

Steiner, R. (2000). 'It is a New Kind of Diaspora': Explorations in the Sociopolitical and Cultural Context of Psychoanalysis. London: Karnac.

Tönnesmann, M. (2008). Panel report: Emigration from Berlin part one: Transfer of theories and institutional regulations. *International Journal of Psychoanalysis*, 89, 413–16.

Weinshel, E. (1986). Report of the 34th International Psycho-Analytical Congress. *Bulletin of the International Psycho-Analytical Association*, 67, 87–130.

Žižek, S. (2005). Neighbours and other monsters: A plea for ethical violence. In S. Žižek, E. Santner and K. Reinhard (eds), *The Neighbor: Three Inquiries in Political Theology*. University of Chicago Press.

Žižek, S. (2006). *The Parallax View*. Cambridge, MA: MIT Press.

3

Sa loob ang kulo: Speaking the Unconscious in the Transformations of a Filipino Proverb

Narcisa Paredes-Canilao

From metaphorical proverb to handy expression

Pent-up anger; hidden mischief

Ang taong walang kibo, nasa loob ang kulo is one of 1592 proverbs from different regions of the Philippines in D. Eugenio's *Philippine Proverb Lore* (1967).[1] It has been translated variously as: 'The quiet person hides a capacity for mischief,' 'A person who is outwardly calm has anger raging inside' and 'A quiet person has anger boiling inside.'[2] The proverb's antiquity cannot be determined for certain, but it was among the 876 Tagalog proverbs, epigrams and idioms collected from the areas of Tanay and Pililla, Rizal by two Spanish friars. It was published for the first time in 1890.[3] Eugenio classified the proverb under her sixth categorization, 'those expressing general truths about life', particularly on the human idiosyncrasy that quiet people have a lot to hide. She translated the proverb as, 'A person who is quiet boils inside,' and offered the interpretation, 'The quiet person hides a capacity for mischief.' The proverb also appears in other Philippine languages: the Bikol, *An matinao; May itinatagong milagro*, and the Hiligaynon, *Ang tao nga mahipos; Sa sulod ang dumot*. Another idiosyncrasy of the quiet person is they are 'slow to anger but terrible when aroused', expressed in the Ilokano proverbs, *Ti saan a matimtimec; Nauyong no macaunget*, and *Annadam ti pungtot ti tao nga naanus* (Beware of the anger of a patient person). Thus, not only mischief, but anger too can be what the quiet person is hiding. Twelve other sayings in the Eugenio collection allude to the proverbial quietude of the natives, which may have pleasantly surprised the colonizers. The quiet person also hides and boils, brews or percolates intelligence, creativity and deep secrets.

The notion of the piled-up, repressed or suppressed inside needing displacement is a common motif in some Philippine proverbs. And paradoxically items for life sustenance are the contents making one wonder whether these proverbs could have been injunctions against greed. The *ganta* – a household measure for rice, beans or corn, equivalent to 5 pints – has figured in these proverbs. The proverb 'An overflowing *ganta* should be levelled to prevent spilling,' is found in seven Philippine languages, including the Tagalog *Kapag napuno ang salop, tatapon pag di kinalos*. The traditional perception related to folk physiology that accumulation of metabolic products in the body results in illness (Tan, 2008, p. 102) may be a more relevant frame to understand vessel tropes: there is a limit to the abuse one can take. To support this reading, V. Enriquez, founding father of *Sikolohiyang Pilipino* ([1977] 2002), disputed the stereotype that Filipinos patiently suffer in silence, and will endure abuse. *Ang tapayan kapag napuno ay umaapaw* (A water jar when filled shall overflow), Enriquez wrote, is proof that Filipinos express their emotions in a step-wise fashion. *Mabuting kaibigan, masamang kaaway* (Good friend, bad enemy) is another saying expressing the same idea.

Not only common household items boil or overflow. The Philippines has been ranked among the most disaster-prone countries, because it is located within the Pacific ring of fire and along the typhoon belt, so pent-up rage/desire/drives can erupt like a volcano, found in the expression *Parang bulkan na sumabog ang kanyang galit* (His/her anger erupted like a volcano). *Sa loob ang kulo* is the calm before the storm too. Thus the expression *Parang bagyo kung magalit* (Like a typhoon when angry).

Social volcanoes

These proverbs, together with the main proverb under study, do not only speak of individuals boiling or overflowing, but also of a community or society seeking ruptures or lines of escape from repressive regimes. As a rule, the pre-Hispanic Filipinos were terse and patient. In contrast the Spaniards were reported to have been hot-tempered and quick to anger. However, by October 1889, a group of Filipinos in exile abroad wrote about what might happen if there was no let-up:

> When a people is gagged; when its dignity, honor, and all its liberties are trampled; when it no longer has legal recourse against the tyranny of its oppressors, when its complaints, petitions, and groans are not

attended to; when it is not even permitted to weep; when even the
last hope is wrested from its heart; then…! then…! then…! it has
left no other remedy but to take down with delirious hand from the
altars the bloody and social dagger of revolution! (Agoncillo, 1990,
p. 102)

Recently, the social volcano theme or shared desire of release from
repression has been invoked in connection with perceived excesses
of the previous dispensation. Social eruptions are usually expected to
bring about a sea of change, and a naturalistic ontology would view
this social phenomenon as contiguous with the physical phenomenon
in thermodynamic systems that the boiling point is a critical threshold that triggers qualitative change (Bonta and Protevi, 2004). Thus on
the commemoration of Philippine Independence Day on 12 June 2009,
then Chief Justice Reynato Puno declared: *Parang bulkan na tila handa
nang sumabog ang ating inang bayan* (Like a volcano ready to erupt, our
motherland).[4] The 2009 Philippine Independence Day became an occasion to recall the sacrifices of generations of Filipinos to free ourselves
from abusive regimes, foreign or native. The daughter of a 2004 presi-
dential candidate, popularly believed to have been cheated, was on TV
news saying *Punong-puno na ang salop ng bayan* (Filled to overflowing, the
nation's *ganta*), a derivation from the proverb *Kapag napuno ang salop,
tatapon pag di kinalos* mentioned earlier. The theme of accumulated
anger that can no longer be contained is evoked as well in the compact outrage: *Tama na, sobra na* (Enough, too much). This outcry during
the dictatorial and martial law regime has become the protest slogan of
contemporary Filipinos whenever government, business leaders, school
administrators or foreign employers become abusive. It speaks of a
threshold of what is humanly endurable.

The stomach or *sikmura* has often been the calculus of what is
humanly endurable, in the expression *Di ko na masikmura* (I cannot
stomach it any more). The website *Kulo sa Loob*,[5] maintained by an
artist-activist, provokes the visitor/surfer with the caption:

> *Bukas na lansangan sa aking sikmura, kumulo, kumukulo, at pinakukulo…*
> A gaping alley inside my stomach, boiled, boiling and being boiled…

This line speaks of a *sikmura* (stomach) empty as a deserted alley, inter-
minably boiling. It has boiled in the past, it is boiling now and being
made to boil by (external forces). The banner picture entitled *Ulingan*
(charcoal furnace) has a sooty, emaciated boy staring from limbo at the

foreground, and a stooped figure of another boy feeding the fires under the charcoal-in-the-making. Everywhere are shanties that are not even finished residences – a wall here, a canvas roof there depicting urban squalor. From the artist's notes, the picture is part of a collection of photos taken from an urban community whose main livelihood is charcoal making. Other photos are of political rallies, labour union pickets, effigies of abusive presidents, Uncle Sam, environmental degradation and other dismal scenes of urban life, and of different personalities from the urban poor who suffer most from the combined impact of inefficient government and globalized capitalism.

The worldview of *kulo*: *ginhawa-kaluluwa*; *labas-loob*

The metaphor 'anger is a boiling' is not unique to Filipinos. It is perhaps a universal metaphor because the system of metaphors for anger evident across languages is based on the physiology of anger (Lakoff and Johnson, 1980, p. 249). A description of the physiology of anger would include rise in temperature causing the body to heat up, faster heartbeat and rise in blood pressure, all similar to the phenomenon of boiling, which is not seen, but must be happening *inside* (*loob*), like a rumbling volcano. Tan (2008, p. 103) has noted the link of blood with emotions invoked in Filipino metaphors *Kumukulo ang dugo ko* (My blood is boiling) and *Natutuyo ang dugo ko* (My blood is drying up or drained). Folk physiology and anatomy figured crucially in the traditional Filipino worldview which resonated with those of the Hindu and Chinese in the centrality of adjusting harmoniously to *kalikasan* (nature) as the bigger reality to which humans belong. Fr Bulatao (1992) and Fr Mercado (1994) described this worldview as transpersonal. The latter has researched similarities of the Filipino worldview to those of other South East Asian and Austronesian cultures and has shown similarities of the Filipino animistic, islander worldview to that of the Javanese, and likewise to the Melanesians of Irian Jaya, Papua New Guinea, the Solomon Islands, Vanuato, New Caledonia and Fiji.

Historical and ethnographic studies indicate that most Filipinos traditionally and up to now believe in an interlinked and non-hierarchical interrelationship of two forces – *ginhawa* (well-being) and *kaluluwa* (spirit-soul) – which have equivalents in different regional and linguistic groups not only in the Philippines but throughout Austronesia and Asia (Paz, 2008b; Salazar, [1977] 1995; Tan, 2008). *Ginhawa*, which is close to, or is, life-giving breath, connotes that well-being means life that is easy, peaceful, comfortable, free from wants and pressures. In a comprehensive study of traditional and modern theories of health and illness, anthropologist Michael Tan (2008) identified naturalistic theories as one theory commonly held among Asians including Filipinos. Humoral pathology holds that illness is caused by 'a disturbance of the balance of forces within the body' (p. 92), thus displaced organs are major causes of sickness.

Kaluluwa traditionally pertained to an unseen fellow traveller, a sort of *twin-spirit* usually born with an individual. *Kaluluwa* can also be the spirits of the departed still wandering on the zone of middle dimensions. The pursuit and maintenance of well-being included harmonious and sustained relationship with the spirit world. The *babaylan/katalonan*, who were probably the first psychotherapists (Enriquez, 1994, 2002), were medicinal priests/priestesses who administered the harmonious relationship between *ginhawa-kaluluwa*. According to Z. Salazar (1996), the *babaylan/katalonan* could have been the Philippines' 'proto-scientists'. They were 'women or anyone with female characteristics' (p. 210) who were central personalities in 'the fields of culture, religion and medicine and all kinds of theoretical knowledge about the phenomenon of nature' (p. 213).

The role of *kapalaran* (fate), or the dimension beyond human control, is prominent within this worldview, and, I note, the gesture of having one's palm read may be a bodily symbol of one's not being in control (resonating the Zen riddle: what happens to my fist [grasp] when I open my hand?). C. J. Paz (2008a) studied the provenance of the notion of *kapalaran* in different Philippine languages, and her respondents identified ability, character, customs and taking risks within the purview of human decision, while the supernatural, beyond the normal, luck, fortune, bad luck and without luck were outside human decision. But Paz averred this is not fatalism because even the effects of matters beyond human control could be mitigated or reversed by human effort.

P. Covar's *construct* of Filipino folk anatomy (1998) spatially divides the parts of the body into: (1) *labas* (outside) of the face, chest, *sikmura* (no English equivalent, it is the higher part of the stomach above the navel, directly outside that which aches when one is hungry), and *tiyan* (outer stomach); (2) *loob* (inside) of the mind, heart, *bituka* (inner stomach) and liver; (3) *ilalim* (deep down inside) of the *kaluluwa* (spirit-soul) and *budhi* (sensibility). In this frame to say that one boils inside implicates the insides, so to speak, that are the mind, heart, inner stomach or liver which are all revved up, notwithstanding that face, chest, etc. are all calm on the outside. More important, the naturalist-immanentist ontology implicit in this folk anatomy supports the vessel metaphors and inside-outside orientation. First, the operative principles are spatiality and consistency with two components of the triad oriented towards inside with less solidity, and the other component towards outside with greater solidity. Second, nowhere do we find an ordering component or an organizing principle. It is as if there are just the parts, nothing has the parts, as Buddhism would put it. Thus the category mistake identified by Ryle (1949) is avoided. Ryle argued that the Cartesian conception of mind suffers a category mistake, because it is not enough that there are mental processes, we must posit a mind that does or has the processes. Third, the body parts or capabilities are not binaries, because there are three spatial orientations whose boundaries are flexible and unfixed. Covar's metaphor of the human person, the *Manunggul* jar (a secondary burial jar from the Neolithic period), could have been a pot, a ganta, the water storage/collector (*tapayan*), or any vessel whose material is one and the same in the inside and outside, and thus the contiguity between the inner and outer part. Fourth, the bodily organs and capabilities are not ordered by a mentalist ontology that leads to mind–body dichotomy and a supremacy of mind, or mind as norm. Neither is soul or spirit a norm. There is no norm that predetermines the functions or arrangement of the parts. It thus makes sense to refer to these parts, in Deleuzoguattarian terms, as *molecular* (there is equality or democracy among the parts) rather than *molar* (organs are organized with reference to a centre, standard or norm).

Other current uses of the proverb turned handy expression

The proverb's more compact and elegant forms, *Sa loob ang kulo* (Inside, the boiling) or *Kulo sa loob* (Boiling inside), have surfaced senses that may have been latent in its previous sayings. Mostly figuring in internet blogs and posts about movie stars, or stars of reality shows – in a word, popular culture – said to boil inside now are still anger, mischief and social unrest, but, in addition, sex-libido, creativity, perversion and quirks. At the same time that the proverb is now floating freely, one might notice circulating in these endless blogs a tendency towards the commodification of an everyday expression by the hegemonic discourse of mindless cultural consumption (Roberts, 2006). Take the narrowly sexual component, for instance, which has predominated in the expression's uses. It is women in reality shows, noontime shows, the movies, who are said to be shy, prudish and well-behaved, but are hot or promiscuous deep inside.

Creativity boiling is associated with the cookery sense of *kulo*. From this alimentary sense of *kulo* had been derived the metaphorical expressions *Kaninong pakulo ito* (Whose simmering [idea] is this?) and *Ano naman kaya ang bagong pakulo niya* (What could he be brewing this time?). The power and efficacy of alimentary boiling (simmering, percolating, brewing) as a metaphor for creative thought have a logic and theory of their own. Percolation theory – a type of heterarchical theory (Kontopoulos, 1993) – is a 'mathematical theory of non-linear transitions named after the surprising, complex behavior of common percolation' (p. 386). The associated meaning of depth in *loob* (inside) cooperates with the creativity connotation of something that is not shallow, and not routinary. Thus *sa loob ang kulo* disrupts the drudgery borne out of the repetitive, that is sometimes culture and society.

Metaphor-metonym, logical grammar and syntax

The analysand as metaphor

In analysing the proverb-turned-handy-expression (henceforth the analysand) as figurative speaking, methods developed by philosophers in tropology, or metaphorology/metaphorics (Black, 1962; Derrida, 1982; Hesse, 1966; Lakoff and Johnson, 1980; Ricoeur, [1977] 2003), are helpful. With the proviso, however, that these speakings are not reduced to mere figures. Among the questions raised by metaphorology are: What is the logical grammar of metaphors? How do they differ from other uses of language? How do we recognize them? What is the point in using them? Do they serve only a decorative function? In what sense or senses are they creative? What and how do they mean? (Black, 1962, p. 25).

The analysand belongs to a seminal assemblage of proverbs and expressions all speaking the unconscious projecting human bodies as vessels whose most significant structure is outside-inside. That these tropes or metaphors were the seminal form of the *kulo* concept affirms the theory of the metaphorical sedimentation of concepts, or the insight of philosophers that all concepts, scientific or philosophical, originated as metaphors (see Derrida, 1982). Furthermore, these enunciations can be seen as interesting accounts of psychosocial individuation, if not perhaps an originary one. Individuals or communities saw themselves or projected themselves as vessels or receptacles: pots, jars, water containers, volcanoes, that are naturally bounded on the inside (the unseen, the mysterious, protected) by an outside (the seen, exposed to vulnerability). Curiously, these enunciations refrain the motif that over-flowing vessels need *levelling*, rather than *emptying*. Emptying is the goal in certain Taoist and Mahayana Buddhist texts as a requisite of enlight-enment. In these Filipino vessel metaphors, on the other hand, levelling is necessary in order for potentially disastrous accumulated energy to be displaced. Lakoff and Johnson (1980) confirmed the preponderance of ontological metaphors where human beings see themselves as ves-sels or containers bounded by the skin. Their explanation is that such metaphors express the 'basic instinct of territoriality' and consequently the putting up of boundaries around one's territory (p. 30). Closely related to container metaphors are what they call *orientational* or *spatial* metaphors of outside-inside (p. 15), which we saw in earlier discussions as the main structuring mechanism of the vessel metaphors, but that, however, there is no inside–outside dichotomy.

Other dimensions of the proverb-turned-handy-expression as a trope emerge when viewed through major philosophical theories of metaphor that developed in the past 50 years. These theories have generally been classified either as semantic, inclined more towards ordinary language and discourse philosophies of language, or as semiotic, more towards structuralist-poststructuralist approaches (see Ricoeur, 1977). I will not play partisan. I consider both streams useful to the aim of exposing the full potentials of the analysand in engendering a concept of the uncon-scious. So I employ a technique known in Filipino as *pamamangka sa dalawang ilog* (boating in two rivers).

First, the analysand can be seen as the resemblance not of a signifier and a signified but of two signifiers. The multiple senses evoked and that can be evoked by the proverb may be due to its open-ended signifying components as metaphor of resemblance (Derrida, 1982). Second, it is an interactive metaphor. Two terms, for example *anger* and *boiling*, are united by the similarity or genus that they are both inside, or unseen. When viewed from the interaction theory not only is there a transfer-ence of meaning from one term (*boiling*) to the other (*anger*), such that anger becomes boiling-like, the two are in a dynamic relation or inter-action, cooperating and inter-illuminating each other such that boiling too is anger-like. *Nag-aalburuto ang bulkan* is a Filipino expression that sees rumbling/erupting volcanoes in terms of human rage. Third, the analysand is a discourse, because the interaction of the two terms results in a changed perspective leading to an understanding of the psychol-ogy of anger, and to changed attitudes and practices in the name of *pakikipagkapwa* (fellow-feeling or being of one heart/mind with others), such as avoiding the abuse of a quiet person's patience, practising anger management, or providing non-destructive vents for anger so that it will not reach a bursting point. Proponents of the discourse theory assert that metaphors tend to create the similarity rather than formulate some already existing similarity. Metaphors (rather, creators of metaphors) select from a broad list what similarities to highlight and what to suppress or de-emphasize, depending on what they want a community of speakers to see, thus the power of metaphors to restructure perception (see Ricoeur, 1977).

Fourth, the analysand uttered by a person in a real-life situation, referring to a real-life somebody, takes on a linguistic force of a directive or mild warning of somebody's state of mind or temperament ('Beware, she's been keeping her anger for days now!'). Thus it is a speech act. First, it does not describe or report something true or false. Second, the utterance of the proverb consists in doing an action, that is, to warn or to remind the listener about somebody's disposition to vent anger. This, notwithstanding the utterance not having to be in the 'first person singular, present indicative active', the most common formula of performatives, though quite flexible, suggested by Austin (1970, p. 57). To be sure, the analysand, being a discourse and speech act, cannot be appreciated in abstraction from the saying/*parole* or event situated in particular and actual locations and intentions of speakers, and listeners. I discussed the parole of the analysand earlier in the first part of this chapter.

The analysand as metonym

What is significant with our analysand and its background of related proverbs and expressions is their being metonyms. The tropes belonging to the intertextuality of the analysand, projecting individuals or societies as vessels, are actually more metonyms than metaphors. But not exactly synecdoches, where part-for-the-whole logic is at work, but rather a type of metonym where product–producer contiguity is operative (see Lakoff and Johnson's classification of metonyms, 1980). The metonymic structure is: products (measuring vessels, cooking pots, water jars and, by contiguity, volcanoes) are the producer (*homo faber*). But this then makes the main analysand a metonym too because inside-outside is possible only if an individual is seen as a vessel or container.

That the figurative enunciations turn out to be bipolar in their being metaphors and metonyms at the same time is a significant finding of this study considering that there has been a growing concern about the lopsided focus of philosophers-metaphorologists on metaphors and the need to restore the bipolarity of not only language (Jakobson, 1956) but desire as well (Irigaray, 1985; Lacan, 1977).

For a brief backgrounder, Derrida (1982) did not only declare all metaphors as cases of resemblance between two signs, he also claimed that this 'authorizes' grouping all tropes under metaphors. He has made a very strong point in calling attention to the way philosophers had *rubbed* concepts of their primitive and elemental sensuousness, ending up with anaemic, lifeless mythologies, or 'white mythologies'. The realization of the metaphorical sedimentation of concepts was not a discovery of philosophers alone. It has been the point made by researchers revealing metaphors as the first expressions or the 'morphemes' of thought, so to speak. That our conceptual system is fundamentally and inescapably metaphorical was the conclusion of Lakoff and Johnson, noting at the same time that metaphors play a central role in defining our everyday realities (1980).

Derrida's fixation on the metaphor to the exclusion of other figures of speech is understandably a result of his view that language is best released from the determination of intentionality and reference. However, this does not have repercussions only on language, but on particular relations of the subject to language as well, which Lacan, relying partly on Jakobson, has made central to psychoanalysis. Jakobson (1956) suggested that language is inherently bipolar, involving two modes of arranging words, phrases or sentences, the pole or mode of combination (metonymy), and the pole or mode of selection/substitution (metaphor). In metaphor words are combined through similarity, while in metonymy through contiguity. The fixation on one pole to the disregard of the other was diagnosed by Jakobson as the cause of speech aphasia. People suffering from similarity aphasia are deficient in metaphor involving a deterioration of metalinguistic operations, while those with contiguity aphasia are deficient in metonymy involving a damage in the capacity to maintain the hierarchy of linguistic units. Jakobson extended the contiguity aphasia to his time noting how poets and artists, notwithstanding their being in control of their signifying practice, had fixated on the metaphoric pole, resulting in 'an amputated, unipolar scheme' (Jakobson, 1956, p. 82).

I want to argue further that the analysand in this study is a metonym not only by its form but also because of its function as a discourse and speech act. If we go by Jakobson's and Lacan's specifications of a metonym – as the pole of language's (or the unconscious's) contiguity with the Other – the analysand as discourse and speech act does not confine itself to language but reaches outside itself, first by intentionality, and second, by reference to an experience, situation, reality, the world and to its own speaker (see Ricouer, [1977] 2003, p. 86). The analysand as parole situated in Philippine sociohistorical and traditional ideology (worldview, folk anatomy, notions of well-being) was discussed in the first section of this chapter.

The unique syntax of Filipino sentences lend further support to the metonymic character of the analysand, that is, of pointing towards the Other, which in this case is the unconscious. It has been a tendency in English translations of Filipino or other Philippine languages to elide the unique syntactical qualities of the language. One who celebrates Filipino transgressions of the Subject-Copula-Predicate sentential form would take care to preserve the dispensability of the copula in Filipino and translate the proverb as, 'A quiet person … inside the boiling'. The ellipsis calls attention to the absent copula in the Filipino original, and the significance of this absence in uncoupling the predicate from the projective determination of the subject. The absent copula reinforces the unconscious as the 'discourse of the Other' (Lacan, 1977, p. 55), or the forces 'in me' that 'act me' (G. Groddeck in Castoriadis, 1997, p. 177).

Another syntactical feature of the analysand, this time contributing to its greater deterritorialization potential, is found in the abbreviation *sa loob ang kulo* ('inside, the boiling'), such that *kulo* ('the boiling') is now predicable of any subject or anything – rage, mischief, creativity, sex-libido, revolutionary fervour or kink. But the syntax of the website *Kulo sa loob* ('boiling inside') rarefies the expression even more, resulting in greater flight potential, because it gets rid of the problematic 'definite description' *ang* ('the'). Defunctionalized, freed from the copula and the definite article, *kulo* can be said to have become 'pure intensity' (Deleuze and Guattari, 1987, p. 4).

Speaking desire in post-Freudian psychoanalysis

A discernible theme in recent reconceptualizations of the unconscious in terms of drives or desire is the move towards more fluid and multiple ways of speaking the concept. The viscous lava and fluid water in Deleuze and Guattari (1983) were natural but contrary forms taken by the qualitative flows and pure intensities that is *desire*, while magma was invoked by Castoriadis (1987, 1997) to characterize the inexhaustible formations the *drives* are capable of, particularly psychic singularity and the institution of society.

Deleuze and Guattari (1983) eschewed the Freudian dictum: 'Where the Id was, there Ego shall be,' because it promoted the singular mastery of the drives by the ego. The philosopher-psychoanalyst duo believed Freudian psychoanalysis could not sufficiently account for 'nonlocalizable resistance' of desire. To them, most essential in the phenomenon of desire are 'the qualitative flows of the libido' (p. 66), which engender subjects whose libidos are both *viscous* and *liquid* (p. 65). The flows of desire therefore behave ambivalently, exhibiting at once the 'irresistible pressure of lava' and the 'invincible oozing of water'. Deleuze and Guattari saw Freudian psychoanalysis to have wrongly diagnosed as disease what is in fact a normal situation, that we all have multiple selves who experience in the flows of desire 'both the lava and the water' (p. 67). However, the partners have always insisted that lava, and water, like their other terms based on naturalism and complexity theories, are not to be taken as mere metaphors, but rather actual descriptions of events in the world.

Another well-developed reconception of the unconscious is the magmatic account of human drives[6] by the Greek philosopher, psychoanalyst and revolutionary theorist Cornelius Castoriadis. Magma is openly acknowledged by Castoriadis as a metaphor, recalling how around 1964–65 he was looking for a term sufficient to the radical imaginary in the human world, and 'after various terminological peregrinations' he ended up with the term magma (1997). Magma has since been central to his thought, serving as 'the launch pad of his attack on all forms of determinism and fatalism, whether materialist or psychoanalytic in character' (Tormey and Townshend, 2006, p. 24). In addition, magma has the capability of speaking about modes of being so new, and heretofore unprecedented, and unthinkable, notably psyche and society. Neither biology nor logic can comprehend the human psyche in its richness and complexity. Likewise with society which cannot be reduced to 'any rational-functional determinations' such as, for instance, economic, or the narrowly sexual. Furthermore, there is a unique mode of coexistence between the psychical sphere and the social sphere such that one is irreducible to, and cannot be dissociated from, the other (Castoriadis, 1997, pp. 290–1).

What characteristics of magmas might have suggested to Castoriadis of their productivity and efficacy as metaphors for unprecedented and unthinkable modes of being? It could be magmas are located at the earth's core, where they lie unconscious, unknown, beneath the surface, the visible or the known. Magmas connote the 'molten', 'primordial', 'protean', 'shifting and unpredictable', 'mysterious, yet creative and productive – that is, productive of meaning'. In short, magma makes thinkable how meaning or reality is originated, how the new is born

(Tormey and Townshend, 2006). But what most attracted Castoriadis (1987, 1997) is the magma's capacity for formings, or formations, which are not to be construed at all as ensembles. Ensembles are wholes that are nothing but their parts. In contrast, the logic of magmas is that they are not ensembles, but have to be described in terms of ensembles for as long as ensemblistic-identitary logic and ordinary language are the only available means of thought and expression. Not all institutions of society are at par with magma's continuous productivity of free formations, one such formation being capitalism which is animated by the unlimited expansion of rational mastery. But no institution should remain stagnant, societies must be open to the irruptions of radical imagination by continuous creation of significations; after all, the psyche and the social are inexhaustible. Novel determinations or formings are engendered each time societies consciously fight for autonomy, by 'breaking the grip of ensemblistic-identitary logic-ontology under its various disguises' (1997, p. 312).

Conclusion: metonymy, desire and psychoanalysis

Irigaray (1985) and Lacan (1977), for psychoanalytic reasons, had issued calls to balance the two poles of language. Irigaray has denounced a 'long-standing complicity' between rationality and a mechanics of solids which has structured psychoanalysis. To prevent the subject from being diminished by a 'systematics that re-marks a historical "inattention" to fluids', she recommended a recourse to metaphors. But metaphors are still 'quasi solid', operated as they are by the laws of equivalence derived from analogy which is a matter-form complex. Metonymy more closely allied to fluids would thus be preferable in speaking 'bodies in process', specifically women and the unconscious, with their internal frictions, instabilities, pressures, turbulence and resistance to solids (Irigaray, 1985, p. 106).

Lacan (1977) posited that it is not the unconscious that is primordial or elementary; it is language. He then attributed to the unconscious Jakobson's idea on the bipolarity of language with some modifications of his own. The bipolarity of the unconscious is exhibited through its functions of condensation (metaphor) and displacement (metonymy). Referring to the figures of style, he asked: 'Can one really see these as mere figures of speech when it is the figures themselves that are the active principle of the rhetoric of the discourse that the analysand in fact utters?' (Lacan, 1977, p. 169). Through this masterful stroke, Lacan thereby *converted* tropes of the unconscious to the very functions of the unconscious, and here I am using *conversion* as a logical operation of turning the predicate into the subject. For Lacan, the symptom is operated by metaphor, and desire by metonymy. In turn, it is metaphor that links the subject to the question of being, and metonymy to the question of lack.

What I hope to have accomplished in this critical exploration which can be located under the field of metaphor studies or metaphorology is the delineation and elucidation of a concept of the unconscious or desire that was originally evoked in metaphors and metonyms which linked vessels and volcanoes with individuals and communities by similarity or contiguity. I started this philosophical study of what might be a Filipino concept of the unconscious with the aim of testing the applicability of the metaphorical sedimentation of concepts, but my most rewarding find is: the seminal forms or the morphemes, so to speak, of the concept *kulo*, are not only metaphors but more importantly metonyms. This discovery is significant for a number of reasons. First, *kulo* being both a metaphor and a metonym contributes to restoring the bipolarity of language and the unconscious. Second, by being a metonym, *kulo* allies itself with the mechanics of fluids thereby advocating the proliferation of infinitely creative and multiple free-form desire. Third, *kulo* as metonym points to the indispensability of reference and intentionality in language. Fourth, *kulo* as metonym evokes the contiguity of individuals and communities with a bigger reality that may even lie beyond language. Hence *kulo*, like lava and water, is not a figure of speech alone, it is an actual description of a natural process that is thermodynamic, physiological, biological or psychical. *Ang taong walang kibo, nasa loob ang kulo* describes the event of bodies seemingly solid and consistent yet which conceal beneath them dynamic drives or desire forever seeking release. The challenge for psychoanalysis is whether to muster a containment or help subjects engage ambivalence productively.

Acknowledgement

The basic ideas for this essay were presented in several forums: the Annual Convention of the Philippine Sociological Society, 15–17 October 2009; the 35th conference of the *Pambansang Samahan ng Sikolohiyang Pilipino*, 25–27 November 2010; Symposium sponsored by the Laboratory for Indigenous Psychological Research, De La Salle University, 16 December 2010. On all occasions I was privileged to gather comments on the viability of the study and how to further refine my arguments. To Aydan Gülerce, editor of this volume, and the two anonymous reviewers, thank you for your critiques and suggestions for the final form of this essay.

Notes

1. Reprinted in 1992, with close to 13,000 proverbs from 36 Philippine languages, revisions in the categorization of the proverbs and more extensive documentation of sources, as Philippine Folk Literature Series, vol. VI.
2. The first translation is by Eugenio, 1967, 1992; the second is from Tagalog Lang: http://tagaloglang.com/Philippine-Literature/Tagalog-Proverbs/proverbs-about-people.html, accessed 13 July 2009; the third from blogspot.com: http://khuletzslapshock31.blogspot.com/2007-12-01-07, accessed 13 July 2009.
3. The friars, Gregorio Martin and Mariano Martinez Cuadrado, arrived in the Philippines in 1874 and 1875 respectively. The collection was first published in a small publishing house in Guadalupe, Manila in 1890 as *Coleccion de Refranes, Frases y Modismos Tagalos* (Mackinlay, 1905).
4. R. Puno, Ang moralidad ng Inang Bayan. Caloocan City: Andres Bonifacio Monument, 12 June 2009: www.scribd.com/doc/16373395/Independence-Day-Speech-by-the-Chief-Justice, accessed 3 December 2010.
5. kulosaloob.multiply.com: http://kulosaloob.multiply.com/photos/album/38/Ulingan, accessed 23 September 2009. To date the artist's true identity, despite efforts to trace him/her, is not known.
6. According to Uribarri, Castoriadis asserts again what other post-Freudians had realized before him, that 'the key concept in psychoanalysis is not the unconscious, but the drive' (Uribarri, 2002, p. 42).

References

Agoncillo, T. (1990). *History of the Filipino People*. Quezon City: Garotech Publishing.

Austin, J. L. (1970). *How to do Things with Words*, ed. J. O. Urmson. Oxford University Press.

Black, M. (1962). *Metaphors and Models: Studies in Language and Philosophy*. New York: Cornell University Press.

Bonta, M. and Protevi, J. (2004). *Deleuze and Geophilosophy: A Guide and Glossary*. Edinburgh University Press.

Bulatao, J. C. (1992). Westernization and the split-level personality in the Filipino. In J. Bulatao, *Phenomena and their Interpretation: Landmark Essays 1957–1989*. Manila: Ateneo de Manila University Press.

Castoriadis, C. (1987). *The Imaginary Institution of Society*, trans. K. Blamey. Cambridge, MA: MIT Press.

Castoriadis, C. (1997). *The Castoriadis Reader*, trans. and ed. D. A. Curtis. Cambridge, MA: Blackwell.

Covar, P. (1998). Kaalamang Bayang Dalumat ng Pagkataong Pilipino. In *Larangan: Seminal Essays on Philippine Culture*. Manila: National Commission on Culture and the Arts.

Deleuze, G. and Guattari, F. (1983). *Anti-Oedipus: Capitalism and Schizophrenia*, trans. R. Hurley, M. Seem and H. R. Lane. Minneapolis: University of Minnesota Press.

Deleuze, G. and Guattari, F. (1987). *A Thousand Plateaus: Capitalism and Schizophrenia*, trans. B. Massumi. Minneapolis: University of Minnesota Press.

Derrida, J. (1982). White mythology: Metaphor in the text of philosophy. In *Margins of Philosophy*, trans. A. Bass. University of Chicago Press.

Enriquez, V. D. (1994). *Pagbabangong-Dangal: Indigenous Psychology and Cultural Empowerment*. Manila: Pugad Lawin Press.

Enriquez, V. D. ([1977] 2002). Filipino psychology in the Third World. In A. B. Bernardo, M. A. Sta. Maria and A. L. Tan (eds), *Forty Years of Philippine Psychology*. Quezon City: Philosophical Association of the Philippines.

Eugenio, D. (1967). *Philippine Proverb Lore*. Quezon City: University of the Philippines Press.

Eugenio, D. (1992). *Philippine Folk Literature: The Proverbs*. Quezon City: The U.P. Folklorists.

Hesse, M. (1966). *Models and Analogies in Science*. University of Notre Dame Press.

Irigaray, L. (1985). *This Sex which is Not One*, trans. C. Porter with C. Burke. Ithaca, NY: Cornell University Press.

Jakobson, R. (1956). Two aspects of language and two types of aphasic disturbances. In R. Jakobson and M. Halle, *Fundamentals of Language*. The Hague: Mouton.

Kontopoulos, K. (1993). *The Logics of Social Structure*. Cambridge University Press.

Lacan, J. (1977). *Ecrits: A Selection*, trans. A. Sheridan. New York and London: W. W. Norton.

Lakoff, G. and Johnson, M. ([1980] 2003). *Metaphors We Live By*. University of Chicago Press.

Mercado, L. N. (1994) *The Filipino Mind*. Washington, DC: The Council for Research in Values and Philosophy.

Paz, C. J. (2008a). *Ginhawa*: Well-being as expressed in Philippine languages. In C. J. Paz (ed.), *Ginhawa Kapalaran Dalamhati: Essays on Well-Being, Opportunity/Destiny, and Anguish*. Quezon City: University of the Philippines Press.

Paz, C. J. (2008b). Sino ang may Pasya. In C. J. Paz (ed.), *Ginhawa Kapalaran Dalamhati: Essays on Well-Being, Opportunity/Destiny, and Anguish*. Quezon City: University of the Philippines Press.

Ricoeur, P. ([1977] 2003). *The Rule of Metaphor: The Creation of Meaning in Language*, trans. R. Czerny with K. McLaughlin and J. Costello. London and New York: Routledge.

Roberts, J. (2006). *Philosophizing the Everyday: Revolutionary Praxis and the Fate of Cultural Theory*. London: Pluto Press.

Ryle, G. (1949). *The Concept of Mind*. New York: Barnes and Noble.

Salazar, Z. ([1977] 1995). Ang Kamalayan at Kaluluwa: Isang Paglilinaw ng Ilang Konsepto sa Kinagisnang Sikolohiya. In R. Pe-pua (ed.), *Sikolohiyang Pilipino: Teorya, Metodo at Gamit*, 3rd edn. Quezon City: University of the Philippines Press.

Salazar, Z. (1996). The Babaylan in Philippine history. In P. D. Tapales (ed.), *Women's Role in Philippine History*, 2nd edn. Quezon City: University of the Philippines Press.

Tan, M. (2008). *Revisiting Usog, Pasma, Kulam.* Quezon City: University of the Philippines Press.

Tormey, S. and Townshend, J. (2006). Cornelius Castoriadis: Magmas and Marxism. In S. Tormey and J. Townshend (eds), *Key Thinkers from Critical Theory to Post-Marxism.* London: Sage.

Uribarri, F. (2002). Castoriadis: The radical imagination and the post-Lacanian unconscious. *Thesis Eleven.* 71, 40–51.

Whyte, L. L. (1969). *The Unconscious before Freud.* London: Basic Books.

4
Beyond Objectivity to Extimité: Feminist Epistemology and Psychoanalysis

Kareen Ror Malone and Shannon D. Kelly

Introduction to a questioning of objectivity

How one conceives of particularity and universality is a question with important social and methodological implications, in addition to being an arbiter of numerous disputes that still exercise academics over historicism, relativism and so forth; such issues have impacted critical psychology, psychoanalysis, cultural studies, political discourse and, as we discuss, modern (Western) science itself (Copjec, 1994; Martin, 1998). Certainly psychoanalysis is rightly included in this conversation by drawing upon its practice and forms of knowledge transmission; psychoanalysis is a matter of the very conceptualization of that interface of particularity with what may be 'transpersonal' or universal.

This chapter is an examination of certain trends in science studies and feminist philosophies of science that challenge science's 'legendary' status as a normative practice (Kitcher, 1993). According to legend, science is seen as an objective and progressive accumulation of facts (Kerr, 2001). However, any cursory readings of its history reveal that this idealized view of science is fallible by dint of the role of the historical, political and subjective elements that advertently or inadvertently organize its aims (Hook, 2007; Harding, 2001).

One may reproach science's failing as a universal method through which one arrives at objective truth through a number of lenses: the political disenfranchisement of articular groups' forms of knowledge through 'expert' interventions, the ecological backwash of scientific progress (see Shiva, 1988), the forms of knowledge (experimental isolation, manipulation and control of variables to make nature produce knowledge) that gain ascendance as the hegemonic form of knowledge creation that ignores its own social embeddedness (Haslinger, 1993). As science is not a metanarrative, it must garnish meanings from other domains to sustain itself, creating a minimum of 'non-scientific' features that function as points of orientation (Harding, 2001; Lacan, 1999; Stepan, 1996).

This essay's challenge to science is less an examination of the political and broadly based historical context of Western scientific practices and beliefs as prototypic modern science, but more a matter of examining critiques of science that refer particularly to how the scientific attitude in the West and questions about 'diversifying' science education and faculties must reckon with a number of social elements that are inherent to knowing and the desire for knowledge. The analysis, like an 'internal' history of science, arises out of the lab itself. The subjective elements, as essential as they are to the motivation and success of the scientist, involve non-rational components that erupt typically when science reaches its own internal limit because diversity entails alterity.

When taking modern Western science as the template, the intrusion of the subjective as a matter of gender and diversity in science education is typically queried from two directions. First, one may question the sorts of conceptualizations of method or specific theories that emerge at a given time in relation to women and minorities (Fedigan, 2001). More practically, one may question why it is that the ranks of scientists are drawn from a too narrow demographic range (Eisenhart and Finkel, 2001; Schiebinger, 1999; Seymour et al., 1997).

In order to investigate why science attracts practitioners from such a limited range and describes the world in such limited ways, one may ask how the presumably capacious methodological tenets of science are coloured by systems of representations and interests ulterior to science – thus the clarity of knowledge about the object is tainted by possibly subjective factors. In this case, science becomes culturally contextualized and loses its claims to universality and neutrality. Critiques of primatologists or examination of broader theoretical metaphors that inform the very possibility of a way of thinking the object are examples of this intrusion of culture into science (Fausto-Sterling, 2000; Morawski, 1994). Feminist scepticism about the results of science regarding men, women or any number of objects also reflects this line of reasoning. Scholars such as Sandra Harding (1996a) can, in this light, outline a stronger objectivity that takes account of just such factors.

Alternatively, a critique of the andocentric biases of science can lead one to examine the processes of scientific inquiry itself. If there is a tilt to the masculine within science, it may not be 'bad' science but rather a certain way 'good' science has not recognized some of its own foundational processes and limitations. This would mean that one might, since such bias is indicative of the subjective, review how the subjective component per se enters into science, and become more reflexive about it (Fedigan, 2001; Rosser, 1999). The presumption is that the subjective emerges within the very process of science itself, is internal to it. There are simultaneous practical and theoretical gains at stake.

This feminist critique gained an ally in the movement of science studies, both empirical and archival, which shed a more realistic light on the processes of science and thus mucked up the normative portrayal of scientific practice. Thus, post-Vienna School, those within philosophy of science often speak to the implications of this reflexive glance. Thomas Kuhn's (1977) historical work in paradigms certainly entertained the question of refounding the place of the subjective, without implying that the project of knowledge generation was hopelessly relative (Nersessian, 2002). Feminists, too, have taken this tack, asking whether gender difference (considered an attribute of a subject) is in any way acted out by one's style of doing science (Rosser, 1999).

This chapter, based within this feminist-become-philosophical reflexivity about science, interrogates the theorization of these subjective moments within the context of science as a universal practice. For example, Donna Haraway (1999, pp. 176–7) speaks of the 'god's eye trick' of seeing everything from nowhere (indifference and distance) as the 'cannibal eye of the masculinist-extraterrestial'. This obviously implicates the location of the subjective/objective division. Keller and Grontkowski (1996) implicate vision as the primary metaphor of the scientist's relation to his object rather than examining the communicative and erotic dimensions that bind the subject–object relation. Helen Longino (1990) and L. H. Nelson (1993) examine the community of knowledge making and its foundational status over the individual knower. Karen Barad (1999) draws from Neils Bohr and Foucault to rethink materiality within a discursive and social frame. All in all, under the auspices of asking if women do science differently (Kerr, 2001; McIlwee and Robinson, 1992), feminists entertain an internal epistemological agitation about science itself. This inward-looking reflection on the processes of science, both normative and empirical, implicates the philosophy of science (Grosz, 1993) as well as research that investigates diversity in science education (Rosser, 1999; Seymour et al., 2004).

Following the work of such authors, the chapter agrees that one might look at how one thinks of the subject/object relation within science. Rather than lean on the subjective as ideological or incidental, the chapter posits other ways of encountering the 'object'. Put differently, examining what an object means also allows for further reflection on the role of the subjective element. It is our presumption that psychoanalysis is well suited to this endeavour. Such an address to the object supposes that psychoanalysis, like science, developed a method of discovery, one that entails understanding the subject's relation to the object – even as psychoanalysis as method may be more or less successful in creating a universal form of knowledge creation and transmission.

Our psychoanalytic referent is one essay, *Extimité* by Jacques-Alain Miller (1994), a major interpreter of the psychoanalytic work of Jacques Lacan. We can ask if the sense of objectivity adduced by Lacanian psychoanalysis, as articulated in this essay, speaks to the debates about a universal practice, which may be called science.

Objectivity in Western science

All Western cultural narratives about objectivity are allegories of the relations of what we call mind and body, of distance and responsibility, and of course of the real and the subject who registers that reality/real in some way. And, as one might suspect, such questions are embedded in the interrogation of science and science practices by feminism. For many in feminist science studies, feminist science practices and thus the status of objectivity refer to *situated knowledge* rather than transcendent and universal knowledge (Haraway, 1999; Harding, 1996b). When one posits about the status of knowledge, one implicates the way in which the subjective interacts with the objective. Feminists are inquisitive about if not sceptical of science's usual strict demarcation of the subject and object (Keller, 1996). Particularly given the utter absence of any Lacanian ideas within feminist science studies, one might note that the psychoanalytic object is understood in terms of a particularity intrinsic to the subject and more generally as structurally necessary for subjective development; in other words, as object, as materiality, the object that draws the attention of the scientist entails an ulterior intimacy. This is recognized somewhat differently but recognized in feminist science studies in the continued influence of the psychodynamic object-relations work of Evelyn Fox Keller and in Keller's recognition of the erotic component of research or even the implication of sexual difference within knowledge (Lloyd, 1993). Insofar as the object within psychoanalysis is virtual – meaning it is critical not to simply conflate the image of the object with its function or what its appearance allows one to decipher – one can also see a similar apprehension of the virtual object in the ethnographic study of labs by Cetina-Knorr (1999) and in the feminist reflections on physics by Karen Barad (1998, 2008).

Despite the many ways that instrumentalism tries to finesse the theoretical questions on objectivity and otherness that are posed by feminist reflections through recourse to a kind of empirical pragmatics, it remains worthwhile to interrogate the practice of psychoanalysis and *its* theory of the object in science studies and in feminist research. Science is after all in a search for an object that appears in discrepancies and unaccountability and which cannot be signified in its current idiom, that is, anomalies (Kuhn, 1977). Science is equally a matter of a scientist's desire in that he or she orchestrates a certain question (Lacan, 1981). Desire caused by an object invites a psychoanalytic turn.

In science studies, a number of feminist philosophers have turned to object relations (Keller, 1996) and to the study of how women literally do science (is it different?) (Schiebinger, 1999). It seems supposed that something is going on in knowledge that needs to be interrogated as an issue internal to science (mostly here tied to gender) but its formulation remains tentative – is it simply a question of how actual women do science, an essential feature of the feminine, or is it something else, and how does this all implicate research? Some feminist articulations of this alternate modality may entail a turn to the 'maternal' as a model of science (e.g. Shiva, 1988), a choice that is not without some disingenuousness about the nature of this maternal.[1] Regardless, the status of the object as encountered by the subject is the issue; scientific methodology is meant to universalize this encounter and make it work with, so to speak, no subjective input.

Jacques-Alain Miller's (1984) essay, *Extimité*, theorizes the object through a notion of alterity located within the subject – of an exteriority lining the interior. Psychoanalysis depends on a sense of truth that does not rely on knowledge in terms of a coherent understanding or to Law to specify the foundation of one's actions. Instead psychoanalysis relies on this object as a logic that structures the psychoanalytic act. The immanence of this real object allows psychoanalytic praxis to maintain a position that seeks an ethics for a subject – a relation to enjoyment and to limit. Outside of Lacan, the most closely aligned renditions of this object are framed in terms of introjections or ingestion or as a lost object, which is given attributes and mourned (Butler, 1993). Yet it is not the character of being lost but a presence as materiality, its virtual status, which determines the object's articulation in terms of a logic rather than an image.

Although hardly a final word on the topic, Jacques-Alain Miller's essay on extimité is devoted to a general explication of this object. Miller's concept of extimité utilizes the Lacanian term of extimaté 'in order to escape the common ravings about a psychism supposedly located in a bipartition between interior and exterior'. In terms of the relationship of extimité to feminist epistemologies, we might wonder, insofar as extimité is tied to otherness and to a certain praxis of subjectivity (the clinic), how this construct could inform the research practices with science as considered by feminism. Such practices reflexively seek to reform the relation of subject to object and attempt to represent an encounter with that which has been excluded and that which, rather than being law-like, is Other (Stewart, 1994). Feminists' imaginings and recounts of science practices challenge the traditional scientific understanding of the object and objectivity as simply dependent on a set form of knowledge creation – Truth or a metalanguage, posing as the reality that we discover and codify. Thus, thinking about extimité might indeed lead to formulations that could seek to inform feminist research and science education.

As we indicated at the beginning, our work looks to the internal structuration of modern science itself. Now we can be less general in specifying our aims. While the work of some feminist philosophers examines the political aspects of women's representation in science and the way that scientific knowledge comes to bear on women's bodies (Haslinger, 1993), the focus of this particular essay is an examination of the role of the object per se as it is constituted and constitutes science itself. Feminist philosophers such as Irigaray introduce some nicely articulated ideas regarding the utility of a feminine voice in the reorganization of knowledge. Such a project obviously implicates the scientific endeavour and the subject's relation to the object. For a similar question but different takes, see also Haraway (1999) and Haslinger (1993). But it is the belief of the authors that Irigaray's method of thinking, at least, delays the interrogation of the function of the object itself by suppressing the logical necessity of an Other. This essay is focused on ways that psychoanalysis might assist the endeavours within feminist science studies to better examine the object as it appears in science in an effort to articulate an ethics that would then inform the political and social imbrications of scientific knowledge, for example the ability to hear diverse voices on the scientific project. To indicate the import of our efforts, the following examines two leading feminist examinations of science epistemology and method.

Helen Longino: philosophy of science and feminism

Helen Longino is a philosopher of science who takes the critical insights of science studies and of feminism to heart. She wants to maintain the normative claims of science – that is, that science makes successful knowledge claims. Yet she recognizes that science may be fundamentally misguided on certain of its points, for example how a subject comes to know something and how claims are validated. Longino acknowledges that the standpoint theory of Sandra Harding (1996b) and the posit of situated knowledges (Haraway, 1999), as well as her own work, are not about women as an object of science or about getting more women in science as it is, but refer to knowledge creation as implicating a type of subject:

> Both standpoint theory and the psychodynamic perspective suggest the inadequacy of an ideal of a *pure transparent subjectivity* that registers the world as it is in itself...I find it most useful to read them as articulating special instances of more general descriptive claims that subjectivity is conditioned by social and historical location and that our cognitive efforts have an ineluctably affective dimension. (Longino, 1996, p. 269, emphasis added)

Although Longino acknowledges an opacity within the subject of science, she sees nothing of the 'object' in psychodynamic accounts. Psychoanalysis is about a certain formation of the subject as is standpoint (gendered for example). She goes on to present misgivings about these accounts, reservations that follow from the way she characterizes standpoint/psychodynamic views in the first place (for example, that they are simply intersubjective accounts):

> [Such accounts] fail to explain how we are to decide...between what seem to be conflicting claims about the character of some set of natural processes. On what grounds can one social location or affective orientation be judged epistemologically superior to another? (Longino, 1996, p. 270)

To counter this feminist option, which is laden with too many undecidable subjective options, Longino introduces a kind of contextual empiricism (Kerr, 2001). Here, the self-transparent consciousness of the individual observer in tandem with an objective world – the model traditionally associated with science – is jettisoned in favour of a 'cognitive democracy'. But is this path of return to objectivity a bit too staid insofar as one simply appends a new set of systems in which 'knowledge is safeguarded from desire' and in which we assume that a subject who is not only safeguarded but really that sort of subject (a sort of half-transparent subject that needs a few buddies) is the ideal and foundation that produces good science (Keller and Grontkowski, 1996)?

According to Longino and other feminists and within cognitive science, there is growing awareness that the individual observer as the foundation of science is considered no longer viable (Hutchins, 1995; Nelson, 1993). The differences reside in what sort of subject comes to serve as the replacement and how does this subject relate to the world. Thus, part of Longino's project is to rehabilitate science so that this 'no longer' self-transparent subject, a half-blind perspectival sort of person riddled by other interested, gendered and ideological pressures, can be corralled into good scientific work. In *Science as Social Knowledge* (1990), she uses Habermas to model a broader community of knowers and thus return to how that community can get back to parsing an objective world – a project made a touch more tentative by the undecidability of possible ultimate pluralism and by the underdetermination of the data (Longino, 1993).

Longino's project *is* perhaps more pluralistic, both in terms of how many scientists it takes to observe the world and in terms of the material world it imagines. It attempts to hold up a universal methodology as the best science can do. So that, for example, rather than attempting to measure via universal standards, it can instead hold up to standards of relative validity. Yet Longino's view quickly flees from what sort of subject it is who can only think if there is a social realm, the subject who is this half-blind individual. What if this sort of individual were the starting point of science or even necessary to science? Instead her model corrects subjective errancy by replacing it with an epistemologically normative community that can be accounted for, used in knowledge production and restored to a more palatable relation to reality, albeit a bit clouded.[2]

In Longino's view, the subject, in concert with similar subjects, is a perspective, and the perspectives add up or counter one another to solve the scientific problem at hand:

From a logical point of view, if scientific knowledge were to be understood as the simple sum of finished products of individual activities, then not only would there be no way to block or mitigate the influence of subjective preference but scientific knowledge would be a potpourri of merrily inconsistent theories. Only if the products of an inquiry are understood to be formed by the kind of critical discussion that is possible among a plurality of individuals about a commonly accessible phenomenon, can we see how they count as knowledge rather than opinion. (Longino, 1990, p. 74)

Such a judgement refers of course to a number of carefully considered logical epistemological requirements outlined by Longino which refer to a way to integrate sociality (subjective) and science. Given that there is not only one community, one may assume that objectivity may have to countenance pluralism. The implied posit of pluralism (which one can also finesse by simply going for instrumentalism), is that knowledge cannot soak up the world.

Longino, acceding this pluralism in principle, then in the name of keeping science as governed by normative practices that create knowledge and feminist claims that show its subjective underbelly, introduces a particular form of social practices. Now a bevy of scientists or practices encounters the material world:

The claim of sociality is the claim that the status of the scientist's perceptual capacity as observations depends on her relations with others, in particular her openness to their challenge to and correction of her reports. This is what enables the transformation in accessibility from 'It seems to me that p' to 'P'. The data are established socially through the interactive discursive processing of sensory interactions. (Longino, 2002, p. 103)

Longino's point in the above refers to an important series of related points about the establishment of intersubjective concordance between subjects. Gilbert and Mulkay's (1984) study of scientists may give one pause about the practicality of this shift to the social in order to overcome the social interests working against the epistemological interests of science. Still, Longino's effort asserts that we can no longer deny that the social is built into the subjective and thus built into how we apprehend the objective. But in a way, her concept of the subject is quite sanitized. The way in which the subject has been rendered half-blind, less than transparent, as unknowable in its determinants (as object, we would suggest), all of these attributes are simply assumed to be screened out by the consensus building of democratic intersubjective relations. For Lacan, by contrast, it is precisely the operation of intersubjectivity on the material world that creates desire and destabilizes reality. The demand of the Other implicates the being of the subject and the restless to rigid constitution of reality through which the Other presence is mollified.

For the authors, there are two queries for Longino: The subject is not really related to the object – it is an intersubjective problem – and the model of the community of practices is simply substituted for the individual scientist. Certainly Longino has particular restraints placed upon this community: measured authority, democracy and so forth. But the kernel of irrationality is removed from both the method and the subject. One more or less continues to treat scientific method as if it were grounded in a rational (some say masculine) subject rather than as perhaps approachable as a problem of sexual difference that produces a divided subject, an erotic object and a factor of something missing. Feminists have traversed the gendered terrain of science, sifting through its history and metaphors (Keller, 1995; Stepan, 1996), and seen the erotic through the study of individual scientists. Obviously, how such a subject can do this thing called science given this stain of non-rationality *may* depend on whether one sees science as a matter of appearances and observations of a reality or a matter of the mathematic mapping and formalization of an unknowable – feminists have seen this (e.g. Barad, 1998; Haraway, 2001; Keller and Grontkowski, 1996).

Psychoanalysis might frame the enterprise as aimed at an unknowable sexual difference (Fink, 2002). There is a reason that one can trace a kind of 'nature as woman' and 'knower as man' in the rise of science. If a methodology and philosophy of science emerged that transformed how knowledge addressed the difficulties of the erotic core of science, this discourse obviously did not eliminate the (a)rationality of the initial foundation. 'If the subject of knowledge is a "blind-spot" in knowledge production and assessment, then all knowledge is necessarily contaminated by an irreducibly arational component at its core' (Grosz, 1993, p. 192). The chapter has suggested that Longino, despite her best efforts, still assumed many of the parameters of science as usual.

The two feminist theorists who most steadfastly have championed this arational problematic are Donna Haraway, whose work is thought of as leading into a postmodern direction, and Evelyn Fox Keller, whose work draws on object relations and psychoanalysis. One actually sees bits of psychoanalysis within science education work (Margolis and

Fisher, 2002), but more of the postmodernist turn within academics, although Haraway's work is creatively unclassifiable, as is Keller's. To introduce Keller's work, we might begin by framing such thoughts in relation to a well-known quotation by Lacan (1999), from his Seminar XX:

> [Science] is a subversion of knowledge. Prior to that, no knowledge was conceived that did not participate in the fantasy of an inscription of the sexual link. One cannot even say that the subjects of antiquity's theory of knowledge did not realize that.
>
> Let us simply consider the terms active and passive...that dominate everything that was cogitated regarding the relation of form and matter, a relationship that was so fundamental...It is visible and palpable that their [Aristotle and Plato] statements are based on a fantasy by which they tried to make up for what can in no way be said, namely, the sexual relationship. (p. 82)

Evelyn Fox Keller: psychodynamics and science

In her work on feminism and science, Evelyn Fox Keller (1995) thinks through the relation of subject and object in terms of the subject's infantile relations to the object. In contrast to Longino's positing of a partially blind subject standing in relation to a distinct object, Keller is attempting to show the ways in which gender construction and the process of sexualization itself create and reproduce a masculinist science driven by a notion of the object as radically separated from the subject that encounters it. Such a conceptualization has interesting implications for science and scientific endeavours as it forces a closer examination of the underlying, perhaps even unconscious, motives of the scientific endeavour as it is currently understood.

Keller's work on gender, science and objectivity addresses some areas that are important in terms of the current project. First, Keller points to the linguistic and metaphorical terms in which science is currently understood. For example, pointing out the demarcation between hard and soft science as relating to masculine and feminine types of knowledge. This seemingly simplistic positing of linguistic productions of gender actually points to a deeper, more constitutive notion of subject/object relations and Keller uses this argument to further interrogate the status of the scientific process itself as necessarily caught up in the gendered understanding of types of knowledge. She states, 'It would be naïve to suppose that the connotations of masculinity and conquest affect only the uses to which science is put and leave its structure untouched' (Keller, 1995, p. 78).

She points to the traditional divide in science between knower and knowable – subject and object that then becomes further understood in terms of subjectivity (feminine) and objectivity (masculine). She points out, however, that within this divide there is also a process that would then generate knowledge about the object. It is this process which interests her insofar as it too bears the mark of the socially constructed notions of masculinity:

> The scientific mind is set apart from what is to be known, that is, from nature, and its autonomy – and hence the reciprocal autonomy of the object – is guaranteed ... by setting apart its modes of knowing from those in which that dichotomy is threatened. In this process, the characterization of both the scientific mind and its modes of access to knowledge as masculine is indeed significant. Masculine here connotes, as it so often does, autonomy, separation, and distance. It connotes a radical rejection of any commingling of subject and object, which are, it now appears, quite consistently identified as male and female. (Keller, 1995, p. 79)

The question arises for Keller, as it does for us – is it enough to understand the scientific endeavour as merely tainted by socially constructed and performative gender ideals? Such an understanding would suggest either that the introduction of more women into the scientific field might alter the process of science and thus neutralize the 'masculine effect', or that science requires, as per Longino, an additional set of eyes from which to view the object.

While not denying that the introduction of women into the field of science may alter science in some way, Keller suggests instead that the dominance of men in science is an effect rather than a cause of the masculinist focus of science. Interestingly, she points to the process itself as generating a solution to a problem encountered by the masculine subject in the construction of his subjectivity. As does Lacan, Keller seems to be pointing to the unconscious fantasies that sustain the erotic dimension of the subject.

More specifically, Keller is pointing out that science, with its explicit separation of subject and object, a guarantee of distance between object and scientist, perhaps provides masculine subjects with a more secure position in relation to the Other; a position which allows them to better manage the infantile anxiety surrounding engulfment by the (m)Other.

Her argument overall attempts to locate subjective constitution as it is understood by psychoanalysis as the starting point for the development of scientific notions of objectivity: this means in terms of the object that it is not a contingent argument based, for example, in a particular family constellation. In doing so she points to the underlying Oedipal conflict that may drive a notion of 'pure objectivity' and thus contaminate the scientific endeavour as a subjective strategy aimed at reinforcing the subject's sense of its own autonomy. Keller brings up two issues here, one of the subjective status of the knower in terms of the ethical position in relation to knowledge, which is understood by science as Truth, and the status of Truth itself as knowledge intrinsically linked to a subjective position.

She is not suggesting that the scientific endeavour itself be abandoned in favour of some notion of ultimate relativity, but instead is suggesting that a more careful interrogation of the play of the erotic within the scientific method may produce a more rigorous science. Such a science, not bound by the exact separation between subject and object, would allow a reciprocity between knower and knowable not currently accepted by traditional science. Proscribing a change in the way science seeks to understand its object, Keller relies on psychoanalytic understandings of subjective constitution in terms of object relations.

Where Keller perhaps falls short in her analysis of the structure of the scientific endeavour is in her failure to follow the subject/object argument to the point of an actual restructuring. She abandons object relations for knowledge relations which, while creating some possibilities for change within science, leaves certain questions unanswered. While recognizing the constitution of objectivity as occurring within the emergence of a subject, she abandons further interrogation of the structural aspects of this emergence in favour of a re-examination of science in terms that allow and utilize alternate ways of knowing. While objectivity becomes problematized as a subjective attitude marred by the unconscious and further complicated by the interpretive aspects of language, the object itself remains external. For example, in rethinking the traditional aim of science as domination related to law or causal interactions, Keller proposes a new relationship to knowledge acquisition – a focus on order rather than law. Such a focus, she claims, would allow scientists to interact with nature such that a more reciprocal relationship would ensue – a relationship where nature would be allowed to express itself to a more 'modest' observer. This she claims would produce an understanding of nature as neither completely causal nor completely chaotic, thus producing 'science as neither objectivist nor idiosyncratic'

(Keller, 1995, p. 134). In this view, the attitude of the scientist becomes primary, as it is what allows the expression of nature to be fully heard. Put differently, she attempts to broker a new sense of object(ivity) and thus gravitates to knowledge construction – assuming that object and knowledge are the same. Thinking through gender and science to its final limit requires a relation both to the object and to knowledge – one cannot be adequately thought without the other.

Keller's shift from traditional forms of scientific knowing to one based on a listening is certainly interesting and would have profound effects on productions of science; however, it does not critically examine the notion of the object as a structural point of alterity within the subject itself. This structural point refers to a lack that cannot be symbolized via the traditional language of science – in fact, resists symbolization per se. Keller notes the flaws in scientific language, and even begins to point to the flaw of language itself in terms of its ability to symbolize the real, but stops short of theorizing this lack of symbolization in terms of its potential effects on scientific praxis.

It is precisely at this point – the point of the not-whole – where Lacan begins to theorize a logical relationship that may be of use in rethinking the trajectory of traditional scientific inquiry. In rethinking the problems with the traditional binary of subject/object, Lacan abandons the established reasoning of science that assumes a Truth to anchor knowledge, he instead proposes another form of knowledge, 'this unknown form of knowledge is not a separate something; it belongs to the Other as well, except it belongs to that part of the Other that is the "not-whole" part, the gap in the Other in which something else of this Other makes its appearance' (Verhaeghe, 2002, p. 110). It is here that the status of the object comes into question in terms of its intimate relations with this subject. And it is also at this point – the point of intimate alterity – that psychoanalysis may seek to inform feminist science studies by re-evaluating the possibilities for a practice that acknowledges the *jouissance* inherent in this production and seeks to understand and include that *jouissance* in an ethical praxis. It is a matter of the object as such and its *jouissance* effects through which one is provoked and organized in knowledge creation.

Psychoanalysis, objectivity, extimité

The usual recourse against any classical reductionistic objectivity in psychoanalysis is to see the object as residing in the imaginary, the image of the historical mother that is held by the physical consistency of the analyst. One then bears a relation to that object within a field of effects ultimately conceived in terms of intersubjectivity (one develops a relationship to the analyst as not mother). But one might also think of this traversal of the analysand's insides as intrinsic to the logic of the 'subject of the unconscious' as that subject exists or comes into being within the artifice of psychoanalysis. This subject is not part of an intersubjective tandem (even at the level of the signifier) nor is it an object in the traditional ontological sense. Extimité as the teleology of Miller's essay and as a position that is exterior yet within the interior pushes this 'subject of the unconscious' to its limits, to a genesis that is outside of itself. This is why one must rethink the 'logic' of the object as well as simply understanding its imaginary appearance.

Extimité and metalanguage

Miller's essay on extimité, on the structure of the object such that 'the subject is, as it were, internally excluded from its object' (Lacan, 1989, p. 10), refers at its beginning to the signifier. Miller speaks of reading Lacan's text 'against itself' and of the analysand's encounter with the analyst as both stranger and intimate. Miller's initial formulation of extimité, one that would be most known, situates this other within as the signifier itself. Language is the intruder that always already mediates our identity, leaving us a day late and a dollar short in our claims to selfhood. Here we are at the edge of Longino's less transparent subject.

But what is the other to this Other of language, what grounds its alterity in relation to the subject? With the introduction of the object *a* within the Other as that which renders its otherness and as that which orients the aims of treatment, we have broached a domain in which one is focused on the failure of the signifier, not simply as an instance, but as a logic. '[T]his *a* as *plus-de-jouir* founds not only the Other's alterity but also what is real in the symbolic Other. It is not a matter of a link of integration, of interiorization, but of an articulation of extimacy' (Miller, 1994, p. 81). So extimité becomes a sort of logic that falls upon the limits of the signifier, and one may see the final pages of this short and condensed essay as following out this logic of the *a* in relation to the Symbolic Order and in relation to the position of the analyst.

It is well known that Lacan asserted there was no metalanguage in psychoanalysis and even that the absence of a metalanguage was the truth of psychoanalysis. Querying science through feminism touches on this question of metalanguage; this is part of their point of speaking of gender and science. But Keller's linking of identity with knowledge sutures this relation again and Longino's construction of a community of knowers performs the same suture, thus closing the relation between knowledge and truth, which is precisely what creates the fantasy of a metalanguage. In psychoanalysis where what is at stake is the status of knowledge without the support of a metalanguage, this fantasy cannot be maintained. A similar assumption may be the price of the challenges to scientific knowledge as well.

Lacan suggests that the truth is posited as an assumption of the object cause of desire. Here one bears the brunt of the division of the subject through an encounter that is saturated with *jouissance*. Keller is astute, for our being overwhelmed by the Other and the 'choice' of self-division over such absorption is a critical structural moment in subjective genesis. The object emerges at this moment as the inchoate remainder of this operation. The turn to the object as so foundational to the subject is intrinsic to the movement away from Law as a guarantor of the subject's relation to the Other and towards *jouissance* as the substance of psychoanalysis, the intimate matter on which the subject's life depends. It is no wonder we might want laws of nature.

Within psychoanalysis, then, there is no metalanguage but that does not mean that one generates an endless hermeneutic circle. The absence of a metalanguage is tied to what must be found as the truth of the subject; truth is not something that psychoanalysts can avoid. Truth is produced within the signifying apparatus that generates a certain sort of encounter with the object. But the object's opacity found in the anomalous inconsistency in the Symbolic, is what must be thought out as *jouissance* if we are to discover the full implications of there being no metalanguage (at least in the terms of psychoanalytic treatment). If in fact the ultimate arbiter in psychoanalysis is *jouissance*, there is no metalanguage, no normative template in terms of which the analysand is (to be) oriented.

Needless to say, this is not the usual approach to the end of metalanguage. The more usual approach is to cultivate interpretative subversion, play for a proliferation of signifiers, reveal the operation of the signifier in seemingly objective discourses, or look to the networks of signifiers to produce conflicting subject positions. So this end to metalanguage is not the occasion for the multiplicity of meanings or subject positions or narrative possibilities wherein the question of truth is infinitely forestalled. In part, as an effect of psychoanalytic practice, one cannot overindulge in interpretation, since one aims to reduce a symptom to enjoyment. 'There is no exaggeration in positing Lacan's teaching as being animated by the difficulty of thinking about the subject as lack-in-being, that is, as a certain kind of non-being, together with *jouissance* as substance' (Miller, 2000, p. 13). In fact, Miller attempts to reach a point of disidentification through the supposition of extimité insofar as the Symbolic Other is evacuated and one is left with how one handles the conditions of one's *jouissance* – one's *savoir-faire*.

It may be inappropriate to ask other fields to engage with the object in this way; this may be the singular project of psychoanalysis. But if psychoanalysis offers its two bits to the 'end of metalanguage' as a theoretical project and as a question of research, it may be most precisely in these terms of the object rather than in terms of a postmodernist imputed relativism. For this object is conjured out of a logic that is enacted in a practice. It is not unthinkable that other practices may be able to also tap the Real within a given set of parameters. In other words, we must think the Real but this Real is as it exits within its failed absorption into the Symbolic order.

It may be then that we are able to return to an understanding of the Real as cause – an understanding that informs the trajectory of Miller's essay. Most importantly, this might inform a number of disciplinary projects, including science itself, in a way that would not 'safeguard' against desire.

We do not think that such speculations are so far away from science and the ideas of those who think about it. Feyerabend (1987) referred to logical positivism as infantile and later more instrumentalist versions of philosophies of science as just as infantile but less clear. The nasty aside may deserve more attention than it gets as it appears in a call for scientists to realize that they cannot have science and a theory of science at the same time, 'All we have is the process of research and, side by side with it, all sorts of rules of thumb which *may* aid us in our attempt to further the process but which may also lead us astray' (p. 283). Feyerabend certainly sees that truth and knowledge cannot be the same and cannot replace the subjective and contingent responsibility of the scientist. Interestingly, his essay on method drifts into how one knows the Other and also whether Evil can be eradicated: these are the questions of knowledge upon which it stumbles. Whether he meant to dredge up the old psychoanalytic troika of sex, death and science is of course an open question. The point is that he articulates a different way of encountering the real as the scientific ethic.

Karen Barad (1998, 2008), a feminist and theoretical physicist, tries to tackle a new approach to the Real where one no longer accords that the object exists separately from the apparatus of measurement. She notes that 'feminist science studies' imply the need for new understandings of objectivity. The object, for her, is created in an 'intra-act' in which an apparatus produces an object, in which subject and object perform as an apparatus together, producing an 'agential realism' (Barad, 1999). In contrast to Miller, the object (*a*) is not a semblance and Barad's aim, as we expect, is greater intelligibility. Nonetheless, for this essay, her work picks up a certain quality, the logic of the encounter, as the generative point that creates the 'cut' (as she calls it, following Bohr) that renders the object. She pulls back from the separation of truth and knowledge.

But our introduction of Barad and Feyerabend refers to more general posits. The object and subject are being rethought through feminist science studies in ways that might dialogue afresh with psychoanalysis. Were this more than an initial articulation, Barad's and Feyerabend's work, as well as that of Donna Haraway's, might join psychoanalytic formulations to get at this issue of the object in science and trace the choreography of the dance that 'normal' science enacts not to *see* so much as to avert its eyes.

Notes

1. For the issue of the maternal see Flax, 1997.
2. Of course, along with the scientist, scientific reality has taken a bit of a drubbing in recent decades. The reality that interested science was one that was seen as a shared world of appearances that given the right method will yield her secrets (Keller and Grontkowski, 1996). Today, reality is that which, given our questions, presents a certain problem. Science then is a sort of instrumentalism rather than a description. But the ideal of knowledge is very similar, if more modest, in terms of its aims and fantasies of representing a real that fits with a sort of conscious knowledge: it works; there is still a fit between subject and object. The subject here as a trouble spot recedes into background noise insofar as that subject may be something ulterior to this system of knowledge and instrumentation.

References

Barad, K. (1998). Getting real: Technoscientific practices and the materialization of reality. *Differences*, 10, 87–128.

Barad, K. (1999). Agential realism: Feminist interventions in understanding scientific practices. In M. Biagioli (ed.), *The Science Studies Reader*. New York: Routledge, pp. 1–11.

Barad, K. (2008). Living in a posthuman material world: Lessons from Schrodinger's cat. In A. Smelik and N. Lykke (eds), *Bits of Life*. Seattle: University of Washington Press, pp. 165–76.

Butler, J. (1993). *Bodies that Matter*. New York: Routledge.

Cetina-Knorr, K. (1999). *Epistemic Cultures: How the Sciences Make Knowledge*. Cambridge, MA: Harvard University Press.

Copjec, J. (1994). *Read My Desire*. Cambridge, MA: MIT Press.

Eisenhart, M. and Finkel, E. (2001). Women (still) need not apply. In M. Lederman and I. Bartsch (eds), *The Gender and Science Reader*. New York: Routledge, pp. 13–23.

Fausto-Sterling, A. (2000). *Sexing the Body: Gender Politics and the Construction of Sexuality*. New York: Basic Books.

Fedigan, L. (2001). Is primatology a feminist science? In M. Wyer, M. Barbercheck, D. Giesman, H. Öztürk and M. Wayne (eds), *Women, Science and Technology*, 2nd edn. New York: Routledge, pp. 239–53.

Feyerabend, P. (1987). *Farewell to Reason*. New York: Verso.

Fink, B. (2002). Knowledge and science: Fantasies of the whole. In J. Glynos and Y. Stavrakakis (eds), *Lacan and Science*. London: Karnac, pp. 167–78.

Flax, J. (1997). Forgotten forms of close combat: Mothers and daughters re-visited. In M. Gergen and S. Davis (eds), *Toward a New Psychology of Gender: A Reader*. New York: Routledge, pp. 311–24.

Gilbert, G. and Mulkay, M. (1984). *Opening Pandora's Box: A Sociological Analysis of Scientists' Discourse*. Cambridge University Press.

Grosz, E. (1993). Bodies and knowledge: Feminism and the crisis of reason. In L. Alcoff and E. Potter (eds), *Feminist Epistemologies*. London: Routledge, pp. 187–216.

Haraway, D. (1999). Situated knowledges: The science question in feminism and the privilege of partial perspective. In M. Biagioli (ed.), *The Science Studies Reader*. New York: Routledge, pp. 172–89.

Haraway, D. (2001) (with Thyrza Nichols Goodeve). More than a metaphor. In M. Mayberry, B. Subramaniam and L. Weasel (eds), *Feminist Science Studies: A New Generation*. New York: Routledge, pp. 81–7.

Harding, S. (1996a). Rethinking standpoint epistemology: What is 'strong objectivity'? In E. Keller and H. Longino (eds), *Feminism and Science*. Oxford University Press, pp. 235–48.

Harding, S. (1996b). *The Science Question in Feminism*. Ithaca, NY: Cornell University Press.

Harding, S. (2001). After absolute neutrality. In M. Mayberry, B. Subramaniam and L. Weasel (eds), *Feminist Science Studies*. New York: Routledge, pp. 291–304.

Haslinger, S. (1993). On being objective and being objectified. In L. Anthony and C. Witt (eds), *A Mind of One's Own*. Boulder, CO: Westview Press, pp. 85–126.

Hook, D. (2007). *Foucault, Psychology and the Analytics of Power*. Basingstoke and New York: Palgrave Macmillan.

Hutchins, E. (1995). *Cognition in the Wild*. Cambridge, MA: MIT Press.

Keller, E. (1995). *Reflections on Gender and Science*, 2nd edn. New Haven: Yale University Press.

Keller, E. (1996). Feminism and science. In E. Keller and H. Longino (eds), *Feminism and Science*. Oxford University Press, pp. 28–40.

Keller, E. and Grontkowski, C. (1996). The mind's eye. In E. Keller and H. Longino (eds), *Feminism and Science*. Oxford University Press, pp. 187–202.

Kerr, E. A. (2001). Toward a feminist natural science: Linking theory and practice. In M. Lederman and I. Bartsch (eds), *The Gender and Science Reader*. New York: Routledge, pp. 386–406.

Kitcher, P. (1993). *The Advancement of Science*. Oxford University Press.
Kuhn, T. (1977). *The Essential Tension: Selected Studies in Scientific Tradition and Change*. University of Chicago Press.
Lacan, J. ([1973] 1981). *The Four Fundamental Concepts of Psychoanalysis*, ed. J.-A. Miller, trans. A. Sheridan. New York: W. W. Norton.
Lacan, J. (1989). Science and truth. *Newsletter of the Freudian Field*, 3, 4–29.
Lacan, J. (1999). *On Feminine Sexuality, the Limits of Love and Knowledge: The Seminar of Jacques Lacan, Book XX, Encore*, trans. B. Fink. New York: W. W. Norton.
Lloyd, E. A. (1993). Reason, science and the domination of matter. In E. Keller and H. Longino (eds), *Feminism and Science*. Oxford University Press, pp. 41–56.
Longino, H. (1990). *Science as Social Knowledge: Values and Objectivity in Scientific Inquiry*. Princeton University Press.
Longino, H. (1993). Essential tensions – phase two: Feminist, philosophical and social studies of science. In L. Anthony and C. Witt (eds), *A Mind of One's Own*. Denver, CO: Westview Press, pp. 257–72.
Longino, H. (1996). Subjects, power, and knowledge: Description and prescription in feminist philosophies of science. In E. Keller and H. Longino (eds), *Feminism and Science*. Oxford University Press, pp. 264–79.
Longino, H. (2002). *The Fate of Knowledge*. Princeton University Press.
Margolis, J. and Fisher, A. (2002). *Unlocking the Clubhouse*. Cambridge, MA: MIT Press.
Martin, J. (1998). Methodological essentialism, false difference, and other dangerous traps. In B. Clinchy and J. Norem (eds), *The Gender and Psychology Reader*, 2nd edn. New York University Press, pp. 34–53.
McIlwee, J. and Robinson, J. (1992). *Women in Engineering*. Albany: State University of New York Press.
Miller, J.-A. (1994). Extimité. In M. Bracher, M. Alcorn, R. Corthell and F. Massardier-Kenney (eds), *Lacanian Theory and Discourse*. New York University Press, pp. 74–87.
Miller, J.-A. (2000). The experience of the real in psychoanalysis. *Lacanian Ink*, 16, 7–29.
Morawski, J. (1994). *Practicing Feminisms, Reconstructing Psychology: Notes on a Liminal Science*. Ann Arbor: University of Michigan Press.
Nelson, L. H. (1993). Epistemological communities. In L. Alcoff and E. Potter (eds), *Feminist Epistemologies*. London: Routledge, pp. 121–59.
Nersessian, N. J. (2002). Kuhn, conceptual change, and cognitive science. In T. Nichols (ed.), *Thomas Kuhn*. Cambridge University Press, pp. 178–211.
Rosser, S. (1999). Different laboratory/work climates: Impacts on women in the workplace. *Annals of the New York Academy of Sciences: Women in Science and Engineering: Choices for Success*, 869, 95–101.
Schiebinger, L. (1999). *Has Feminism Changed Science?* Cambridge, MA: Harvard University Press.
Seymour, E., Hunter, A., Laursen, S. and Deantoni, T. (2004). *Establishing the Benefits of Research Experiences for Undergraduates in the Sciences: First Findings from a Three Year Study*. www.interscience.wiley.com, accessed 16 December 2003.
Shiva, V. (1988). *Staying Alive: Women, Ecology and Survival in India*. New Delhi: Kali for Women.

Stepan, N. (1996). Race and gender: The role of analogy in science. In E. Keller and H. Longino (eds), *Feminism and Science*. Oxford University Press, pp. 121–36.

Stewart, A. (1994). Toward a feminist strategy for studying women's lives. In C. Franz and A. Stewart (eds), *Women Creating Lives*. Denver, CO: Westview, pp. 11–33.

Verhaeghe, P. (2002). Lacan's answer to the classical mind/body deadlock: Retracing Freud's beyond. In S. Barnard and B. Fink (eds), *Reading Seminar XX: Lacan's Major Work on Love, Knowledge, and Feminine Sexuality*. Albany: SUNY Press, pp. 99–139.

5
Knotted Subjectivity: On Lacan's Use of Knot Theory in Building a Non-universal Theory of the Subject

Stijn Vanheule and Abe Geldhof

In this chapter, we explore Lacan's use of knot theory and highlight how this brings him to elaborate a theory in which the subject is thought of as an effect of knotting the registers of the Real, the Symbolic and the Imaginary. In doing so, we review Lacan's discussion of James Joyce's life and work. We argue that his suggestion that Joyce created a so-called 'sinthome' is most innovative in that it refers to a purely singular and non-universal way of creating connections between the Real, the Symbolic and the Imaginary. As Lacan's knot-theoretical model provides a most valuable tool for further reflection we illustrate its usefulness by introducing the case of David Nebreda, a Spanish photographer who severely mutilated his body and took pictures of it, which he called 'photographic doubles'. These photographic doubles are a singular invention by means of which the artist gains subjective consistency as well as access to shared discourse. To conclude we address the social and political implications of Lacan's later theory on the subject. However, first we provide an overview of how Lacan's use of knot theory fits within his conception of the subject.

Lacan's shifts in conceptualizing the subject

Guided by a return to the work of Freud, in the 1950s and 1960s, Lacan formulated a theory of the subject that focused on the structuring role of language. His proposal was that Freud's ideas on the functioning of the unconscious can be better understood within the context of linguistic theory. In this respect he devoted much discussion to how language functions in the inauguration and expression of human desire. From this perspective, the unconscious is made up of so-called signifiers which, following de Saussure (1916), Lacan (1957b) considers as the most elementary units of language. At the level of the unconscious signifiers are combined in terms of linguistic tropes, such as metaphor and metonymy, which convey how defences take shape. To emphasize the organizing role of language, during this period Lacan proclaimed that the so-called register of the *Symbolic* – that is, language and the internal structure of speech – determines mental functioning. Inspired by the structuralist perspective of his French contemporaries such as Claude Lévi-Strauss, he proposes that the contents of mental representations should not be studied as such, and that psychodynamic and phenomenological approaches to human subjectivity are far from adequate. In his view psychodynamic theory and phenomenology focus too strongly on what he calls *Imaginary* phenomena, or people's lived experiences. Such a focus is inadequate because it neglects what really matters, that is, the structure of signified articulation which comes to the fore in speech. These structures are thought to give shape to psychic reality, which is why Lacan advocated a direct study of speech.

Within this view, subjectivity is conceptualized as a pure effect of speech. The signifiers we use, especially pronouns, connote us as speakers and define the social world we are living in, and the subject is nothing but the net result of these connotations: 'a signifier is what represents the subject to another signifier' (Lacan, 1960, pp. 693–4). This viewpoint is radical in that it implies that the subject is not a mental instance or a 'being' that has any reality beyond language, but a strict effect of symbolic articulation (Parker, 2003). Hence the idea that the subject is divided: no signifiers ever exactly denote who the subject is, and subjectivity is to be found only in the scattered diversity of signifiers. Some signifiers are embraced and give shape to identification and to identity; others are repressed and give rise to symptom formation (Vanheule and Verhaeghe, 2009).

Inspired by Lévi-Strauss' structural approach to myths, Lacan reformulates the Freudian Oedipus complex (Verhaeghe, 2004). Whereas Freud mainly described the Oedipus complex in developmental terms, and characterized it as a conflict all human beings live through and remain marked by throughout their life, Lacan (1959) believes that what actually takes place is a metaphorical transition. In his interpretation a special signifier is installed during the Oedipus complex: the paternal signifier or 'Name-of-the-Father'. This signifier names the desire of the maternal figure with which the child is first confronted, and it opens up the dimension of the law for the subject. Through the Name-of-the-Father people understand themselves and others in terms of rules and standards that one should obey. They use this signifier to make sense of desire and it helps them to experience permanency in social relations.

Actually, the Name-of-the-Father is a most remarkable concept in Lacan's work from the 1950s, in that it is a signifier that both makes part of the Symbolic and functions as the element that guarantees the consistency of the Symbolic register (Lacan, 1957–58). When the paternal signifier is installed the Symbolic contains an orderly structure by means of which the subject can be articulated in consistent ways. If, by contrast, this signifier remains lacking, psychosis is the result (Lacan, 1959). At the level of subjectivity, such non-installment of the Name-of-the-Father has dramatic effects; the articulation of the subject is rendered chaotic and can only be stabilized through the construction of a delusion. To the extent that a delusion helps make sense of the world in terms of idiosyncratic laws, it enables the creation of subjective consistency. Within this view the Name-of-the-Father has the status of a *universal operator* in the process of creating subjectivity. Either people acquire this signifier and enter the world of shared neurotic convention, or do not acquire the Name-of-the-Father and end up in psychosis, which prevents them from participating in the world of convention. This viewpoint is universal in that it posits a model trajectory: the Name-of-the-Father is the ultimate reference against which subjectivity needs to be checked and the unique password for getting access to shared discourse and desire.

From his tenth seminar onwards, Lacan (1962–63) progressively searched for other concepts to elaborate the notion of the subject and aimed at theorizing aspects of subjectivity that cannot by grasped by means of the Symbolic. In those years he still believed that the Symbolic determines the Imaginary, but added that the impact of the Symbolic is limited. Picking up from Freud's concept of the death drive he then argued that human functioning is marked by a *jouissance*, a mode of satisfaction or drive gratification that is beyond pleasure and should be thought of as dialectically opposed to the Symbolic. As *Jouissance* resists signification, Lacan qualifies it as the *Real* against which the Symbolic collides.

An important concept that Lacan introduced during this period is the object *a*. The object *a* denotes the element of corporeal *jouissance* that, despite all dialectical tension, cannot be inserted into the order of the Symbolic. Lacan (1960) says that it is in relation to such an object that the subject, which is still conceptualized as an effect of the signifier, takes shape. More specifically, in the subject's relation to the orifices of the body such as the oral, anal, scopic and invocative registers, objects *a* can be found (Lacan, 1962–63, 1964). Henceforth, it is no longer the signifier, but the object *a* that is seen as that which sets the subject in motion, and inaugurates desire. For example, whereas in his seminar on 'The purloined letter' (1957a) Lacan situated the cause of desire in the field of the signifier and demonstrated that the signifier obeys strictly probabilistic rules, in his 1964 seminar he argued the opposite. He then proposed that the true cause of desire and Symbolic articulation is to be found in the failure of the Symbolic. He states 'there is cause only in something that doesn't work' (Lacan, 1964, p. 22); that is, what is Real to the subject sets the Symbolic in motion.

As he included the dimension of the Real in his theory, Lacan's ideas on the unconscious and the Name-of-the-Father changed substantially. In the 1950s he conceptualized the unconscious in strictly Symbolic terms. For example, following Freud (1900) he stated that condensation and displacement are crucial in the formations of the unconscious, and that metaphor and metonymy adequately reflect the transitions signifiers make in these processes (Lacan, 1957b). From the 1960s onwards, when he elaborated his theory on the object *a*, his focus on the unconscious changed (Lacan, 1964). The dimension he begins to emphasize then is what Freud (1900, p. 603) called the 'core of our being'. His thesis is that not everything of the unconscious can be interpreted, and that there is a Real part to the unconscious that cannot be understood in terms of metaphor and metonymy. Next to the Symbolic 'transferable unconscious' he henceforth distinguishes and a 'Real unconscious' that is not open to interpretation (Miller, 2007).

In the same vein, there comes a shift in Lacan's privileging of the Name-of-the-Father as the ultimate guarantee of subjective consistency. From the early 1960s on, Lacan argued that what structures the subject is not so much *the* Name-of-the-Father, but *a* Name-of-the-Father. Starting from the idea that only an act of faith elevates a signifier to the status of guarantee he then says that multiple paternal signifiers exist (Lacan, 1962–63, 1963, 1964). In this view Names-of-the-Father are still thought to be the only operators that offer access to the Symbolic and lead to the articulation of desire in terms of shared discourse. The paternal signifier is no longer seen as a unique signifier with inherent lawful qualities but as a uniquely used signifier that people believe in (Vanheule, 2011). Moreover, from then on Lacan (1962–63) sees a clear link between the Names-of-the-Father and the object *a*, in that the function of the Father consists of clearing the path for a subject in having access to the object *a*. The Name-of-the-Father sets the standard in how desire takes shape in relation to an object *a*, and in this respect it cannot be missed.

These conceptual changes in the 1960s are important in that the basis of subjectivity is no longer the unique paternal signifier, but a corporeal element in relation to which a Name-of-the-Father only has an orienting function. The hallmark of the subject that provides consistency to the subject is no longer situated within the Symbolic register, but in the dialectical tension between the Symbolic and the Real.

However, a theory in which a Name-of-the-Father is no longer seen as strictly necessary to obtain subjective consistency only comes to the fore in the 1970s (Miller, 1993), when Lacan begins to use knot theory as a model for conceptualizing the relation between the registers of the Real, the Symbolic and the Imaginary. We believe that with this model from the 1970s Lacan built a truly non-universalist theory of the subject. Contrary to his Oedipus-inspired model from the 1950s and 1960s he no longer suggests that a Name-of-the-Father is indispensable for the subject to have access to shared discourse. Multiple 'knottings' between the Real, the Symbolic and the Imaginary are thought to be possible, and in order to create subjectivity a shared Symbolic law is no longer seen as crucial.

Knotting with Lacan

Lacan's use of knot theory is controversial. Several authors, both insiders (Borch-Jacobsen, 1991; Roustang, 1990) and outsiders (Sokal and Bricmont, 1998) to psychoanalysis, are most critical of Lacan's work from the 1970s and have attempted to ridicule his use of knot theory, arguing that it bears witness of his eccentricity and the abracadabra nature of his work. A popular example of such a criticism can be found in Sokal and Bricmont's (1998) book *Fashionable Nonsense*. The authors argue that Lacan offered no empirical or conceptual argument for the analogy he draws between psychoanalysis and mathematics, rendering this link arbitrary at the very least. However, despite their commendable scepticism, the authors fail to demonstrate precisely *what* is problematic in Lacan's use of mathematics. The mere fact that Lacan draws an analogy between psychoanalytic concepts and mathematical formulae is not sufficient criticism. Social scientists make use of mathematics frequently, and necessarily equate their nominal categories with mathematical categories despite the fact that nomination is always arbitrary. A most interesting question that Sokal and Bricmont do not address, however, is *how* and *why* Lacan makes use of topology. In line with Badiou (2009) it is our opinion that by using knot theory Lacan addressed a number of theoretical problems that are prominent in his earlier work, and established a new language for reflection on psychoanalysis that implies, among other things, an innovative notion of the subject.

Lacan was familiarized with knot theory in the early 1970s through his association with a number of young French mathematicians, such as Thierry Soury and Michel Thomé. In his seminar of 1975–76, he gave a detailed explanation of mathematical knot theory and its relevance for psychoanalytic theory. With knot theory he found a new means to define recurring theoretical problems. It was considered to be a discursive framework with axioms and rules, and exploring them in depth offered him the means to reformulate complex psychoanalytic concepts.

This trajectory brought Lacan to use mathematical knots and links to serve as a model to reflect on the relation between the Real, the Symbolic and the Imaginary (Lacan, 1975–76, p. 130). Whereas before the 1970s Lacan largely conceptualized the relation between these registers in terms of dialectical oppositions between two elements, and focused on tensions between the Symbolic and the Imaginary or between the Symbolic and the Real, in the 1970s he concentrated on how these registers are mutually connected. Henceforth dialectical oppositions no longer hold his interest. What comes to the fore is the question of how in the relation between these *three* elements a *connection* can be created, such that the whole is more than the sum of the parts. Indeed, Lacan's (1975–76) knot theory is most valuable since it opens up a three-dimensional way of thinking that moves beyond two-dimensional representations. Henceforth the question is no longer how, in the dialectical tension between two registers, a third element is created, like the object *a* is created in the dialectical tension between Symbolic and the Real. The key question Lacan is working with in the 1970s is how, in the relation between the Real, the Symbolic and the Imaginary, which he abbreviates as R, S and I respectively, a fourth element is created. This fourth element is the knot, or the link that connects R, S and I. In Lacan's psychoanalytic interpretation the knot refers to that which creates stability in the relation between R, S and I, such that consistency in the articulation of the subject can be obtained.

The choice of knot theory was as surprising for his students as it was for his contemporaries: nobody before had used this branch of topology to facilitate reflection on the structure of human subjectivity. However, when one examines the trajectory of Lacan's work this progression makes sense. General mathematical theory, such as algebra and projective geometry, was a frame of reference that Lacan had been using long before his interest in topological knot theory. He believed that the rigour of mathematics guaranteed a certain scientific exactitude that escapes language and thus made frequent use of arithmetical terminology to more precisely define basic psychoanalytic concepts, such as the relation between the subject and the Other, or the relation between demand and desire. His subsequent interest in knot theory emerged largely because algebra had reached the limit of its usefulness at this point in his work (Lacan, 1975–76, p. 42). Overall, Lacan's use of knot theory comes alongside his concern with the scientificity of psychoanalysis; it is a matter of finding a foundation outside the conceptual language of psychoanalysis or its clinical practice, and not lapsing into imaginary speculation on the relation between the registers R, S and I. For Lacan, working with knots has the status of a novel form of 'writing' that enables logical reflection (Lacan, 1975–76, pp. 131, 144).

The knot-theoretical model Lacan most frequently makes use of for conceptualizing the relation between the three registers R, S and I, are the Borromean rings. The Borromean rings are three topological circles that are linked in such a way that a mutual connection is created: ring B lies on top of ring A; ring C lies on top of ring B; but ring C lies under ring A. Removing any of these rings results in the disconnection of the other two rings as well. Lacan uses the Borromean rings (Figure 5.1) as a model for conceptualizing the relations between R, S and I, whereby he represents the Real by a blue circle, the Imaginary by a green circle and the Symbolic by a red circle.

An important characteristic of the Borromean rings is that it consists of *non-hierarchical* circles: 'the three circles from the Borromean knot are, from their status as a circle, equivalent'[1] (Lacan, 1975–76, p. 50). None of the registers is superior or inferior; none is anterior or posterior in relation to the others (Lacan, 1975–76, pp. 50, 52). What is particularly interesting about this non-hierarchical model is that it made Lacan abandon his idea that the Symbolic is the ultimate reference point from which the Imaginary or the Real take shape. Henceforth, the Symbolic is just one component of the broader composite that is created by connecting R, S and I.

A further conclusion Lacan draws from the model of the Borromean rings is that what gives consistency to the Symbolic is not an exceptional or exceptionally used signifier within the same register, like a Name-of-the-Father, but the fact that S is linked with R and I. His idea then is that it is the register of the Imaginary that adds consistency to the link

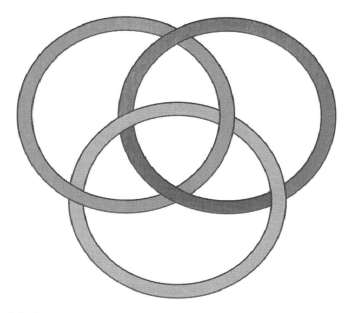

Figure 5.1 Borromean rings

between R, S and I, and that it is because of being included in this link that the Symbolic is stabilized (Lacan, 1975–76, p. 36). This viewpoint is important in that it implies a further step away from a purely signified model of subjectivity. In the Borromean model the subject is no longer seen as a mere effect of references between signifiers in the Symbolic, but as a production within S that only comes to the fore because R, S and I are linked. His point then is that the link between the three registers is the support of the subject (Lacan, 1975–76, pp. 50, 53), meaning that the connection between R, S and I makes up the condition for a subject to appear in the Symbolic.

By formulating this idea on the structuring role of the knot Lacan radically dethroned the Oedipal account of subjectivity he had been using until then. With the Borromean rings subjectivation is considered in purely logical terms that have nothing to do with a normative developmental psychological trajectory. Also, by situating the basis of a lawful functioning of the Symbolic in the mere connection between S with R and I, Lacan no longer assumes that the incorporation of a law that is external to the subject is needed for the articulation of the subject. As long as Lacan stuck to the idea that the Name-of-the-Father or a

Name-of-the-Father is needed for a coherent articulation of subjectivity, his theory stressed that without the transmission of a dominant cultural discourse in which one has faith, the subject cannot be articulated. By emphasizing the role of knotting this changes. Henceforth a belief in the law of the Father is no longer seen as the critical foundation of the subject. What counts is the *singular* way in which the knot takes shape. Of all possible ways in which R, S and I might be linked, believing in the Father and in convention is only one option. It is the option by means of which neurosis takes shape, and discourse gets reproduced, but certainly not the only solution for obtaining a stable mode of subjectivity.

Parallel to this shift in ideas on how the subject takes shape, Lacan (1975–76) also adjusts his ideas on how the object *a* is coined. In line with what he had previously said, Lacan considers the object *a* as the foundation of desire that has a crucial role for the subject. Yet, contrary to his work from the 1960s he no longer assumes that this object is created in the dialectical tension between S and R. Henceforth the knotting between R, S and I is the basis from which the object *a* takes shape. In terms of the Borromean rings he situates the object *a* in the common intersection between the three topological circles (Lacan, 1975–76, p. 72).

James Joyce: knotting via an artist ego

In elaborating his theory on the singular knotting of R, S and I, Lacan takes James Joyce as a source of inspiration. What Lacan (1975–76) finds most striking in Joyce's work is that spanning from the autobiographical novel *A Portrait of the Artist as a Young Man*, to *Ulysses* and *Finnegans Wake*, the father is represented as a broken and worthless figure. In his interpretation *Ulysses* shows that Joyce cannot have faith in the father. Whenever a paternal figure comes to the fore he negates the structuring role that fathers usually play, and presents his protagonist as an 'artificer' who makes his way alone (Lacan, 1975–76, pp. 96–7).

In terms of the connection between R, S and I Lacan (1975–76) more specifically says that in Joyce's case the Imaginary plays a peculiar role. In terms of his literary style this can be seen in his non-narrative and cryptic way of writing, which became more prominent as his oeuvre progressed. Consistency in content and storylines is remarkably poor, such that his later work is almost unreadable (Lacan, 1975–76, p. 151). Another point Lacan (1975–76, pp. 148–9) considers as indicative of the peculiar way in which the Imaginary functions, are the anecdotes from *A Portrait of the Artist as a Young Man* (1965) in which Joyce states that when Stephen was beaten by a group of friends, or by the prefect at school, he was actually not distressed. In a remarkable way the physical impact of the beatings has no subjective counterpart. In Lacan's interpretation Stephen disconnects from his body and neutrally bows to the pain the other's violence induces, as if his body is an external instance to which he is not attached.

However, the eccentric status of the Imaginary does not imply that at the level of the subject consistency could not have been experienced. Lacan (1975–76, p. 87) indicates that although R, S and I were not linked via a belief in the father, the topological rings were not untied or intermingled. On the contrary, Lacan (1975–76, p. 88) believes that by cultivating his position as an artist Joyce most adequately compensated for his poor embedding in convention. Joyce aimed at making a name for himself as a writer, and wanted to be the kind of artist everyone is fascinated by. In Lacan's interpretation this self-made-man attitude provided him with a way of living that counterbalanced his poor insertion in established discourse. He quickly cultivated his enigmatic way of writing, which bears witness of a mixture between R and S, and assumed the ego of being a great writer, which Lacan (1975–76, p. 152) qualified as an Imaginary mode of self-cultivation.

Indeed, in Lacan's interpretation Joyce's active cultivation of his artist ego is a true alternative to neurotic belief in the Father function. It is the binding principle starting from which R, S and I become linked in a stable composite (Lacan, 1975–76, p. 152). Given the fact that this 'invention' (sic, Miller, 2004) is tailor-made, and does not build on pre-established standards and customs, we can consider it as strictly singular (Lacan, 1975–76, p. 17). Joyce's cultivation of his artist ego zeroed in on the uncharacteristic way in which R, S and I functioned, and was successful because it compensated for his spontaneous lack of connection with the Imaginary. As he characterized Joyce's ego and style, Lacan (1975–76, pp. 19, 152) said that these have the status of a sinthome. This is to say that they are kind of symptomatic, but in a strictly positive sense. They bear witness of Joyce's 'sins' or frailties, but at the same time act as a most elegant solution for peculiarities in the relation between R, S and I (Lacan, 1975–76, p. 13). Contrary to a symptom, a sinthome cannot be understood in terms of metaphor and metonymy, and it does not imply a suffering subject. Its principal function resides in tying together reality, which is why Joyce's active cultivation of this sinthome is considered useful.

What we find particularly interesting about Lacan's discussion of Joyce is that it underscores a mode of subjectivity that does not build on a universal operator like a Name-of-the-Father, but that at the same time does not imply exclusion from the social bond. Using the model of the Borromean rings Lacan emphasized that by inventing an art of living, stability can be created in the relation between R, S and I, such that a stable platform for the articulation of the subject is created. Furthermore, Joyce's case shows that a sinthome has a social function. No matter how little support established discourse might have given him, his art and his way of living connect Joyce to shared discourse.

David Nebreda: knotting via photographic doubles

To further explore the pragmatic usefulness of knot theory and subjectivity, and to move beyond the discussion of cases Lacan worked with, we now switch to the Spanish artist David Nebreda. Nebreda is a self-educated photographer, born in 1952, who since the 1980s made an art of photographing diverse forms of self-injury on his emaciated body. He uses knives, cords and red-hot objects to mutilate his body, puts excrement on his face and writes texts with his own blood. A first series of photos was taken between 1983 and 1989. After a serious mental crisis, diagnosed as schizophrenia, and two psychiatric hospitalizations, a second series of photos was taken in 1997, and a last series of photos, accompanied by drawings, was completed between 1998 and 1999. The pictures were published in three books, accompanied by personal notes in which the artist comments on his own work (Curnier and Surya, 2001; Nebreda, 2000, 2004, 2006). The majority of Nebreda's pictures are self-portraits, and are completed with a degree of technical perfection and a feel for composition reminiscent of classic painters, such as Caravaggio or Goya (Guillo, 2002).

In our interpretation these photos, which Nebreda (2000) calls 'photographic doubles', are far from pathological symptoms of a disorder, but inventions that fulfil the function of a sinthome. His art helps him experience consistency, and it topologically 'knots' the registers R, S and I. His problem in experiencing a personal feeling of identity seems to be regulated by photography. Moreover, just like Joyce's sinthome, Nebreda's art has a social function as it connects him to the scene of contemporary art. Although Nebreda (2000; Guillo, 2002) argues that his work is not inscribed in any artistic movement or tradition, his exhibitions and publications do not pass unnoticed. Some describe his oeuvre as unacceptably obscene, others, like Jones (2005), describe it as avant-garde and challenging: 'Nebreda, like Orlan, creates a critical turbulence within normative discourses of the body, representation and the aesthetic.' The artist himself indicates feeling honoured by the attention people pay to his work, which suggests that his work functions to integrate him into social bonds. Throughout his personal notes and in interviews (Guillo, 2002; Millet, 2000) Nebreda says that his basic position in life consists of a profound detachment from convention and from others. In this sense, the socially inclusive power of his work should not be underestimated. Nebreda writes that his life is marked by an absolute 'absence of norms' (Nebreda, 2000, p. 183) and that he feels no connection at all with the reality other people share (Guillo, 2002), which regularly leaves him in deep despair about what is real or not. By means of his art, this spontaneous lack of social inclusion seems to be compensated.

A singular difficulty Nebreda struggles with is the experience of identity. He says that he feels a 'lack of identity' and he questions his very existence, which brings him to refer to himself in the third person (Guillo, 2002, p. 75). This is not done for stylistic reasons, but as a 'health exercise' (p. 75), and it is by such means that he seems to avoid a confrontation with his basic feeling of being 'the one who is not' (Jones, 2005; Nebreda, 2000, p. 177).

The first strategy Nebreda uses in dealing with his difficult position in life is adhering to strict self-imposed rules, like sticking to silence and isolation, eating only eight or nine pieces of vegetarian food, never taking drugs, not looking into mirrors, refusal to wear glasses despite his poor eyesight and absolute refusal to take up anything from art history or culture. These guiding principles seem to create a Symbolic framework by means of which Nebreda organizes the unstructured way in which corporeality comes to the fore. By mutilating his flesh in a variety of ways, the physical experience of the Real is regulated, which creates a bearable sense of life: 'the absence of norms can be compensated by taking refuge in rituals, and this contributes to creating a certain sense of order' (Nebreda, 2000, p. 183). This self-mutilation constitutes an 'eye-catching' strategy that Nebreda makes use of to give shape to his life. Rather than being problematic, Nebreda (2000, p. 132) describes these as 'acts of life' that take out the 'beast', the 'Bad' or the 'absolutely negative' from his body (Guillo, 2002, p. 72). Through self-injury he extracts the otherwise intolerable dimension of his self-experience.

The self-portraits Nebreda makes pick up on these self-injuries, which are not staged for artistic reasons. The photos show snapshots of lesions and bruises imposed upon his disciplined body. Nebreda (2000) qualifies these portraits as 'photographic doubles', and says that they compensate 'the renunciation of the first person' (Guillo, 2002, p. 75): 'one gives

them a status of surrogate identity, in the sense of attributes that contribute to a better definition of the kernel' (p. 73). Given the fact that
Nebreda no longer looks into the mirror, these pictures are his only
source of self-image: 'When I say that I haven't looked in a mirror any-
more, I affirm at the same time that the only references I have from my
image are these that my photographic double gives me' (Curnier and
Surya, 2001, p. 13).

Conceptually speaking, we suggest that Nebreda's dramatic self-
portraits knot the registers R, S and I, and that, by doing so, an object *a*
is extracted. The pictures Imaginarily depict how Symbolic rituals discipline Real corporeality, and by doing so an unbearable element is
drained from the artist's self-experience. Crucial to the photographic
doubles is that they externalize the dimension of the unbearable, and
place the agonizing element Nebreda suffers from in a space between
the artist and an audience. Nebreda's photography creates a distance
between him as a subject and the pain he lives through. By transferring
the unbearable corporeality of being to the medium of photography,
his private experience starts functioning as an uncanny *visual* element.
It installs a lack in relation to that which he intimately experiences as
intolerable. The photographic doubles incarnate a gaze *outside* of the
body, and they free Nebreda from an element that was previously only
known as internal agony. In the social bond the element Nebreda pho-
tographically extracts has a fascinating effect. Any aesthetic admiration
of the human body will encounter his pictures, and early twenty-first-
century discourse on art and photography cannot but be challenged by
what this artist produces.

Conclusion

With his switch to knot theory Lacan opened up a field for reflection on
subjectivity that does not adhere to a presumed indispensable reproduction of established discourse. Contrary to his theories from the
1950s and 1960s, his work from the 1970s does not take the Freudian
Oedipal account for granted. Henceforth, a shared Name-of-the-Father
is no longer seen as the foundation of the subject. What counts is
the singular way of knotting the registers R, S and I. As we hope to
have demonstrated with our review of Lacan's interpretation of Joyce,
and with our discussion of Nebreda, a sinthome can henceforth be
seen as the element in the relation between R, S and I that provides
a platform for the articulation of the subject, and for the extraction of
an object *a*.

An important implication of Lacan's use of knot theory in his conception of the subject is that it calls into question the categorical division made in Western psychiatry between sanity and insanity, or between normality and the disorder. Such a categorical attitude encourages us to think in terms of deviance from a so-called norm, and turns our attention away from the singular. From a Lacanian point of view, it is not the case that belief in the father function would be more 'sane' than not making use of established discourse in the articulation of the subject (Miller, 1993). On the contrary, what Lacan's discussion of Joyce indicates is that people, and the problems they present, should not be considered in terms of what is socially normal. Instead one should focus on the characteristics that make their functioning and their suffering unique.

Note

1. 'Les trois cercles du noeud borroméen sont, à titres de cercles, tous trois équivalents.'

References

Badiou, A. (2009). *Pocket Pantheon*. London and New York: Verso.

Borch-Jacobsen, M. (1991). *Lacan: The Absolute Master*. Stanford University Press.

Curnier, J.-P. and Surya, M. (2001). *Sur David Nebreda*. Paris: Éditions Léo Scheer.

Freud, S. (1900). *The Interpretation of Dreams*, SE, vols 4–5.

Guillo, A. (2002). 'J'espère que mon travail sera toujours innocent.' Entretien avec David Nebreda. *La Voix du regard*, 15, 72–7.

Jones, D. H. (2005). The body eclectic: Viewing bodily modifications in David Nebreda. *Reconstruction: Studies in Contemporary Culture*, 5(1): http://reconstruction.eserver.org/051/contents.shtml, accessed 7 November 2010.

Joyce, J. (1965). *A Portrait of the Artist as A Young Man*. Harmondsworth: Penguin Books.

Lacan, J. ([1957a] 2006). Seminar on the purloined letter. In *Ecrits: The First Complete Edition in English*, trans. B. Fink. New York: W. W. Norton, pp. 11–48.

Lacan, J. ([1957b] 2006). The instance of the letter in the unconscious or reason since Freud. In *Ecrits: The First Complete Edition in English*, trans. B. Fink. New York: W. W. Norton, pp. 412–42.

Lacan, J. ([1957–58] 1998). *Le Séminaire, Livre V, Les Formations de l'inconscient*. Paris: Seuil.

Lacan, J. ([1959] 2006). On a question prior to any possible treatment of psychosis. In *Ecrits: The First Complete Edition in English*, trans. B. Fink. New York: W. W. Norton, pp. 445–88.

Lacan, J. ([1960] 2006). The subversion of the subject and the dialectic of desire in the Freudian unconscious. In *Ecrits: The First Complete Edition in English*, trans. B. Fink. New York: W. W. Norton, pp. 671–702.

Lacan, J. ([1962–63] 2004). *Le Séminaire, Livre X, L'Angoisse.* Paris: Seuil.

Lacan, J. ([1963] 2005). Introduction au Noms-du-Père. In *Des Noms-du-Père.* Paris: Seuil, pp. 67–104.

Lacan, J. ([1964] 2004). *The Seminar, Book XI, The Four Fundamental Concepts of Psychoanalysis.* London: Karnac.

Lacan, J. ([1975–76] 2005). *Le Séminaire, Livre XXIII, Le Sinthome.* Paris: Seuil.

Miller, J.-A. (1993). Clinique ironique. *La Cause Freudienne,* 23, 7–13.

Miller, J.-A. (2004). L'Invention psychotique. *Quarto,* 80/81, 6–13.

Miller, J.-A. (2007). La Passe bis. *La Cause Freudienne,* 66, 209–13.

Millet, C. (2000). David Nebreda et le double photographique. Entretien avec Catherine Millet. *Art Press,* 255, 49–55.

Nebreda, D. (2000). *Autoportraits.* Paris: Éditions Léo Scheer.

Nebreda, D. (2004). *Chapitre sur les petites amputations.* Paris: Éditions Léo Scheer.

Nebreda, D. (2006). *Sur la révélation.* Paris: Éditions Léo Scheer.

Parker, I. (2003). Jacques Lacan, barred psychologist. *Theory and Psychology,* 13, 95–115.

Roustang, F. (1990). *The Lacanian Delusion.* Oxford University Press.

Saussure, F. de (1916). *Course in General Linguistics.* New York: Philosophical Library.

Sokal, A. and Bricmont, J. (1998). *Fashionable Nonsense.* New York: Picador.

Vanheule, S. (2011). *The Subject of Psychosis: A Lacanian Perspective.* London: Palgrave Macmillan.

Vanheule, S. and Verhaeghe, P. (2009). Identity through a psychoanalytic looking glass. *Theory and Psychology,* 19, 319–411.

Verhaeghe, P. (2004). *On Being Normal and Other Disorders.* New York: Other Press.

6
Beyond Identification: The (Im)possibility of Loving thy Neighbour

Calum Neill

In the fifth chapter of *Civilization and its Discontents* Freud broaches the directive that 'Thou shalt love thy neighbour as thyself' (King James Bible: Leviticus 19:18 and Matthew 19:19) and responds to this with what we might, following Lacan, characterize as 'horror' (Lacan, 1992, p. 186). For Freud, love of one's neighbour is something which would impose as an excess, an affront to the love that one would give to those closest, one's partner, one's friend, one's community. Where the sexual relationship can be understood as being the paramount case of relating to another, for Freud, the love given therein cannot be extended beyond the pair involved to encompass a wider world of people:

> sexual love is a relationship between two people, in which a third party can only be superfluous or troublesome, whereas civilization rests on relations between quite large numbers of people. When a love relationship is at its height, the lovers no longer have any interest in the world around them; they are self-sufficient as a pair, and in order to be happy they do not even need the child they have in common. In no other case does Eros so clearly reveal what is at the core of his being, the aim of making one out of more than one; however, having achieved this proverbial goal by making two people fall in love, he refuses to go further. (Freud, 2002, p. 45)

Consequently, for Freud, the pre-eminent question which arises in the face of this injunction to love one's neighbour as one's self is 'how shall we manage to act like this? How will it be possible?' (p. 46). Freud's initial refusal of the directive is centred around the fact that it appears to advocate a non-preferentiality which would, for him, deny the very possibility of love that it sets out to promote. Love for one's neighbour, which would be love without preference, is wrong, 'for my love is prized by my family and friends as a sign of my preference for them; to put a stranger on a par with them would be to do them an injustice' (p. 47). It is, for Freud, the very distinguishing qualities of the object of love, most notably those qualities in which the lover can find a point of identification, which confers on love the value which would be proper to it:

> If I love another person, he must in some way deserve it...He deserves it if, in certain important respects, he so resembles me that in him I can love myself. He deserves it if he is so much more perfect than myself that I can love in him an ideal image of myself. I must love him if he is my friend's son, for the pain my friend would feel if any harm befell him would be my pain too; I should have to share it. But if he is a stranger to me and cannot attract me by any merit of his own or by any importance he has acquired in my emotional life, it becomes hard for me to love him. (p. 46)

This chapter will seek to explore the contestation here, initially through consideration of three different perspectives on the biblical directive, with a view to considering the place of identification in the approach to the other. We will then extend this question of identification by exploring Husserl's influential and apparently intuitive argument that we relate to the other on the basis of analogy. As a corrective to this position, the chapter will draw on Lacan to emphasize the crucial dimension of that which irrecuperably escapes identification. It is in this beyond of identification that a space for an ethical approach is opened up, a space which can be reduced neither to a prescription nor an absorption, a space where the other is properly other.

Loving one's neighbour

Freud's horror in the face of the great commandment to love thy neighbour as thyself can be understood as a fairly straightforward insistence on the reality principle. Such a directive is not, he suggests, realistic. It is not possible. Žižek, not usually one to be tied to notions of possibility, extends Freud's opposition in his 'Afterword' to *Revolution at the Gates* (2002), where he critiques Kierkegaard in a manner which allows us to see him as falling on the same side of this argument as Freud, in favour of preferential love. In *Works of Love*, Kierkegaard argues that the love attested to in the directive to love one's neighbour is the highest form of love precisely because it does not distinguish on the basis of preference. For Kierkegaard, the love one might have towards one's partner, the beloved, or one's friend is but a form of self love:

> self-love and passionate preferential love are essentially the same, but love for the neighbour – that is love ... For this reason the beloved and the friend are called, remarkably and profoundly, to be sure, the *other self* and the *other I*. (Kierkegaard, 1995, p. 53)

In opposition to exclusively preferential love, Kierkegaard advocates love of one's neighbour as non-preferential, as a love which renounces distinctions. Such love is the perfection of love precisely insofar as it is not dependent on any extraneous perfection in the object. Love predicated on an object perceived to be perfect cannot, for Kierkegaard, be perfect love because it is by definition limited to and by the object which would condition it. He compares such limited love to the health of a person which only subsists in one particular and favourable location. Clearly, Kierkegaard argues, we would not consider this person's health to be particularly excellent. We may consider the conditions or arrangements excellent, insofar as these conditions and arrangements are what allow the person's health to subsist. But the person's health itself we would no doubt find frail in that it is utterly dependent upon these limited conditions. So it would be for love reserved only for persons who would display the kinds of excellences that Freud advocates as the proper aim for love. Such love is limited and, thus, while perfection may well reside in its object, the love itself is by definition poor, imperfect:

> Thus, the perfection of the object is not the perfection of the love. Because the neighbour has none of the perfections that the beloved, the friend, the admired one, the cultured person, the rare, the extraordinary person have to such a high degree, for that very reason love for the neighbour has all the perfections that the love for the beloved, the friend, the cultured person, the admired one, the rare, the extraordinary person does not have. (p. 66)

Love for one's neighbour, in Kierkegaard's understanding, is perfect love precisely because it does not distinguish. It is perfect as love in that it is not dependent on the qualities of the object on which it befalls. Indeed, as perfect, it falls on every object equally.

Concerning himself with the object here, Žižek contends that, following Kierkegaard's argument, the only good neighbour is a dead neighbour. Death might be understood as that which would remove all distinctions and thus, in death, the neighbour can be fully loved, can attain to that perfected love which renounces distinctions. Žižek, accurately, perceives in Kierkegaard a desire to delimit a non-pathological love, in the Kantian sense of non-pathological, where there would be no subjective incentive or attachment in the act of love, where love is 'motivated not by its determinate object, but by the mere *form* of love – love for the sake of love itself, not for the sake of what distinguishes its object' (Žižek, 2002, p. 213). In order to do so, Kierkegaard is not advocating that the only good neighbour is a dead neighbour. To do so would be to treat death as the distinction *par excellence* and thus to miss the very point at which he aims; a love which is not predicated on any distinction at all. This would properly be, as Žižek claims, the love of the poet who can valorize the object of his love in death, not because this erases distinctions, but precisely because death here distinguishes the beloved above all else. What Žižek sees Kierkegaard as advocating is that we treat the neighbour, that is, each individual, equally, as 'already dead, erasing his or her distinctive qualities' (p. 214). This, Žižek maintains, indicates the failure of Kierkegaard's argument, this is 'where Kierkegaard cheats' (p. 214). This non-pathological love, for Žižek, would precisely miss what is difficult in love, the work of love which would describe it as authentic. Kierkegaard's love for the neighbour, devoid of any particularity, is, for Žižek, an 'easy feast' (p. 214). Against this, and we can perhaps understand this as a support for Freud's rejection of the directive to love one's neighbour, Žižek suggests that we 'love the other *because of his or her very imperfection*' (p. 214). What Žižek clearly has in mind here is that some*thing* in the other which would render them different.

Contra both Freud and Kierkegaard, Žižek isolates the imperfection as that which would render the other as worthy of love, the difficult work of love. Kierkegaard and Freud appear to be very much in agreement on the fact that that which commonly renders someone worthy of love is their identification with the lover. For Freud someone deserves love when he 'so resembles me that in him I can love myself' (Freud, 2002, p. 46). Similarly, for Kierkegaard, 'passionate preferential love is another form of self-love' (Kierkegaard, 1995, p. 53). We can clearly understand this identification in self-love which Freud defends and Kierkegaard criticizes as the imaginary objectification of the other. One loves the other here, as Kierkegaard and Freud both point out, inasmuch as the other resembles oneself. Or, to be more precise, one loves the other inasmuch as one perceives the other as resembling what one perceives in one's self. It is useful to recall Lacan's theory of the Mirror Stage here as a clarification of the loop this process of recognition entails. In 'The Mirror Stage as Formative of the Function of the I' (Lacan, 2006) Lacan argues that an infant, not yet a subject, yet to cohere an image of itself, an identity, only begins to form such on the basis of an encounter with that which is outside or beyond itself. Held before a mirror, the child does not recognize the image which appears before it as an already evident reflection of itself. The mirror stage rather describes the formation of an anticipation which marks the difference between the child's experience of itself and the image it has before it. The lack of motor-control, the incohesiveness, the otherness with which the child experiences itself is contrasted with the seeming coherence of the image in the mirror. This is then to say that the child's idea(l) of itself is fashioned on the basis of a desire to resemble, or become, that which is external, that which is other. Moreover, it illustrates the necessary alienation at the core of self identity. In Rimbaud's terms, 'je est un autre' (Rimbaud, 1963, p. 268). Lacan terms this process *méconnaissance*, misrecognition, to emphasize the force of the imaginary in the identifications made. It is not only that the subject misrecognizes itself in the other, but it misrecognizes the other and forges its fragile image of itself on the basis of such a misrecognition of the other, setting in play a life of interminable misrecognitions:

> it is from this fellow as such that the misrecognitions which define me as a self are born. (Lacan, 1992, p. 198)

Against such identification on the basis of misrecognition, Žižek would appear to advocate a love which, difficult as this may be, is predicated on difference, a love which would celebrate that in the other which could not be reduced to or recuperated to an identification. This resistant some*thing*, he argues, is *objet petit a*:

> Lacan's name for this 'imperfection', for the obstacle which makes me love someone, is *objet petit a*, the 'pathological' tic which makes him or her unique. (Žižek, 2002, pp. 214–15)

Where Žižek's argument falters is that what he identifies as that which would constitute the other as the proper object of love is precisely the fantasy object which would shield the 'annoying excess' (p. 214) which would render the other imperfect and deserving of authentic love. Žižek confuses the object of fantasy with that which it would serve to conceal.

In the course of his reading of Freud's *A Project for a Scientific Psychology*, Lacan makes the argument that the encounter with the other can be separated into two aspects, 'one of which affirms itself through an unchanging apparatus, which remains together as a thing, *als Ding*' (Lacan, 1992, p. 51) 'while the other can be *understood* by the activity of memory – that is, can be traced back to information from [the subject's] own body' (Freud, 1966, p. 331). That is to say, in the encounter with the other there is necessarily a process of identification and there is necessarily some *Thing* which cannot be reduced to this process of identification. Without the process of identification, the other would not be recognized as another person. Without the remainder, that which would resist identification, the other would not constitute an*other*. In the terms of Lacan's reading here, we can understand that what in Freud we might term 'deserving love' and what in Kierkegaard we might term 'love of the self in the other' are both commensurate with that in the other which can be 'understood by the activity of the memory – that is, [that which] can be traced back to information from [the subject's] own body' (p. 331). That is, it is love based on (mis)identification with the other, identification of the other as the counterpart of one's ego. Against this, however, *objet petit a* is not the 'unchanging apparatus' (Lacan, 1992, p. 51) but rather that which would simultaneously be indicative of and protective against the 'unchanging apparatus' (p. 51). To fixate on the object of fantasy and, moreover, to impute this object to the other, to make of this object a distinctive *part* of the other, is precisely to refuse to acknowledge one's own part in the constitution of this object in the relation of fantasy.

It is that in the other which refuses identification which, paradoxically, for Lacan, is necessarily already the *same*, that which would lie beyond the positive distinctions the subject would draw between itself and the other. It is not the same, however, in the sense of a recuperation to the self, but rather because it is that which is in the subject more than the subject itself, that which is extimate to the subject. It is that which both insists upon the subject and cannot be reined within the subject. It is precisely that which would lie beyond all distinctions.

In this sense, we can see, contra Žižek, that, despite its apparent morbidity, Kierkegaard's claim is perfectly valid. Where Kierkegaard might be understood to falter himself is in the idea that such removal of all distinctions might be possible. Though, to be fair, it is not clear that Kierkegaard is actually making this claim at all. The love for the neighbour which would be a love oblivious to all earthly distinctions is, in his own words, not something which should 'abolish dissimilarity, neither dissimilarity of distinction nor of lowliness' (Kierkegaard, 1995, p. 88). Rather, he advocates that dissimilarity should be seen, in loving the neighbour, as hanging 'loosely on the individual, as loosely as the cape the king casts off in order to show who he is' (p. 88):

> In other words, when the dissimilarity hangs loosely in this way, then in each individual there continually glimmers that essential other, which is common to all, the eternal resemblance, the likeness. (p. 88)

Kierkegaard seems not to be so much advocating a renunciation of the recognition of positive differences, those aspects of the other which would set that other apart in their unicity, their particularity, as he is indicating that such differences are necessarily an imputation of the subject who would perceive them. Kierkegaard's point is to admonish those who would seek to validate self-love on the illusory ground that it is love of the other in all their individuality. In indicating that dissimilarity may be made to 'hang loosely' on the individual, Kierkegaard is indicating precisely that this is no easy feast. Relations with the other are such that they are bound in a logic of identification. The danger lies in allowing such identification, such love (or hate) of the '*other I*, the *other self*' (p. 53) to be mistaken as true recognition of the other's 'particular characteristic' (Žižek, 2002, p. 214). To refer to one of Žižek's preferred examples, the mole on Cindy Crawford's lip is not her *objet petit a*, it is precisely Žižek's *objet petit a*, that which Žižek perceives in her which renders her unique and desirable for him, that which allows her to be escalated to the status of an object of fantasy *for him*. For Kierkegaard, we should struggle to allow, to remain with this example, Cindy Crawford's mole, to 'hang loosely', that is precisely to acknowledge the objectifying perspective in which we might place 'her', to accept that the other necessarily exceeds the image, and thus the relation with the image, we would have constructed of them.

This is to suggest that the relation with the other entails a certain impossibility, an aporia wherein the other can neither be reduced to a point of identification nor experienced exclusively in their otherness. Any relation with the other is such that it would necessarily entail a process of identification, but an identification which is necessarily a recuperation to the *méconnaissance* of the subject in the form of the ego, an identification, that is, which is necessarily a misidentification which cannot but point to its own limitations. In so pointing to the limitations of identification, both in the sense that such identification is limited to recuperation and in the sense that such identification is necessarily *not all*, any relation with the other necessarily entails a beyond of identification but a *beyond* which must be understood as entailing a *with*. It is beyond identification and recuperation that we would experience the otherness of the other but such a beyond cannot be experienced in itself, that is, it can only insist at the limits of the symbolic and imaginary frameworks and, thus, only figure in subjective experience as the limitations of the symbolic and imaginary frameworks.

Imaginary identification

The logic of the conjunction of the same and other, the impossibility of either reduction to the same or the reduction to exclusive separation of otherness, can be adduced in Husserl's phenomenological investigation of the experience of the other in his *Cartesian Meditations*:

> *How* can my ego, within his peculiar ownness, constitute under the name, 'experience of something other,' precisely something *other* – something, that is, with a sense that excludes the constituted from the concrete make-up of the sense-constituting I-myself, as somehow the latter's analogue? (Husserl, 1991, p. 94)

If the experience of the other is precisely something differentiated from the subject's own experience of his or her self, then what is there that would substantiate such an experience while still marking it as distinct from the experience of an object? On the one hand, if it were possible to experience subjectively the very subjectivity of the other, then there would be nothing to differentiate such an experience from one's own experience of one's self. On the other hand, if the other is merely experienced as *being there*, as another object in the world, then on what basis would one be justified in assuming its attributes to extend beyond this physical appearance?

> if what belongs to the other's own essence were directly accessible, it would be merely a moment of my own essence, and ultimately he himself and I myself would be the same. (p. 109)

In response to these dilemmas, Husserl argues for a deduction of the other on the basis of an analogy with the subject. The subject, for Husserl, experiences itself 'as *uniquely* singled out' (p. 97):

> there is included in my ownness, as purified from every sense pertaining to other subjectivity, *a sense, 'mere nature'*, that has lost precisely that 'by everyone' and therefore must not by any means be taken for an abstract stratum of the world or of the world's sense. Among these bodies belonging to this 'Nature' and included in my peculiar ownness, I then find my *animate organism* as *uniquely* singled out – namely as the only one of them that is not just a body but precisely an animate organism: the sole Object within my abstract world-stratum to which, in accordance with experience, I ascribe *fields of sensation…*, the only Object 'in' which I '*rule and govern*' *immediately*, governing particularly in each of its 'organs'. (pp. 96–7)

That is, the subject perceives its own 'psychophysical self' as the only *noema* which is not merely the perception of a physical body but is conceived as that which is 'reflexively related to itself' (p. 97). In order to conceive of the other as similarly capable or productive of such self-experience, such governing, the subject must conceive of the other analogically as the same but different. The essence of the other cannot be directly experienced without this effectively amounting to a recuperation to the self of the subject. It can, however, according to Husserl's argument, be deduced as existent through the logic of recognition and analogy.

The analogy here would be one drawn by the subject on the basis of its recognition in the imaginary of a similarity between the appearance of the other and the image it, the subject, has of itself. This would be what in Lacan's terms we might call 'ego identification'. It is, however, not, in Lacan's understanding, so easily reducible to an identification by analogy of the other with the self. As we have seen in the above brief comments on the mirror stage, the subject can be understood to have constituted its own image of it*self*, what Lacan will term the ideal ego, on the basis of a misrecognition of the other. Any identification with the other on the basis of an analogy with the self is thus necessarily an identification of the other with the ideal ego, rendering the other analogous, not with the subject as such but with the subject's misrecognition of itself which was necessarily already constituted in misrecognition of the other as something other than the subject.

That is to say, the (mis)recognition of other on the basis of imaginary identification, precisely because it is misrecognized on the basis of imaginary identification, cannot account for the other in all its alterity. As imaginary identification would be, by definition, partial, that is, as it is only identification with the ideal ego, the other so comprehended or so constituted on the basis of such identification is necessarily not all. Something of the otherness in the other still persists as unknown. The very possibility of encountering the unknown in the other arises from this possibility of a point of perceived resemblance. Without such, there would be no suggestion of encountering the other as anything other than an object. It is insofar as the other is encountered as analogous to the subject that it is encountered as other than or more than an object. Insofar as the other is encountered as a speaking being or potentially speaking being, the otherness perceived in it insists on the subject.

Significant in Husserl's discussion of the possibility of intersubjectivity is his emphasis on the point of perception. True to the phenomenological method, Husserl's assertion of a distinction between himself and the other noemata is based on his own role of perceiver. As he perceives or intends the objects of his consciousness, he, as perceiver, is already there, already engaged in the conscious act. Such apperception of course speaks only of consciousness. The noema of the physicality of the self is concluded through the consciousness of his own body being governed by himself. Through the perception of his touching an object and the contrastive perception of his touching a part of himself, Husserl concludes his relation to the body doing the touching and the thing touched is not the same. The analogous deduction of the other as another self must then also follow from the logical priority of the perceiver. The other as other is necessarily logically subordinated to the self insofar as the self is construed as the perceiver.

Where the Lacanian formulation complicates such a picture is in the theorizing of the subjective basis upon which any such analogous deduction might be said to take place. Any identification configured as an identification on analogy is dependent on the starting point with which the analogy is made. *Other* is necessarily thought as *other than*. *Same* is necessarily thought as *same as*. Either renders itself logically dependent upon that which would be located at the point of comparison. Whether *A* is other than *B* or *A* is the same as *B*, in both cases the identity in question is determined by *B*. The task in such a formulation would be that of initially identifying *B* in order to, subsequently, determine the otherness or sameness of *A*. What Lacan allows us to do is to understand that such a starting point is only ever a pure assumption.

Insofar as the encounter with the neighbour brings with it that which can be recuperated to the understanding, the familiar, and that which remains alien, *das Ding*, we can understand that in such a formulation, to remain with our simplified terms, A^1 is the same as B and A^2 is other than B insofar as A^1 is that which is taken to be recuperable to an identification with that of B which was constructed on the basis of a misrecognition of or misidentification with a prior term and A^2 is taken to be irrecuperable to such an identification. By recognizing this bifurcation or separation in B, that there is a B^1 and a B^2, where B^1 would represent that which had been constructed on the basis of misrecognition and B^2 would represent that which refused any reduction to such an identification on the basis of misrecognition, that which would be excluded from any such identification, we can understand that A^1 is (taken to be) the same as B^1 and A^2 is (taken to be) the same as B^2 with the proviso that it is only as A^2 and B^2 are only identified by their non-identity, by the impossibility of construing them as such, that A^2 and B^2 can be understood to be the same. So far, within such an abstraction, the terms of each pair, $A^1 = B^1$ and $A^2 = B^2$ would appear to be quite reversible. What renders the pairings irreversible is the fact of perception, or the starting point. A^2 and B^2 cannot strictly speaking be construed as reversible insofar as they are, effectively, the same thing. There are not two points here to reverse. From the point of view located in the symbolic order there is that which cannot be known, that which would resist all representation. The insistence of this unrepresentable excess, *das Ding*, is what would be indicated in A^2 and B^2, the insistence of a beyond of the symbolic and the imaginary both in or with the subject and in or with the other. As such, the two terms are not so much reversible as never reducible to two terms as such in the first instance. It is only from the question of perspective that the separation of the points into two might arise, a separation which would be properly understood as a misconstrual. The very question, 'His or mine?' (Lacan, 1992, p. 198), asked of the indeterminate 'interior or emptiness' (p. 198) is, properly, inappropriate insofar as there is nothing which 'indicates they are distinct' (p. 198). The otherness, the alien in the other as neighbour, is irreducible to a reversible relation not because of a fixed priority of one term over the other but rather because of a radical impossibility of distinguishing two points at all. That which is not known is not known.

It is thus only in the case of A^1 and B^1 that a reversibility might be considered possible. Here, however, reversibility is only conceivable on the basis of the hypothesis of a third, external vantage point, one which would consider both elements from an equal distance. It is in the very impossibility of such an external vantage point that the irreversibility of the elements in question imposes itself. The only possible vantage point is one of the elements itself. Consequently, regardless of the formal identity of the two components, a formal identity which is at best illusory, constituted as it is on the basis of a double misrecognition, there imposes a contextual dissymmetry insofar as one point is necessarily the point of perspective, a requisite condition which necessarily repudiates the hypothesis of reversibility. Where A^1 stands for the other, the neighbour, and B^1 stands for the ideal ego, the subject's misrecognized self image, we can understand that, beyond the insistence of *das Ding*, both A^2 and B^2, where these terms are understood to be not so much formulated on the basis of an identity as to be misconstrued as two separable terms, there is another factor which renders the pair irreversible: that of the point of perception.

This is not, however, to suggest that the point of perception is in any way a pure given, that there is something which would independently insist apart from misrecognition or *das Ding* which would radically differentiate the other (*a*) from the subject's ideal-ego (*i(a)*). The point of perception is rather that point which must be assumed.

In reading Freud's famous dictum, *Wo Es war, soll Ich werden*, which Strachey translates as 'Where id was, there ego shall be' (Freud, 1973, p. 112), Lacan argues that where Freud habitually attached an article to *Es*, the id, here he does not. Lacan maintains that this lack of an article indicates that *Es* here does not refer to the id at all but rather to the unconscious subject. This allows Lacan to reconsider the significance of the phrase which he now reads as an ethical injunction, the very core of ethics; ' "Where (it) was itself" ... "it is my duty that I come into being" ' (Lacan, 2006, pp. 347–8). We should understand the I which will be assumed here as the point of perception in our model, which is to underscore the fact here that we are not discussing a natural or immanent status but rather a fragile position which entails the burden of responsibility.

What differentiates *a* from *i(a)* is the fact that *i(a)* is constituted as the image of what *I* would be, the ideal image one would have of oneself, and *a*, as the other, is constituted as what would be other than *me* for *me*. Both points are constituted as *for* but inadequate to the subject, but, in being so constituted, both points are located or imagined separately for the subject.

What this allows us to understand is that in any attempted or projected identification between the subject and the other, there is

(1) imaginary identification on the basis of misrecognition, $i(a) \to a$; (2) *das Ding*, as that which insists but refuses recuperation to identification and thus refuses any allocation to either the subject or the other; and (3) a necessary point from which the other is perceived as identifiable. What ought to be clear here is that the point of perception cannot be reduced to $i(a)$, that on the basis of which (mis)identification with the other is construed. It is rather because of the inherent proximity of $i(a)$ to that which would perceive it, that $i(a)$ is constituted as an (illusory) image of the self, that the process is deemed irreversible.

Symbolic identification

It is important here to acknowledge that this imaginary identification must also part-take of symbolic mediation. That is to say, beyond or in addition to identification in the imaginary order, the subject, in order to be constituted as a subject, must enter the realm of the symbolic. This *'secondary identification'* (Lacan, 2006, p. 95) can be understood to emerge in the process of the Oedipus complex with the intervention of the father, in the process of castration which would be synony-mous with the subject's emergence in the field of the symbolic. The initial stage of the Oedipus complex (though, this, for Lacan, should be understood as a logical rather than a chronological sequence) can be understood to be commensurate with the imaginary identification we have been discussing. In encountering the mother as lacking, the child seeks to situate itself as the object of her desire. Since the child is incapable of accomplishing this, is incapable, that is, of completely sat-isfying the mother, it encounters itself as also lacking. The 'second stage' of the Oedipus complex would be characterized by the intervention of the imaginary father, that is, the perception of desire as prohibited. It is in the 'third stage' that the Real father is understood to intervene and display that he has the 'phallus', that which would satisfy desire. Crucial here is the point that the various fathers are functions for the infant and none is essentially bound to or dependent on the biological father. The Real father would be defined precisely in terms of that which is under-stood to possess the phallus, 'the signifier of the desire of the Other' (Lacan, 2006, p. 583), that which would satisfy the mother's desire. The intervention of the Real father can be understood as allowing the child access to the symbolic through the process of renunciation of the always failed attempt to situate itself as the cause of the mother's desire. This can be understood as the inauguration of law and, thus, the Real father can be understood in terms commensurate with the mythical father of

Freud's primal horde; he who would satisfy the women of the group, he who would be without lack. Through identification with the Real father, the subject can be understood to have adopted and internalized the prohibitionary strictures understood to have been imposed by the father. This is the moment of incorporation to which Lacan points in his reading of the myth of the primal horde:

> Freud shows us that the need for a form of participation, which neutralizes the conflict inscribed after killing him in the situation of rivalry among the brothers, is the basis for identification with the paternal Totem. Oedipal identification is thus the identification by which the subject transcends the aggressiveness constitutive of the first subjective individuation ... it constitutes a step in the establishment of the distance by which, with feelings akin to respect, a whole affective assumption of one's fellow man [neighbour] is brought about. (Lacan, 2006, pp. 95–6)

This 'secondary', symbolic, identification can be understood to be constitutive of the ego ideal $(I(A))$, that on the basis of which one would internalize the law and the symbolic order. In identifying with the father, in incorporating the father as prohibitory force, the subject locates itself in terms of the phallus, the signifier of desire which would be understood to be inaugural of the signifying chain. The position so assumed is one of symbolic identification. The phallus, as the signifier of desire, would be that in relation to which the subject would symbolically constitute itself:

> It is in so far as the function of man and woman is symbolized, it is insofar as it's literally uprooted from the domain of the imaginary and situated in the domain of the symbolic, that any normal, completed sexual position is realized. (Lacan, 1993, p. 177)

It is the different positions adopted in relation to the phallus which would determine the symbolic and sexual identity of the subject. This can be seen most clearly in the formulae Lacan adopts in his schema of sexuation in his twentieth seminar. Where the subject who would be structured as male would be understood to be wholly determined by the signifier, the subject who would be structured as female is not. Where the phallus is understood as the signifier of desire and thus, inseparable from this, the signifier which would be understood to introduce lack, it can be understood to be constitutive of the subject. Where the male-obsessional subject would be such that $\forall X \Phi X$, that is, the whole of x is such that it is subject to the phallic function, the hysteric-female subject would be such that $\overline{\forall X} \Phi X$, that is, not all of x is such that it is subject to the phallic function. This is not to suggest that hysteric-female subjects would be such that they would be excluded from the symbolic order; $\overline{\exists X}\,\overline{\Phi X}$, that is, there is not one instance of x which is not (in part) subject to the phallic function (Lacan, 1998).

It is thus only through symbolic identification that the subject can come to 'be' in the symbolic order and the precise manner in which this identification is undertaken or experienced is determinative of the particular (sexed) position the subject will take up. It is only from such a position that the misrecognition on the basis of the *same* and *other* can be understood. That is to say, without symbolic structuration there is, properly, no position from which to perceive the (mis)identification in question. The subject as symbolically constituted, as barred, $, is the position of perception which would be assumed, not an already constituted or existent position in front of which such processes of identification would unfold. As we have seen, though, *das Ding*, as that which is beyond both imaginary and symbolic recuperation, would be that which would persist beyond both imaginary and symbolic identification.

The impossibility of identification

Where the Husserlian conception of adduction of the other through the process of empathy is such that there is the suggestion of the other as a mere reduplication of the ego, in a Lacanian conception what stops such a reduplication is the persistence of that which cannot be recuperated to such an identification, that which was never reducible to the ego and, where the *and* here does not necessitate any suggestion of consequence, is not reducible to any alter-ego. That the irreducibility of *das Ding* in either instance is not predicated on a logic of consequence is attested to by the fact of the impossibility of any firm exterior starting point. If, as is suggested in Husserl's formulation, the alter-ego were construed or apperceived on the basis of an originary ego, then it might be possible to claim that that which insists as an excess in impossible relation to the ego is subsequently or consequently read into the apperception of the alter-ego construed on analogy with the original model. The problematic to such an understanding that Lacan allows us to grasp is the fact of there being no clear-cut original from which to work. As the mirror stage indicates, not only is the ego itself construed upon a misrecognition of some exterior model – the child's own image, the parent or even a toy – but also the whole scenario of (mis)recognition is only ever received in a retroactive movement. That is to say, there is not available any comfortable, linear progression from ego to analogous ego formulated on a basis of identification of similarity but rather a disrupted circle or reductio ad infinitum of misrecognition from $i(a)$ to a to $i(a)$ to a to $i(a)$ and so on. What would disrupt such a knit of misrecognition is not only the fact of misrecognition, that is, that each moment would entail an encounter with that for which there is no accounting, *das Ding*, but also the fact of the point of perception. In order for the process of (mis)identification to be seen to have taken place, there must be, no matter how obfuscated, a point from which the process is seen to have taken place. Both $i(a)$ and a, the ideal ego and the other, are such that they are only ever taken to be. They are imaginary effects. They are construed by the subject and, as construed by the subject, form part of the psychical make-up of the subject. Such a subject is by no means a pregiven unity but rather a position which must be assumed. The subject in coming to be can be understood as the very split between the imaginary self-present ego and the indeterminable, unfathomable otherness within itself. It is this location of the subject as not so much *in* as *as* the very disjunction of these two positions, which should be seen as the point of perspective. What this indicates is that the point of perspective is not in any predetermined sense the truth of the subject, its original or proper position. Rather, the point of perception is the position the subject would come to assume and thus from which the subject would retroactively posit the very disjunction it could not inhabit.

Clearly here such a point cannot be stable. The assumption of the *I* in *Wo Es war, soll Ich werden* is only ever pulsational. It is not a matter of an assumption once and for all, but rather an assumption to be made again and again.

When, then, one is directed to love thy neighbour as thyself, the injunction might be properly understood to entail a radical impossibility. This is the horror from which Freud recoiled. And yet, might we not find instead in this impossibility the very crack which might suggest the possibility of ethics? Where insistence and reduction to the same implies an originary certainty, it implies an expectation that the other must conform in order to earn one's love. It is all very well enjoining to love the good neighbour, the neighbour who is, after all, much like us. It is all very well professing an openness to that which one can recuperate to a closed identity. It is the truly other, the incomprehensible, the ungraspable, the abhorrent that demands the true work of love. What Lacan allows us to appreciate is the illusion inherent to the identification we tend to start with. If the very premise of our identification, of ourselves and with another, is fragile and false, then might not this suggest the possibility of a prizing open of the constricts of the same to make room for the possibility of the utterly other?

References

Freud, S. ([1895] 1966). *A Project for a Scientific Psychology*, SE, vol. 1.
Freud, S. (1973). *New Introductory Lectures*, trans. J. Strachey. London: Penguin.
Freud, S. ([1929] 2002). *Civilization and its Discontents*, trans. D. McLintock. London: Penguin.
Husserl, E. ([1950] 1991). *Cartesian Meditations: An Introduction to Phenomenology*, trans. D. Cairns. London: Kluwer Academic Publishers.
Kierkegaard, S. ([1847] 1995). *Works of Love*, trans. H. V. and E. H. Hong. Princeton University Press.
Lacan, J ([1986] 1992). *The Ethics of Psychoanalysis: The Seminar of Jacques Lacan, Book VII, 1959–1960*, trans. D. Porter. London: Routledge.
Lacan, J. ([1981] 1993). *The Psychoses: The Seminar of Jacques Lacan, Book III, 1955–1956*, trans. R. Grigg. London: Routledge.
Lacan, J. ([1975] 1998). *Encore – On Feminine Sexuality, The Limits of Love and Knowledge: The Seminar of Jacques Lacan, Book XX, 1972–1973*, trans. B. Fink. New York: W. W. Norton.
Lacan, J. (2006). *Écrits: The First Complete Edition in English*, trans. B. Fink. New York: W. W. Norton.
Rimbaud, A. ([1871] 1963). *Oeuvres complètes*, ed. A. Guyaux. Paris: Gallimard.
Žižek, S. (2002). Afterword. In S. Žižek (ed.), *Revolution at the Gates: Selected Writings of Lenin from 1917*. London: Verso.

7
Desire in the Time of AIDS

Grahame Hayes[1]

Introduction

There is no precise way of specifying what psychoanalysis is, and the answer to what it is lies in who one reads, or what one thinks one wants to do with this body of knowledge. This lack of precision seems to be a good thing as the pursuit of a stable and resolute body of knowledge of the unconscious does not sound sustainable or desirable. However, a lack of conceptual precision within, and especially between, 'schools' of psychoanalytic thought is not the same as saying that anything goes, and that we can make psychoanalysis mean whatever we want it to. And on a surprisingly large number of topics there is considerable agreement and consensus among the many theoretical approaches within psychoanalysis.

It seems what we can say about psychoanalysis is that it has to do with the unconscious, with repression (and hence conflict), with sexuality and with death (non-being). Psychoanalysis also has to do with, or in my view at least should also have to do with, a dialogue, or relationship, with the body of work that Freud inaugurated. For example, Adam Phillips, in discussion with Anthony Molino, asks the interesting question of what we think we are doing when we read Freud's work, and he suggests:

> We can use him to stop ourselves thinking. Or we can use him to have all sorts of thoughts, and in this sense, I really do believe that the Freudian thing is not remotely over. In fact, it's just beginning. I think it is just beginning to dawn on people what they might be capable of thinking, as a consequence of noticing Freud. (Phillips, in Molino, 1997, p. 144)

Thus 'noticing Freud', especially in the domain of the sexual, does not mean an unwavering commitment to all of Freud's theorizations, nor thinking that nothing has changed, in the realm of either the real or theory, since Freud's time. However, what it might mean is taking seriously the *history* of psychoanalytic thought since Freud's time, and more importantly locating ourselves within Freud's *theoretical problematic* which it seems we still have a long way to go to fully comprehend. This is precisely André Green's (2001) approach in his text, *The Chains of Eros*, where he argues for the 'coherence' of Freud's formulations regarding the significance of sexuality in symptom formation (see chapter 2 – Freud's coherence). There is also more at stake than merely asserting Freud's theoretical coherence, or even his continuing relevance, in the (psychoanalytic) theory of sexuality. For instance, Green (2001, pp. 14–15) states that there are important consequences for psychoanalytic theory with regard to the marginalization of sexuality and writes:

> [It] is an urgent matter to consider the consequences of the *desexualisation* of the theory and practice of psychoanalysis. Up to the present, this movement has not, it must be noted, found any room for any systematic and reasoned critique of the theoretical function Freud ascribes to the sexual. We have limited ourselves to retracing Freud's terrain step by step, yet without feeling any astonishment at the falling-off which has accompanied this 'forgetting'.

This 'forgetting' or 'de-sexualisation' obviously has consequences for psychoanalytic *theory*, but is potentially disastrous for the psycho-politics of *everyday life* in the time of HIV/AIDS, and especially so in southern Africa, an area devastated by high HIV infection rates and calamitous AIDS deaths.

Psychoanalysis and the social, psychoanalysis of the social

For the purposes of this chapter I would like to claim the sociality of sexuality for both politics and psychoanalysis, and suggest that Freud and psychoanalysis can help us extend some of what we know and understand about the sociality of sexuality, in this time of HIV/AIDS. As Deborah Posel (2004, p. 62) recently remarked, 'Discursively, the imagery of sex as freedom, as symbol of a virile new lease on life, *jostles* with that of sex as menace, sex as death' (emphasis added). It is on this jostling – between life and death, between demand and desire, between *jouissance* and consideration – that I think psychoanalysis might be able to say something interesting, even helpful.

So while on the surface it might seem obvious that psychoanalysis would have an important role to play in the social world of sexuality, and especially where the politics of sexuality leads so easily to sickness and death, it still seems necessary to demonstrate its social value outside the clinic, beyond the couch. Psychoanalysis' roots are in the individual case study, and as Anna Freud (1978, pp. 268–9) says, 'In its clinical applications Freud's psychoanalysis never was anything but an "individual psychology" in the best sense of this term.' But does this mean that psychoanalysis is more at home in the individual case history, and, as some would argue, should stay there? Does this mean psychoanalysis is merely the theorization of the formation of symptoms, an account of the unconscious dynamics involved in the development of psychopathology?

It is true that in their early clinical work Freud and Breuer were trying to *explain* hysterical symptom formation, while at the same time also trying to give some coherent rationale to their therapeutic interventions and practice. We need to remember that this early clinical practice was a lot more messy and hit-and-miss than the later systematization of psychoanalytic theory would sometimes have us believe. The early concepts of psychoanalysis were born and tested in the clinic, in the consulting room, which is not to say that the presentation of these early patients of psychoanalysis did not have a social basis – we just have to remind ourselves that they were mostly (youngish) women from bourgeois (and patriarchal) backgrounds to see the obviousness of the social enmeshed in the symptomatology of hysteria. The feminist appropriation of psychoanalysis has sought to ground the 'female malady' of hysteria in its historical and social context, thus contributing to a more complex account of the origins of hysteria in particular, and the neuroses in general (see for instance the classic text by Juliet Mitchell, 1976; and more recently Showalter, 1998). And although Freud is not a thinker unaware of the social articulation of human misery, and hence of psychopathology, it would be inaccurate, to say the least, to suggest a *social interest* in these originary moments of psychoanalysis. This is not to suggest an epistemological foreclosure based on the site or history of a system of thought's origins, but rather to caution the over-exuberance of the applicability of psychoanalytic concepts in social analysis. Psychoanalysis is not primarily a social theory, but it certainly can and should be *part of* social theory. One could go further and suggest that if psychoanalysis, or some other theoretical variant of human individuality, is *not* part of social theory, then social theory is at least incomplete. In other words, a work of translation needs to be done – psychoanalytic concepts need to be 'translated', made applicable to the social domain. Kelly Oliver (2004) refers to this as a project of transformation, and bemoans the fact that psychoanalytic concepts have not been transformed into *social* concepts when applied in the analyses of social phenomena. This is a slightly different point from denying the important body of work of (post) Lacanian thinkers, or the immense contribution of Slavoj Žižek, and Žižekian-influenced thinkers (see Stavrakakis, 2007; and the 'British school' of psychosocial studies, Frosh and Baraitser, 2008).

However, psychoanalysis has a specificity, and lays claim to being the knowledge of a particular object. Psychoanalysis can be defined as

> a method of investigation which consists essentially in bringing out the unconscious meaning of the words, the actions and the products of the imagination (dreams, phantasies, delusions) of a particular subject. (Laplanche and Pontalis, 1973, p. 367)

It can be added that the *content* of the unconscious for psychoanalysis is also quite specific: it has to do with sexuality and aggressivity. What is clear in this definition of psychoanalysis from Laplanche and Pontalis (1973) is that it incorporates both pathological and normal developmental processes. This would be common cause in many other accounts and definitions of psychoanalysis (see e.g. Rycroft, 1972, pp. 129–30).

Even Anna Freud, not well known for her social application of psychoanalytic ideas, locates her father's work in particular, and psychoanalysis more generally, in the terrain of human and social studies. Referring to Freud's *The Question of Lay Analysis* (1926) where he tries to open up the social applicability of psychoanalytic ideas, Anna Freud (1978, pp. 261–2) writes that the

> exclusion [in the training of psychoanalysts] of educators, clergymen, social workers, lawyers, historians, and those interested in literature and art has led to an increasing narrowing of psychoanalytic interest to pathology and a growing alienation from the humanities and social sciences to which psychoanalysis after all belongs.

And again she says that surely psychoanalysis would not 'have disturbed the sleep of the world' (Hebbel, cited by Freud) 'if it had not gone beyond working with neurotic suffering to the general problems of [hu]mankind and the development of humanity, which it clearly illuminated and discussed anew' (Freud, 1978, p. 263).

In a slightly different vein, Tauber's (2010) recent study makes a particularly strong argument for seeing Freud's work as concerned with 'philosophical issues and questions'. Tauber is not the first to note an (unresolved) ambivalence in Freud, on the one hand as the man of medicine and science, and on the other as a thinker deeply immersed in the existential dilemmas and aporias of the human condition.

If we start with psychoanalysis as a theory of sexuality, and even recognizing that clearly there are a lot of problems with Freud's theory of sexuality, it certainly cannot be accused of being placatory of the prevailing social values. Relying on Freud's daughter again, Anna Freud (1978, p. 229) notes:

> That Freud questioned his neurotic patients about the details of their sexual life offended the conventions of the bourgeois world in which he lived and worked, without sharing its hypocritical denials.

There is an inherent ambiguity in psychoanalysis' critique of sexuality, which can be harnessed for a radical rethinking of sexual morality, and sexual practices more generally. An instance of the operation of the sexual unconscious in the social domain is in the area of AIDS. The lack of information about HIV infection cannot adequately account for the range of myths surrounding AIDS. The fact of AIDS confronts us as a stark reality, *and* as unconsciously projected fears and phantasies. After all, AIDS encapsulates sex, promiscuity, drugs, morality and death. What more could we ask for psychoanalytically as far as an appropriate object of investigation is concerned?! Unless one gets to the basis of the formation of sexual morality, as psychoanalysis has the potential to do, there is little prospect of making AIDS a problem which affects all of us, in other words, a truly *social* problem, but rather of maintaining the view that AIDS is something that happens to other people, literally people who are *other* (gays, blacks, drug addicts).

In an ordinary developmental sense, psychoanalysis could be said to be a theory which accounts for the formation of identity, in terms of the dialectics of other-ing. Following Lacan (1977a), and defining the unconscious as 'the discourse of the other', psychoanalysis can begin to offer theoretical insights into the myriad of social others of modernity. This in any case is the origin of psychoanalysis in its critique of bourgeois sexual morality. That Freud studied the *effects* on (and in) the individual of social life, does not mean that psychoanalysis cannot be extended to an analysis that is less hypostatizing of individual and inner life. The separation of the personal and the social reflects theoretical and political moments, rather than the experience and lived-reality of human life. For all we might say about identity formation, the least we can say is that it is a social and moral process. Our 'socializers' (parents, usually) are hardly *neutral* about how we turn out, about what identities we adopt, and early psychoanalytic discourse even reflected the moral dimension of our socialization in the now 'out-of-date' notion of *character* development. It is a psychoanalytic commonplace to recognize that our identity/identities are formed in the interplay of psychosexual development, the social mores that accompany sexual morality, and the consequent repression attendant to any particular person's psychobiography. On this account the unconscious is inextricably social *and* personal.

The psychosocial and psychosexual dimensions of the unconscious are also a central feature of Lacanian thinking. For instance, the Lacanian insistence in training that an important question to consider is 'the analyst's *desire*' (Lacan, 1977b, p. 9), is not merely another way of talking about transference and countertransference issues in practice. Questioning the analyst's desire is simultaneously a highly personal matter, intrapersonal in fact, and also a social and moral matter. Commenting on Lacan's phrase of 'the dialectics of desire', Evans (1996, p. 39) writes: 'The most important point to emerge from Lacan's phrase is that desire is a social product. Desire is not the private affair it appears to be but it is always constituted in a dialectical relationship with the perceived desires of other subjects.'

Desire is a social product because it arises, emerges originally in the field of the Other, and we become *subjects* of the discourse of the Other. It is social in the sense of being intersubjective. Using ordinary parlance, we can ask: what's in it for us? Or what do we make of being involved in an endeavour that, to paraphrase Freud, attempts to turn neurotic misery into everyday unhappiness? It seems, to me at least, that Lacan's teaching focused on making sense of circuits of desire so as to undermine psychoanalysis becoming an unwitting *moralizing* discourse and practice. As Lacan says in the beginning of his seminar on the ethics of psychoanalysis:

> It is my belief that no one who is involved with psychoanalysis has not been drawn to treat the subject of its ethics. I am not the one who created the expression. Moreover, it is impossible not to acknowledge

that we are submerged in what are strictly speaking *moral problems*. (Lacan, 1992, p. 2, emphases added)

Psychoanalysis, sexuality and HIV/AIDS

Having made some introductory comments about what I think psychoanalysis is, and that a case can be made for including certain psychoanalytic concepts as part of our social theoretic analyses, I would now like to apply a very limited range of psychoanalytic concepts to the issue of sexuality and HIV/AIDS. I am going to do this in a highly specific way by engaging with Jonathan Berger's (2005) seminal article entitled 'Re-sexualising the Epidemic'. Berger's article appeared at a time when many people working in the field of HIV prevention were having to deal with two troubling social realities. The first being the Mbeki[2] presidency's AIDS denialism, and the second the fact that (overly) rational, information-based intervention strategies seemed to be having little effect on people's sexual practices and consequent HIV infection rates. It is worth reminding ourselves that South Africa has one of the highest HIV infection rates in the world. Also noteworthy is the disjunction between what people know about sexual practices and HIV infection, and the anticipated change in 'high-risk' sexual activities. Amongst other things, Berger's (2005) important article was a challenge to predominantly rationalist conceptions of sexuality, and in particular sexual desire, as well as a challenge to foreground sexuality in the fight against AIDS.

It seems that we can find anything to say about sex, and thinking psychoanalytically this is not surprising. Berger (2005, p. 62), referring to Berer (2003), says that 'human beings are sexual by nature', whatever that means, and 'with sex often being about nothing more than satisfying need and desire'. Need and desire – that sounds like quite a lot really, and certainly is the basis for understanding the psychosexual development of (gender) identity. Quoting Berer further, Berger (2005, p. 62) notes: 'If nothing else, one thing seems certain – people will never stop having sex or wanting to have sex'!; and then adds that 'In other words, pleasure-seeking explains much sexual behaviour.' Somewhat at the other end of the scale, Joyce McDougall (1995) notes that 'human sexuality is inherently traumatic'. I could have found other statements about sex and sexuality, and positioned them in relation to their objectives and moral registers: for example, what account of sex and sexuality is there in contemporary Freudian psychoanalytic theory?; or in relation to Lacan's notion of *jouissance*; or the white right in the USA proclaiming the evils of abortion; or the research on sexual practices for the purposes of health education; and so on. It is a banality to note that more so than any other biological, natural or bodily dimension that sex is inherently inscribed in a moral universe, and in fact according to psychoanalysis it is through the process of psychosexual identity formation that a moral consciousness (super-ego, if you will) develops.

It is no accident that I choose to contrast, or rather juxtapose, the views of Berger and McDougall as this forms the thrust of what I am doing in this chapter. I would like to think psychoanalytically about the many challenges Berger presents us with in his fascinating and provocative paper – 'Re-sexualising the Epidemic' – which just as easily could have been titled 'Sexualising the Epidemic', given the current levels of repression of sexuality in the HIV/AIDS field in the South African context. The discourses around HIV/AIDS are mostly about infection, about health, about medication, about prevention interventions, about condoms and sanitized notions of safe sex – the ABC slogan: Abstain (for as long as possible); Be faithful; and Condomize. Too seldom are they about sex, sexual practices, sexual enjoyment, sexual taboos and myths, and the broad range of psychosexual relationships among people, and especially *young* people. Until we start to talk about sex differently especially when working with the youth in HIV/AIDS prevention programmes, and thus do sex differently, we shall continue to be alienated by the other-ing of our sex lives.

Posel (2004) is right to note that since 1994 there has been a radical opening up of public discussions and debates about sex and sexuality. The new democracy has been an important catalyst in 'getting the nation talking about sex'. There is no doubt that we need to keep the nation talking about sex, but it matters too what it is we say about sex, and presumably *how* we talk about sex. Well-meaning national television advertisements in the mid-2000s implored us to talk to our children about sex: 'If you love them, talk to them about sex.' The 'them' being referred to in the television advertisements were young teens, presumably 14 and 15 year olds. Obviously parents and guardians should be more open to the issues of sex and sexuality with their children, but what should these hoped-for conversations be about? Should parents talk to their children about whether to have sex or not?; about the range of possible sexual practices?; about the dangers of unprotected sex?; about the fun and awkward anticipation of sexual desire? And while *some* parents might be happy to talk to their children about sexual matters, it seems clear that children do not really want to talk to their parents about sex. This is not to say that they do not talk about sex amongst themselves, quite the contrary in fact, as the research evidence in this area demonstrates. The reserve and reticence on the part of young people about talking to their parents, or other adults for that matter, is entirely understandable from a psychological point of view. Young teenagers are psychosexually negotiating a transition from childhood to adulthood, and hence their identity is at stake, and not just in relation to being sexual or sexually active beings. In any case, seeing as sex is not just one thing, what else is it that we should be talking about when we talk about sex?

It is about sex, sexuality and relationships generally that we need to keep talking, and not only the priority of what Berger refers to as 'dirty sex'. In wanting to make sense of vulnerability and risk, Berger (2005) suggests that we need to consider two issues mainly. First, we need to speak about the *reality* of our sexual lives, and this includes 'dirty sex'. In writing about 'dirty sex', Berger (2005, p. 48) says:

> [T]here are two categories of 'dirty sex' that we ordinarily choose to ignore: those that involve 'unacceptable' sexual partners, such as people of the same sex and commercial sex workers, and those that involve 'unacceptable' practices, such as anal sex and sado-masochism.

The second issue with regard to vulnerability and risk that Berger (2005, p. 50) is interested to explore is 'why some people fail to *place themselves in safety* when having sex in circumstances where they are in a position to do otherwise – in other words, why they make "bad" choices or "fail to choose rationally" ' (emphases added).

Elaborating on the importance of getting hold of 'information' about the reality of our sex lives, Berger (2005, p. 49) writes: '[The] spotlight on sexuality should ... attempt to paint an inclusive, non-judgmental and accurate picture of the diverse and varied ways in which we have sex and why we do so.'

Clearly Berger is hoping for a Kinsey or Hite Report for South Africa. Are we all prepared to paint this (accurate) picture of our diverse and varied sexual practices and motivations, not to mention our fantasies? This seems doubtful, and not because we are uncooperative, prudish and especially reserved about our so-called 'private lives', but more to do with the particular forms of sexual repression, the problematic masculinist notions of male gender identity, and the persistence of patriarchal relations that still pertain in South Africa. Even so, the getting of accurate and reliable 'information' about our sex lives is an extremely complex issue, and has to do with the 'beyond language', 'beyond speech' dimension of sex and sexuality. There appear to be two assumptions behind the reasons for a lack of accurate and detailed accounts of our sexual lives. The one has to do with certain social and cultural inhibitions that are not conducive to open and frank discussions about sexuality, and Berger (2005) clearly challenges these inhibitions by being bold enough to state what he thinks 'dirty sex' is, and why we need to acknowledge and talk about it. The second assumption that accounts for our lack of talk about our sex lives, which Berger (2005) does not discuss, is psychological repression. By definition, what is repressed is unconscious, and what is unconscious is not known by us. In other words, desire is not something easy to talk about, or another way of putting this is to say that the dialectics of desire are discursive rather than lexical.

Expanding on the Lacanian notion of the 'dialectics of desire', Benvenuto and Kennedy (1986, pp. 165–6) suggest:

> One of the most important discoveries of psychoanalysis has been the nature and function of unconscious desire, for example as can be seen in dreams and symptoms. But Lacan was the first to try to put this discovery within a philosophical context, and to examine the relation between the subject and the kind of knowledge with which he [she] has to deal, both within and outside of psychoanalysis.

And noting that the philosophical context for Lacan was mostly to do with language, with discourses, with intersubjective meanings, Benvenuto and Kennedy (p. 176) further argue:

> According to Lacan, analytic experience shows that it is the property of language to slide around its own incapacity to signify an object, and the object exists then only as a *lacking object* (desire follows this movement).

And so what would it be that I would be trying to signify when I talk about my sexual practices and motivations, and surely it would matter to whom my speech was directed? It matters whether we are talking as interviewees to a researcher; or to a therapist in a psychotherapeutic session; or to a friend; or to our lover, or potential (hoped-for) lover. As mentioned above, sex is not just one thing, nor does it have a stable meaning across culture and time, and hence signifying (sexual) desire envelopes language while sliding through it 'in disguise'.

On the constitution of desire, Lacan himself (1977a, p. 311) says:

> Desire begins to take shape in the margin in which demand becomes separated from need: this margin being that which is opened up by demand, the appeal of which can be unconditional only in regard to the Other, under the form of the possible defect, which need may introduce into it, of having no universal satisfaction (what is called 'anxiety').

However, Laplanche and Pontalis (1973, see pp. 482–3) locate the psychoanalytic reading of desire, and this particular inflection, to Freud's notion of wish (*wunsch*), *with Lacan*. Laplanche and Pontalis (p. 483) are correct to note the centrality of the notion of desire in Lacanian psychoanalytic theory, and aptly summarize the distinctive conceptual meaning that Lacan gives to desire, when they write:

> This perspective [of reading wish as desire] ... led Lacan to distinguish desire from concepts with which it is often confused, such as need and demand. Need is directed towards a specific object and is satisfied by it. Demands are formulated and addressed to others; where they are still aimed at an object, this is not essential to them, since the articulated demand is essentially a demand for love. *Desire appears in the rift which separates need and demand*; it cannot be reduced to need since, by definition, it is not a relation to a real object independent of the subject but a relation to phantasy; nor can it be reduced to demand, in that *it seeks to impose itself without taking the language or the unconscious of the other into account*, and insists upon absolute recognition from him. (Emphases added)

The disjunction between desire and language that psychoanalysis alerts us to, forces us to think about what talking about sex might add up to, and how we might 'access' those elements of desire that exceed speech. In this regard, Evans (1996, p. 36) in writing about Lacan's notion of desire states:

> However, there is a limit to how far desire can be articulated in speech because of a fundamental 'incompatibility between desire and speech'; it is this incompatibility which explains the irreducibility of the unconscious (i.e. the fact that the unconscious is not that which *is not known*, but that which *cannot be known*). Although the truth about desire is present to some degree in all speech, speech can never

articulate the *whole* truth about desire; whenever speech attempts to articulate desire, there is always a leftover, a surplus, which exceeds speech.

The implication of this seems to be that we can talk about sex until we are blue in the face, and unless we acknowledge that talking about sex involves both conscious, and *unconscious*, elements, our talk will not take us much beyond a surface understanding of our sexual behaviour. For our 'sex talk' to have recuperative effects in terms of our sexual behaviour, we need to acknowledge and understand the link between talk and unconscious desire. This is not the same as saying that we should not talk about sex because we cannot 'capture' desire in speech, or that the irreducibility of desire renders the verbal accounts of our sexual practices as meaningless. It is rather to remind us that 'sexual knowledge' is a bit of a misnomer, that the 'truth' of sexuality is not waiting in the wings of empirical research or in lots of so-called 'straight talk' about sex, and that much to do with our sexual lives is both non-rational and irrational. For instance, one particular form of talk – flirting (and hinting) – operates precisely to keep the desire of our desire alive without us really knowing what we are doing, or satisfying. Flirting, which is a way of keeping ourselves interesting, or interested, is attractive or appealing because we do not know what the outcome will be, and it allows us to *play* with desire while not risking too much! But who is going to be convinced to take flirting seriously as a sexual practice, and yet it is the safest sex we are likely to have (see Phillips, 1993)? Psychoanalytically speaking flirting is safe sex because the risk of personal vulnerability, and possible rejection, are significantly curtailed, and the pleasure that is bound to desire is not really in danger of becoming 'too much', *jouissance*, in other words. Again, psychoanalytically speaking, within the discourses that circulate around HIV/AIDS there is no such thing as safe sex. Medically, bodily, we can have safe sex, but not psychologically. Psychologically, safe sex, like military intelligence, is an oxymoron, and much of our (persistent) interest in sex has to do with its edgy excitement, vulnerability, risk, desire, *jouissance*, and not its inherent safety! Would this not be even more the case for awkward, inexperienced and mostly 'incompetent' teenagers? The issue of course, especially for young people 'starting out' active sex lives, is to maintain an interest and enjoyment in sex, and to continue talking about sex, because sexuality seems to have more to do with *relationships* and the *recognition and respect* of our partners than just some base selfish pleasure, and at the same time being able to restrict the risk of HIV infection.

To move now to talk briefly about Berger's (2005, p. 58) second main concern and that is 'why people "choose" not to place themselves in safety and engage "knowingly" in high-risk sex'. In this regard, Berger (2005, p. 58) adds that to 'translate knowledge about the potential danger of exposure to HIV into action, one needs to feel that one is at risk of infection'. While this assertion might be partly true, it seems more accurate to suggest that the *risks* of having sex are mostly psychological, and not primarily about bodily infection. For instance, do young people have a conception of infection associated with sex, when HIV positive infections are *so invisible*? There are a range of interesting 'gaps' and 'connections' between the above terms of Berger: choice; safety; high-risk; danger; infection. And yet there seem to be two terms that are displaced, hidden, lurking, that I want to briefly touch on, namely pleasure and death. The first one – pleasure – comes to mind often when we are thinking or talking about having sex; and the second one – death – hardly ever, even in a time of AIDS. The notion of pleasure, and especially coupled to unpleasure, is given expression in Freud's concept of the pleasure principle, one of the two principles of mental functioning, the other of course being the reality principle.

Considering the complex links between pleasure, *jouissance* and death, it is worth quoting (at some length) the Lacanian commentators Benvenuto and Kennedy on this issue:

> Lacan considered that pleasure sets the limits on jouissance, 'pleasure as that which binds incoherent life together, until another, unchallengeable prohibition arises from the regulation that Freud discovered as the primary process and appropriate law of pleasure'. Pleasure, for Lacan, is bound to desire as a defence against jouissance, and is a prohibition against going beyond a certain limit of jouissance. Jouissance, like death, represents *something whose limits cannot be overcome*. In Lacan's thought the 'other' of life, the negativity to be overcome, non-being (in Freudian terms the death drive) paradoxically becomes the centre of life. (Benvenuto and Kennedy, 1986, p. 179)

Continuing, Benvenuto and Kennedy (p. 180), also note: 'Death is the "beyond" of desire, the forbidden, i.e. death is equivalent to enjoyment, jouissance. The unconscious strives to express what is forbidden to the speaking subject – jouissance and death.'

These are highly abstract and complicated ideas, but what they point to are some of the problems connected to the so-called practice of safe sex. If the pleasure principle is always struggling against the pull of *jouissance*, as the prohibition of 'too much pleasure' and the unbearable slide into non-being, how then do we pull back from the attraction of what is forbidden, the allure of what is prohibited? In this sense, the 'dirtier' and riskier the sex the better, and at the same time the attraction to the 'transgressive' is what is too much, what 'terrifies'. Supposedly what is at stake then is finding the *jouissance* of the forbidden that will not kill us. At the level of unconscious desire at least, the *jouissance* of non-being, makes us beholden to the forbidden, to what is beyond. Sex and desire, and the desire of sex, in a time of AIDS bring together *jouissance* and death in a macabre and real way. And yet it seems that what people fear is *symbolic* death, more than biological death.[3] The 'death' of not being the object of someone's desire, the 'death' of desiring what we lack, in short the absence of being able to be part of the signifying (and desiring) practices that constitute our identity. Ironically, then, the positive messages of HIV/AIDS campaigns and intervention programmes, about 'always wearing a condom', and 'practising safe sex', are destined to be the 'kill-joys' of our sex lives. In encouraging 'safe sex practices' we need at the same time to ensure that we do not 'kill' the enjoyment of sex, or the mystique surrounding our desire, and somehow make the *practice* of safe sex *sexy*.

A milder way of approaching this problem of being safe in our sexual relationships, although it is not clear whether Paul Verhaeghe's (1999) views are ultimately any less pessimistic than what I have been suggesting up till now, concerns what he calls 'the internal division between pleasure and desire'. So, in writing about some of the difficulties in sexual relationships, Verhaeghe (1999, p. 25) says:

> The question about the reasons for the difficulties in sexual relationships concerns the problem of the internal division between pleasure and desire. This internal division was the starting point for Freud's work and throughout his life he attempted to formulate it in several ways.

One of these internal divisions is what Freud described as 'the contrast between what he calls the affectionate and the sensual aspects in people' (Verhaeghe, 1999, p. 25).

Pursuing this idea of the internal division between affection and sensuality, Verhaeghe (p. 26) notes:

Too much tenderness on the part of the man does not really do much
for his erection, and a tender wife cannot really expect much hard sex
from her man – let alone ask for it – because it is not the done thing.
This difficult combination can also be understood as the continually
problematic marriage between the sexual drive and love, so that we
will have to go in search of a practical definition of each. What is this
drive? What is love?

Verhaeghe's (1999) context is not HIV/AIDS, and in the above
example he is presuming a husband and wife relationship, but the issues
are not at all dissimilar to what concerns Berger (2005). Berger is particularly motivated by a need to improve and redirect current HIV/AIDS
prevention interventions, and focuses his attention on high-risk sex,
what he identifies as 'dirty sex'. He does not want us to hide behind
taboos of what we can or cannot talk about in terms of sexual practices, and especially wants to find out what our (dangerous) sexual
activities are. Given the current extent of the HIV/AIDS epidemic in
southern Africa it might seem somewhat obscene to suggest, following Verhaeghe, that we need to answer questions like, what is love?;
what is the sexual drive? But, as we all know, HIV/AIDS is not just about
sex, and is much more comprehensively about *relationships*, about various forms of intimacy and not only sexual intimacy, about the division
between affection and sensuality, about who lives and who dies, about
dignity and respect, and about what it means to be human in this precarious new century. And so for instance if the split between love and
sensuality is not 'resolved' in particular partnerships, then Verhaeghe's
seemingly genteel questions about 'love in a time of loneliness' can easily find themselves displaced into the world of Berger's (2005) 'dirty sex'
activities.

This discussion is not intended to create the impression that a
psychoanalytic take on desire and the politics of sexuality is some kind
of 'good news' story that unproblematically helps us rethink the social.
The all too brief discussion of some of the issues raised by Berger's (2005)
article is surely more troubling and pessimistic than that. Given the
enormity of the problems in human social and sexual relations that are
thrown up and exposed by the HIV/AIDS epidemic, I am often rendered
thoughtless, literally unable to think (to paraphrase a comment of Bion).
In this sense I do think, *sometimes*, that HIV/AIDS is an atrocity that is
beyond words, beyond speech.

However, the last thing we can afford is to be silent on the psycho-
politics of sexuality in the time of AIDS, and yet it is disappointing that

psychoanalysis is often too silent on many social issues that it could say a lot more about, and this surprisingly, according to two authors at least (Phillips and Green), even in the area of its expertise, namely sexuality. In an essay on sexuality Adam Phillips (1995, p. 87) writes:

> Most psychoanalytic theory now is a contemporary version of the etiquette book; improving our internal manners, advising us on our best sexual behaviour (usually called maturity, or mental health, or a decentred self). It is, indeed, dismaying how quickly psychoanalysis has become the science of the sensible passions, as though the aim of psychoanalysis was to make people more intelligible to themselves rather than to *realize how strange they are*. When psychoanalysis makes too much sense, or makes sense of too much, it turns into exactly the symptom it is trying to cure: defensive knowingness. But there is nothing like sexuality, of course, for making a mockery of our self-knowledge. *In our erotic lives, at least, our preferences do not always accord with our standards. We are excited by the oddest things, and sometimes people.* (Emphases added)

This is precisely the point, referred to early, that André Green (2001) was making when he bemoaned the absence of sexuality and the erotic in current psychoanalytic theory and practice, and it is in this sense that we need to be wary of the 'etiquette book' approach to our understanding of sexuality and sexual practices. On this score Berger (2005) is right to go after 'dirty sex', and yet by so doing actually creates what he is trying to resist, and that is seeing certain practices as 'dirty', as taboo, as forbidden, and hence especially desirable, but at the same time disavowed. It is a very simple point in fact: knowledge about sexuality is not really what might be called positive knowledge, and in any case the positive knowledge is not what gives us such a tough time in making sense of sexuality and desire. Sexuality and desire do not seem to be primarily about knowledge at all, but seem to be more about lived experience, of how we try to live amongst people in the midst of the dialectics of desire, and how when acting on our sexual desires we do not risk too much and become HIV positive.

Finally, Phillips (1995, p. xi) says that 'Psychoanalysis affirms that there is something unmanageable about being a person, and it is this that makes a person who he or she is.' And one of the unmanageable aspects of our lives is other people, our desire for other people, our desire for other people's desire, and especially our (futile) attempts to control others' desires for / of us. Hopefully, a psychoanalytically informed psycho-politics of sexual desire might make some aspects of HIV/AIDS work more 'manageable'. By acknowledging that a significant amount of our everyday thinking and talking about sex and sexuality is *not* rational, we might 'manage' HIV/AIDS intervention programmes differently as we engage communities, and especially the youth, about their sexual practices, behaviour and attitudes. Furthermore, a socially attuned psychoanalysis reminds us that to talk about sex and sexuality is also to talk about relationships, respect for others and the quest to live decent lives. So, and maybe somewhat surprising, is the fact that socially applying some psychoanalytic concepts – in this instance, desire – could have 'practical' effects.

Notes

1. This is a substantially revised and extended version of a paper first presented at the WISER Symposium 'Rethinking the Social: Psychoanalytic Perspectives', University of the Witwatersrand, Johannesburg, 25–26 August 2005.
2. Thabo Mbeki, South Africa's second democratic president (1999–2008), after Nelson Mandela, espoused two very problematic views concerning HIV/AIDS. First, he claimed that HIV did *not* cause AIDS, and that the *main* cause of AIDS was related to the material conditions of poor people's lives. Second, he accused many AIDS activists of racism, suggesting that the attributing of high HIV infection rates among black (African) South Africans was evidence of a (racist) view that Africans were sexually promiscuous and depraved.
3. I am indebted to Peter Hudson for making a related point in discussion at the WISER symposium in 2005.

References

Benvenuto, B. and Kennedy, R. (1986). *The Works of Jacques Lacan: An Introduction.* London: Free Association Books.

Berger, J. (2005). Re-sexualising the epidemic. *Development Update*, 5(3), 45–67.

Evans, D. (1996). *An Introductory Dictionary of Lacanian Psychoanalysis.* London: Routledge.

Freud, A. (1978). A study guide to Freud's writings. In A. Freud (1982), *Psychoanalytic Psychology of Normal Development, 1970–1980.* London: Hogarth Press.

Frosh, S. and Baraitser, L. (2008). Psychoanalysis and psychosocial studies. *Psychoanalysis, Culture and Society*, 13, 346–65.

Green A. (2001). *The Chains of Eros: The Sexual in Psychoanalysis.* London: Karnac (1997 in French).

Lacan, J. (1977a). *Écrits: A Selection.* London: Tavistock Publications (1966 in French).

Lacan, J. (1977b). *The Four Fundamental Concepts of Psychoanalysis.* London: Hogarth Press (1973 in French).

Lacan, J. (1992). *The Ethics of Psychoanalysis – 1959–1960: The Seminar of Jacques Lacan*, ed. J.-A. Miller. London: Tavistock / Routledge (1986 in French).

Laplanche, J. and Pontalis, J.-B. (1973). *The Language of Psycho-Analysis.* London: Hogarth Press (1967 in French).

McDougall, J. (1995). *The Many Faces of Eros.* London: Norton.

Mitchell, J. ([1974] 1976). *Psychoanalysis and Feminism.* Harmondsworth: Penguin Books.

Molino, A. (ed.) (1997). *Freely Associated.* London: Free Association Books.

Oliver, K. (2004). *The Colonization of Psychic Space: A Psychoanalytic Social Theory of Oppression.* Minneapolis: University of Minnesota Press.

Phillips, A. (1993). *On Flirtation.* London: Faber & Faber.

Phillips, A. (1995). *Terrors and Experts.* London: Faber & Faber.

Posel, D. (2004). 'Getting the nation talking about sex': Reflections on the discursive constitution of sexuality in South Africa since 1994. *Agenda*, 62, 53–63.

Rycroft, C. ([1968] 1972). *A Critical Dictionary of Psychoanalysis.* Harmondsworth: Penguin Books.

Showalter, E. (1998). *Hystories: Hysterical Epidemics and Modern Culture.* London: Picador.

Stavrakakis, Y. (2007). *The Lacanian Left: Psychoanalysis, Theory, Politics.* Edinburgh University Press.

Tauber, A. (2010). *Freud, the Reluctant Philosopher.* Princeton University Press.

Verhaeghe, P. (1999). *Love in a Time of Loneliness: Three Essays on Drive and Desire.* London: Rebus Press (1996 in Dutch).

8
Fanon and Libidinal Economy

Derek Hook

proud, lazy, treacherous, thievish, hot and addicted to all kinds of lust, and most ready to promote them in others, as pimps, panders, incestuous, brutish and savage, cruel and revengeful, devourers of human flesh, and quaffers of human blood, inconstant, base, treacherous and cowardly; fond of and addicted to all sorts of superstition and witchcraft; and, in a word, to every vice that came their way... They are inhuman, drunkards, deceitful, covetous and perfidious to the highest degree... It is as impossible to be an African and not lascivious as it is impossible to be born in Africa and not an African... [Their] faculties are truly bestial, no less than their commerce with other sexes; in these acts they are libidinous and shameless as monkeys, or baboons. (Edward Long (1774), cited by Mbeki, 2007, pp. 111–12)

Approaching libidinal economy

In this chapter I want to unfold and develop the *affective logic* of racism that Frantz Fanon presents in *Black Skin, White Masks* (1986) and do so in a way that pays particular attention to the regular and conventionalized affective operations he details, demonstrating thus how Fanon outlines a particular libidinal economy. This is a line of critical analysis which has its contemporary representatives in postcolonial critique (I discuss an instance of libidinal economy in Gilroy's work, below). It also brings with it the benefit of sidestepping many of the shortcomings long associated with applications of psychoanalysis to the political field such as the epistemological and political problems that arise from attempts to use psycho-diagnostic categories as means of making prognostications of existing sociohistorical and political conditions (Frosh, 2010). Whereas

the political application of diagnostic language results in a sliding to-and-fro between registers of individual and society, a libidinal economy is, by contrast, always *necessarily trans-individual.*
It pays here to refer to the libidinal economy of the mass that Freud (1921) outlines in *Group Psychology and the Analysis of the Ego.* The reason for the irreducibly social focus of this concept soon becomes clear. Libidinal economy, for Freud, is a fundamental vector of group identification; the push-pull cohesion of its (symbolic) ego-ideal and (imaginary) ideal-ego investments is precisely what proves constitutive of social bonds. Of course a libidinal economy, like political fantasy itself, permits for a degree of individual variation. Not everyone enthralled by the same fantasy dreams the same dream, just as not everyone in the hold of fantasmatic racist notions is as invested, as passionate in such beliefs. That being said, the fact such an economy remains tied to the Other (of prevailing societal-historical norms, ideological values, etc.) means that a regularity of sorts is nonetheless obtained in such fantasies. Rather than existing in a primary or unmediated form affects always 'find their feet' within a symbolic universe that is thoroughly saturated by laws of custom, structure, exchange.
Alcorn (2002) suggests that we need be attentive to the libidinal power of language in 'its potential for attachments, attraction, organizations, repulsions and bindings that create . . . stable sites of identification' (p. 105). This description informs a provisional definition of libidinal economy as a force-field of affects; a set of regular patterns and distributions of libido underwritten by a symbolic frame; which entails relations of passionate attachment and exclusion; that affirms types of group identification and holds certain social formations in place.

Libidinal social ties

In relation to colonial notions of 'blackness' Fanon identifies a whole spectrum of derogatory values (vividly deployed in the historical extract cited by Mbeki (2007) above), values that European culture has wished to distance itself from. All that this culture considers undesirable, that it does not wish to admit about itself, it projects onto others as a means of attaining its own 'emotional equilibrium'. The black man is hence for white culture the 'object capable of carrying the burden of original sin' (Fanon, 1986, p. 192). It is already clear that Fanon is utilizing a series of rudimentary economic terms in his discussion – relations of production and distribution feature strongly, as do descriptions of the compensation and balancing of libidinal force. One should avoid limiting the terms of such an analysis to the level of individual psychical functioning. An adequate psycho-political engagement with existing formations of affect, an attention that is to the location, management and intensity of prevailing social affects, cannot exclude the issue of social identification.

Tracing the ebbs and flows of libidinal economy is not simply a case of identifying a given 'social passion', of registering the upsurge of drive impulses within a mass. Nor is it simply a task of noting disproportionate investments of love and/or hate that a group exhibits in respect of certain social objects – although clearly all these types of observation have an important role to play. A libidinal economy necessarily works to substantiate a community, to establish the elementary social ties without which a coherent social group fails to exist. In addition to attempts to name and describe social configurations of affective force, we must consider the role of such affective currents in consolidating processes of group identification. A libidinal economy should thus take into account the narcissistic, imaginary *ideal-ego* image a given community has of itself, that is, the 'narrative ensemble' of likeable, heroic and often fairly grandiose self-representations that it promotes and identifies itself with. Likewise important are the more symbolic components of a group identification, the long-standing pantheon of ego-ideals that link the history of a given group or nation to its present, and that include a vast array of symbolic resources (cultural codes and values that bond a community, the traditions, structures and historical mandates that ground it).

What Fanon gives us then in his account of how colonial anxiety is managed by racist culture is an identification strategy (as strongly substantiated in declarations of what one *is not* as by assertions of what one *is*) which is simultaneously a placement strategy, a 'treatment' of anxiety by means of an outward-focused series of attributions that leads to the fortification of a group identity. This much is apparent in Long's eighteenth-century description of Africans cited above. Such a litany of deprecations and complaints is also a point-by-point assertion of the subject culture's own (supposedly superior) traits. With this theoretical context in place, let us now turn to Fanon's description of what he calls 'negrophobia'.

Negrophobia

The phobic object, Fanon notes, is essentially that which arouses a sense of subjective insecurity in the subject. This object unsettles and provokes anxiety within the phobic subject who finds it loathsome, repugnant. While Fanon clearly draws on conventional clinical literature in order to trace the phenomenology of phobia, it is easy enough to see how the description he is building is always broadly social in its concerns, how it dovetails with the *intersubjective* parameters of political fantasy. 'The choice of the phobic object is ... *overdetermined*,' says Fanon (1986), this object 'does not come at random out of the void of nothingness' (p. 155). It is instead the 'latent presence' of a previously evoked affective association that has now become fixed, that now lies at the root of a given view of the world: '[T]here is an organization that has been given form ... the phobic is governed by the laws of rational prelogic and affective logic' (p. 155). Fanon's phobogenic model of racism is thus very clearly socially structured, 'conventionalized'; it is what we might term a 'structure of colonial feeling'. This is a point worth reiterating: any affect that occurs within a given libidinal economy maintains a symbolic intelligibility; never naively 'spontaneous' nor exclusively individual, such libidinal components always maintain a symbolic-societal basis, a logic. It is for this reason that Fanon's experiment with the trope of phobia – and it is just that I think, an *experiment* – must be introduced with the clear proviso that racism cannot be reduced to phobia. Racism is not to be seen as a sub-variant of an affect more readily recognizable in other contexts (hate, envy, fear), even though the dynamics of phobia provide profitable analytically, alerting us to a relatively stable pattern of affect – a libidinal configuration – that makes it possible to predict trends in racism as a social formation.

The phobic object, continues Fanon, induces a powerfully irrational reaction, a response which exceeds any reasonable fear or justifiable anxiety. 'In the phobic', he insists, 'affect has a priority that defies all rational thinking' (1986, p. 155). The phobic moreover endows the object with 'evil intentions and ... the attributes of a malefic power' (p. 155). In referring to the 'laws of prelogic', Fanon nicely designates the role of fantasy as a type of 'pre-emptive structuring' of ideas and affects. The paradox of 'affective prelogic' alerts us to the presence of a type of social-discursive intelligibility *within* what is felt. The constellation of affective values Fanon pinpoints is thus extended: the fear we are concerned with possesses a markedly paranoid quality, which is to say that it lays the ground for an idea-system, a series of beliefs that one is being systematically undermined, compromised, undone, by a 'bad object' intent on damage.

A clinical observation proves useful here. A phobia can be considered a domestication of anxiety, a means of stabilizing a free-floating type of nervousness by localizing such affects to a particular designated object. I mention this for two reasons. Firstly, to make the point that a phobia could be expected to *intensify* relative to the proportion of general anxiety a given subject or community is experiencing. Secondly, to stress that a spiralling set of grievous ideas and suspicions – the paranoid quality of the idea-system in question – would be the likely result of anchoring so large a quantity of anxiety to a single object. Colonial anxieties thus may be said to fuel the fire of imaginary racist ideation.

The phobic object is not only a source of fascination and attraction but of markedly prurient interest, indeed of repressed sexual desire, or as Fanon more accurately puts it, of 'sexual revulsion' (p. 155). It is here that Fanon's theory of racism becomes properly psychoanalytic: his attention to the symbolic density of racism is now linked to that mainstay of Freudian preoccupations, *sexual drive*. The psychoanalytic notion of ambivalence alerts us to this possibility, namely that ostensibly contrary currents of affect exist in composite, dynamic conjunctions in which each is a condition of the other. This is an example of psychoanalytic thinking at its most counter-intuitive and it has clear bearing on the topic of racism, a discursive and affective formation which is never exclusively an instance of its typically cited causes: ignorance, hate or inter-group antagonism. What such clear-cut categories fail to capture is the ambivalent libidinal quality of racist sentiments.

So, while it is true, as Bollas (2003) notes, that the 'negative hallucination' of treating the other as invisible is itself an instance of racism, it is nonetheless true that there is typically considerable affective investment by the racist in their object. Never merely apathetic or indifferent, the 'hate' of racism always connotes a more active involvement, a far greater imaginative interest. Ahmed (2004) makes much the same point in her analysis of racism: hate is a form of intimacy which involves powerful negative attachments to others. She cites Holbrook: 'where there is hate there is obviously an *excessive need* for the object' (p. 36). It is for this reason that we need be wary of implying, as is often the case in more intuitive ideas about racism, that the racist maintains a kind of exalted exteriority from their object. Fanon's idea of the phobogenic object of racism makes this perfectly clear: the target of racism remains criss-crossed not only with relations of disgust, repulsion and denigration, but with potent relations of allure, exoticism and desire. Each such aspect of this ambivalent object-relationship needs to remain in place if we are to understand anything of the volatility of racist affect: the multiple paradoxes of anxiety yet attraction, contempt yet desire, abjection yet sexual curiosity. The anxious, fearful, paranoid and hateful impulses of racism are thus thought to be conditioned by an unregistered attraction which is so unpalatable to the subject in question that it must be fended off at all costs, remaining unconscious in form.

Race in the field of vision

The topic of anxious sexuality lies at the heart of one of the most original contributions Fanon makes as regards the analysis of colonial racism. This is of course a multifaceted theme, but I want to focus briefly on the particular prioritization he affords practices of visuality in the colonial sphere and, more specifically, the link he identifies between racism and the scopic drive (the gaze). The notion of the colonial gaze represents a convergence of key Fanonian themes: the violence of de-subjectivizing racist objectification, firstly, and the role of desire and sexual anxiety in the etiology of colonial racism, secondly.

Nigel Gibson (2003) prefaces his description of the racial gaze by noting that the subjugating colonial subject has – even without their realizing it – transferred domination into unconscious sexual fantasy. This subject

> desires and fears the Black, who is perceived as the source of virility... The [racial] gaze is simultaneously haunted by hate, fear, anxiety, and sexual desire of the Black body. The racist gaze... suffers from double consciousness, the consciousness of superiority and the consciousness of inadequacy, incompleteness, an incompleteness that is manifest in the visual desire of the... Black Other... The racial gaze of the White seals the Black into a 'crushing objecthood'... The White puts the Black together as a phobogenic object... The racial gaze is both a polymorphous perverse sexual desire, and sexual projection. The innermost repressed and sadistic and masochistic desires are externalized and projected onto the Black. (pp. 22–3)

Vital to stress here is that these twin trajectories of subjectivity, desire and identification, unfold together, in an overlapping and often jointly problematizing manner. The gaze is thus a vehicle of both identification (or apparent counter-identification) and desire.

Stuart Hall, another of Fanon's contemporary interlocutors, is likewise attentive to this interweaving of desire and objectification. He emphasizes both the eroticization of the pleasure in looking and Fanon's recurring motif of the paralysing 'look' from the place of the 'Other':

It is the exercise of power through the dialectic of the 'look' – race in the field of vision... – which *fixes* the Negro from the outside... by the fantasmatic binary of absolute difference... caught, transfixed, emptied and exploded in the fetishistic and stereotypical dialectics of the 'look' from the place of the Other... he/she *becomes* – has no other self than – this *self-as-Othered*. (Hall, 1996, pp. 16–17)

Elsewhere Hall offers another treatment of this topic:

[R]acism appears in the field of vision... [Fanon points to] the sexualized nature of the look. Looking always involves desire; there's always the desire not just to see, but to see what you can't see, to see more than you can see... The reaction in racism between black and white partly arises when the white looker becomes aware that he is... attracted to the black subject. The act of racism is a denial of that desire which is in the gaze itself. (Hall, in Julien, 1995)

The important qualification added here is that the desiring impulse within racism does not emerge in a recognizable form as such, but remains tacit, repressed, defended against whilst nonetheless powerfully conditioning the fierce disavowal of the racist act itself. The paradox at hand is that the presence of desire in the white onlooker often takes precisely the form of *the violent repudiation of desire*.

Sexual anxiety

We are justified here in asking the obvious question: why the relentless prioritization of sexuality in his analysis of colonial racism? More generally put: why is sexuality – or if not that, some phallic attribute – so frequently at the heart of the libidinal economy of racism? Must we always seek the role of sexuality in racism, and thus fall prey to the critique so often made of psychoanalysis by its detractors, that is, its alleged pan-sexualism? This is a question I want to explore in some detail as we continue.

My own doubt as to the veracity of Fanon's account – of the omnipresence of sexual anxiety in contexts of severe racism – vanished after attending an exhibition entitled 'Without Sanctuary' in Atlanta, Georgia in 2002, which was comprised in large part of lynching photographs. This was something I had not realized until then: a lynching, certainly in the Southern States of the USA at the beginning of the twentieth century, often took on the qualities of a social gathering, a spectacle. This was perhaps the most disturbing feature of the exhibition: many of the photographs on display were postcard images in which white spectators posed alongside the dead body of the victim. Similarly affecting was the list of alleged offences committed by those who had been lynched, a case in point of a racist fantasy frame overwriting perceptions of social reality. Apart from the odd citations of violence, the offence alleged again and again, in what read like a series of surreal variations on the same basic formula, was violent or threatening sexual behaviour towards a white woman (the charge of having assaulted or raped a white woman; making inappropriate sexual overtures; being caught in a white woman's house, etc.), the crime, in other words, of perceived sexual desire.

One way of approaching this issue is not by looking simply to affirm the omnipresence of sexuality within the colonial domain, but to be aware of the omnipresence of another theme, that of *radical asymmetries of power* within this sphere which make the prospect of 'interracial' sexual contact such a worrying idea, at least (but presumably not only) for the colonizer. So, rather than a crude psychoanalytic insistence on how everything is sexual, one should proceed by a more refined attention to how power itself sexualizes, and engenders forms of sexual propriety and sexual anxiety.

The white man's double difference

Fanon offers a further means of shedding light on the complex issue of sexual anxiety in racism. His initially puzzling pronouncement that 'the Negrophobic man is a repressed homosexual' (1986, p. 156) alerts us not only to the allure of the other but to the fact that such an attraction might run across gender-lines, posing thus the issue of homosexual desire. As above, the issue of how lines of identification and desire (of otherness and sexuality) intersect proves instructive. Let us then, in a fairly deliberate fashion, play through the steps of the argument that would enable us to illuminate Fanon's pronouncement.

We have in the colonial environments the production of racial and sexual difference alike. These modes of difference are produced in tandem, and, typically, in a relation of opposition. Bearing in mind the psychoanalytic contention that (imaginary) identifications are often supported by types of physical likeness, we should be unsurprised to learn that in many racist societies patriarchy is also powerful, that we have a reiteration of difference in the division of races and sexes alike. Differently put: if it is on the basis of categories of difference that white masculinity separates itself off and subordinates other races, then – on much the same basis – women are also made other, treated as secondary, even if according to a different (sexual as opposed to racial) logic. Perhaps unexpectedly then – and as Fanon was at pains to emphasize – the most feared of all relationships in patriarchal colonial settings is the sexual relationship between the white woman and the black man.

Now, to follow a certain way of thinking, this seems odd, because from the perspective of the white man, we have a relation that epitomizes a double difference. My differences to both these categories of subject would thus, as a white man, seem to be affirmed, my separateness and distinctness from each member of the relationship secured, the co-ordinates of my own identification reinforced: unlike him I am *white*, unlike her I am *male*. As such, this relationship should leave him unconcerned, indeed, doubly affirmed. 'Unconcerned' of course is the opposite of what occurs in situations such as these, where the very possibility of such a relationship comes to represent a massive influx of anxiety, a vexation of the white man's desire and identifications alike.

The problem with the explanatory route taken above is that it neglects the question of desire, in particular it neglects the ways in which desire problematizes the relation of difference. What in fact occurs, taking a psychoanalytic perspective, is that this relationship between the white woman and 'the man of colour' returns to the white man both his desire and his identification in inverted forms. I should reiterate here that not only do identification and likeness support one another, so do desire and difference. Here lies the problem: the protection of desire *through difference*, and the protection of difference *through desire* are both troubled in this example, each playing one another off in a vicious circle of pre-emptive defence. Let us trace here the perspective of the white male subject in racist/patriarchal/heterosexual society: you, the black man, must not desire the object (the white woman) of my (white man's) desire. Why? For if I understand that you also desire this category of object, then I am forced to admit a similarity between us, by virtue of our *shared* desire for this object. The likeness of your desire, in other words, questions the distinctness of my racial identification as separate, especially considering how important I take this desire to be in constituting my identity as a heterosexual man. The apparent anxiety uncovered here is that of the problematization of (apparently distinct) racial identifications through the undeniable similarity of (heterosexual) desire. There is more of a basis for identification with the black man than the white man may care to admit.

There is a second and intersecting line of anxiety, which, by now, is easy to anticipate. If desire can problematize difference, then difference can likewise problematize desire. We return to the perspective of white male colonial subjectivity. Both the black man and the white woman are, to me, objects of difference. They are – despite many apparent differences – alike, at least in this respect: *they are fundamentally other*. She, the female subject, operates as an object of desire, and does so, at least partly, on the basis of certain (imaginary) aspects of visual difference. Nowhere else is my difference to an other more powerfully reiterated than relative to the black subject. If the black man and the white woman are thus somehow aligned, and I desire her, might I not also *desire him*? So whereas above the fact of shared heterosexual desire (between white man and black man) questioned my assumption of racial difference, here the apparent fact of overriding racial similarity (between white men and women) poses troubling questions of desire.

The racial other is able to problematize both (white, colonial, racialized) desire and identifications by showing up the fact that both of these are potentially more inclusive categories than the desiring subject might wish them to be. Not only is it the case that prospective lines of identification and desire extend beyond the categories of appropriate objects as set by the terms of racist/patriarchal/heterosexist discourse. This state of affairs is further compounded by the fact that desire (or, its flipside, the perception of lack) is typically amplified by attributions of difference. Given that the segregations, divisions and underlying rationality of colonial power is premised upon the constant reiteration of difference, one can understand how the colony is also a domain where the conditions of unexpected desire are being relentlessly produced. This does not of course mean that the whole colonial system of differences is threatened with collapse, although it certainly does mean that this domain is threaded through, layered with anxiety. It suggests that this 'system of difference' is constantly in defence mode, potentially explosive, willing to sanction whatever measures are necessary to fortify its world of difference.

Sexuality, enjoyment and phallic loss

There is a further clarification that needs to be made as regards the relation of sexuality and racism, a clarification that will help set the scene for the next step in Fanon's exposition of negrophobia. The lynchpin in the racist imaginary is not simply the *sexuality* of the other taken in the most conventional or normative sense. In most instances, as in the Edward Long extract above, it would serve us better to pinpoint traces of abhorrence, pronouncements of disgust. Fanon, after all, is careful to qualify that it is 'sexual *revulsion*' he has in mind when speaking of phobogenic attractions. The reviled reaction, the element of repugnance, indeed, the *abject* quality of the sexuality Fanon describes, prove crucial. The litany of features cited by Long all have this in common: they are illicit enjoyments. It is more the obscene stuff of *jouissance* than sexuality alone that we are here concerned with, although, as always, sex appears in its most privileged form, its irreducible component. So despite the variation of Long's catalogue of evils, which moves from criminality, to baseness, savagery and immorality, the inherent sexual problematic always returns.

This historical example of racist discourse helps us draw an important conceptual distinction. The threat to which the subject is beholden, and which brings their own lack to the forefront, is presented in two modalities. Firstly, in the other's unacceptable enjoyments and libidinal excesses unmarked by the renunciations and prohibitions that the civilized subject has been subject to. So although such enjoyments are despised and resented, they enable the denigrating subject to locate *jouissance* somewhere other than in themselves, to purify themselves of the stains of their own enjoyment. Secondly, the apparent 'nature' of the other shows something that the desiring subject hankers after; it exemplifies the displaced element of their being that they experience as unjustly lost to an intruder. If in the first case we are dealing with the obscene enjoyment, the attributed *jouissance* of the other, in the second we are dealing with a phallic component, a precious quality around which the existence of the desiring subject pivots and which defines their lack.

There are two fundamental aspects that must be noted as regards this phallic attribute. The phallic component is not merely a token, and it is always shadowed by loss. In other words, whatever it may be in a given sociohistorical context, the phallus does not simply connote but effectively *is* a kind of power, at least within the parameters of the prevailing social fantasy. Moreover, to invoke this phallic quality is simultaneously to evoke the potential loss – the castration – of the imagined attribute. To risk a psychoanalytic aphorism: the phallus only appears on the horizon of castration. Bringing these two components together leads us to the following hypothesis. Identify a prevailing signifier of power (of desirability) – be it wealth, sexual endowment, violence, etc. – and, inasmuch as this property is capable of engendering envy, and can viably be located in an other, you will have the germinal point for a form of bigotry. It is to a consideration of this phallic component within Fanon's theorization of racism to which we now turn.

The logics of racist affect

Fanon asserts that there are, unexpectedly perhaps, a set of positive, even *idealizing* associations to be found, albeit in distorted forms, in the logic of racism. Let us ground this assertion in an example Fanon provides, an example which draws together many of the arguments discussed above. I have in mind here Fanon's argument that a chief stereotype of blackness is that of unrestrained sexual appetite, a postulate he attempts to verify with reference to association he conducted with white Europeans. When his subjects came to associate to the signifier 'Negro' he was confronted with the following string of ideas: biology, penis, strong, athletic, potent, boxer, savage, animal, devil. A particular anxiety came to the forefront in the fear of 'the raping Negro': 'The white man is convinced that the Negro is a beast...if it is not the length of his penis, then it is the sexual potency that impresses him' (Fanon, 1986, p. 170). There is a certain concealed respect and/or jealousy at work here for Fanon, a 'rapturous admiration of black...prowess' (p. 174). It is through the projection of sexual anxiety and/or guilt onto the figure of the black, he claims, that the European avoids a neurotic sense of their own sexuality. There is, however, a 'return effect' of this fantasy – the perceived sexual potency of the black man is enough to engender a sense of inadequacy and insecurity within the white man as regards his own sexual abilities. There is a form of envy underlying this racism, reiterates Fanon; the white man wishes he possessed what he considers to be the black man's primitivism, his joy for life, his unrivalled sexual capacities.

Here then is the more general hypothesis we are presented with: each variant of racism contains within it the identification of a highly valued social trait. This trait is desired, the racist subject or community covets this particular quality, wants to possess it, but comes to hate and resent it, or more directly, *the other*, for possessing it. There is already here a clue to the logic of this affective operation. The positive virtue cannot be rejected outright, certainly not if it has attained the status of a societal ideal. Not being able to attain this ideal thus necessitates the narrative insertion of an object that prevents the subject from attaining the ideal in question; something is taken to stand in the way of the subject's realization of this ideal; there is some*one* who capsizes the possibility of the subject's ever fully possessing it.

The case of anti-Semitism serves as one of Fanon's examples. 'The Jew', he says, drawing here on Sartre, 'is feared because of his [or her] potential for acquisitiveness' (1986, p. 157). We have a case in point then of a desired phallic attribute – the ability to make money – which, despite being demonized in others, is a highly prized, even valorized quality that the racist would dearly love to make their own. In *The Wretched of the Earth*, Fanon (1967) provides an additional example of this phallic anxiety. Speaking of European anti-Muslim sentiment in Algeria at the time of the war of independence, Fanon claimed that the European's belief in the Muslim's apparent proclivity for violence revealed a hidden admiration. In the case of colonial and white supremacist racism, the perceived attribute that represents such a repository of anxiety is that of a *sexual potency*. Crucial here is the fact that the idealizing component in racism, that is to say, the *phallic stereotype* around which its logic turns, is hopelessly overstated, excessive, *fantasmatic*, despite apparent empirical evidence suggesting otherwise. Fanon is at pains to emphasize that this assumption of white colonialists is unrealistic, that there is no evidence to suggest that the sexual powers of blacks is in any way superior to that of whites. Importantly of course it may well be the case that there are elements of empirical reality which appear to affirm such fantasies. Take for example the dominance of black male athletes in many long- and short-distance running events, an apparent affirmation of the essential athleticism that racializing discourse identifies in black masculinity. Such a conjunction of objective fact and fantasy is not uncommon. Our response should be to query why *this particular facet of reality* has been seized upon and prioritized. There are presumably a variety of equally truthful generalizations which could be made as regards white men; the fact that such generalizations have less of a role to play in securing a given political fantasy goes some way to explaining why such truths are taken to be of less significant value. Younge (2004) employs parody to make this point, rhetorically demonstrating the 'laws of prelogic' that govern which questions – which facets of reality – come to be prioritized as opposed to others:

> Now the Olympics are over, can we finally admit that white people are genetically equipped to excel in archery and rowing? . . . Shouldn't the police be doing more to tackle white-on-white crime? . . . What do you make of the tribal conflict in Ukraine? . . . Isn't it a shame that white people cannot pick more responsible leaders? Why aren't you doing more to check the rise in Christian fundamentalism? . . . [W]hy are white men so aggressive? (p. 3)

The feature of inverted admiration within racist discourse can, as a rule, be identified in that quality that best epitomizes the threat the others in question pose, indeed, in that attribute which most infringes upon the space, the vitality, the prosperity of the dominant group. What is most feared in racist discourse is also unfailingly a token of anxious lack, of something intensely wished for. The absence of secular rationality that so vexes Western modernity about Islamic fundamentalism might, for example, be viewed in light of the failure of any metanarratives, the pronounced insecurity generated by the postmodern 'risk society' whereby there are few if any certainties. In much the same way, the (apparently) troubling spread of Islam across Europe should be grasped alongside the failure to develop any real viable discourse of cohesive intra-European identity. This leads us to an interesting conclusion: if racism is (in part) the negative reflection of the particular anxieties of a given culture projected onto another, then subtle shifts in cardinal anxieties and perceived societal lacks will be reflected in what is most angering, most menacing in today's other. What such a postulate emphasizes is that we need guard against viewing the process in static terms, as a sequence of 'stuck' historical images, but rather as an operation subject to historical flux, subject to continual amendment and variation.

Formulations of racist lack

The logic of racism hence seems to be something like: 'I blame you for something that I perceive myself to lack, something that I imagine you, the other, to have in abundance and that represents a threat to my livelihood or enjoyment.' A type of symbolically mediated social jealousy is apparent here. One way of managing this jealousy, of downplaying the apparent phallic power of the other, is through caricature. The other possessing the desired attribute, be it the Jew, the Muslim, the black, is *reduced* to this particular quality, condensed to an offensive phallic feature, as if it exhausted all there was to know about them. '[T]he Negro is eclipsed,' says Fanon. 'He is turned into a penis. He *is* a penis' (1986, p. 170). In the logic of racism, even the apparent 'racial virtue' can be twisted into a corrupting vice; the once-prized feature takes the form of an 'ideal gone bad'. There is a double gain to this logic. For a start, it becomes easier to mask one's own apparent inability to secure the cherished object. Secondly, the other thought to possess the object has been objectified; their intimidating phallic endowment has been converted into a single deplorable trait beyond which nothing else is worth knowing. This problematizing factor thus becomes the key to the other; it is *the* salient feature which overrides any other positive attribute they may be thought to possess. The Jew, to stick with Fanon's example, is nothing more than the love of money.

One should note the lethal feature noted above. Not only is the desired object exaggerated, spoiled by its apparent excess, it is now twisted into a threat to my well-being – a way of life, a type of enjoyment is now at stake. Here then we confront the paranoid element in racism, *the sense of personal threat*, the danger of my 'coming undone' that the other comes to embody. This is the elementary racist fantasy writ large: the other is taking something away from me, that they are somehow stealing my livelihood, my vitality, something of immense value to my existence. *That* is why I hate you: because you threaten to imperil my way of life and to ruin all the things I hold dear. The other thus seems always to pose the threat of moral corruption, the degeneration of values, the violation of law and order, of 'the way things are meant to be'. As Fanon puts it, 'The Negro destroys, brings to nothing, ruins, damages . . . [he is] the detriment of what we have of our civilization' (1986, p. 180).

Affective procedures

The affective logic of racism that we have been plotting involves a series of evasions and distortions that prevents the subject from confronting a variety of associated, anxiety-provoking ideas. To appreciate this is to understand that racism is not an emotion, but an affective economy that shores up a particular identity. It is worth briefly recapping the affective procedures underlying the fantasmatic logic in question. There is, firstly, the emergence of a desire associated with the other. This may be a desire for the other, or a desire for something that the subject themselves lacks. (In each such case, it is worth noting, the other comes to embody the subject's lack.) Secondly, there is a lingering sense of inadequacy – the lack here is intensified – of not being able to possess the desired phallic attribute. The best way to sidestep these realizations is to represent both such troubling sets of ideas as threats emanating from the other. It is thus *the other* who is thought to possess a series of problematic desires *rather than myself*. Furthermore, it is not that *I lack a particular quality*, it is rather that *you have this quality in an excessive and hence dangerous quantity*. In this distorted logic of racism, I, the racist subject, hence become *the victim* of you, the other, who undermines and threatens my existence. You, on the other hand, become *my persecutor*, that which represents all that is threatening to me. Hence, I deserve protection *against you*, and *you*, on the other hand, *deserve punishment*.[1]

If there is a truth of the racist subject (or community) that the affective logic of racism distorts and conceals, then it is one that involves several operations of disguise, operations that Fanon's libidinal economy of negrophobia enables us to identify. There is, firstly, an ego-to-other displacement (a projection) which enables the racist to believe that the problematic attributes in question are most fundamentally about *the other* rather than about the subject themselves (the subject community's own disavowed qualities). A defensive reversal is also present: the feared and threatening object also exerts an attraction – it maintains a sexual charge, it piques the subject's interest and proves to be an object of their curious desire. There is, thirdly, a transformation of the object, a transformation which follows a virtue-to-vice trajectory. A once-prized phallic quality is reduced to something tainted by the other's *jouissance*; a devalorization which functions to cover over the subject's own perceived lack.

A melancholic libidinal economy

I want now to briefly introduce another example of libidinal economy, namely Gilroy's analysis of post-imperial melancholia. Doing so helpfully extends the type of theorization offered by Fanon; it likewise helps bridge the time of Fanon's analysis and our own.

Gilroy's (2004) analysis of contemporary formations of British cultural identity reveals a central tension, a push-pull relation between amnesia and aggrandizement. This dynamic is the result of juxtaposition between two powerful yet contrary cultural imperatives. On the one hand there is a largely unconfronted colonial past, an entire epoch of Imperial dominance that remains repressed, avoided, relegated to the 'dead history' of that which is not easily retrieved within popular cultural memory. For Gilroy, this is a pathological orientation, born out of the inability to face up to, let alone mourn, 'the profound changes in circumstances and moods that followed the end of the Empire and consequent loss of imperial prestige' (Gilroy, 2004, p. 98). Running counter to this cultural trend is another: the incessant imperative of rejuvenating a vision of British greatness. Such an outlook 'dictates that conflicts against Hitler and Hitlerism remain imaginatively close while Britain's many wars of decolonisation . . . are to be actively forgotten' (Gilroy, 2004, p. 8).

These two contrary imperatives must be in conjunction, indeed, read dynamically. The regretted fact of Britain's 'lost greatness' must necessarily be linked to a narcissistic self-image that has been wounded and that must now, in some or other form, be retrieved. What results is an anxious regime of self-affirming images that need continually be reiterated. The resulting cultural conjunction, for Gilroy, exhibits all the patterns of neurotic blockage (to-and-fro undulations of ambivalence, repetitive assertions of certain historical events, the denial and elision of others), particularly so in view of its attempted adjustment to the changing conditions of a multicultural society. The popular imaginary of Britishness is thus underwritten by a 'postimperial melancholia', a libidinal formation which denotes a lopsided approach to British cultural identity which selectively idealizes aspects of its past while effectively erasing others.

The contradictions evident even in liberal-sounding proclamations of equality in Britain today should thus be viewed as symptomatic. They represent the psychological costs of the constant denial of repressed colonial pasts. Given that such denials – always underlined by a niggling sense of complicity – are coterminous with the need to assert a redemptive image of British greatness, we are able to understand Gilroy's characterization of a defensive cultural attitude of contemporary Britishness. Hence the fact that outward commitments to non-racism can occur alongside exclusionist rhetoric, just as apparent compassion for immigrants and asylum-seekers can exist alongside xenophobic loathing.

A political analytics of desire, fantasy, affective logic

Contrary to the problem that characterizes many attempts at societal psycho-diagnostics, that is, a sliding between registers of the individual and the social (as critiqued by Frosh, 2010), an analysis of libidinal economy remains focused on what constitutes a group, a cultural mass. The standard argument that psychoanalysis is not a social theory does not hold up here. As noted above, the notion of libidinal economy is most accurately understood as a theory of mass identification. We are concerned here with the 'glue' of a collectivity, with its routine bindings and repulsions, with how such affective operations interact with and, typically, support given social formations. Libidinal economy is, in this respect, precisely an account of the *formation of the social*.

What I hope the above account of Fanon's and Gilroy's work makes clear is that to accurately pinpoint a libidinal economy is to do more than indulge in a descriptive exercise, to dabble in psychoanalytic concepts that do not properly fit the sociopolitical domain. An analysis of libidinal economy is attentive to societal flows of affect; to how such distributions are characterized by certain points of blockage and fixity; to how such arrangements of libido enable a type of identification; to how they sustain a particular regime of images. Such an analysis is never simply tantamount to a collection of representations; nor can it be considered an instance of psychological description. Such flows, circuits and transactions of affect possess a logic – that of the fantasy frame with which they accord – and they pertain to a larger-scale system than that of the isolated subject. The patterns of affect in question are not of a free-floating, individual or intra-psychic sort that has been cut adrift from societal context and the parameters of the symbolic. They are instead profoundly conventionalized, habituated.

I have noted elsewhere that racist discourse is always locked into a relationship with 'extra-discursive' factors, factors that provide a fuller means of understanding the dynamics and limitations of discursive processes themselves (Hook, 2006). In tackling the topic of libidinal economy, this chapter has proposed an answer to this conceptual challenge. The above discussion of libidinal economy provides a way of responding to a broader methodological problem, that of how a psychoanalytic approach might fruitfully supplement a discourse analysis without succumbing to the reductive psychologism of 'intra-psychic' explanations of the unconscious of individual subjects. The analysis of the libidinal economy underlying specific discursive formations would move us away from attempts to fix such discursive patterns as merely the outcome of intra-psychic processes, of individual psychopathology. Used in conjunction with discourse analysis it would, I think, provide a non-reductive analytical strategy, one asserting that discourses themselves maintain the coherence, the repetitiveness – indeed, the cycles of *jouissance* – that mark certain well-established patterns of libidinal functioning.

Apprehending the libidinal economy of a given discourse might enable us to answer questions along the lines of why certain signifiers come to be locked into patterns of repetition, why some are so historically persistent, 'sticky', difficult to shake off. It may likewise assist us in understanding how certain regimes of representation are so effective in, to paraphrase Glynos (2001), fuelling identification processes and creating effects of discursive fixity. My above description of the various psychical operations present in the logic of racist affect hints at something of the difference of approach between discourse analytic perspectives and those aiming to trace a given libidinal economy. The analysis of racism, that is to say, concerns more than grappling with the constructive and rhetorical features of texts. It should aim also to grasp the governing fantasmatic logic of the discourse; the 'infrastructure' of regularly occurring patterns of affect; and the involved psychical operations (reversal, projection, repression, selective aggrandizement and amnesia, etc). It is these features which help us better understand the bridge between discourse and identification and that enable us to explain what gives such discourse their tenacious hold, their particular intensity.

Note

1. One is reminded here of the paranoid logic that Freud (1911) discerns in the Schreber case. He traces the transformations underpinning the progression from the (unacceptable) affective proposition '*I (a man) love him (a man)*' to its opposite '*I do not* love *him – I* hate *him!*' This proposition is itself subject to further transformation, that of projection: 'He hates (*persecutes*) me, *which will justify me in hating him.*' Freud's conclusions – which he claims holds for all types of paranoid delusions – are worth reiterating:

   > The mechanism of symptom-formation in paranoia requires that internal perceptions – feelings – shall be replaced by external perceptions...the impelling unconscious feeling makes its appearance as though it were the consequence of external perception: 'I do not *love* him – I hate him, because HE PERSECUTES ME.' (1911, p. 63)

   Freud insists further that 'Observation leaves room for no doubt that the persecutor is some one who was once loved' (p. 63). The pertinence of his analysis to our current concerns is clear, particularly so given that he is interested in a form of erotic love (homosexual desire) which, within prevailing social norms, is unacceptable to the subject.

References

Ahmed, S. (2004). *The Cultural Politics of Emotion*. Edinburgh University Press.
Alcorn, M. (2002). *Changing the Subject in English Class*. Carbondale: Southern Illinois University Press.
Bollas, C. (2003). Introducing Edward Said. In E. Said, *Freud and the Non-European*. London and New York: Verso.
Fanon, F. (1967). *The Wretched of the Earth*. London: Penguin.
Fanon, F. (1986). *Black Skin, White Masks*. London: Pluto.
Freud, S. (1911). *Psycho-analytic Notes on an Autobiographical Account of a Case of Paranoia (Dementia Paranoides), SE*, vol. 12, pp. 1–79.
Freud, S. (1921). *Group Psychology and the Analysis of the Ego, SE*, vol. 18, pp. 65–144.
Frosh, S. (2010). *Psychoanalysis Outside the Clinic*. London and New York: Palgrave.
Gibson, N. C. (2003). *Fanon: The Postcolonial Imagination*. Cambridge: Polity Press.
Gilroy, P. (2004). *After Empire: Melancholia or Convivial Culture?* London: Routledge.

Glynos, J. (2001). The grip of ideology: A Lacanian approach to the theory of ideology. *Journal of Political Ideologies*, 6(2), 191–214.

Hall, S. (1996). The after-life of Frantz Fanon: Why Fanon? Why now? Why black skin white masks? In A. Read (ed.), *The Fact of Blackness: Frantz Fanon and Visual Representation*. London: ICA, pp. 13–37.

Hook, D. (2006). 'Pre-discursive' racism. *Journal of Community and Applied Social Psychology*, 16, 207–32.

Julien, I. (Dir.) (1995). *Frantz Fanon: Black Skin, White Mask*. Arts Council of England: BFI/K Films, UK.

Mbeki, T. (2009). 30th commemoration of Steve Biko's death. In *The Steve Biko Memorial Lectures 2000–2008*. Braamfontein: The Steve Biko Foundation and Macmillan, pp. 101–22.

Younge, G. (2004). No offence, but why are all white men so aggressive? *The Guardian*, 1 December, p. 3.

9
Violent Crime in Post-Apartheid South Africa

Bert Olivier

Among the advantages of psychoanalytic theory for rendering a sociohistorical critique of social and political phenomena is the fact that it unavoidably works with 'quasi-universal' psychic structures. This means that psychoanalytic theory is predicated on the assumption that the psychic ontogenesis of *all* human subjects proceeds 'universally' via a succession of the 'same' structural phases, as exemplified by what Freud dubbed the Oedipus complex, or by what Lacan termed the 'mirror phase'. 'Universally' has to be qualified by the prefix 'quasi', however, given humanity's inescapable subjection to historical processes. Hence, 'quasi-universal' indicates that, while all human beings are constituted in terms of similar psychic structures, the functioning of these structures is itself historically reconfigured via changing social, economic and political circumstances. In cultures where there are no mirrors, for example, infants negotiate the 'mirror phase' in ways that do not involve mirrors in the literal sense, but the place of which is taken by a different medium of 'self-reflection', such as the reflecting surface of water, the ritual assessment of the self by others ('You are correctly dressed') and so on. Or, to bring it closer to the contemporary era, the 'social dialectic' of secondary identification (e.g. in a school situation) that follows in the wake of the mirror phase is complicated, today, by the ubiquity of the mass media, where thousands of celebrity images offer themselves as sites of identification for subjects. One could also employ the term '*quasi*-transcendental' to indicate that these (interrelated) psychic structures facilitate certain relational modes and actions ('*universally*') on the part of subjects, but simultaneously comprise the conditions of possibility of their *particular* embodiment, *as well as* their distortion and perversion, in their specific articulation in individuals' lives. Conversely, the historical conditions of individuals' lives provide the indispensable 'material' anchoring points for these quasi-transcendental structures, without which they could not function, or even be said to exist.

Concepts marking crucial junctures in psychoanalytic theory therefore do not lose their explanatory power in the course of social evolution, but are inescapably subject to time or history. Here I propose to employ the theoretical 'grid' of Jacques Lacan's three registers of the *imaginary*, the *symbolic* and the '*real*', the explanatory efficacy of which does not, in my judgement, diminish with time, but which, simultaneously, are (re)configured in new and different ways at various stages of social, economic and political development. More specifically, I believe that they provide the theoretical means to comprehend the violent crime that has been plaguing South African society since the advent of democracy in 1994.

I should further point out, at the outset, that my 'quasi-transcendental' use of these concepts in the context of violent crime in South African society should not be read as indicating an intention to analyse 'causal' connections in terms of 'group psychology'. I do this because a helpful critic has questioned whether 'the study [is] meant to trace the psychic causes of violent crimes at the individual level the accumulation of which is the community, or [is the analysis] meant to be at the community level'. Given what my critic describes as the 'problematic methodological individualism [in] Lacanian psychoanalysis', I want to stress that I see no contradiction between my claim (to be elaborated below) that, analytically speaking, one may posit a causal link between the constitution of individuals in terms of the historically mediated registers in which their subjectivity is articulated – the (Lacanian) imaginary, symbolic and 'real', which are further subject to specific historical conditions for their specifically 'weighted' configuration in individuals' lives – and the manifestation of unspeakably violent crimes in the society. While it is the case that the symbolic is the repository of societal values, or of the social (as opposed to the distinctively individual, inscribed in the imaginary register), crimes are perpetrated by *individuals* in this society, and the causal nexus I shall attempt to uncover therefore bears on actions performed by individuals *within* this society, but motivated by their *particular* experience of, or insertedness in, an historical situation by the intertwined roots of the 'real', the imaginary and the symbolic.

Violent crime in South Africa

Violent crime is ubiquitous in South Africa today. Not only does it figure daily in South African and often also international news media, television documentaries which report on this phenomenon in an investigative manner have also been broadcast – a recent example of which is Paul Theroux's BBC documentary, *Law and Disorder in Johannesburg* – and several fiction films have explored it from various perspectives, including Gavin Hood's Oscar-winning *Tsotsi* (2005) and Ziman's *Jerusalema* (2008). Moreover, 'everyone' in South Africa is constantly talking about it; whether it is within families or at other social gatherings, stories are constantly being exchanged about the way that violent crime has touched the lives of family members or friends.

All this sustained attention notwithstanding, it seldom happens that news reports and commentary surpass mere verbal description, sometimes accompanied by popular-psychological or economic discussions concerning violent incidents involving assault, robbery, rape, murder or car hijacking; illuminating accounts of the grounds of their provenance remain scarce. Such an enlightening grasp is usually made possible by a certain reflective distance, the most productive kind of which is encountered in theoretical or philosophical perspectives. Johann Rossouw's (2006a, 2006b) philosophical appropriation of this disturbing phenomenon in South Africa is therefore a welcome interpretation of violent crime, insofar as he has designed a conceptual framework for the identification of the 'causes' of violence.

In the first of two articles, Rossouw (2006a, p. 2) draws attention to specific events which, from a psychoanalytical perspective, are significant for an adequate understanding of violent crime in South Africa. The first of these is the agreement between the ANC[1] and the South African corporate sector in the mid-1990s to adopt a neoliberal economic policy which has enabled government and business elites to become 'fabulously rich', and without hiding this fact from the covetous eyes of the vast majority of South Africans, who were consequently thrown into a state of helpless envy and unfulfillable desire (Rossouw, 2006a, p. 2). The other two important matters raised by Rossouw are related to the first one. He alludes to what he calls (my translation) 'the enormous orgy of unrestrained consumption in which the black middle classes, following and exceeding their white counterparts, have participated' (Rossouw, 2006a, p. 2) since that time, as well as to the fact that the industrial model implemented in South Africa is the obsolete nineteenth-century one that benefits only the small circle of 'owners' disproportionately.

This is the case, despite the availability of 'postmodern' technology that the 'circle of owners' clings to, notably in the communications industry – unnecessarily, because it could enable many more people to improve their 'material and symbolic' position, for example by means of cultural production (Rossouw, 2006a, p. 2). It is important to note that these issues pertain to the economy.

Rossouw's second article on crime is more encompassing and analytically differentiated than the first one. At the outset (Rossouw, 2006b, p. 1) he poses the pertinent question, why crime in this country is so frequently not restricted to mugging, robbery, burglary-related theft or to car hijacking (which one might expect in a country where poverty is widespread), instead of which assault, the infliction of serious bodily harm or mutilation and even murder are common occurrences. He alludes to the historical phases of Western society's modernization, where at various stages different societal spheres have occupied the preponderant position *vis-à-vis* the others. Among the three societal spheres of existence distinguished by him (Rossouw, 2006b, pp. 1–14), first *religion*, then *politics* and finally *economics* has functioned as the most important or dominant organizing societal principle in the lives of people, from the institutional to the individual level. To be sure, all of them play an enduring structuring role in every society, but their respective positions of dominance and subordination in relation to one another vary from time to time. In Western society the religious sphere was dominant in the premodern middle ages, the political prevailed during the modern era, and the contemporary (postmodern) age is governed by the economic order (Rossouw, 2006b, p. 14; my translation):

> In the economy which emerges after the Second World War, the market is the cornerstone of value. All those virtues which promote the growth of the economy are regarded as being valuable, including productivity, wealth and consumption. It is the 'market' which makes it possible to say 'we', and those who form part of this 'we' inaugurate community in the institution of consumer society, where surrender to consumption and ownership comprises the most important virtue.

His insightful analysis of the relevance of the never-satisfiable market notwithstanding, I believe that a psychoanalytical poststructuralist framework could fulfil an important complementary and deepening role in understanding the 'causality' implicated in the epidemic of violent crime sweeping through South Africa.[2]

Lacan's theory of the subject

Turning to Lacan's theory,[3] his conception of the human subject as a being who is precariously articulated in and between the different registers of the imaginary, the symbolic and the 'real', supplies one with the requisite structural means to arrive at a nuanced comprehension of the kind of subjectivity which is compatible with acts of violence inflicted on human beings by others in a specific social and historical situation. The psychic anatomy of the subject in terms of these three registers can be briefly summarized as follows. Firstly, each person, as subject, occupies an *imaginary* position – that is, you have a 'self' or ego-identity, an image-appearance, as well as a self-image. All acts of identification occur at this level, and Lacan (1977c; Olivier, 2009) notes that this invariably, if paradoxically, involves alienation on the part of the subject, whose act of identifying is directed at an imaginary entity functioning as a powerful lure towards (spurious) wholeness and unity. Secondly, one has a *symbolic* subject-position – in other words, every subject also has a discursive identity in language, as a shared system of signification. This means that the 'symbolic' is not a neutral system of meaning(s), but functions as *discourse* in the constitution of subjects' subjectivity – in other words, upon the acquisition of language, subjects are simultaneously inscribed in asymmetrical axiological and power relations (Lacan, 1977a, 1977b, 2007; Olivier, 2005a). Thirdly, there is the '*real*' that structures subjectivity – the most puzzling aspect of the subject's identity, comprising the paradoxical, ineffable, foreclosed 'thing' in every person (and in language). It cannot be symbolically represented (Copjec, 2002, pp. 95–6; Lacan, 1981, pp. 54–5), is both 'more' and 'less' than the imaginary and symbolic subject-positions, but nevertheless has concrete effects on the latter.[4] In a Lacanian developmental schema the 'real' names the subject's earliest mode of being, which precedes the mirror phase and the acquisition of language, and subsequently remains impervious to symbolization.

By way of clarifying the meaning of these three registers in terms of which the complex configuration of human subjectivity may be understood, one may elaborate on it as follows. As with everything human, the three societal spheres distinguished by Rossouw lend themselves to being comprehended in terms of Lacan's three orders or registers. This means that there is an imaginary, as well as a symbolic and a 'real' side to the religious, the political and the economic mode of social being. In the religious sphere (specifically Christianity), for example, Christ has traditionally been depicted iconically (that is, in the imaginary register) by means of diverse stylistic figures in art, in addition to which the Christ figure is associated with humanity as a whole via symbolic articulations (such as the doctrine of the reconciliation between humanity and God through Christ as mediator), and at the same time Christ's martyrdom on the cross may fill one with an inexpressible dread, which words are powerless to express (an instance of the 'real').

The same Lacanian interpretation applies to the political and the economic spheres. Realistic painting in the nineteenth century – for instance that of Courbet (Baumer, 1977, p. 308) – in which the pro-letariat is glorified, is but one relevant political embodiment of the imaginary register, while political utterances and writings, such as man-ifestoes and pamphlets, as well as countries' constitutions, are located at the level of the (political) symbolic. The 'real' in the political sphere may be detected – albeit not face to face – where one comes up against the limits of language and iconic representation: after all, how does one symbolize or otherwise represent the deepest desires and survival imperatives which give rise to the 'social contract', whether the lat-ter is conceived in monarchical, democratic or primitivist (for example Freudian) terms?

In the case of the economic societal sphere, it may come as a sur-prise that, over and above its imaginary manifestations (the image of an elated consumer, brandishing the latest top-of-the-range model cellphone, among others), and its symbolic counterpart (including economic theories of various stripes, such as Keynesian, Marxist or neoliberal ones, as well as economic policies or laws), it also harbours a 'real' dimension that exceeds representation of any kind, notably, today, the unrepresentable aspect of capital as a limitless, all-devouring pro-cess which, in Marx's famous phrase, causes 'all that is solid, [to] melt[s] into air' (Žižek, 2000, p. 12). Few people ever consider that capital as such is nothing concrete, but instead instantiates a 'purely' abstract pro-cess. No matter how accurately an accountant may calculate one's assets and liabilities, the numbers representing these are abstract ('exchange value'), and do not coincide with the actual 'use-value' of the things subsumed under 'fixed assets', for example. Nevertheless, because these numbers are subject to fluctuations at various levels and registers (some of which are situated in cyberspace), such as financial markets, the stock exchange, the property market, crime statistics, droughts, international tensions, the oil price and so on, any changes in these would have an impact on the overall (use-) value of the things abstractly represented by them. Hence the psychoanalytical insight, that the 'real' cannot be represented, but nevertheless, like the abstract play of cyber-capital, has concrete effects in the imaginary and symbolic registers – such as when the economic lot or condition of individuals, or even of nations, is determined by 'abstract' speculation on the world's financial markets (Žižek, 2000, p. 15; 2005; 2009, pp. 10–11).

Regarding the relation between the 'real', the symbolic and the imaginary, it is significant that Lacan characterizes *trauma* as an 'encounter' with the 'real' that somehow does not take place (Lacan, 1981, p. 55):

> The function . . . of the real as encounter – the encounter in so far as it may be missed, in so far as it is essentially the missed encounter – first presented itself in the history of psycho-analysis in a form that was in itself already enough to arouse our attention, that of trauma.

Is it not remarkable that, at the origin of the analytic experience, the real should have presented itself in the form of that which is *unassimilable* to it – in the form of the trauma, determining all that follows, and imposing on it an apparently accidental origin?

The relevance of Lacan's theory for South Africa

What does this have to do with violence in contemporary South Africa? First I should emphasize that, although the three Lacanian orders of the imaginary, the symbolic and the 'real' are *distinguishable* as psychic registers which co-constitute the subject's complex identity *as* a subject, they are *all* necessary for the subject's 'normal' functioning – should one be absent, one could not speak cogently of a 'human' subject. Someone lacking the imaginary register, for instance, would not 'have' an 'ego-identity', but only symbolic (social, linguistic) and 'real' (infra- and supra-imaginary and -symbolic, 'thing'-) 'identities', which would 'short-circuit', without the imaginary as a mediating register, to render something like a reification of the collective in the psyche of the person concerned.[5] Given the relations of necessary intertwinement among these three registers, the ubiquity of violent crime in South Africa may be traced to the traumatic 'breakdown' of relations among them at an individual level, with far-reaching consequences at a collective level.

To be able to understand my psychoanalytical interpretation of the phenomenon of violence, an elaboration on the concept of 'trauma', linked with the 'real' by Lacan in the excerpt above, is needed. Insofar as 'trauma' is described as a 'missed encounter' by Lacan, it may be conceived of as the disintegration of the symbolic and imaginary horizon within which a person's self-understanding is located. When one loses a child in a car hijacking, or is subjected to rape, one experiences the full impact of trauma, manifesting itself in a paralysing condition of shock, followed (or accompanied) by an involuntary, blind 'repetition' or reliving of the traumatizing event, as if one were desperately trying to prepare oneself, in retrospect, for something that has caught one by surprise, in a completely unprepared state (Freud, 1968, pp. 12, 31–2).

Such 'repetition' is symptomatic of what Freud (1968, pp. 47, 53) named the 'death drive' – the 'conservative' aspect of which aims at restoring 'homeostasis' to the psyche in its interactive relation with concrete reality. Hence, such 'blind' repetition has the function of preparing the way for, or rather of initiating, the integration of the traumatic event with the fabric of one's life, no matter how difficult or (strictly speaking) impossible it may be. What 'causes' the trauma proves, in the final analysis, to be elusive, the necessity of *having* to confront it notwithstanding – hence the displacement of the confrontation with the 'source' of the trauma from the register of the unsymbolizable 'real' to the registers of the imaginary and (mainly) the symbolic, where one attempts to come to terms with the shattering event.

This attempt to confront, elaborate on and make sense of trauma happens as a synthesis of an imaginary and symbolic appropriation of it. In other words, trauma – whether individual or collective – leaves one no option but to try to make sense, via imagination and language, of what is completely senseless.[6] With this characterization of trauma in mind, it should be remembered that South Africans have experienced two successive, collective (although individually registered) 'traumas' in the psychoanalytical sense outlined here. First there was the imposition of the policy of apartheid or legal racial segregation (with its own symbolic framework, no matter how unjustifiable) on black people for more than four decades, followed, in 1994, by the new 'trauma' of the transition to a radically new symbolic order, minimally in the form of the new constitution of post-apartheid South Africa, which demanded that citizens leave behind the 'exclusive' symbolic 'order' of apartheid and commence thinking and acting in terms of the new, 'inclusive', human rights-oriented symbolic order as enshrined in the constitution. It is here that the effects of collective trauma (as index of the 'real') on the registers of the symbolic and the imaginary, seen in conjunction with the domains of the political and economic, can be perceived, as extensive symbolic productivity in, among other cultural practices, art and literature testifies.[7]

The structural consequence of apartheid as an institution was that the *humanity* of black people – something that functions at the level of the symbolic in universalistic conceptual terms – was traumatically 'banished' from the symbolic sphere. The consequence of this was the neutralization of the mediating universalizing function of language as discourse – that is, language insofar as it is the point of convergence between meaning and values, or sense and power. In light of the earlier account of the constitutive role (for subjectivity) of the inter-linking of the three Lacanian registers, it therefore appears that, under apartheid, the socially pathological situation was created where, because of the exclusion of blacks from participating in a symbolic human-ity as inclusive nationhood, a kind of 'short-circuit' occurred between the imaginary and the 'real', so that blacks appeared, for all intents and purposes, as 'reified others', that is, others as mere (inhuman) 'things'.

This is an important structural consideration for the understanding of violence in contemporary, post-apartheid South Africa. Today the pat-tern of exclusion of some people from the (inclusive) symbolic order of 'humanity' repeats itself, but this time via an exclusivist, hegemonic economic discourse, instead of a political one.

Not that this involves a simple, monocausal state of affairs, then or now – on the contrary: a complex set of relations is at stake, which crucially implicates the contemporary priority of the economic sphere over the political and the religious. This is the era of 'globalization', that is to say one where a reciprocal global 'flow' occurs among different countries at economic, political and cultural levels, something that is promoted by the operation of 'postmodern' electronic means of com-munication, or 'informatization' (Hardt and Negri, 2001, pp. 280–94). In fact, electronic communication systems and the labour skills required for their operation comprise the area where employment opportuni-ties and employability are optimal in the context of globalization. Add to this the adoption of global, neoliberal economic principles in post-1994 South Africa, and it should be clear that those people who are least equipped with communicational and informational productive capacities would be the most economically vulnerable.

It is interesting to note the pertinence of Naomi Klein's chapter on South Africa[8] in *The Shock Doctrine* regarding the post-transition eco-nomic conditions in this country, epitomized by what Peter and Favret (1982) call 'the abstract violence of money' (Foucault, 1982, p. 187). In her discussion of the transition from apartheid-rule South Africa to 'democratic' government under the ANC, combined with the adoption of a neoliberal economic programme of privatization and other free market reforms, she observes (Klein, 2007, p. 198):

rather than meeting in the middle between California and the Congo, the ANC adopted policies that exploded both inequality and crime to such a degree that South Africa's divide is now closer to Beverly Hills and Baghdad. Today, the country stands as a living testament to what happens when economic reform is severed from political transformation. Politically, its people have the right to vote, civil liberties and majority rule. Yet economically, South Africa has surpassed Brazil as the most unequal society in the world.

This situation described by Klein is germane to what has been argued so far. Because of the priority accorded the economic sphere, as argued by Rossouw, the reconfiguration of the collective symbolic order, demanded by the traumatic exchange of an old symbolic order for a new one, has proceeded chiefly, if not solely, in exclusivist *economic* terms (Gumede, 2005, pp. 97–122, 215–33), despite the fact that South Africa's new constitution, which is one of the most progressive in the world, holds the potential of being elaborated on at various inclusive levels, probably with salutary consequences. It is important to remember, here, that such a reconfiguration of the symbolic order *in predominantly economic terms* is not merely something that happens at the innocuous level of 'mere' language; it comprises a discourse, or, more accurately, a discursive *practice*, which has transformed South African society fundamentally. Here I am thinking of extensive economic legislation on what is known elsewhere as 'affirmative action', but in South Africa is subsumed under the euphemistic name of 'Broad-Based Black Economic Empowerment' (BBBEE)[9] (which has benefited only a comparatively small elite group of blacks; Gumede, 2005, p. 223), of economic development initiatives and related policy issues, much of which has been absorbed into everyday parlance, *as well as economic practices*, regardless of the accompanying, comparatively degraded, social and political noises about the 'rainbow nation', Africa nationalism, the 'African Renaissance' and so on.

Needless to emphasize, only a relatively small percentage of the South African black population (who have not already been economically empowered as political representatives at central or provincial government level) has been actively involved or drawn into the globalization-susceptible economy; the rest – mainly unskilled labourers – fall outside this production net. William Gumede (2005, p. 215) points out that, although there were only about 150 white ultra-millionaires in 1994, in the first decade of democracy this figure escalated to 690 of all races, and by 2004 so-called dollar-millionaires in South Africa numbered 25,000, possessing more than $300 billion privately – more than the GDP of the Southern African Development Community. His next comment is significant for the theme of this essay (Gumede, 2005, p. 215): 'In itself, this might not matter much, but the other side of the coin is that 22 million South Africans eke out an existence in abject poverty.'

Against this background, the violence, which has been a phenomenon concomitant with the rapid growth of a black economic elite in South Africa, may be explained as follows in terms of the Lacanian psychoanalytical theory of the subject, outlined above. The crux of the matter is that, under 'normal' circumstances, the symbolic, the imaginary and the 'real' are structurally distinguishable; different, but interdependent, triadically of necessity imbricated, and this structure is a prerequisite for 'normal' individual functioning and interpersonal relations. Under current socio-economic conditions, however, the kind of *'short-circuit'* that was referred to earlier occurs between the imaginary and the 'real', insofar as the symbolic register does *not* fulfil its indispensable function, of mediating discursively between the other two registers in an encompassing, universalizing and community-inaugurating manner. Consequently, *'humanity' is not constituted inclusively*. What does this mean?

The first thing to remember is that, as far as the human subject is concerned, the 'real' paradoxically names the unnameable, unsymbolizable (infra- *and* supra-sensible), irretrievably foreclosed 'thing' in every person – that which cannot be rationalized or colonized in any way, and is therefore not susceptible to moral judgement. (Thus the moral law is ineluctably framed in universalist, that is, conceptual-linguistic terms.) Hurst (2007, p. 2) describes the 'real' as: 'the mysterious, disgusting, noumenal "Thing"' in (or, for that matter, outside) the subject.

Second, recall that, in contrast, the imaginary register is that of the particular ego, which finds its counterpart in the 'other ego' or 'alter ego' (your neighbour). Hurst (2007, p. 2) refers to it as 'a powerful mirror image or alter-ego' in our psyche, but also points out that, in social terms, in 'the imaginary mode, other humans come to represent the alter-ego'. It is also the sphere of alienation of the subject via acts of primary and secondary identification (Lacan, 1977c; Olivier, 2009).

Third, the symbolic represents the 'universal' discursive domain of language and conceptuality, without which one could never surpass the realm of the imaginary, where the irreducible singularity, and also the alienating semblance of each individual subject as supposedly whole and 'unified' ego, are located. This is also the domain of normativity and the 'moral law', insofar as the moral law (as well as the whole panoply of positive laws) is inconceivable without the universalistic signification of language in the symbolic register. The latter is a prerequisite for a sense of community or society – what Freud called the 'Oedipus complex' is nothing less than the psychic mechanism by means of which every child enters the network of kinship relations (by virtue of having a name), and simultaneously the symbolic realm, in this way subjecting her- or himself to the authority of the 'law', represented by parents as authority figures. Hurst (2007, p. 3) remarks that: 'the symbolic order...is associated with the power of abstract thinking and the universally communicative self, [and] our primary concern is to engender a global belonging together'.

Keeping in mind that, for non-pathological human subjects, these three registers are necessarily imbricated – each fulfils an indispensable, interdependent role in the constitution of the subject, as indicated above – the obvious question is whether the 'belonging together' towards which the symbolic order tends can indeed be engendered in contemporary South Africa, given the dominant position occupied by the economic sphere in relation to other societal domains.

I have already indicated that, in my judgement, the answer to this question is negative, but to be able to provide a more extensive answer, I should point out that an across-the-board, instead of a severely limited, elaboration of the symbolic sphere (in conjunction with the other two) in post-apartheid South Africa is indispensable for the cultivation of a 'new', inclusive sense of community. As remarked earlier, however, a 'short-circuit' – in the precise (metaphorical) sense of 'a low resistance-connection across which an excessive current flows' – is bound to occur between the alienated ego (imaginary) and the foreclosed 'thing' ('real') in the absence of symbolic mediation. As a result, instead of being able to perceive the 'other' as an 'other (alter) ego', who is also, like myself, subject to the moral law (encountered in the symbolic register) – through which the inhuman 'thing' is in effect held in check – symbolic moral mediation, in principle valid for *all* people, is severely curtailed, and the 'other ego' is increasingly perceived as a mere 'thing'. This entails a kind of 'double alienation' – the imaginary order being constituted in terms of alienation, and the foreclosed 'real' resisting symbolization. In other words, in the absence of the inclusive universalistic functioning of language, which implies the general validity of the moral law for all humans, the imaginary ego-function and the 'real' thing-function of the subject 'fuse', as if in a doubly alienating short-circuit, facilitating violent behaviour towards others, and complicating the work of the symbolic register, effectively weakening its capacity to weave a discursive canopy beneath which all South Africans could find a symbolic home.

Explaining violent crime

Given the growing gap between the rich and the poor in South Africa, the desire of the latter for the wealthy 'lifestyle' of the former, with whom the poor identifies in imaginary terms, is bound to be left unsatisfied, first because such secondary identification occurs in an essentially alienating register, and second because this register is infused with capitalist promises of enjoyment which, in principle, cannot be kept. As Kovel (2002, p. 52) points out, capitalism introduces 'a sense of dissatisfaction ... so that it can truly be said that happiness is forbidden under capitalism, being replaced by sensation and craving'. It should be noted that this presupposes a more fundamental 'lack' as fertile soil for capitalism's superimposition of an artificial dissatisfaction, namely the 'lack' that Jacques Lacan singles out as the most fundamental characteristic of the human subject. Human 'desire', for Lacan, is a manifestation of this lack, but ironically individuals who understand that 'lack' is a fundamentally unalterable human condition would be most resistant to capitalism's false promises of finally fulfilling all desires and removing all lack (Kovel, 2002; Olivier, 2005b). Those who identify with capitalist images of fulfilment are therefore subject to an additional alienation from their own character as lacking subjects.

This explains why crimes in South Africa since 1994 have been marked, as in early nineteenth-century France, where a similar political and economic transition occurred (Foucault, 1982; Olivier, 2003), by unbelievable, inhuman gruesomeness – why parents have burnt or mutilated their children, or each other, and why robbers or hijackers (superfluously) murder or maim their victims.[10] As long as the restrictive, 'exclusive' economic sphere comprises the preferential order for establishing a new symbolic domain in South Africa, subordinating other levels of symbolic activity such as the political, this slaughter is bound to continue, in my judgement, because some members of the South African population are excluded from such symbolic activity, an exclusion exacerbated by capitalist desire, identification and concomitant imaginary alienation.

To be sure, symbolic work has been, and is being, done in other areas of social and cultural life (including the political and the aesthetic), but not nearly with such extended constructive effect that it could surpass the economic in importance. Besides, given the socially fragmenting nature of neoliberal economic practices[11] (which ultimately lead to the enrichment of a relatively small number of individuals via the promotion of an ethos of economic self-importance), any possible experience of solidarity among South Africans of all cultural groups is further undermined by the economic advantage and benefit of a relatively small group of people (Gumede, 2005, pp. 215, 223). In fact, such economic elitism actively works *against* the creation of any sense of shared community which might have emanated from symbolic activity (of a different kind) in the sphere of economic discourse.

By way of confirmation of the preceding (largely) psychoanalytic interpretation, which amounts to the diagnosis of a 'dissonance' of sorts in the psyche of subjects, Rossouw identifies two kinds of desire on the part of South Africans, in the context of the contemporary privileging of neoliberal economic values of self-enrichment and consumer practices (2006b, p. 15; my translation):

> On the part of those who are able to buy a 'good life' – the middle and upper classes – a condition of *disturbed desire* arises, which is manifested as a feeling of 'not enough yet', tendencies towards suicide, depression, drug- and entertainment-addiction, eating disorders and so on. On the part of those who are unable to buy this 'good life' – the poor class – a condition of *frustrated desire* comes into being, which manifests itself as feelings of extreme humiliation and despair, which, in some instances, eventually result in violence, especially and precisely there, where the web of community relations starts to tear, and individuals are left to their own desperate devices.

What Rossouw does not place under the magnifying glass in this excerpt is the Lacanian 'real', albeit under a different name, which is exactly that which, in the absence of the symbolic community circle, presses the already alienated imaginary ego into showing itself as being 'desperate', specifically in brutal, inhuman guise.

It does not follow, of course, that only the poor are capable of 'reified' violence along the trajectory of this 'connectivity-disturbance', because of their inability to see others as 'humans like myself'. Everyone in the social situation where the exclusion of some people from the limited domain of (predominantly) economic symbolic activity takes place, is susceptible to being caught in the grip of such violent behaviour. Under these circumstances, therefore, the wealthy cannot escape the perceptual disruption manifested in the brutal, violent reification of others, either.

Conclusion

What is to be done, in light of the findings of this interpretive analysis? The construction and elaboration of an *inclusive* symbolic sphere is, I believe, the only possible antidote for the present situation of widespread violent crime in South Africa at this stage of its social and political history – this much follows from what I have argued with the help of psychoanalytic theory. There is an important caveat, however. My argument should not be construed as an appeal for the formulation of an encompassing, inclusive political *ideology* – the symbolic elaboration of an alienating imaginary locus of identification – as distinguishable from the well-camouflaged ideology of neoliberal capitalism, which does *not* function inclusively. In the long run, nothing could be more detrimental for the country and its people, insofar as (given the role of nationalist ideologies of various stripes in history) it would probably lay the foundation for a totalitarian state, with all its accompanying consequences, such as a hypertrophy of nationalism (which is already latent in South Africa because of the ruling ANC's support for the idea of Africa-nationalism), as the twentieth-century history of fascism has taught us.

My reason for claiming this, is that such an ideology would imply that an overarching framework could be furnished for addressing and supposedly 'finally solving' all existing problems, as well as satisfactorily responding to all questions, demands and needs. In contrast, what I mean by the phrase 'inclusive symbolic sphere' is a *commonly shared, but in principle incomplete discursive vocabulary* – one that bears on the meaning of a *radical social democracy* in everyday social and political practices, a vocabulary by means of which questions and problems might be addressed with no illusions concerning 'permanent' solutions. On the contrary, built into such a discursive vocabulary would be an affirmation of conceptual and phenomenal complexity, itself predicated on the knowledge that – in the face of the open-endedness of history and of language – no 'solution' of problems, or answer to perplexing issues, is ever conclusive, and that tomorrow will inevitably bring new problems that will have to be approached with newly forged symbolic means.

The 'inclusive vocabulary' at stake here, would always, incessantly, dwell creatively on the edge of the precipice above the Lacanian 'real'. As such, it would inescapably have to operate in the shadow of human finitude and fallibility – a shadow that falls on even the very best of

human ventures and projects. Symbolic activity of this kind would not easily fall prey to the illusions and delusions of ideology.

Notes

1. For an informative discussion of the ANC's move from a party that championed nationalization of key industries while still in exile to one that embraces free market policies, see Klein (2007, pp. 194–217) and Gumede (2005, pp. 97–122, 215–33). Briefly, in pre-democracy negotiations with the Nationalist (apartheid) government, the ANC initially sacrificed economic for political power, only to find itself hamstrung after coming into power in 1994. Every time it seemed to move towards 'left' policies, the market punished it severely. When Mbeki took over as President from Mandela, however, he moved decisively to *impose* (Klein, 2007, p. 209) an economic programme that entrenched free market principles on the ANC, and simultaneously convinced the white South African business sector that they have nothing to fear from ANC economic policy. True to his word, in 1996 Mbeki announced a neoliberal economic programme of privatization and government spending cutbacks, freer trade and relaxed control on national and foreign currency flows. As a result, both white and black business and government elites have profited hugely in financial terms.
2. This interpretation will not focus on crime *vis-à-vis* the religious sphere, but only consider the relevance of the political and the economic. For earlier elaborations on the phenomenon of violent crime in South Africa, see Olivier (2007a, 2007c and 2007d).
3. For an elaboration, see Lee, 1990; Bowie, 1991; Olivier, 2004, 2005a, 2006.
4. See Žižek (2009, pp. 10–11; 2000, pp. 14–15; 2005) regarding capital as 'real', which has far-reaching effects on the concrete lives of people across the social and economic spectrum. He says (2009, p. 11): ' "reality" is the social reality of the actual people involved in [economic] interaction and in the productive processes, while the Real is the inexorable "abstract", spectral logic of capital that determines what goes on in social reality'. The 'real' that has an impact on one's concrete life in the event of trauma, therefore also has effects in (personally relevant) social reality.
5. The 'Borg' in the science fiction series *Star Trek* exemplifies this, insofar as a representative of the 'Borg', while ostensibly possessing an individual identity, does not really have one, but always acts as a 'direct' embodiment of the collective.
6. This is what Freud's famous 'talking cure' amounts to, as Derrida evidently knows where he comments on the requisite linguistic response to the trauma of 9/11 (2003, pp. 87–8; Olivier, 2007b, 2008).
7. As literary embodiment of the phenomenon of elaborating on trauma via language, Antjie Krog's *Country of My Skull* (1999, pp. 320–7; Olivier, 2008) includes a moving and illuminating account of the traumatic impact of apartheid practices on an old shepherd's life.
8. 'Democracy born in chains: South Africa's constricted freedom' (Klein, 2007, pp. 194–217).

9. For a useful summary of BBBEE legislation and the 'measurement' of companies' compliance, see: http://en.wikipedia.org/wiki/Broad-Based_Black_
Economic_Empowerment.
10. See the BBC television documentary on crime in South Africa by Louis
Theroux, *Law and Disorder in Johannesburg* (2008/9), which uncovers the
monstrous face of crime in South Africa mercilessly.
11. See in this regard Kovel (2002) and Olivier (2005b).

References

Baumer, F. L. (1977). *Modern European Thought: Continuity and Change in Ideas,
1600–1950*. New York: Macmillan.
BBBEE. *Broad-Based Black Economic Empowerment Legislation*. http://en.wikipedia.
org/wiki/Broad-Based_Black_Economic_Empowerment, accessed 13 October
2010.
Bowie, M. (1991). *Lacan*. London: Fontana Press.
Copjec, J. (2002). *Imagine There's No Woman: Ethics and Sublimation*. Cambridge,
MA: MIT Press.
Derrida, J. (2003). Autoimmunity: Real and symbolic suicides – A dialogue with
Jacques Derrida. In G. Borradori (ed.), *Philosophy in a Time of Terror*. University
of Chicago Press, pp. 85–136.
Foucault, M. (ed.) (1982). *I, Pierre Riviere, Having Slaughtered My Mother, My Sis-
ter, and My Brother ... A Case of Parricide in the 19th Century*, trans. F. Jellinek.
London: Bison Books.
Freud, S. (1968). *Beyond the Pleasure Principle*, SE, vol. 18, pp. 7–64.
Gumede, W. M. (2005). *Thabo Mbeki and the Battle for the Soul of the ANC*. Cape
Town: Zebra Press.
Hardt, M. and Negri, A. (2001). *Empire*. Cambridge, MA: Harvard University Press.
Hood, G. (Dir.) (2005). *Tsotsi*. Miramax Films.
Hurst, A. (2007). *Hoe Moet Ons Oor Geweld Dink?*, trans. B. Olivier, 'How Should
We Think About Violence?' Presentation, Klein Karoo Nasionale Kunstefees.
Litnet Seminaar-kamer/Seminar Room. www.litnet.co.za/cgi-in/giga.cgi?cmd=
cause_dir_news_item&cause_id=1270, accessed 10 November 2009.
Klein, N. (2007). *The Shock Doctrine: The Rise of Disaster Capitalism*. London:
Allen Lane.
Kovel, J. (2002). *The Enemy of Nature: The End of Capitalism or the End of the World?*
London and New York: Zed Books.
Krog, A. (1999). *Country of My Skull*. London: Vintage.
Lacan, J. (1977a). The agency of the letter in the unconscious or reason since
Freud. In *Écrits: A Selection*, trans. A. Sheridan. New York: W. W. Norton,
pp. 146–78.
Lacan, J. (1977b). The function and field of speech and language in psycho-
analysis. In *Écrits: A Selection*, trans. A. Sheridan. New York: W. W. Norton,
pp. 30–113.
Lacan, J. (1977c). The mirror stage as formative of the function of the I as
revealed in psychoanalytic experience. In *Écrits: A Selection*, trans. A. Sheridan.
New York: W. W. Norton, pp. 1–7.

Lacan, J. (1981). *The Four Fundamental Concepts of Psycho-Analysis* (Seminar XI), trans. A. Sheridan. New York: W. W. Norton.

Lacan, J. (2007). *The Other Side of Psychoanalysis* (Seminar XVII), trans. R. Grigg. New York: W. W. Norton.

Lee, J. S. (1990). *Jacques Lacan*. Amherst: University of Massachusetts Press.

Olivier, B. (2003). Discourse, agency and the question of evil. *South African Journal of Philosophy*, 22(4), 329–48.

Olivier, B. (2004). Lacan's subject: The imaginary, language, the real and philosophy. *South African Journal of Philosophy*, 23(1), 1–19.

Olivier, B. (2005a) Lacan and the question of the psychotherapist's ethical orientation. *SA Journal of Psychology*, 35(4), 657–83.

Olivier, B. (2005b). Nature, capitalism, and the future of humankind. *South African Journal of Philosophy*, 24(2), 121–35.

Olivier, B. (2006). Die kompleksiteit van identiteit in demokrasie: Lacan. *Tydskrif vir Geesteswetenskappe (Journal of Humanities)*, 46(4), 482–97.

Olivier, B. (2007a). Geweld in Suid-Afrika: 'n psigoanalitiese perspektief'. *Tydskrif vir Geesteswetenskappe*, 47(4) (Supplement), 46–58.

Olivier, B. (2007b). The question of an appropriate philosophical response to 'global' terrorism: Derrida and Habermas. *Freiburger Zeitschrift für Philosophie und Theologie*, 54(1/2), 146–67.

Olivier, B. (2007c). Waarom ons vir mekaar 'n 'ding' word. *Die Vrye Afrikaan*, 16 February, p. 16.

Olivier, B. (2007d). Why SA violence turns horrific and brutal. *Comment and Analysis, Mail & Guardian Online*. www.mg.co.za/articlePage.aspx?articleid=303071&area=/insight/insight_comment_and_analysis/, accessed 27 March 2010.

Olivier, B. (2008). Trauma and literature: Derrida, 9/11 and Hart's *The reconstructionist. Journal of Literary Studies*, 24(1), 32–58.

Olivier, B. (2009). That strange thing called 'identifying'. *South African Journal of Psychology*, 39(4), 407–19.

Peter, J.-P. and Favret, J. (1982). The animal, the madman, and death. In M. Foucault (ed.), *I, Pierre Riviere, Having Slaughtered My Mother, My Sister, And My Brother...A Case of Parricide in the 19th Century*, trans. F. Jellinek. London: Bison Books, pp. 175–99.

Rossouw, J. (2006a). Misdaad. *Die Vrye Afrikaan*, 20 October, pp. 1–2.

Rossouw, J. (2006b). Waarom geweld SA oorspoel. *Die Vrye Afrikaan*, 17 November, pp. 1, 14–15.

Theroux, L. (2008/9). *Law and Disorder in Johannesburg*. BBC Two television documentary.

Ziman, R. (Dir.) (2008). *Jerusalema*. Muti Films and Moviehouse Entertainment.

Žižek, S. (2000). *The Fragile Absolute – or, Why is the Christian Legacy Worth Fighting For?* London: Verso.

Žižek, S. (2005). Revenge of global finance. *In These Times*, 21 May, www.inthesetimes.com/article/2122/, accessed 7 July 2007.

Žižek, S. (2009). *Violence: Six Sideways Reflections*. London: Profile Books.

10
The Violence of an Idealized Family: A Kleinian Psychoanalytic Reading of *Te Rito*

Peter Branney, Brendan Gough, Anna Madill and Mandy Morgan

While Aotearoa/New Zealand is a world leader in the arena of family violence policy, it has a long history of violence between its Māori and Western inhabitants that continues to manifest in its policy-making structures. In this chapter, we shall introduce the Aotearoa/New Zealand cultural context and relate it to Kleinian psychoanalytic concepts (paranoid-schizoid position, splitting, idealization and introjection); describe a specific family violence policy called *Te Rito* before using Kleinian concepts to help us read this text. Finally, we shall critically reflect on the processes used in this chapter and explore implications of this analysis for family violence policy internationally.

Aotearoa/New Zealand

Contemporary discourse within and about Aotearoa/New Zealand often constructs it as a country consisting of two cultures: the descendants of the British (white and Western) colonizers known as 'Pākehā' and the indigenous Māori. Te Tiriti o Waitangi/The Treaty of Waitangi[1] is a site of contested meaning and is evidence of the separation into two cultures. As Morgan, Coombes and Campbell (2006) note, the Tiriti/Treaty has been largely ignored by the structures of state (i.e. the British Crown) in a benevolent and violent vein of a progressive colonization benefiting the colonizers. More importantly, the British took the Tiriti/Treaty as having a singular meaning, which was that the signatories were acceding Māori sovereignty to them. In contrast, Māori have an oral tradition where decision-making occurs through dialogue and, as such, decisions are not fixed (in the written word). Indeed, it is possible that the Tiriti/Treaty is still known today because Māori have kept it alive through their discourse. It would appear that Māori continued to talk about Tiriti/Treaty because many understood it as offering a partnership where they would be equals (Kawharu, 2003) with their autonomy intact (Durie, 1996) when the British Crown used it to claim land and kill those who opposed such moves. As such, colonization was not progressive for Māori but a violence done to their differences from the colonizers (Bell, 1996) contentiously referred to as a holocaust (Turia, 2000, cited by Morgan et al., 2006).

Notwithstanding that this separation into either colonizer or Māori is an oversimplification and contested, it still forms the basis for much contemporary policy-making. Since the 1970s, there have been actions on the part of the Aotearoa/New Zealand Government giving greater recognition to Māori concerns particularly in relation to the Tiriti/Treaty. The 1975 Treaty of Waitangi Act recognized the Tiriti/Treaty in Aotearoa/New Zealand law by establishing a tribunal for considering transgressions of the agreement. The Waitangi Tribunal was open to much criticism because it could only consider events after 1975 even though the Tiriti/Treaty had been signed 135 years earlier. Yet even in those cases that the tribunal could hear, it could merely recommend rather than enforce solutions. The 1984–90 Labour Government started openly promoting biculturalism, purportedly legitimizing Māori concerns as policy issues (Wilson and Yeatman, 1995).

More recently, a health policy from the Aotearoa/New Zealand Ministry of Health (2001) incorporated the principles of partnership, participation and protection between Māori and the British Crown in an explicit reference to the Tiriti/Treaty. Nevertheless, this policy was a strategy for Māori health, which would seem to limit these principles somewhat to matters of Māori concern instead of, for example, seeing them as relevant for how everyone provides for and deals with their health. Furthermore, the Ministry of Health's advocation of the three Ps (partnership, participation and protection) looks more like paternalism because they were developed in the absence of negotiation with Māori about what they might mean or how they could be implemented (Morgan et al., 2006).

Cultural splitting

It is possible to make comparisons between the cultural context of Aotearoa/New Zealand and conceptualizations in Kleinian psychoanalysis where a subject splits complex reality. Let us explain by introducing a little of the work of Melanie Klein.

Kleinian psychoanalysis provides a model of early infanthood that attempts to theorize how, from the very first few months of life, children develop a sense of themselves and the world around them. Over her lifetime, Klein presented a two-stage developmental model where dealing with the first stage (the paranoid-schizoid position; Klein, [1946] 1986) allows the infant to move onto the second (the depressive position; Klein, [1930] 1986). That is, as the first stage is negotiated the concerns and attempts to deal with the second gradually become more important (Klein, [1946] 1986). Klein's development of the depressive position was the start of her journey away from classical psychoanalysis (Hinshelwood, 1991b) although it still relied heavily on Freudian notions of the formation of a self or 'ego', primarily through the Oedipus complex. Drawing upon the work of Fairbairn (1941, [1944] 1952, [1946] 1952), Klein subsequently turned to develop the paranoid-schizoid position and ended up challenging Freudian ideas of ego development because she argued that there was a stage prior and prerequisite – or propaedeutic – to the depressive position. While the 'paranoid-schizoid position' is a 'stage' in infant development and its resolution will affect the infant throughout its life (Klein, [1946] 1986; Laplanche and Pontalis, 1983), Klein preferred the term 'position' in her latter work to emphasize that it is something that the adult will come to again and again. In this chapter, we have insufficient space for detailed exploration of the depressive position, so we will keep our focus on the paranoid-schizoid position.

In the first stage, the infant interacts with the outside world and slowly develops a sense of self, of an outside world and of relationships between the two (specifically, between the self and objects in the world; Klein, [1946] 1986). The infant will therefore have overlapping experiences of both its inner (psychic) and outer worlds. Klein draws particularly upon the gratification of feeding from the mother's breast and the frustration when it is taken away (or merely absent). We can imagine that as an infant feeds, hunger is removed and it sees a connection between the experience of itself as gratified and the contiguous cornucopia of sights, smells, sounds, tastes and touches that we know of as the breast. For Klein, this as-yet unnamed 'good object' (the breast) is taken (*introjected*) into the infant's psychic world and helps it to integrate its experiences of itself and the world into a coherent identity (Klein, [1946] 1986). We can imagine too, that when the breastfeeding ends, the infant's experiences of the world change; it may be uncomfortable with the new movement, become cold or still be a little hungry. The infant may connect these new experiences with the breast, so that it is experienced as if it is under attack (from an as-yet unnamed 'bad object') (Klein, [1930] 1986). Fearing that it is under attack from the breast, the infant may be unable to maintain the introjections that was helping it to develop a coherent identity, and its fragile self falls apart and it feels as if it is 'in bits' (Emanuel, 2000; Klein, [1946] 1986, p. 184). Differentiating between the gratifying and persecutory aspects (hence, the good and bad object) of its experiences in relation to the breast (*splitting*), is one way in which the infant can deal with the anxiety and therefore continue to develop a coherent identity. Indeed, splitting allows the infant to exaggerate (*idealize*) the good aspects and imagine 'an inexhaustible and always bountiful breast' (Klein, [1946] 1986, p. 182). It is these anxieties of persecution and attempts to manage (e.g. introjection, splitting and idealization) them that define the paranoid-schizoid position.

Returning to Aotearoa/New Zealand, we can compare a number of binary cultural separations – between Pākehā and Māori, colonizer and colonized, state and subject – with the Kleinian splitting. This helps us to consider two alternative but complementary notions.

First, Pākehā and Māori are part of the same object. Not only do Pākehā and Māori constitute the population of Aotearoa/New Zealand but they also share attributes usually associated with only one of them. While Māori have an oral tradition, the written words of Pākehā are open to discussion, negotiation and reconstruction. Additionally, Pākehā are the colonizers although Māori have a number of migration stories (Craig, 1989) recounting how they left their homeland and found the land of the 'Aotearoa' (long-white-cloud).

Second, the population of Aotearoa/New Zealand is multiple and complex; that is, the split between Pākehā and Māori fails to represent adequately the complexity of Aotearoa/New Zealand life. There are, for example, people seeking asylum, immigrants from other Australasian countries, and tourists who do not easily fit into these categories and yet are recognized and marginalized by institutional structures in various ways. Furthermore, people do contest designations as Pākehā or Māori. If we were to name someone Pākehā, he or she could be offended. The term 'Māori' is applied so widely that it inaccurately represents a large unified cultural group whereas there is much variation. Indeed, some would reject the designation 'Māori'. Nevertheless, separations between Pākehā and Māori are dominant in political and social life in ways indicative of Kleinian splitting (and we shall illustrate more of the New Zealand contexts throughout this chapter).

In making a comparison between Aotearoa/Zealand life and the concept of splitting, we are making a conceptual shift from the infant of Kleinian analysis and theory, to the level of groups. While this is a complex shift, we would argue that there is interplay and mimicking between individuals and groups. The practices of mind (such as introjection, splitting and idealization) effect the interaction between individuals and hence the constitution and action of groups. Furthermore, the practices of groups effect the development of identity and the sense an individual has of the world around them. In shifting from individuals to groups, we mean more than the collection of individuals, which we signal by using the word 'culture'.

Culture

Culture can be conceptualized as occurring at some, or all, of a number of different levels: the cross-cultural, intra- and interpersonal (Price-Williams et al., 2002) and supra-individual (Smith et al., 2002). Alternatively, culture can be conceptualized as some type of meaning, such as the meaning of emic concepts or the differences between the meanings of concepts (Triandis et al., 2002). These two conceptions of culture – culture *occurring at different levels* and culture *as meaning* – are not mutually exclusive and we may combine them for a broad understanding of culture as shared meaning, which has three particular implications for the study of culture.

First, it is through language that meaning is made and therefore language should be the object of the study of meaning (Phoenix, 2004). Psychology has been developing its use of discursive methods since a turn-to-language in social science during the 1980s (e.g. Henriques et al., 1984; Hollway, 1989) although the detailed study of words and what they mean has long been a concern of psychoanalysis. Discursive methods focus on what we do with language (Potter and Wetherell, 1987) and what language does to us (Parker, 1992). Take, for example, a shared understanding of 'family' as private and something that requires protection from government intrusion. Such a sentiment would seem to be expressed in the saying 'an Englishman's home is his castle', which is not a mere meaning without material importance but one of the basic concepts of English common law (Morris and Morris, 1988). This sentiment is also evident in the US Constitution's Bill of Rights where citizens have a right to be secure in their homes from unreasonable interference from the government.

Second, while meaning may be made through language, the failure to make meaning may be just as important (Frosh, 1999, 2001). For example, introducing oneself as a psychologist may result in the oft-made statement, 'so you can read my mind then'. For the psychologist, being seen as having an ability to read minds may be a misunderstanding but is more than likely part of the shared meaning of psychology. What is important in this example is that the misunderstanding, the failure to be adequately identified, could be part of the shared meaning of what it is to be a psychologist. Psychoanalysis offers many different ways, such as repression, to understand how things are a) not done and b) still have effects in group dynamics (Bion, 1955) and institutions (Jacques, 1951, 1955). The seminal work of Menzies Lyth (1988) is particularly apt because it suggests that the repetitive, structured nature of the work of nurses can be understood as the enactment of a cultural defence mechanism that allows nurses to maintain a safe emotional distance from the anxiety of dealing with illness and death, but which leaves many of them dissatisfied with their working environment.

Third, understanding shared meaning as something that is made – discursively, psychoanalytically or psycho-discursively – provides a focus on the processes and practices through which a particular meaning becomes shared and, by implication, through which other meanings are not shared. While a broad concept of culture as shared meaning means that many cultures can co-exist as people take up and live multiple shared meanings, it does not mean that all meaning can become culture, that all meaning will be shared. For example, in the 1840 founding document (Te Tiriti o Waitangi/The Treaty of Waitangi) of Aotearoa/New Zealand, the English version accedes 'sovereignty' to the British Crown whereas the Māori version protects *tino rangatiratanga*. Both English and Māori translations of The Treaty of Waitangi continue to be a focus where cultural meaning making occurs, particularly over the meaning and relative juxtapositions of sovereignty and *tino rangatiratanga* over ownership of land, foreshore and seabed (Tuffin, 2004). It would seem prudent to provide a definition of *tino rangatiratanga* but the point is that any accepted definition, as well as an accepted definition of sovereignty, would be a cultural meaning that precludes another possible meaning or meanings.

As a country where different (mis)understandings or conflicting shared meaning have led to, for example, mass bloodshed in the seizure of land, Aotearoa/New Zealand is perhaps the *nec plus ultra* or most extreme example where symbolic differences have resulted in material violence. Compared to the treaty, *Te Rito* is a more mundane and recent illustration of the dynamics in Aotearoa/New Zealand.

Te Rito

Te Rito, Aotearoa/New Zealand's key family violence policy (Ministry of Social Development, 2002), is an important policy in the social psychological domain because it operationalizes a pivotal international civil rights initiative and comes from a country with a recent history of model domestic violence legislation. Aotearoa/New Zealand, along with 60 other countries, has ratified (Office of the High Commissioner for Human Rights, 2004) the Convention on the Elimination of All Forms of Discrimination against Women (CEDAW), and, like, for example, England, India and the USA (except Louisiana), has a system of common law. In such a system, parliament makes law and the judiciary interpret it. Should a judge find a law to contravene, for example, CEDAW, they may ignore that law and make their findings in light of CEDAW. Having ratified CEDAW, Aotearoa/New Zealand is required to report, at least every four years, to the committee on the elimination of discrimination against women (CEDAW) on the measures adopted to effect CEDAW. In their fifth periodic report (considered at the 29th session of CEDAW, 2003), the Aotearoa/New Zealand Minister for Women's Affairs presented *Te Rito* as a landmark strategy to implement CEDAW.

Aotearoa/New Zealand is also a world leader in domestic violence work. Aotearoa/New Zealand was the first to develop domestic violence specific legislation, the Domestic Violence Act 1995 (DVA), which makes provision for the protection of victims[2] (through civil protection orders) and attempts to treat perpetrators (through court orders to attend anti-violence programmes). Indeed, the UK's domestic violence legislation, the Domestic Violence, Crime and Victims Act 2004 (DVCA), mimics the DVA's use of protection orders and anti-violence programmes while deliberately opposing the creation of a piece of legislation specific to domestic violence. The Bradford Reducing Anger and Violent Emotions (BRAVE) project is apposite as a small, local, anti-violence programme in the north of England, which is informed by Aotearoa/New Zealand violence prevention work with boys and young men (Dominey, 2006). In the USA, the Leitner Center for International Law and Justice at Fordam Law School in New York sent out a delegation of 11 to review the Aotearoa/New Zealand legislation, producing a lengthy and critical report (2009). Consequently, *Te Rito* is a policy that many other countries have been looking to as a model for the implementation of CEDAW.

Consequently, *Te Rito* is not just about violence but is an attempt to do something in relation to family violences in Aotearoa/New Zealand. It is in and through the text of the policy that the sharing and not sharing of meanings will have material effects. Specifically, we shall argue that we can make comparisons between *Te Rito* and the *paranoid-schizoid position* proposed by Klein ([1946] 1986).

Splitting

In the following extract, taken from the introduction of *Te Rito*, family is constructed as both victim and perpetrator of violence:

> Extract 1: Family violence in Aotearoa/New Zealand is a *significant social issue*. It directly affects the well-being of families/*whānau* and the extent to which they can participate in society. It creates high personal costs for those affected and significant social and economic costs to society as a whole [includes reference to footnote given in Extract 2]. (p. 6; emphasis in original)

The importance of family violence is asserted as a social, and therefore not simply private, problem (first sentence, Extract 1). The presentation of this statement as unquestioned acts as a counter to the ideological separation of public (social) and private (personal) space. The next sentence in Extract 1 adds to this by noting that it is the families' well-being that is damaged. The later part of the sentence then suggests that a family with well-being is one that can participate in society. Each successive line of text serves to clarify, retroactively, that which came before and the policy asserts that the good in a family lies with its societal participation. What exactly these participative functions are is depicted as the text turns to describe what is so bad about family. In the third sentence, family violence is presented as something that creates costs: personal, social and economic. However, as with participation, costs are never specified. Their specification is developed through the opposition of costs and participation. Hence, the understanding of each is created in a circle of meaning; costs are losses in participation, be that personal, social or economic, and participation is the lack of costs. Yet, the term 'costs' favours what is often called an 'economic metaphor' (Bracker and Herbrechter, 2005). That is, cost is an active giving or surrendering of something for something else. It is the price paid to acquire something, or have it produced or maintained. Participation is therefore constructed as a finite means of exchange. Violence is paid for with participation. However, violence is bad because it costs; because it squanders this means of exchange. Consequently, the absence of violence means that participation can continue and accumulate: wealth can be created. Family is good when its participation leads to the continued creation of wealth (well-being/wealth-being) but bad when it frustrates that.

Te Rito refers explicitly to money and the following is a footnote to Extract 1, above, presented as an aside to the main text:

> Extract 2: [*footnote to* Extract 1] *For example, Suzanne Snively's 1994 study*[,][3] *New Zealand Economic Cost of Family Violence*[,] *conservatively estimated the potential economic cost of family violence at* [*NZ*]$1.2 billion *a year.* (p. 7)

The 1.2 billion was indeed Snively's (1994) most conservative estimate with an upper limit of over 10 billion. This is compared to the one and two and a half billion made in wool and forestry exports respectively; however, in *Te Rito* there is no attempt to make the 1.2 billion reported understandable to the reader. It is presented as an unimaginably large amount and the point is clear: Family Violence costs *a lot!* of money. Hence, the emphasis of the good family moves from the absence of violence to the accumulation of wealth. Some, particularly Connor (2005), relate such metaphors of economy to a Freudian notion of the libido in attempts to go beyond a generalized economic perspective but for here it is enough to point out that the economics of exchange are privileged over preventing family violence.

The textual presence of the good and bad family in *Te Rito* is certainly indicative of the Kleinian concept of splitting ([1946] 1986) but alone is insufficient to justify our reading. Nevertheless, there is a subtle difference in wording that adds greater weight to comparing *Te Rito* with splitting: the use of the word '*whānau*' and its presence or absence alongside the word 'family'. 'Family/*whānau*' is a combination used in *Te Rito* that is part of a practice of combining, in a gesture of biculturalism, Māori and New Zealand English languages to signify difference, for example the different names for the country 'Aotearoa/New Zealand'. In the case of 'family/*whānau*', both terms name the smallest unit of kinship relationship recognized by the respective cultures. Nevertheless, Te Puni Kōkiri, a government body concerned with Māori affairs, argues (2004) that the mere citation of family and *whānau* together does not evoke difference and the two words in *Te Rito* can be '*viewed as the same constructs with different languages used to describe them'* (p. 12). The implication is that *whānau* is Māori for family. However, in *Te Rito* it is not used as if the interchange between the two can be taken for granted. In fact, where *Te Rito* names violence, *whānau* is omitted. In the title of *Te Rito* (New Zealand *Family Violence* Prevention Strategy), as well as in the following extracts, Family Violence is named without recourse to the term *whānau*:

> Extract 3: Family violence is a major issue affecting the lives of far too many New Zealanders. (p. 3)

> Extract 4: [T]he *effects* of family violence on individuals, families/*whānau*, communities and society as a whole are *wide ranging and multidimensional*. (p. 9; emphasis in original)

In both extracts, 'family violence' is used as a name for certain violences and relations. Where family and *whānau* are combined, violence is left out as something separate. In the following extract, violence is internal to family/*whānau* – it is 'in' and 'within' – but it is still something other.

> Extract 5: [V]iolence in families/*whānau* further contributes to the continuation of violence within families/*whānau* and in society in general. (p. 9)

It is difficult to read the presence or absence of the word *whānau* alongside the 'family' as a stylistic attempt to use different words throughout the policy document because it appears so strategic. *Whānau* is only absent when family is used to name violence, which suggests an unconscious process of splitting family. Admittedly, the mere presence of good and bad is insufficient because splitting occurs to preserve a sense of good/defend against something bad. In the next step, we get a sense that something is being preserved/defended against.

Idealization

There is only one place where *whānau* is not separated from violence, which will help introduce the next step, from splitting to idealization. In the 'Area of action 5', the 'plan of action for preventing violences in Māori communities', *whānau* is used to name violence (p. 26). *Te Rito* refers to a report by Te Puni Kōkiri entitled *Whānau Violence* (2004).

Hence, *whānau* and violence are only combined as a noun when the focus is Māori. Family is left out and *whānau* used as a concept peculiar to Māori. Had family and *whānau* been combined it would have continued to construct them as bilingual synonyms, as names, from different languages, for the same construct. However, family is absent and *whānau* is left open to meanings outside of this text. That is, *Whānau Violence* is the domain of Māori and *whānau* may mean something different to family. Yet in family/*whānau*, *whānau* is family.

We would suggest that it is possible to read the use of family/*whānau* as a form of cultural domination that assumes a fundamental similarity in the reference point of the two signifiers, family and *whānau*, but which privileges the first. In addition, through the splitting of family/*whānau*, *Te Rito* is avoiding conscious awareness of the implication that if *whānau* is to mean family, then it must also mean family violence. That is, splitting makes idealization possible and preserves a sense of goodness about family. From a Kleinian perspective, the splitting and idealization suggests that *Te Rito* is anxious about the possibility that, by suggesting that Māori are, or can be, violent, they will be denigrating Māori. That is, that *Te Rito* wants to avoid *appearing* racist or colonialist. Domestic violence is recognized to be an issue for Māori in a number of places and this is frequently done by also considering the violence British colonization of Aotearoa/New Zealand has done to Māori, for example in a report from Te Puni Kōkiri (e.g. 2004) and in Māori theological writing (Shirres, 1994). However, *Te Rito* appears deliberately to avoid discussing British colonialism or Māori violence, and we consider this later.

Family/*whānau* divides the people that *Te Rito* concerns itself with into two separate cultures, and idealization (Klein, [1946] 1986) occurs in the representation of Māori. Each word calls forth its own language: family is English and echoes Aotearoa/New Zealand's colonial roots in Europe. New Zealand English is a language of European descent and its people may be called Pākehā. Wetherell and Potter (1992) define Pākehā as white New Zealanders, and Shouksmith (2005) calls Pākehā non-indigenous New Zealanders, although 'Pākehā' is a contested term which would be rejected by many white New Zealanders. The word Pākehā mixes skin colour, historical origins, belonging (to New Zealand), and responsibility for a colonial past, present and future (for a fuller exploration see Ranford, 2003). The implication with both uses is that Pākehā is a Māori name for a group of people and a name that Others them. However, the practices utilized in developing *Te Rito* – focus groups, prevention strategy, report writing and publication – culminate in a New Zealand English written language document.[4] That is, *Te Rito* is Pākehā and its use of the word *whānau* calls forth Māori as a language and a people that is Other.

The forward slash between family and *whānau* further separates, showing Pākehā and Māori to be different, divided. It is a dualistic practice that constructs two cultures as distinct and yet offers the possibility of merging – or recognizing that they were the same in the first place. Yet this is contested, with Te Puni Kōkiri arguing that 'using these terms synonymously in social policy indicates that they are...not well understood' (2004, p. 12). *Whānau* is (re)presented as a Māori language word, for which Te Puni Kōkiri claim ownership and the power to define. At the same time, they disown the use of *whānau* in *Te Rito*. Recognizing that *whānau*, like any other word, may have multiple meanings is important. Rather than trying to seek a correct interpretation from Māori to English, the point is to consider how its meaning is constructed in *Te Rito*. In *Te Rito, whānau* is a signifier for two signifieds: (a) Māori, a culture split from Pākehā by the binary Othering processes of the English language, and (b) family, a Pākehā concept. *Whānau* summons up Māori but is collapsed back into Pākehā, to signify *family*.

It is difficult to understand Klein's concept of splitting without also drawing upon idealization ([1946] 1986). When an object is split, the good part, lacking anything bad, is easily idealized. For example, the breast that only gratifies would seem to offer unlimitless love and nourishment. The use of *whānau* in *Te Rito* ties family in with Māori where *whānau*, split from the violent family, is the violence-free family for which *Te Rito*, as policy, is aiming. The point is that, as *whānau* collapses back into Pākehā, to signify *family*, it retains a link to Māori as a culture where there is violence-free family. Hence, Māori in *Te Rito* can be read as having families that live free from violence. That is, Māori are idealized and in a postcolonial country idealization is a process through which the colonial subject can be denied full agency under the pretence that they are no longer colonized (see e.g. Fanon, 1963).

Introjection

The development of *Te Rito* was one that used a collaborative approach and there is an account of this process in *Te Rito*, which presents collaboration in terms of an extended family/*whānau*. A Family Violence Focus Group (FVFG) was established from organizations within and outside of government in order to produce the document:

Extract 6: The strategy has been developed by government and non-government agencies working together in partnership. There has also been significant input from a wide range of individuals and different sectors in the communities ... Continuing and building on these relationships are integral to achieving the strategy's vision, goals and objectives. (p. 3)

The lead body and publisher of *Te Rito* is the Ministry of Social Development (MSD), but many more government ministries and departments were involved. These included those for criminal justice, education, health, women, Pacific Islanders, Māori, and children, youth and family, as well as internal affairs, which, in this case, were the treasury, ethnic affairs and accident compensation. Non-governmental organizations (NGOs) included charities and collectives providing refuges, rape crisis, relationship counselling, support for children and elder adults, and services to help perpetrators change. In addition, interviews and community workshops were conducted to feed into the policy development. The FVFG's aim was to establish strategy for government and to do so by involving all that may, in the end, help implement that strategy. *Te Rito* presents the relations between the organizations as harmonious and egalitarian:

Extract 7: The strategy is a product of the positive, collaborative working relationship between government and non-government organizations. (p. 54)

Consequently, *whānau*, the idealized violence-free family, is introjected (Klein, [1946] 1986) into *Te Rito* as a way of doing public policy. Introjection is similar to identification, in which an object – the characteristics of another – is taken within the self. However, introjection is also, for Klein, a defence mechanism to deal with a hostile internal world (Hinshelwood, 1991a; Klein, [1946] 1986). For example, Klein theorizes that the infant experiences the drinking of breast milk, in a process of introjection, as the replacement of the hunger (the bad internal object) with the good mother (the external good object). As such, it is important to consider signs of disharmony that would question the idealization and internalization of *whānau*.

Te Puni Kōkiri was part of the FVFG that put *Te Rito* together, yet they still denounced the use of *whānau* in *whānau*/family in this document (Te Puni Kōkiri, 2004). This, or indeed any conflict, is absent from the written document of *Te Rito*. The following extract, like the last sentence in Extract 6, shows the relations between the diverse groups in the FVFG group to be essential to the continued and successful formation of *Te Rito*:

> Extract 8: Principle 6: *Approaches to family violence prevention must be integrated, co-ordinated and collaborative*: Cross-sectoral co-ordination, collaboration and communication are essential to providing an integrated and comprehensive approach to family violence prevention. (p. 13; emphasis in original, which is used for the title of all nine principles)

Te Puni Kōkiri's disagreement about the use of *whānau* in *Te Rito* suggests the policy-making group is not free from violent relations. Rather, it would appear that the policy-making of *Te Rito* is like the policy's object (family), which is both good (violence free) and bad (violent). Indeed, *Te Rito*, in terms of both process and product, is like a family who keeps its violences hidden (see Fahey, 1995).

Equating such disagreement with violence is deliberate. Domestic violence is more than physical assault and covers a continuum (Kelly, 1988) including insidious and often repeated actions such as jokes. *Te Rito's* use of *whānau* as if it is synonymous with family – while presenting the policy process as harmonious – can therefore be interpreted as an act of violence. At the very least, it does suggest that *Te Rito's* presentation of the relations between the organizations as harmonious is untenable. It may be that the discussion of the meanings of *whānau* was not deemed significant or relevant enough to be included in *Te Rito*. Nevertheless, for Te Puni Kōkiri (2004), it was important enough to disagree with *Te Rito's* use of *whānau* in their framework for *whānau* violence. The domination over the meaning of *whānau* in *Te Rito* would seem to be a symbolic violence in which Māori are idealized and where discussion of violences done to Māori through colonialism and acts of the Aotearoa/New Zealand government are actively avoided.

Conclusions

As the analysis in this chapter has focused on a policy text, it is somewhat at odds with the Māori oral tradition where decision-making occurs through dialogue. The implications of this can be seen in the importance given to a document by Te Puni Kōkiri to demonstrate conflict over the meaning of *whānau*. Te Puni Kōkiri is a ministry of the Aotearoa/New Zealand Government and as such part of its work includes the production of reports. The first implication is that it could appear as if Te Puni Kōkiri represents all Māori but this would inaccurately present a unified singular cultural group. Second, it would seem as if Te Puni Kōkiri were the only member of the FVFG representing Māori views, whereas it is possible that Māori considerations were brought up by other FVFG members. Last, we are aware that our interpretation is that a Pākehā perspective dominated the FVFG and that we base this on an analysis of policy documents that are largely a product of a Pākehā (white colonial) culture. At this point it is important to remember that the split between Pākehā and Māori is a cultural representation of something that is much more complex and therefore that we should expect any product of Aotearoa/New Zealand, including policy documents, to include a mixture of cultures. Consequently, Te Puni Kōkiri have been utilized because they presented views that were different to those in *Te Rito*. Nevertheless, future research would do well to avoid a sole focus on textual sources (see Parker and Bolton Discourse Network, 1999), particularly when dealing with oral traditions, and should certainly consider the benefits that strategies for developing cultural sensitivity in research could offer to engaging with culture and language (see Tuhiwai Smith, 1999).

It may be possible to stay within the theoretical confines utilized in this chapter to suggest a resolution to the anxiety we argue is located around family in *Te Rito*. The response suggested by questioning *Te Rito* for hiding conflict in the process of its development seems to be greater openness about the struggles of policy development. For Klein (1935), being able to deal with anxiety in such a way would suggest a progression from the paranoid-schizoid to the depressive position. This position is depressive because the good, idealized object is recognized to be also the bad object, that is, that objects contain both good and bad features and the idealized object is therefore lost. In the case of *Te Rito*, this would mean working with a complex, but perhaps more realistic, concept of family and of relating (see e.g. Barrett and McIntosh, 1982) and, specifically, a view of family/*whānau* that, despite colonial oppression, can recognize violence. Indeed, the collaboration conducted in the process of developing *Te Rito* appears a serious attempt to consult relevant organizations and individuals to develop policy – in contrast to the more trite, and perhaps more common, process of consulting after policy is developed (Maynard and Wood, 2002). Unfortunately, the depressive position risks apathy, as it implies that families are inherently both good and bad and that the attempt to eradicate violence is futile. Yet the strength of the Kleinian depressive position is its realism in being able to bring the good and bad together even if this does not leave one feeling especially happy. For domestic violence policy generally, particularly where connected to international human rights initiatives, such as the Convention on the Elimination of All Forms of Discrimination against Women (CEDAW), this is an important point. It means that policies are challenged to engage with cultural contexts, such as ethnicity or colonialism, or the possibility that idealization is another form of colonial control. In Aotearoa/New Zealand this would mean that colonialism is given greater weight in domestic violence policy rather than being limited to Māori-only policy.

Acknowledgements

We are grateful to anonymous reviewers for comments on this chapter. Earlier drafts of the analysis in this essay were presented at seminars at the 19th International Congress on Law and Mental Health, Paris, 2005, and the Institute of Psychological Sciences, University of Leeds, UK, 2005. Versions of the methodological and theoretical work in this essay were presented at a departmental seminar at the School of Psychology, Massey University, Aotearoa/New Zealand, 2004, and the 3rd International Interdisciplinary Conference on Sex and Gender, Wrocław, Poland, 2004. We would like to thank attendees for their feedback. We are also grateful to the UK Economic and Social Research Council (ESRC) for an overseas fieldwork grant which supported this research.

Notes

1. Te Tiriti/Treaty is an agreement between the British Crown and 540 Māori rangatira/chiefs that was officially 'signed' on 6 February 1840 in Waitangi. The British had been settling in Aotearoa/New Zealand since the 1830s and their government reluctantly realized that annexing the country would help to secure their commercial interests and allow them to regulate the settlers' unruly behaviour. The Treaty was written in English, then translated into Māori, and debated for a day and a half before the first 40 signatures were given on 6 February. The British declared sovereignty on 21 May 1840 while an additional 500 rangatira/chiefs signed copies that circulated around the country (although some refused or had no chance to sign). There are important differences in the meaning between the translations, which have long been debated, but the Māori interpretations were largely ignored until the 1975 Treaty of Waitangi Act recognized Te Tiriti/Treaty as a constitutional document (Morgan et al., 2006; Pryor, 2007).
2. Consistent with the terminology of government policy, this chapter utilizes legal terms that lack gender specificity. We acknowledge that gender-neutral terms mask how domestic violence is gendered.

3. The square brackets are used to show that we are editing the quote. In this case, we are adding punctuation to make the quote easier to read.
4. Providing a translation of the report would miss the point because many of those that see themselves as Māori have an oral (rather than written) tradition.

References

Barrett, M. and McIntosh, M. (1982). *The Anti-social Family*. London: Verso.
Bell, A. (1996). We're just New Zealanders: Pakeha identity politics. In P. Spoonley, D. Pearson and C. Macpherson (eds), *Nga Patai: Racism and Ethnic Relations in Aotearoa/New Zealand*. Palmerston North, New Zealand: Dunmore Press, pp. 144–58.
Bion, W. R. (1955). Group dynamics: A re-view. In M. Klein, P. Heimann and R. E. Money-Kyrle (eds), *New Directions in Psychoanalysis: The Significance of Infant Conflict in the Pattern of Adult Behaviour*. London: Tavistock Publications, pp. 440–77.
Bracker, N. and Herbrechter, S. (eds) (2005). *Metaphors of Economy*. Amsterdam: Rodopi.
Connor, S. (2005). Destitution. In N. Bracker and S. Herbrechter (eds), *Metaphors of Economy*. Amsterdam: Rodopi, pp. 9–26.
Craig, R. D. (1989). *Dictionary of Polynesian Mythology*. New York: Greenwood Press.
Dominey, S. (2006). *Winston Churchill Fellowship 2005: Research Carried Out in New Zealand and Australia: 'Violence Prevention Work With Boys and Young Men'*. Bradford: BRAVE.
Durie, E. T. (1996). Viewpoint: Taku titiro – Waitangi Day Address, Wellington, 6th February. *He Pukenga Kōrero*, 1(2), 8–10.
Emanuel, R. (2000). *Anxiety*. Cambridge: Icon Books.
Fahey, T. (1995). Privacy and the family: Conceptual and empirical reflections. *Sociology*, 29(4), 687–702.
Fairbairn, W. R. D. (1941). A revised psychopathology of the psychoses and psychoneuroses. *International Journal of Psycho-Analysis*, 22, 250–79.
Fairbairn, W. R. D. ([1944] 1952). Endopsychic structure considered in terms of object-relations. In *Psychoanalytic Studies of Personality*. London: Routledge & Kegan Paul, pp. 82–136.
Fairbairn, W. R. D. ([1946] 1952). Object-relations and dynamic structure. In *Psychoanalytic Studies of Personality*. London: Routledge & Kegan Paul, pp. 137–51.
Fanon, F. (1963). *The Wretched of the Earth*. New York: Grove Press.
Frosh, S. (1999). What is outside discourse? *Psychoanalytic Studies*, 1, 381–90.
Frosh, S. (2001). Things that can't be said: Psychoanalysis and the limits of language. *International Journal of Critical Psychology*, 1, 28–46.
Henriques, J., Hollway, W., Urwin, C., Venn, C. and Walkerdine, V. (1984). *Changing the Subject: Psychology, Social Regulation and Subjectivity*. London: Methuen.
Hinshelwood, R. D. (1991a). *A Dictionary of Kleinian Thought*. London: Free Association Books.

Hinshelwood, R. D. (1991b). Paranoid schizoid position. In *A Dictionary of Kleinian Thought*. London: Free Association Books, pp. 156–66.

Hollway, W. (1989). *Subjectivity and Method in Psychology: Gender, Meaning, and Science*. London: Sage.

Jacques, E. (1951). *The Changing Culture of a Factory*. London: Tavistock Publications.

Jacques, E. (1955). Social systems as a defence against persecutory and depressive anxiety. In M. Klein, P. Heimann and R. E. Money-Kyrle (eds), *New Directions in Psycho-Analysis: The Significance of Infant Conflict in the Pattern of Adult Behaviour*. London: Tavistock Publications, pp. 478–98.

Kawharu, I. H. (2003). *Conflict and Compromise: Essays on the Maori since Colonisation*. Auckland, New Zealand: Reed.

Kelly, L. (1988). *Surviving Sexual Violence*. London: Polity Press.

Klein, M. (1935). A contribution to the psychogenesis of manic-depressive states. In *The Writings of Melanie Klein*, vol. 1: *Love, Guilt and Reparation and Other Works 1921–1945*. London: Hogarth Press, pp. 262–89.

Klein, M. ([1930] 1986). The importance of symbol formation in the development of the ego. In J. Mitchell (ed.), *The Selected Melanie Klein*. London: Penguin, pp. 95–111.

Klein, M. ([1946] 1986). Notes on some schizoid mechanisms. In J. Mitchell (ed.), *The Selected Melanie Klein*. London: Penguin, pp. 175–200.

Laplanche, J. and Pontalis, J. B. (1983). *The Language of Psychoanalysis*. London: Hogarth Press and the Institute of Psycho-analysis.

Leitner Center for International Law and Justice (2009). *'It's Not OK': New Zealand's Efforts to Eliminate Violence against Women*. New York: Fordham Law School.

Maynard, K. and Wood, B. (2002). Tatou tatou – working together: A model for government/non-government collaboration. *Social Policy Journal of New Zealand*, 18, 79–91.

Menzies Lyth, I. (1988). *Containing Anxiety in Institutions: Selected Essays*. London: Free Association Press.

Ministry of Health (2001). *He Korowai Oranga: Maori Health Strategy*. Wellington, New Zealand: Ministry of Health.

Ministry of Social Development (2002). *Te Rito: New Zealand Family Violence Prevention Strategy*. Wellington, New Zealand: Ministry of Social Development.

Morgan, M., Coombes, L. and Campbell, B. (2006). Biculturalism, gender and critical social movements in Aotearoa/New Zealand: Still speaking from psychologies' margins. *Annual Review of Critical Psychology*, 5, www.discourseunit.com/arcp/5.

Morris, W. and Morris, M. (1988). *Dictionary of Word and Phrase Origins*. New York: Harper & Row.

Office of the United Nations High Commissioner for Human Rights (2004). *Status of Ratifications of the Principal International Human Rights Treaties*. Office of the High Commissioner for Human Rights, UN.

Parker, I. (1992). *Discourse Dynamics: Critical Analysis for Social and Individual Psychology*. London: Routledge.

Parker, I. and Bolton Discourse Network (1999). *Critical Textwork: An Introduction to Varieties of Discourse and Analysis*. Buckingham: Open University Press.

Phoenix, A. (2004). Extolling eclecticism: Language, psychoanalysis and demographic analyses in the study of 'race' and racism. In M. Bulmer and J. Solomos (eds), *Researching Race and Racism*. London: Routledge, pp. 37–51.

Potter, J. and Wetherell, M. (1987). *Discourse and Social Psychology: Beyond Attitudes and Behaviour*. London: Sage.

Price-Williams, D. R., Lonner, W. J., Dinnel, D. A., Hayes, S. A. and Sattler, D. N. (2002). Cross-, intra-, inter-, and just plain cultural. In *Online Readings in Psychology and Culture*. http://orpc.iaccp.org/index.php?option=com_content&view=article&id=8%3Aprice-williams&catid=3%3Achapter&Itemid=2.

Pryor, J. (2007). 'The treaty always speaks': Reading the Treaty of Waitangi/Te Tiriti O Waitangi. In *Constitutions: Writing Nations, Reading Difference*. London: Birkbeck Law Press, pp. 85–124.

Ranford, J. (2003). Pakeha: Its origin and meaning. www.maorinews.com/writings/papers/other/pakeha.htm.

Shirres, M. (1994). A Māori theological response to violence. *Colloquium of the Australian and New Zealand Theological Review*, 26(2), 94–103.

Shouksmith, G. (2005). Psychology in New Zealand. *The Psychologist*, 18(1), 14–16.

Smith, P. B., Lonner, W. J., Dinnel, D. A., Hayes, S. A. and Sattler, D. N. (2002). Levels of analysis in cross-cultural psychology. In *Online Readings in Psychology and Culture*. http://orpc.iaccp.org/index.php?option=com_content&view=article&id=73%3Apeter-b-smith&catid=3%3Achapter&Itemid=2.

Snively, S. L. (1994). *The New Zealand Economic Cost of Domestic Violence*. Wellington, New Zealand: Family Violence Unit, Department of Social Welfare.

Te Puni Kōkiri (2004). *Transforming Whānau Violence: A Conceptual Framework*. Wellington, New Zealand: Te Puni Kōkiri.

Triandis, H. C., Lonner, W. J., Dinnel, D. A., Hayes, S. A. and Sattler, D. N. (2002). Odysseus wandered for 10, I wondered for 50 years. In *Online Readings in Psychology and Culture*. http://orpc.iaccp.org/index.php?option=com_content&view=article&id=5%3Aodysseus-wandered-for-10-i-wondered-for-50-years&catid=3%3Achapter&Itemid=2.

Tuffin, K. (2004). Analysing a silent discourse: Sovereignty and tino rangatiratanga in Aotearoa. *New Zealand Journal of Psychology*, 33(2), 100–8.

Tuhiwai Smith, L. (1999). *Decolonizing Methodologies: Research and Indigenous Peoples*. Dunedin, Aotearoa/New Zealand: University of Otago Press.

Turia, T. (2000). Keynote speech. *New Zealand Psychological Society Conference*. 29 August, University of Waikato, Hamilton, New Zealand.

Wetherell, M. and Potter, J. (1992). *Mapping the Language of Racism: Discourse and the Legitimation of Exploitation*. London: Harvester Wheatsheaf.

Wilson, M. and Yeatman, A. (1995). *Justice and Identity: Antipodean Practices*. Wellington, New Zealand: Bridget Williams Books.

11
Maternal Publics: Time, Relationality and the Public Sphere

Lisa Baraitser

I took the image in Figure 11.1 on my mobile phone in the East End of London, on a familiar 'desire path' across an urban landscape between home and taking my kids to one of their endless after-school activities. In this case it was their karate class, somewhere on the border between the London Borough of Tower Hamlets and the London Borough of Hackney, where I have been living for the past 15 years. It is an area that has undergone dramatic gentrification recently, shifting from being characterized by extreme poverty, unemployment and socio-economic stagnation, to being an area in which those conditions still prevail, but now alongside, and somewhat veiled by, a throbbing middle-class street culture focused around the local park and a vibrant weekend organic farmers market. As I trampled along my desire path each week, children and equipment trailing behind me (quite literally, in the case of the white karate suit regularly dragging through the mud, and one red boxing glove already missing, abandoned irretrievably somewhere en route) I walked past this site, watching a derelict 'public house' going up for sale, watching no one buy it for years, and then eventually seeing a notice for planning permission for the development of 15 ubiquitous new apartments overlooking the park. The building was then partially demolished, and, for a brief period of time, one wall was left standing. It was during this moment that someone, or a group of someones, felt compelled to climb over the fence of the now privatized site and make this intervention. This was not a small job – not a passing act of graffiti with an aerosol. This would have needed tools, possibly noisy tools to cut these letters into the plaster of the remaining wall. It must have taken a considerable time to do – hours certainly, perhaps all night. The letters are over 2 metres high; the wall stretches for about 8 metres in length. It was a transitory intervention. I think of it as a scream: 'MOTHER' across the urban landscape, and a week later, it was gone.

Figure 11.1   MOTHER

Psychoanalysis in the age of globalization

One of the questions this volume raises is how we understand the significance of developments in the theoretical perspectives we loosely group together under the term 'psychoanalysis', especially through its cross-fertilization with social theory. This question, in its turn, raises the issue of how this evolving and heterogeneous set of perspectives can affect some critical leverage on an epoch defined as the 'age of globalization'. Our current age is variously characterized by post-Fordist immaterial labour (Hardt and Negri, 2000; Virno, 2004); precarity (Butler, 2004a); transnational migration; and the development of what Brian Holmes has termed 'flexible personality' (Holmes, 2008). The process by which the market has spread to every aspect of contemporary global life through co-optation of creativity, flexibility, mobility and cooperation – that is, the very stuff of the material practices of artists (Boltanski and Chiapello, 2005; Holmes, 2008; Rolnik, 2006) – could be seen as paradigmatic of the way capitalism absorbs the modes and practices of difference, opposition and resistance, and re-territorializes them for profit. 'Regeneration', for example, is a term that signals both the kinds of creative and generative practices of social and public art, and the workings of a market that creates middle-class enclaves that displace, but do not address, underlying poverty. The result, as Rosi Braidotti's cartography attests to, is a picture of the globalization process that extends beyond nation-states; is headless and centre-less, yet hegemonic; mobile and flexible, yet fixed and very local; inherently violent and therefore prone to self-destruction; and illogical and without an end-point, aiming only at self-perpetuation (Braidotti, 2004, 2006). It is a system that has produced 'the homogenization of commodity culture in terms of consumeristic practices, coupled with huge disparities and structural inequalities' (Braidotti, 2004).

Many agree that we have now entered a new phase of capitalism, one that we know little about. Saskia Sassen stated in 2006 that: 'the future we are entering may turn out to be very, very bad, or it may turn out to be reasonable. We don't know, partly because it will be shaped not only by technology and power but also by the dispossessed' (Sassen, 2006, unpaginated). But the chances of it turning out to be reasonable are difficult to hold onto in the light of the world financial crisis of 2008, and the real dangers of reaching the tipping point of climate change, making the tropes of newness, uncertainty, widening inequality, power, technology and the return of the dispossessed currently apt. What both Braidotti and Sassen focus on is the sheer complexity of current conditions, its inherent paradoxes, and the need for an almost myopic, detailed attention to the internal contradictions of this phase that must be constantly mapped and remapped. Braidotti, in particular, calls for adopting non-linearity in our critical cartographies, to match the non-linearity she sees in the web-like, scattered and poly-centred operations of neoliberal global capitalism.

Why evoke psychoanalysis to contribute to our understanding of this new era? The question might be framed as to whether psychoanalysis, with its insistence on myopic attention to singularity, its focus on the machinations of fantasy and desire, its championing of the non-linear,[1] and its very specific approach to temporality, can bring anything new to an understanding of these contemporary conditions. I want to state from the start that this is, and must remain, an open question. Whether or not psychoanalysis has something to offer to a social analytics cannot be assumed, and what it may have to offer as its theoretical propositions evolve must be constantly critically assessed. One of the contradictions inherent in turning to psychoanalysis as 'a way forward', for instance, is that one of its most important insights is the impossible paradox of the altogether new, as the workings of *Nachträglichkeit* clearly illustrates. *Nachträglichkeit* shows us the double temporal movement captured by combining both the English translation (deferred action) and the French (après coup), in which the developmentally later of two scenes gives retroactive meaning to an earlier repressed or very early unrepresentable scene (Faimberg, 2007), and the earlier scene renders the later scene both traumatic and understandable. Somewhere between anticipation (the 'already there' of the early scene) and assignment of retroactive meaning (the later scene), between the future and the past, is the present of the analytic session, of interpretation and the potential for psychic change. But it is a potential premised on this double movement as both past and future traverse the present-time of analysis, and not on the fantasy of the altogether new. In other words, psychoanalysis often struggles to accord the present a time of its own.

Another contradiction in turning to psychoanalysis in order to understand the present moment is that psychoanalysis not only offers a theory of melancholia (an account of what cannot be given up, that constitutes the ego through an accumulation of identifications with lost objects), but is itself a melancholic field. Although psychoanalysis does continue to revise its theoretical and practice base, although it evolves and develops, and in this sense we could articulate a 'contemporary psychoanalysis' that might be up to the task of understanding 'contemporary conditions', it also regularly appears as the ongoingly 'dying' profession (Bornstein, 2001; Mills, 2002; Shorter, 1998; Stepansky, 2009). It is a field, as Ranjana Khanna has shown, that emerges at the height of European colonialization, and remains haunted by its 'othering' of colonial difference, figured as the primitive, sexual and feminine (Khanna, 2004). In discussing the field of postcolonial studies, she writes:

> Debate concerning field formation and its demise is often accompanied by language of birth, newness, and radical hopefulness in the first instance, and melancholia, disappointment, and outdatedness in the second. (Khanna, 2006, unpaginated)

Outdatedness is certainly something that clings to the field of psychoanalysis too, and, from Khanna's perspective, should be embraced rather than repudiated. One way, then, that psychoanalysis is linked to anachronism is through its theorization of chronological misplacement – the way, as Lacan would have it, that future events control the meaning of events in the past, and, through après coup, give rise to the past itself. But more importantly, psychoanalysis is also an anachronistic and melancholic profession due to an unacknowledged 'othering' constantly at work in its theoretical antecedents, and which we must make visible, but not entirely work through. The 'work of melancholia' (as distinct from the work of mourning) requires a stubborn attachment to a traumatic historical past that is important for both the colonized and the colonizer, as forgetting constitutes a denial of this shared, though unequal history. So it is as a melancholic discipline in both senses that I have outlined above that we should approach the issue of contemporary psychoanalysis in the era of globalization.

Maternal publics

In this chapter I want to perform an analysis of a transitory intervention into the urban landscape that I stumbled across, and that took the form of what I am going to call a 'maternal monument'. The creation of this monument, the word MOTHER carved into a derelict wall, caught my attention because it seemed to pose a series of questions: questions about the current status of the 'private' and 'public'; the temporal frame of late global capitalism; 'regeneration'; the ethics of care; the ongoing question of the status of the maternal in psychic, as well as public life; and the potentials for psychoanalysis to respond to these questions, given that the maternal remains one of the key markers of unacknowledged 'othering' at work in psychoanalysis – indeed, the melancholic object of psychoanalysis, *par excellence*. In other words, this maternal monument seemed to knot together the maternal, psychoanalysis, temporality and the public in a dense and interesting way. My intentions here are to try to loosen this knot a little, so that the relations between these four terms can be understood in their contemporary manifestations.

When I use the term 'the maternal' I mean it in its widest sense – to include motherhood as an embodied and embedded relational and material practice (the very literal daily labour of raising children), through to its figural, symbolic and representational forms. As the meaning of the maternal widens, it comes to signify both as an unanswered theoretical question about the vanishing point of knowledge, and as a structural and generative dimension in human relations, politics and ethics. This very broad arena that the maternal alludes to takes seriously Luce Irigaray's early claim, in *Speculum of the Other Woman* (Irigaray, 1985a), that the excluded and murdered maternal-feminine provides the ground for all signification in a Symbolic that reduces difference to the 'one' of the masculine–feminine binary pair. This binary, as Judith Butler says, institutes a quantitative approach to 'sex' – the one plus one plus one that can only ever add up to one (Butler, 2004b).

In *This Sex which is Not One* (Irigaray, 1985b), Irigaray shows how femininity must be understood as precisely what cannot be captured by number, re-instituting the 'excessive' feminine-maternal of the feminine imaginary. Although I have written elsewhere of the difficulties with running the maternal and feminine together in this way (Baraitser, 2006, 2009a), Irigaray's early work helpfully highlights the maternal as a murdered figure that both psychoanalysis and public culture more generally retains a melancholic attachment to. Irigaray's response to this is to point us towards a feminine genealogical imaginary, one that is premised on our first relations with our (m)Other which links us vertically to other figures and symbols within a female hierarchy that can be transcended, as well as horizontally to lateral relations with both men and women.

This melancholic attachment to the maternal is perhaps best exemplified in the psychoanalytic writings of Julia Kristeva. Early in her work on motherhood, Kristeva (1977) described the maternal as an 'ambivalent principle' in contemporary Western thought, strung out somewhere between biology and meaning, providing the conditions for the movement from one to another without fully signifying in either. Maternity was a placeholder, marking the borders of the social contract, of what was imaginable at the edges of the Symbolic where we are confronted with the limits of language as it gives way to the body, biology and the regeneration of the species. Kristeva argued that the maternal figure 'warrants that *everything is*, and that it is representable' (Kristeva, 1975, p. 302, original emphases), helping to patch over an unassailable gap in our thinking: our difficulties with conceptualizing the threshold of culture, the point at which biology is instilled into 'the very body of a symbolizing subject' (Kristeva, 1975, p. 305). As such, the maternal is also the way we conceive of 'place' – the maternal comes to represent the unthinkable and unnamable place we come from and return to, and yet itself remains a threshold or ill-defined border space. In her more recent writings on motherhood, Kristeva takes up this theme again, speaking of a violent passion in maternal experience that paradoxically allows the mother to sublimate her aggression into love, on the one hand, and into detachment towards her child on the other. She states:

> The mother is at the crossroads of biology and meaning as early on as the pregnancy: *maternal passion de-biologizes* the link to the child, *without becoming completely detached from* the biological, yet already the emotions of attachment and aggression are on the way towards sublimation. (Kristeva, 2005, unpaginated)

It remains the mother's capacity to step aside from the child, to detach, that constitutes her subjectivity. As I have argued elsewhere (Baraitser and Tyler, 2010), this account continues a psychoanalytic tradition of positioning the maternal somewhere between madness and the sublime, between maternal passion and its sublimation, and therefore constitutes a discourse of 'maternal disappearance', of the maternal as threshold and therefore non-place.[2]

And yet what is put into circulation by the maternal monument is not just the return of this theoretically troubling question, but the ways that we have seen a dramatic 'making public' of the maternal and motherhood in recent years that is quite different from previous eras. As I will argue below, the maternal has never been so public, so 'in your face'. One sideways route into the question of the effects of living in late global capitalism might be to ask 'why is the maternal so public now?' and to ask this in relation to a body of thought and practice that figures the maternal as a lost, murdered or disappearing subject, the threshold of meaning and culture.

There is also a methodological issue at work here. My approach to thinking about monolithic, 'masculine' and unwieldy notions like 'globalization', 'capitalism', 'neoliberalism' is deliberately myopic, akin to what I have previously articulated as an 'anecdotal theory' (Baraitser, 2009a) that takes its cue from Jane Gallop's work on the same theme (Gallop, 2002). The use of anecdote as a starting point for theoretical thinking is a way of doing feminist research that refuses to uncouple theory from the singular, the 'personal' or the everyday – that is, from the intricate, mobile, embodied, affective and downright mundane material realities that constitute a life, whilst at the same time putting the materiality of those realities 'on trial' through an engagement with what we call theory. Anecdote is a useful literary trope as it sits at some distance from 'autobiography' without being fully 'fiction'. Anecdotes are also usually funny, a bit silly, told for effect, so they aim to lighten up theory, whilst allowing theory to sober up the analysis of usually overlooked aspects of marginal and marginalized experience (Baraitser, 2009; Gallop, 2002). This deliberate overvaluing of the anecdotal is also echoed in Khanna's approach to historicizing psychoanalysis by 'parochializing' it. The strategy of 'provincializing' a colonial discipline is not just to bring it down to size (as anecdotal theory attempts to force an appreciation of the mundane or ordinary through subjecting small incidents to intense theoretical reflection), but to sharpen the power of psychoanalysis to illuminate postcolonial dilemmas. In this sense thinking about maternal publics aims to interrogate the public through the lens of the mundane and ordinary aspects of mothering in public space, and at the same time there is a hope that this interrogation will in turn tell us something about the maternal, temporality and psychoanalysis itself.

Public mothers

I am proposing that one of the sites that the contradictory processes internal to late global capitalism get played out is across the maternal body. For the mother of neoliberalism, despite being asked to affect her own disappearance, is not merely responsible for detaching from her child, but for actively producing the next generation of flexible workers and consumers. As such, she remains the linchpin of neoliberalism, as many a Marxist feminist pointed out in previous generations in relation to earlier forms of capitalism. From reality TV, film and print media through to Mumsnet, we live in cultures veritably saturated with representations of the maternal, and awash with fierce debates about parenting more generally, and mothering in particular. As Imogen Tyler states:

> young working class mothers are still routinely demonised in political discourse and are stable television comic fodder, older mothers are censured and reviled for perverting 'nature', working mothers are routinely castigated for failing their children, mothers who don't work outside the home are rebuked for failing themselves, their families and the economy. (Tyler, 2009, unpaginated)

And at the same time as these forms of denigration circulate, the idealization of motherhood continues apace (Parker, 2005). The 'pampers' mother of 20 years ago has given way, however, to the glamorized pregnant and post-pregnant celebrity body, as Tyler has so aptly put it:

> The visual backdrop to these terrorising maternal figurations is an unending parade of images of beautiful, young, white, tight pregnant and post-partum celebrity bodies. Indeed, the sexual objectification of the maternal body, a subject matter deeply taboo as recently as the 1990s, is now routine to the point of banality. In short, the maternal has never been so very public, so hyper-visible, but the wall of commentary which surrounds the maternal and the images which represent it, are deeply incoherent. (Tyler, 2009, unpaginated)

This incoherence reveals public cultures that target mothering and mothers in relentlessly intensive ways, rendering motherhood a site of high anxiety and brutal control, and of course played out in predictably uneven ways, so that, as Tracey Jensen has argued, the poorest and most disadvantaged mothers are inevitably the most intensively regulated, as well as held the most responsible for the reproduction of social ills, including the very social disadvantage they find themselves in (Jensen, 2010).

Despite this flooding of the public sphere with these static and oppressive maternal discourses, there are of course very particular and nuanced ways that women take up their roles as reproducers of the next generation of flexible workers and consumers, and inhabit them in complex affective and embodied ways. On the one hand, as Val Gillies (2007) has argued, it is perilously easy to mis-recognize the intricate patterns of working-class parenting, unless we fully situate our investigations in particular social, historical and geographic locations, as mothers with limited resources and power draw on extraordinary levels of resourcefulness and creativity to produce relational webs that help to mitigate against material disadvantage. These forms of working-class maternal labour all too easily remain invisible in dominant maternal discourses that seek to render working-class motherhood as failed and deviant, in need of 'super-nanny transformation' (Jensen, 2010). On the other, as Ruth Quiney has argued, for middle-class professional women, reproductivity in the context of advanced global capitalism becomes 'a curious and urgent mixture of career (with its own regimes of training, information, and on-the-job surveillance) and sacrificial moral vocation' (Quiney, 2007, p. 20). Within the context of an insistent regime of self-surveillance and professional advice that constitutes the discipline of motherhood, she argues, middle-class women with professional work experience prior to becoming mothers experience a *traumatic loss of productivity* that is then covered over and denied through the uptake of this maternal career-vocation that effectively defers lost productivity onto the future citizen who must, in this psychosocial economy, come first. From this view, 'reproductive futurism' (to borrow Lee Edelman's term) might be produced as a defensive covering over of traumatic loss – loss of these women's own productive futures, which give way under the pressure to become carriers of the cultural, national and now global future.

So what emerges from this account is that the maternal is no longer simply strung out across the border of the 'social' and 'psychic' realms, but that she who was once the placeholder of the 'private sphere' has become very *public*, and within the public sphere her visibility is uneven, as maternity, like all regulated practices, is made intelligible according to the production and operation of social norms. To talk of 'maternal publics' is to pose a question about the relationship between the maternal whom psychoanalysis proposes as *the* principle of an edge or threshold between social and psychic life, the guarantor of the Symbolic, and a quite different discourse of motherhood that is now intensely bound up with public life and its regulation.

Judith Butler helpfully works across psychoanalytic and social theory, elucidating the difference between a Lacanian account of the symbolic law and a discourse of 'norms' that may help us see the relationship between the psychosocial mother and this new public mother more clearly. In 'Gender Relations' (Butler, 2004b), Butler states that a norm is 'not the same as a rule and it is not the same as a law' (p. 41). Although one can theoretically separate the norm from the practices in which it is embedded, it is impossible to fully decontexualize its operation. A norm is a form of *social* power that governs and produces the social intelligibility of an action, though it is also not identical with this action itself – it at least *appears* to be indifferent to the actions that it regulates. In this way it resembles a law. However, this indifferent and yet embedded norm is categorically different from the universal cultural law – the set of rules we are meant to follow in our public speech – that is maintained by the Law of the father in Lacan's account of the Symbolic. Butler's argument is that the Lacanian Law enjoys a quasi-timeless quality that, through the iteration 'this is the law', assumes the very force of law that it is said to be exercising. The Law is called upon through this utterance to put an end to the anxieties that circulate about variable and conflicting laws in the social sphere:

> If there is a Law that we cannot displace, but which we seek through imaginary means to displace again and again, then we know in advance that our efforts at change will be put in check, and our struggle against the authoritative account of gender will be thwarted, and we will submit to unassailable authority. (p. 47)

Given the Lacanian Law is the principle of a limit that allows all social laws to operate, Butler's argument is at the level of negotiating how change can occur in relation to that principle (not the social laws themselves), a principle which she sees as produced to deal with anxiety about social laws. Her turn to norms rather than the Law and its laws, is to insist that 'the norm in its necessary temporality is opened to a displacement and subversion from within' (p. 47). It is important to note that her term is 'temporality' rather than variability. It is the temporality of the norm, against the quasi-timelessness of the Law, that is at issue here. Butler argues that without understanding how the Law itself is *produced through the sedimentation of social practices*, the daily social rituals of bodily life that are lived in situated ways *across and through time*, we can have no real notion of change. Just as Butler reminds us of Spivak's insistence that the unitary category 'woman' must fracture in its exposure to public discourse, so I would add that 'the maternal' of psychoanalysis must do the same as we chart the myriad ways that motherhood is lived and experienced in specific geopolitical terrains. Butler's analysis helps us mark a shift from the psychosocial mother (the maternal that guarantees the Symbolic) to a public mother, by moving us from the Law to norms (that is, the conditions of recognition and intelligibility), and in doing so opens up the possibility for reconfigurations of those norms that themselves produce the Symbolic that the maternal is supposed to guarantee.

Maternal monuments

In 'Mothers who Make Things Public' (Baraitser, 2009b) I tried to address the incongruence between the ways that mothers are out of place in the public sphere, despite how they saturate public cultures, through tracing the mundane desire paths that mothers make, particularly in urban landscapes, as they venture forth with their children in tow, beyond the local spaces of home, neighbourhood and community and yet not quite arriving at the public spaces of employment, decision-making or authority; somewhere, that is, in between weak and strong publics (Fraser, 1989). In doing so, I tried to map a maternal 'counter-public', one that hovered in those spaces Marc Augé (1995) describes as non-place (places of solitude in the contemporary West, such as the airport lounge, the area by the cash-point machine, the car park or shopping mall), but perhaps closer to what in French is termed 'terrains vagues' (Wright, 2009), vague terrains in which the relational and duration work of maternal labour that entails an encounter between mothers and children in non-places could be noticed, and in this noticing, called forth into the public domain – publicized, if you will. I was also interested to know what this visible maternal labour in these non-places did to the public itself. What we are tracking here are the contradictory ways that the maternal both disappears (theoretically) and is simultaneously overexposed (in public), which itself is part of the contradictory workings of late global capitalism. My point is that this disappearance and simultaneous overexposure takes place not just in spatial terms (representations of the maternal in the public sphere), but in temporal terms – the maternal, after all, exists in the 'interval' between postponement (her postponed productivity) and an anticipated future that is not hers (that of her child). However, if we notice the ways the maternal occasionally intrudes into what Stephen Wright has called 'the public time', we can begin to see how the maternal deforms, in very minor and transitory ways, the time of late global capitalism.

So, what might it mean to see a blank derelict wall, and desire to carve MOTHER into it? And what kind of scene of address does it create?

I and the children stop, look, check the back of the wall to see if the expected counter-part, 'FUCKER', is lurking behind, and in its absence, I can only think to raise my phone to this maternal monument and capture it. Had it read MOTHER FUCKER, we would have been in familiar terrain, not vague at all, the terrain of the denigration, repudiation and hatred of the maternal that is always on the edge of seeping into speech. But with only MOTHER we are pulled up short in the face of an anomalous appearance, a curiosity, a defacement of a 'public house' but also of the conjunction MOTHER FUCKER itself – severing language as well as 'defacing' the wall. A few years earlier, before having children, I would have walked on past. The cry of MOTHER would have struck me as a little desperate. Of course we all want our mothers! I have read my psychoanalysis! Of course we remain haunted, for the rest of our days, by a lost maternal imago whom we must repudiate if we are to enter into symbolic relations, and yet whose loss continues to fracture our psychic lives. But now, as I stand there with my children, I feel compelled to respond. MOTHER, shouts the sign. 'Yes'? I tentatively reply as I fumble for my phone. The sign calls forth a maternal public – a gathering of anonymous mothers who feel compelled to witness and record this peculiar event.

Should we read this single linguistic term, carved temporarily into a building site, as a sign, however, or as a symbol, a trace, that is, of a material practice that necessarily disappears in the process of memorialization? It is surely a symbol in that the word MOTHER takes the form of a public monument, and remains therefore radically undecidable, its meaning in doubt. But it is also a public monument that takes the form of a sign, a linguistic signifier. And if it is a public monument, especially perhaps one in the form of a sign, what is being marked or memorialized here? What memory and what forgetting is being gestured towards? Memorialization is precisely a public means of forgetting, a strategy of amnesia, a kind of fetishization in which an object is over-invested with meaning allowing us to ward off memories, thoughts and wishes of a much more threatening nature – I will remember this so I can forget that. And what relation does this memory and forgetting have to the parade of 'tight white pregnant bodies' (Tyler, 2001) that pass through London Fields a few metres away, literally crowding out the working-class teenage mums who walked their prams, kids and dogs through the park only a few years previously? When the word MOTHER is arduously carved out in large letters in urban public space, to whom is this address made, and what kind of response is required?

Psychoanalysis has been saying something a little different about mothers lately. The psychoanalyst, writer and painter Bracha L. Ettinger, in particular, has sustained an account of the maternal that places compassion alongside abjection as a primary affect, one that allows psychic access to the other (Ettinger, 2006). Repudiation of the maternal, Ettinger has long argued, is not the only symbolic substrata to psychic life. Through her concept of the matrixial, she reconfigures the archaic m/Other as not 'a Thing becoming object which is then lost' (the Freudian/Lacanian trajectory) but what she names an Encounter-Event that draws on the figure of the mother pregnant with the not-yet other for its form. This Encounter-Event is a borderlink – it occurs across a border between I and non-I which is also a linking process, the establishment of a border that subjectivizes. ' "Lack" ', she writes, 'isn't a sufficient term to process and absorb the traces of the string-like joint subjective instance, and castration isn't the proper mechanism of passage that it requires' (Ettinger, 2010, unpaginated). Instead, Ettinger refers to 'the transjective traces of the incapacity for a total cut from the Other-mother in a certain subjective sphere' (Ettinger, 2010, unpaginated). Alongside the subjective sphere that is conditioned by lack and castration there is a complementary substratum of psychic life that is conditioned by the *incapacity* for a total cut from the mother. No longer in the realm of subjects and objects, with the mother in her traditional place of bringing subjects into existence through her capacity to put herself forward as an object in the psychic life of the child, here Ettinger offers us a subject that is 'transubjective', and an 'object' that is a transject, and this transject leaves its traces as we enter into relations with other 'objects' in later life:

> What we might call the 'positive' experiencing of the maternal-matrixial is usually absorbed by the psyche of the I: its traces are inscribed unremembered, but they have nourished, and they continue to nourish the I all throughout life. (Ettinger, 2010, unpaginated)

So we could reread the address of the monument MOTHER, not so much as an expression of an irrecoverable loss that can only be signalled through the gap between signifier and signified alluded to by the production of the sign MOTHER, but as an invitation to acknowledge she who was never lost, but through a primary connectivity that is generative, is therefore never forgotten, and who has continued to sustain us in positive terms. This account works against the conjunction of the maternal and melancholia by refusing to render even the imaginary pre-Oedipal mother as the primary lost object. The maternal monument would surface as what *sustains* as well as what *remains*, not just in psychic life, but in the very fabric of sociality.

Time without qualities

This idea of the public sphere as something to do with remains, as well, perhaps, as that which sustains, informs a body of work that conceptualizes the public sphere as a site for contesting both collective memory and its erasure. In the context of discussions of post-socialism, for instance, Angela Harutyunyan (2009) writes about the ways the public circulation and representation of both historical memory and oblivion are affected by ideological metanarratives of power. These metanarratives are continually at work, underlining not just their spatial embodiments (such as monuments, symbols or shrines) but also 'the temporal dimensions of the public sphere in the post-Fordist era of capitalism – in a way, the public time' (Harutyunyan, 2009, p. 8). This theme of public time is taken up by Stephen Wright in the same volume (Wright, 2009), who discusses how the term 'the public sphere' prescribes the object it is supposed to describe – that by articulating the public sphere in spatial terms, it erases what is primarily at stake 'when memory and forgetting well up in the present', which is better described as the 'public time'.

If we think through such ideological metanarratives of power that underline public time, rather than public space, we would have to include the time of neoliberal global capitalism – just-in-time manufacturing, flexi-time, continuous working time, working across time-zones, 'time-starvation', the 'accelerated society', 'time banking', time as a commodity that can be lost and saved, bought and sold, doubled and trebled with no additional pay, what some have called the tyranny of real time, or of the continuous present. Against this grain, Wright argues for time 'without qualities' (taking his lead from Robert Musil's *Man without Qualities*) – for public time that carves out 'breathing spots, intervals, transitory breaches in the very core of collective existence, time slots still unfettered by moral or political discipline ... breathing spaces in an increasingly frenetic regime of urgency' (Wright, 2009, p. 129). Like Augé, Wright is describing temporal equivalents to spaces of solitude. His argument is that this regime of urgency is premised on the blurring of the boundary between public and private time, and, in doing so, it contributes to the ongoing privatization of the public sphere. We are heading, he argues, through total penetration of the logic of capital into every aspect of life itself, towards 'total work' – that is, totally qualified time.

Whilst there is no doubt that motherhood is now thoroughly capitalized,[3] there might be a way to think about the scene of address produced by carving MOTHER into a derelict wall as a kind of interruption in totally qualified time – a breathing space that paradoxically re-establishes something once thought of as private within the public time, resists their merger, producing a borderlink, in Ettinger's terms, that reminds us of the intimate and relational, the matrixial indeed, disrupting the continuous present that otherwise can only co-opt maternal labour for the proliferation of profit. MOTHER cries the monument in this reading, neither in order to recuperate the lost object of psychic life, nor as an act of memorialization of the impossibility of adequately representing the maternal in the public time, but as, simply, a bid for time without qualities. Through the arduous carving of MOTHER into a wall to create a temporary monument made through 'wasteful labour', what is made visible is the equally unproductive, tedious, monotonous and, let us say, deliciously unqualified time of the maternal. For what is inscribed by the 'unproductive' labour of the artist as their tools move across the surface of the wall is the fact that in capitalist terms, *motherhood simply takes too long*. It cannot be rushed. It cannot be speeded up. It cannot be made more 'productive'. The reproductive, I am arguing, is curiously resistant to productivity. It can only proceed at the pace of the developing child (the one whose karate suit drags each week through the mud, and whose red boxing glove is irretrievably lost somewhere in the wilds of urban Hackney). We cannot simply choose to 'skip a stage', or move this form of productivity to a cheaper location;[4] indeed motherhood may be best described as a *practice of waiting*. If, as I have argued elsewhere, the maternal subject is a subject of interruption – both subjected to relentless interruptions in her going-on-being, and yet the subject whom interruption enunciates (Baraitser, 2009b) – then here the maternal monument signals an interruption, performing this paradoxical breach of unqualified time into qualified time, through the arduous and 'useless' carving of MOTHER into a wall. The way the maternal intrudes into the public is through her capacity to reinstall, and make visible, unqualified time.

Lee Edelman, in *No Future: Queer Theory and the Death Drive*, describes the organizing principle of current communal relations as 'reproductive futurism', whereby the fantasy that underlies the social and public image of the Child shapes the logic within which the political can come to be thought. It is when reproductive futurism is interrupted with what is deemed 'useless' or 'wasteful' (which is then rendered 'queer') that heterogeneity, in its wonderfully unproductive form, can emerge (Edelman, 2004). 'Queerness names the side of those not "fighting for the children"' (Edelman, 2004, p. 3), and constitutes a refusal to suppress the death drive. Now, I would be the first to admit that I have arrived at a rather queer place – that is, at the pronouncement that the maternal (of all things!) should be articulated as the *nether side of reproductive futurism*, cutting across it, in much the same way as queer, under the banner of *not* fighting for the children. But it is precisely the non-productivity of maternal time – the way that mothering always takes too much time with respect to the other faster flowing streams of 'real' time, the way it continually fails to be shoehorned into career or vocation – that leads to the conclusion that the loss of productivity associated with the maternal (its 'uselessness', its 'wastefulness' in temporal terms) is perhaps due to the ways maternity forces a kind of 'waiting' that everyone knows (like a very public secret) the workings of late capitalism depend upon. In this sense, the maternal queers public time.

But do we want to return to the relation between the maternal and the death drive? Does this not fold us back into the most traditional trope of them all – the linking that psychoanalysis performs between the maternal and death that feminism has worked so assiduously to uncouple? I argued earlier in the chapter that psychoanalysis traditionally fails to recognize maternal subjectivity through positioning the maternal at the border between culture and biology, a place that contributes to her erasure. Irigaray's maternal genealogy goes some way towards restoring a vertical relation between mothers and daughters that is not premised on matricide, and Ettinger extends this by arguing for the matrixial as what remains and sustains both (trans)subjectivity and the capacity for the ethical in both sexes. Perhaps now we can add to this the contribution that the maternal makes in keeping open 'unqualified time', not as a way of overturning the death drive, but as an alternative temporal order to that of either repetition and return, or the barely containable time of eternity. I am referring here to Kristeva's early influential essay 'Women's Time' (Kristeva, 1981) in which she offers a model for thinking about masculine and feminine time. Time as 'project, teleology, linear and prospective unfolding; time as departure, progression, and arrival – in other words, the time of history' is assigned as masculine, and both cyclical time (the time of menstruation, pregnancy, repetition) and monumental time (the time of the reproduction of the species, and the genetic chain) are accessed through the feminine:

> female subjectivity would seem to provide a specific measure that essentially retains repetition and eternity from among the multiple modalities of time known through the history of civilizations. On the one hand, there are cycles, gestation, the eternal recurrence of a biological rhythm which conforms to that of nature and imposes a temporality whose stereotyping may shock, but whose regularity and unison with what is experienced as extrasubjective time, cosmic time, occasion vertiginous visions and unnameable jouissance. On the other hand, and perhaps as a consequence, there is the massive presence of a monumental temporality, without cleavage or escape, which has so little to do with linear time (which passes) that the very word 'temporality' hardly fits. (Kristeva, 1981, p. 16)

What I am proposing is an appreciation of the multiple modalities of maternal time that includes the time of waiting for childhood to unfold – the time, that is, of duration. This aspect of maternal time is distinct from its cyclical or monumental forms (from repetition and eternity). Rather, maternal time retains a Bergsonian sense of time as radical heterogeneity, time as force, as material rather than spatial. Bergson's 'duration' is not so much a temporality 'without cleavage or escape', this kind of timeless time, but more of a means of 'invention, creation of forms, continual elaboration of the absolutely new' (Bergson, 2005, p. 9). The universe *endures*, according to Bergson, because of an 'ascending movement' that 'corresponds to an inner work of ripening or creating'. It is here, perhaps, that psychoanalysis may think the new through the maternal and the maternal may contribute to psychoanalytic theory in ways 'otherwise' than through a figure for containment or an object for repudiation and abjection.

Notes

1. This could be simply understood in classical psychoanalysis as the figure of the unconscious, or as Guattari's schizoanalytic notion of the transversal, for instance.

2. Many feminists have taken issue with Kristeva's apparent endorsement of the non-place of the maternal in psychic and cultural life, realigning maternity and femininity as 'positive' difference, where relationships between women, particularly mothers and daughters, give rise to feminine imaginaries that can act as positive structuring principles, rather than this threshold which is, in effect, the place of disappearance (e.g. Braidotti, 2002; Howie, 2010; Irigaray, 1985; Jacobs, 2007).
3. I am referring to international 'maternal markets' that trade not only in clothes and beauty products, but in fertility treatments, eggs, foetuses, children and, crucially, maternal migrant labour (Baraitser and Tyler, 2010).
4. This is not to deny the reality of transnational domestic care markets, in which mothers from locations in the global South leave children out of economic necessity, in order to take up the care of the children of mothers in the global North. My point, however, is to notice the affective work in making this translocation, and acknowledge the difficulties in uprooting children and families, or in separating mothers from children, that this work entails.

References

Augé, M. (1995). *Non-places: Introduction to an Anthropology of Supermodernity*, trans. J. Howe. London and New York: Verso.

Baraitser, L. (2006) Oi mother keep ye' hair on! Impossible transformations of maternal subjectivity. *Studies in Gender and Sexuality*, 7(3), 217–38.

Baraitser, L. (2009a). *Maternal Encounters: The Ethics of Interruption*. London and New York: Routledge.

Baraitser, L. (2009b). Mothers who make things public. Special Issue: Birth. *Feminist Review*, 93, 8–23.

Baraitser, L. and Tyler, I. (2010). Talking of mothers. *Soundings: A Journal of Politics and Culture*, 44, 117–27.

Bergson, H. (2005). *Creative Evolution*. New York: Barnes and Noble.

Boltanski, L. and Chiapello, E. (2005). *The New Spirit of Capitalism*. London: Verso.

Bornstein, R. (2001). The impending death of psychoanalysis. *Psychoanalytic Psychology*, 19, 580–90.

Braidotti, R. (2002). Becoming woman: Or sexual difference revisited. *Theory, Culture, Society*, 20(3), 43–64.

Braidotti, R. (2004). Critical theory as cartography of g-local powers. *Critical Theory Today: Perspectives and Practices' Conference*, 29 January, Utrecht, The Netherlands.

Braidotti, R. (2006). *Transpositions: On Nomadic Ethics*. Cambridge: Polity Press.

Butler, J. (2004a). *Precarious Life: The Powers of Mourning and Violence*. London and New York: Verso.

Butler, J. (2004b). Gender relations. In *Undoing Gender*. London and New York: Routledge, pp. 40–56.

Edelman, L. (2004). *No Future: Queer Theory and the Death Drive*. Durham, NC: Duke University Press.

Ettinger, B. L. (2006). *The Matrixial Borderspace (Theory out of Bounds)*. Minneapolis: University of Minnesota Press.

Ettinger, B. L. (2010). The 'ready-made mother-monster', m/other re-spect and maternal subjectivity: The production of mother-hate and 'basic fault' by empathy-without-compassion. *Studies in the Maternal*, 2(1). www.mamsie.bbk. ac.uk, accessed March 2011.

Faimberg, H. (2007). A plea for a broader concept of nachträglichkeit. *Psychoanalytic Quarterly*, 76, 1221–40.

Fraser, N. (1989). *Unruly Practices: Power, Discourse and Gender in Contemporary Social Theory*. Minneapolis: University of Minnesota Press.

Gallop, J. (2002). *Anecdotal Theory*. Durham, NC and London: Duke University Press.

Gillies, V. (2007). *Marginalized Mothers: Exploring Working-Class Experiences of Parenting*. London and New York: Routledge.

Guattari, F. (1984). Transversality. In *Molecular Revolution: Psychiatry and Politics*, trans. R. Sheed. Harmondsworth: Penguin Books.

Hardt, M. and Negri, A. (2000). *Empire*. Cambridge, MA: Harvard University Press.

Harutyunyan, A. (2009). Preface. In A. Harutyunyan, K. Hörschelmann and M. Miles (eds), *Public Spheres after Socialism*. Bristol: Intellect Books, pp. 7–9.

Holmes, B. (2008). *Unleashing the Collective Phantoms: Essays in Reverse Imagineering*. New York: Autonomedia.

Howie, G. (2010). Feminist histories: Conflict, coalitions and the maternal order. *Studies in the Maternal*, 2(1). www.mamsie.bbk.ac.uk, accessed March 2011.

Irigaray, L. (1985a). *Speculum of the Other Woman*, trans. C. G. Gill. Ithaca, NY: Cornell University Press.

Irigaray, L. (1985b). *This Sex which is Not One*, trans. C. Porter with C. Burke. Ithaca, NY: Cornell University Press.

Jacobs, A. (2007). *On Matricide*. New York: Columbia University Press.

Jensen, T. (2010). 'What kind of mum are you at the moment?' Supernanny and the psychologising of classed embodiment. *Subjectivity*, 3, 170–92.

Khanna, R. (2004). *Dark Continents: Psychoanalysis and Colonialism*. Durham, NC and London: Duke University Press.

Khanna, R. (2006). Post-palliative: Coloniality's affective dissonance. *Post-colonial text*, 2(1): http://postcolonial.org/index.php/pct/issue/view/9/, accessed 6 November 2011.

Kristeva, J. (1975). *Desire in Language*, trans. T. Gora, A. Jardine and L. S. Roudiez, reprinted in K. Oliver (ed.), *The Portable Kristeva*. New York: Columbia University Press, 1997, pp. 301–7.

Kristeva, J. (1977). Stabat mater. In T. Moi (ed.), *The Kristeva Reader*. Oxford: Blackwell, 1986, pp. 161–86.

Kristeva, J. (1981). Women's time, trans. A. Jardine and H. Blake. *Signs*, 7(1), 13–35.

Kristeva, J. (2005). *Motherhood Today*. www.kristeva.fr/motherhood.html, accessed March 2011.

Mills, J. (2002). Re-examining the psychoanalytic corpse. *Psychoanalytic Psychology*, 19, 552–8.

Parker, R. (2005) *Torn in Two: The Experience of Maternal Ambivalence*, 2nd edn. London: Virago.

Quiney, R. (2007). Confessions of the new capitalist mother: Twenty-first-century writing on motherhood as trauma. *Women: A Cultural Review*, 18, 19–40.

Rolnik, S. (2006). *The Geopolitics of Pimping*. http://transform.eipcp.net/transversal/1106/rolnik/, accessed March 2011.

Sassen, S. (2006). The ideas interview: Saskia Sassen, with John Sutherland, *The Guardian*. www.guardian.co.uk/world/2006/jul/04/globalisation.comment, accessed March 2011.

Shorter, E. (1998). *The History of Psychiatry: From the Era of the Asylum to the Age of Prozac*. New York City: John Wiley & Sons.

Stepansky, P. E. (2009). *Psychoanalysis at the Margins*. New York: Other Press.

Tyler, I. (2001). Skin-tight: Celebrity, pregnancy and subjectivity. In S. Ahmed and J. Stacey (eds), *Thinking Through the Skin*. London and New York: Routledge, pp. 69–83.

Tyler, I. (2009). Why the maternal now? *Studies in the Maternal*, 1(1). www.mamsie.bbk.ac.uk, accessed March 2011.

Virno, P. (2004). *A Grammar of the Multitude*. New York: Semiotext(e).

Wright, S. (2009). Time without qualities: Cracking the regime of urgency. In A. Harutyunyan, K. Hörschelmann and M. Miles (eds), *Public Spheres after Socialism*. Bristol: Intellect Books, pp. 129–32.

12
Psychoanalysis and *Türban*: Self-castrating Objects, or Transformational-Transformative Subject-Objects of Historical Time-Soci(et)al Discourse-Political Imaginary Spheres?

Aydan Gülerce

> I suspect that we have not yet got rid of God, since we still have faith in grammar.
>
> – Nietzsche

> It rests by changing.
>
> – Heraclitus

Wittgensteinian maxims 'meaning is/as use' and 'nothing is hidden' might serve as a couple of general departure and arrival points of this overdetermined essay. Because I basically intend to suggest flexible and responsibly (re)constructive 'uses' of a multitude of psychodynamic knowledge-practices that relate more 'inclusively' to diverse human intelligibilities, lived experiences, social conditions and creative imagination. It is ironic, perhaps, that in both of the arguments, the prominent philosopher of language was particularly critical of psychoanalysis. He referred to the interpretation of dreams and words with fixed meanings (a 'way of speaking') in the former, and unconscious determinism based in mythology (a 'way of seeing') in the latter. Yet, Wittgenstein was (ambivalently) fond of the third aspect of psychoanalysis as a 'way of thinking' (Bouveresse, 1995). That is where, perhaps, I also find its sociopolitically transformative and underutilized potentials. Psychoanalysis went through 'considerable changes' in various directions after both Freud and Wittgenstein. However, its significance as a unique hermeneutic resource towards more egalitarian and *dialogical* knowledge-practices of/for/with contemporary human *life forms* within their particular *glocal* historical contexts do require its further substantial revisions and more intelligible uses.

To state right at the outset: first, I have been (over)reading psychoanalysis (in 'solitude'?) as such a dynamic ('transformational') and critical ('transformative') way of relational thinking and acting about the richness of human imagination within the complexities of real life conditions. I see psychoanalysis, before anything else, as a holistic attitude and a reflective 'way of life'. Thus, some of my own insights from the past 25 years of research and professional experience form the basis of this essay. Second, the avoidance of complexity itself seems just another *sign* of strong *interpellation* of, 'doing politics' within, the so-called Western modernist disciplinarity and its particular soci(et)al order. Otherwise, the usual practices simply do not suffice to 'subvert' psychoanalysis/culture/society for they do not facilitate crucial radical/substantial transformations in 'all' political micro/macro geographies to make the world a better place for 'all', particularly in our age of rapid *glocalization*. Also, in an attempt to fix a singled-out issue in isolation and in a counter-reactive fashion, it seems much too easy to (unwittingly) re/produce other forms of omission/oppression in discourse and society at large, in addition to the ones which were objected to in the first place. Therefore, I here wish to address the interplay between the epistemological-ontological (form-and-content) issues and structural-systemic sociopolitical problems all at once, at all levels of knowledge and praxis at once, from within the 'same' (deep-and-broad) imaginary and dynamic conceptual 'matrix'. Thus, the essay prioritizes a need to 'locate' the problem/meaning/action in the 'invisible' web of connections and the relational void, or silence, admittedly at a cost of in-depth discussions in its limited space.

So, first I sketch an alternative 'framework' at the 'meta'/theoretical level (how, the 'form' of knowledge), rather a *perspectival* perspective, which might serve as a conjoint meeting/potential meaning sphere – as if a common denominator for 'formal transformations', or a pidgin language for 'conceptual translations' – for *transformative trans(sub)disciplinary dialogues* to bring together various disconnected discourses within psychoanalysis as well as various other related fields. Second, at the level of theory (what, the 'content' of knowledge), I point at multiple (re)defining junctures and crucial concepts within its dynamic theory building though being cautious against *casual eclecticism* (Gülerce, 1997). In order to accentuate psychoanalysis' significance as an inspirational source for historical/narrative conceptualizations of human psychosocial development in particular terms of objectivization-subjectivization processes, and to illustrate the point, I give a brief account of *transitional phenomena*. I also expect to draw attention to various dis/continuities in in/direct conversations with current critiques (i.e. feminist, poststructuralist, postmodernist, social constructionist, postcolonialist, postmarxist, ecosystemic philosophical, literary, social, cultural and political arguments which are influenced by psychoanalysis) in the background, by making quick references, or by implications only, which would be familiar to the reader. After this 'detour', I then turn to the *türban*, a type of women's headcovering in Turkey, to short-circuit psychoanalysis, patriarchy, feminism, sexuality, sexuation, post/modernity, alterity, (Western) capitalism, globalization and neoliberalism at once, by a rapid conceptualization and contextualization of its emergence. In so doing, I hope to invite a fresh look at the *transformational-transformative political sphere* that this 'subject-object' of enormous political cathexis offers to theory and *glocal* praxis.

Natural/material reality – soci(et)al/symbolic discourse – political/cultural imagination

Distant reflections on metatheory

Although Freud (1933) disagreed with the idea of psychoanalysis as *Weltanschauung*, his psychoanalysis did have a metapsychology. Freud (1937, p. 326) stated: 'There is nothing for it but summon help from the Witch – the Witch metapsychology. Without metapsychological speculation and theorizing – I had almost said "phantasy" – we shall not get a step further.'

Thus, like Lacan and Ricoeur (despite the former's strong objection to the latter), both of whom read Freud's psychoanalysis as a philosophy, I reread his 'Witch metapsychology' as a comprehensive trans(sub)disciplinary system of ('wishful') thought involving distinct approaches to reality/to distinct realities in the present intermediate context of modernist–postmodernist tensions. Having invited further reflections on our current hegemonic philosophical presumptions of various sorts as to what still has been repressed or missing in the Western(ized) thought and its critique, I have given elsewhere various accounts of my *prospective perspective* as an integrally pluralistic, (post)metaphysical and (post)meta/theoretical orientation that is grounded only *in principle* (e.g. Gülerce, 1997, 2010a, 2010b). There is no need, nor space to repeat here, how I envisage sufficiently inclusive and dialogical ways to relate to and to coordinate multiplexity with critical engagements. Nonetheless, a brief outline of a few interrelated core notions of this *conceptual matrix of (potentially) self-reflective transformative-transformations* which partially draws from a 'revisioned' psychoanalysis might be in order. Its *transformational epistemology* (e.g. Gülerce, 1987, 1992b) is indispensably intertwined with four other philosophical resources that are, in the (artificially split and isolated) terminology of modernist metascience, *critical (psychogenetic-sociogenetic) ontology, ethical attitude, aesthetics of change and political praxis.*

The *natural/material*, the *soci(et)al/symbolic* and the *cultural/imaginary* realms that I (re)described put a particular emphasis on the (re)insertion of the latter which claims more space for psychoanalysis. While these domains are inseparable, they are highly differentiated in terms of their *ontology–epistemology–semantics*, intra-paradigmatic dialectical negotiations between their micro- and macro-poles in their own pace and type of times, and other critically inherent characteristics of their *dialectically communicational* and *time-dependant self-organizing complex systems*. The resemblance to Lacanian knot theory of singularity and his poststructuralist terminology (which is derivative of Freud's 'structuralist' terminology of Id-Ego-Super-ego) of Real-Symbolic-Imaginary calls for a note of differentiation: Lacanian analytic discourse/discourse analysis corresponds only to the symbolic realm and activity in my redefinitions of psychoanalysis' patriarchal 'trinity' (as in Son-Father-God) which are functionally much closer to original (albeit re-formed and reconfigured) Freud. This way, I expect to 'reopen' psychoanalysis for 'intra' (i.e. pre-Oedipal–Oedipal–post-Oedipal: adult, embodiment-identity-self: reflexive subjectivity), and 'extra' (i.e. natural sciences-social sciences-arts and humanities: transformative philosophy) dialogues and renovations. Unlike Lacan and other current literal and narrow readings of psychoanalysis, Freud's subject matter was not human desire and its unconscious manifestations, but its conflicting relationship with a world of culture (Ricoeur, 1965/1970).

Methodology of reflective connectivity

My transformational thinking is concerned not only with connectivity between the individual and the soci(et)al, between the micro and the macro, between the inner and the outer, between the material/biological ecology, the soci(et)al/symbolic discourse and the cultural/political imagination, and so on. It is also interested in 'simultaneous translations-back-translations' between 'socially avoidant' intellectual analysis and transformative praxis, and between Rorty's (1989) modernist *metaphysicians* and postmodernist *ironists* in our confusing r/evolutionary times of intellectual 'transition', or of paradigmatic 'rupture'.

Hence, a critically enabling (deconstructing-reconfiguring-reconstructing) strategy that I employ follows a deductive-inductive-abductive 'methodology'. That is beyond mere *isomorphisms* between the intra/individual and the soci(et)al, and is not *analogical*, is not even only *transferential*, rather, is *transformationally transformative*. Thus, it necessitates, on the one hand, some radically subversive premises, redefinitions and reframings of psychoanalysis 'from within' its metapsychological and theoretical *discourse*, but also from a broader and dialogically reflective philosophical *perspective* 'from without'. On the other, it seeks links for two-way transfers to connect individual-collective psychic imaginations, symbolic discourses and actual relational experiences at various abstract 'structural layers', and 'systemic levels', of conceptual analysis, by zooming-in-and-out micro-macro cosmoses in present forms of knowledge and real conditions.

I introduced the *triopus*[1] as a generic metaphor of (internal/external) connection for *communica(tive ac)tion* in place of the classical notions of 'unit of analysis' and 'unit of intervention'. It is in an ongoing transformation of highly specialized movements of its 'legs', each of which corresponds to/makes up/is made by one of the three realms described which co-constitute each other. It does not have a 'head' of its own to employ 'executive functions' to coordinate its legs as in the 'central processor' of interiorist hegemonic knowledge/practice. Nor does it have an omnipotent 'conductor' exterior to itself other than the choreographies that are *critically intrinsic* to each realm. *Transformational trialectics* of these inseparable realms make up/are made by the human condition (see Figure 12.1). *Triopus is not a universally fixed ensemble, rather it is a contextually contingent prototype for (potentially) self-reflective transformative-transformational coordinations of the three distinct realities.* So, it is necessarily dressed in praxis as a 'singular' *punctuation* of specific historical conditions of possibility at its any given historical time and actual place.

Since (psychoanalytic) knowledge/practice is as yet another *triopus*, I also offered *transformative triangulation* and *reflexive consilience* as other conceptual tools of this dialogical hermeneutic praxis that I propose which is not even *non-dualistic* as in Bhaskar's *critical*

Figure 12.1   Transformational trialectics of the *triopus'* historical/material Real-soci(et)al Symbolic-political Imaginary

epistemology, to begin with, in the sense of negating a 'Cartesian I-centric worldview'. Alternative possibilities for (re)constructive imagination, discourse and collective political action for the subject/person and society/culture are sought in/for our 'new'(/old) world of 'multiplicity'. I basically suggest 'revitalization' of psychoanalysis by rephrasing it as a non-essentializing, non-totalizing, non-linear, non-normative and 'interminable' psychological-societal historical theorizing of *contiguity, similarity, difference* and of *agency*. That is preferred over its reproductions as an elitist method of individual/collective 'therapy' which aimed at 'common unhappiness', an 'impossible' profession, a deconstructive and/or normative developmental theory, an elementalistically analytic discourse of the individual psyche, a grand narrative (of unconscious truth), an overarching blue-print meta/theory and so forth.

Psychoanalytic objects and object(-subject-subject)-relations in the transitional phenomena

Freud's principle of *overdetermination* (*multiplicity, multifinality* and *equifinality*) is useful for the 'revolutionary' historical/developmental theoretical interests of this essay. It also has been valued and appropriated by Althusser, and later by Gramsci, in social theory towards Marxist ends. More relevant to our immediate concern is a discussion on some early traces of 'objectivization-subjectivization' as a rapid illustration of a weaving of our pluralist and polysemic narration. How we theorize human be(com)ings' co-constructive relations with the historical-material physical/biological ('object-ive') reality in psychoanalysis is extremely relevant to many contemporary problematics concerning embodiment, destructiveness, reparation, agency, political resistance, ecological ethics, technology-based culture, computer-mediated communication, commodity fetishism, manic culture of consumerism, machination, schizoculture and so forth. I here focus particularly on the theorizing of the 'in/human object attachment' and the 'transitional phenomena'.

Infants and their caregivers always 'use' just about any object in the potentially *communicative* and *existentially dialogical* context of human interaction, including, for example, gaze, voice, smell, face and other body parts, and objects like pacifiers, blankets, toys, sound, music in the physical surrounding, and nature itself. Nonetheless, cathexis to a particular in/animate object as the infant's 'possession' caught more attention in the early theory. From the *classical* point of view, any attached object was no different from other cathectic *fetish* objects (Sperling, 1963; Wulff, 1946). Freud (1927, p. 154) defined the *fetish* as 'the token of triumph over the threat of castration and a protection against it'. Although the primary function of fetish was to resolve *phallic-Oedipal* conflicts towards sexual identity formation, it was thought to create an obstacle for gaining independence from the mother. Bak (1953) emphasized the role of *separation anxiety* and the weakness of *ego structure* in this attachment, yet maintained that the *fetish* arises as defence in the phallic phase. Greenacre (1953, 1955), as an *ego psychologist*, initially focused on the *body image*, but later (1969) argued that the infant's discovery of separateness and the appearance of the object are synchronic events, for the child brings magical solutions to the anxiety which the awareness of the mother's absence created. He argued that if the separation anxiety eases as *object constancy* develops and that the infant gives up illusory omnipotence, then the object is a 'normal' *transitional object*. Otherwise, the object becomes an essential contributor to the sense of *body self*, and is an 'abnormal' *fetish*.

Winnicott (1953), who first coined the term *transitional object*, posited that the infant gains a mother substitute as it transfers the attachment to the mother('s breast as the primary object) to this new object (as the first 'not-me possession') which usually provides warmth and tactile comfort. The transition meant turning the object gradually from being something subject to 'his/her/its' omnipotent control, to being destroyed or banished, to surviving this destruction and coming into its own existence as a distinct entity. Hence, *me* (subject) is differentiated from *not-me* (object) as *subjective experience* (inside) is differentiated from *objective reality* (outside). Since the discovery of *transitional object* was prior to the subject-object differentiation, and the gender identity formation, sexual difference followed the actualization of the object. Winnicott also claimed that *transitional objects* were gendered as they were usually soft stuff for the girls, and hard toys for the boys. But, perhaps more usefully, he theorized that all cultural experience, including art, science and religion, are products that appear as extensions of this shared vague area of 'creative play'.

On the other side of the Atlantic, Mahler (1972; Mahler et al., 1975) moved further away from *drive theory* and defined the distinct developmental subphases of the process of *separation-individuation*. She posited that *transitional object* helped the infant to hold onto a part of the Mother symbolically, while moving away from her physically in the *rapprochement* subphase. Thus, the transition referred to the move from the infant's symbiotic merger with the Mother to independence. From a *self psychology* perspective, Tolpin (1971) applied Kohut's (1971, p. 50) concept of 'transmuting internalizations' that help the self develop as a *tension regulator*. While the inanimate object represented the caregiver to these theorists, Brody (1980) contended that the infant perceives the transitional object not as part of the mother but as his/her own body. For her the object attachment occurred because of the infant's heightened wish for skin-and-body contact and to experience its own body boundaries.

For Lacan (as a 'French self psychologist'), the separation of the infant from the mother rather seems invariably traumatic, as in Freud. Whilst the *good-enough mother* eases the separation process in Winnicott's formulation, in Lacan it is the *father('s Name)* who enforces the infant–mother separation. For Winnicott, the *transitional object*, on which the infant lavishes both its affection and its destructive cruelty, represents the mother's breast. For Lacan, *le petit objet a* represents that which the child has lost from 'itself' in being separated from the mother and that which the mother seeks to complete herself; namely, the *phallus*. For Winnicott, the object serves a temporary function in guiding the infant into appropriate relationships with real people and objects in his/her surroundings. Whereas for Lacan, the object persists forever in sublimated form, either as the external object of desire or as oneself embodying the other's desire.

For some, it may be conceivable that the (Lacanian) *phallus* is the theoretical equivalent of the (Winnicottian) breast. Although Winnicott himself distinguished a *male element breast* ('active', 'doing') from a *female element breast* ('passive', 'being'), however, this equation would be false. Simply for Lacan's insistence that *objet a* is not what the mother *has*, but that which she *desires* (lacks). The infant perceives that the mother has lost her desire for 'itself' because of something that the infant has lost. Worded differently, in Winnicott, the *lost object* is not what the mother desires and searches for, but what the infant desires and has now been detached from him. Segal (1952) wrote that *symbol formation* occurs as the creative product of pain and work of mourning as the giving up of the real breast is internalized. That is much closer to the formation of the Symbolic in Lacan as they both talk about tragic longing for what is lost.

Let me quickly bring together these seemingly 'competing', yet potentially complementary, formulations. First, this theoretical diversity among the positions does not refer to a contradiction in reality. However, it might appear as inconsistency or discontinuity within the discourse only if viewed from a static, universalist, totalizing, flat, unidirectional, unidimensional, linear and essentialist perspective. Otherwise, all these arguments are (partially) correct in their different and particular knowledge-practice contexts and within (their inherent) limits. Hence, neither do I suggest that 'anything goes' (albeit in close affinity with Feyerabend) at all times in every context, nor solipsism. As is well known, Freud and Lacan were primarily engaged with the issues of 'Oedipal/symbolic' determination from the perspective of the *thing/phallus*, sex(ed) identity, super-ego formation/social order, how *internal fantasy* distorts/shapes *external reality*, social/Other's representation, *Eros/desire* and so forth. Other post-Freudians' focus was more on the 'pre-Oedipal/real' determination, the mother–infant dyad, preverbal ego/self identity formation, how phantasy creates internal reality, the differentiation between internal and external realities, partial self and other, good/bad representations. The developmental/historical period in question corresponds to Freud's *oral-aggressive* and *anal-sadistic*, Lacan's *narcissistic mirror stage*, Kohut's *fragmented archaic self and self-objects* and Mahler's *separation-individuation* phases. The difference in terminology, more crucially perhaps, should reflect that their views of ego-self differ. While *ego psychologists* place the self within the ego as representation (i.e. Anna Freud, Hartmann), for *object-relations* theorists the (Freudian) ego was precursor of the self (i.e. Fairbairn, Guntrip). Kohut (1971, 1977), as an *American self psychologist*, actually adopted Mahler's view that self and ego were separate structures in co-existence. He further argued for self's separate line of development as 'healthy narcissism'. I will not mention further of the differences concerning the primary interest, fixation points, type of patients seen or infants observed, socio-cultural context including intra-institutional and international politics, therapeutic/transference-countertransference issues, and so on, between these 'schools', since I left those topics outside this text. It might be useful to note, however, that many 'cross(sub)disciplinary' analy-ses mix the 'units', 'levels' and 'registers' of analysis, and use various (psycho-analytic/logic-al) concepts interchangeably.

At the final analysis, I draw the following comparative conclu-sions in order to introduce my notion of *transformational-transformative (self)subject-(other)object* (*T-T S-O*) which is a modification and expansion of the *transitional (other)object*:

(1) *T-T S-O is not a consequence, nor has a teleological direction*, unlike *fetish* or *TO*. It is not an *object-cause of desire* in Lacanian terminology either. As in Winnicott, this object has a 'special status' precisely for being ambiguous that is to be accepted, not to be challenged by the 'adults'.

(2) *T-T S-O* is not a (m/other, nor infant/self) substitute. It is neither a *symbol*, nor is *representational*. It has no fixed identity, assigned meaning or pre-given function. Thus, it provides a paradoxical inter-mediate space, which is created by both the infant-subject and the caregiving agents.

(3) *T-T S-O* gains a meaningful function as 'non-identity', reflecting a *relational pattern* (i.e. *exciting*/rewarding or *rejecting*/frustrating), including the void itself (as in Fairbairn), or time interval such as the *pace* (as in 'musical' Freud) and *scheduling* (as in Erikson), which can be 'abduced'.

(4) If it gains, contingently on the context, a fixed meaning and some certainty in function, then the object is already *fetishized by all parties involved in order to (‘hopelessly’) fill a (‘permanent’) gap*. This gap is not real, but imaginary. Just like the object is actual as penis/breast, the lack/absence is mythical as Lacanian phallus. That is how the satisfaction of (‘objectless’) desire is a permanent impos-sibility, regardless of the number of enjoyment/*jouissance* (by losing and refinding the *thing* as in *Fort! Da!*).

(5) This is also to say that the 'potentially' *transformative-transformational object-subject* has already stopped 'transforming/liberating' the material-symbolic-imaginary political sphere, definitely including the caregivers' intersubjective relationship, and is objectivized. Thus the (dead) *fetish object is a consequence of the 'joint communication failure' in the shared sociohistorical system which then invites interpretation as a symptom.*

Further resources and revisions towards transformative politics

Multiplexity and indeterminacy of transformations

An earlier examination of the prevalence of the inanimate object attachment across nations, and in various sub-societal contexts in Turkey, gave no evidence at all that it is a universal phenomenon, or that the object choice was 'gendered' (Gülerce, 1990, 1991a). I, then, employed some of the premises of my *transformational view* of 'development', and proposed a 2X2(X2) grid for conceptual/empirical analysis, to cross-fertilize, so to speak, attachment theory (i.e. Bowlby and Sroufe) and object-relational transitional object theory as the first step (Gülerce, 1991b, 1991c, 1992c). Thus the first two 2s signify the extreme positions of (otherwise 'continuous variable') infants' negotiation styles (i.e. *easy/difficult*), ranging between Mahler's passive 'autistic'/'symbiotic' newborn and Klein's 'pseudo-autonomous'/'actively participant phantasmatic' *object-directed* infant, Winnicott's *unintegrated* infant being somewhere in the middle. While all infants have both *life and death drives* (originally *epistemophilic instinct*, which is not necessarily read as 'biologization') as in Klein, so do the parents/caregivers. Thus, values of the caregiving relational styles (i.e. *responsive/unresponsive*) also show variability *as they are dialogically defined in co-constructive relation to the infants' relational styles.* The dialogical match or mismatch is speculated to correspond to *secure, anxious/resistant, avoidant* and *failed* attachment types.

Intersubjective, dialectical (e.g. infant's life drive vs parent's death drive, or vice versa) and imaginary (e.g. love and hate, oneness and separateness) dialogues through this object within each cluster (which is not exclusively dyadic, and includes other intimate people and the in/animate world around) vary contingently on the third 'continuous variable' that the last 2 of the grid points at: 'Western(ized), modern(ized), individualist, consumerist'/'non-Western(ized), traditional, collectivist, enoughist' (e.g. Campbell, 1987; Etzioni, 1986; Fromm,

1976) sociohistorical-cultural contexts in regards to the occurrence, the meaning and the function of the object from both the infants' and the caregivers' points of view. In brief, all significant possibilities of 'un/known difference' *in principle* are 'installed' as the *initial conditions* of negotiations. I posit further multiplicity in resemblance to Fairbairn's separate developmental lines (which appeared in Kohut for 'self' only). These 'individual differences' of all parties involved in the negotiations might refer to many differences (inside/outside the psy-research), including 'perceptive styles' such as the so-called 'hysterical'/'holistic' vs 'obsessive'/'detailistic' and 'context-dependent' vs 'context-independent' styles, other than the temperamental ('drive') characteristics. Nonetheless, 'structural/functional' differences are expected to be universally distributed positions as they cross-cut all sex and other externally 'identified' identity categories for both the infants and their caregivers. However, irrespective of the personal styles, sociocultural *habitus* (re)produces a certain *grammar, rules to be followed*, including ethnotheories of, and everyday knowledge on, parenting (Gülerce, 1993, 1994a). They prepare the caregivers in a certain way to 'read' the infant's gaze, signs, gestures and the void in their 'relationship' to be channelized 'communicatively' (Gülerce, 1994b).

Theorizing difference and otherness

The dominant belief/ideology at all levels of *folklore, common sense, science* or *religion* (in Gramsci's categorization) of the Western world imposes certain biases and constraints. For instance, not all micro/macro cultures around the world (including the West) are *self-centred* and are 'cathected' on the dichotomic boundaries and *splitting*, such as the self/other, inside/outside, affect/cognition, etc. Some are characterized as 'other-centred', altruistic, 'self-less', 'spiritualist', 'collectivist', 'communal' and so forth (e.g. Gergen et al., 1996). Also, Kleinian pre-Oedipal and 'paranoid/depressive' engagement and the feminist 'political' preoccupation with matricentricity leave out the paternal, just as the Freudian Oedipal patricentricity and Lacanian 'structuralist' phallocentricity leave out the maternal, not to mention the neglect of the sociohistorical reality on the macro scale (Gülerce, 1996). Despite the significance of m/Other as primary caregiver in most contexts, and irrespectful of the actual co-parenting conditions, an 'intimate third' is always present, at least within the conjoint Imaginary/phantasy space of the mother–infant dyad, since the very first moment of historical/psychic negotiations.

I here cannot give a full account of how my *theorizing of difference/otherness* differs from still unchallenged positions within the hegemonic theory, but it should suffice to draw attention to only three interconnected points in relation to these three types of socio-cultural diversity for us to move on: An infant who is born in such an *other-centred* micro/macro cultural context (as a 'whole' personal spirit, albeit not an 'autonomous entity'), let us suppose as a 'rebellious character', would be 'tamed' towards 'obedience', 'loyalty', 'hospitality', 'responsibility' and 'care for others' (which are valued, and define 'intelligence', not 'stupidity' or 'lack of agency' in that milieu). I also posit that not in all cases do infants start negotiations with *splitting* the (single) Other and form self/other part-objects as intrapsychic representations. Rather, simultaneously present (multiple) parental others are differentiated (split?) from one another and introjected differently, based on the relational qualities and patterns of intersubjective interactions. These alone will create different mis/match dynamics for the *S-O* negotiations at different levels than the monolithic, flat and normative psychoanalytic developmental theory suggests.

If *T-T S-O* signals anything, first of all, that would be any affective-cognitive and verbal-non-verbal discrepancy between the 'parental others' within the entire sociohistorical context that creates the paradoxical double bind of that particular *triopus*. Therefore, the 'object' is not only used for transit, as Kristeva (1984) discussed, from the *semiotic chora* to the Lacanian Symbolic. Her discussion is in similar fashion to Davidson's (1992) description of the 'triangulating process' of language acquisition. My argument is also for another function of the object that is developmentally much earlier than that. *T-T S-O* is also used as the private anchor of 'meaning' to truth ('faith'), and serves as a 'litmus test' for basic trust/intentionality/authenticity and desire/love. I am here thinking more in line with dialogical ethics of love/care, responsibility, solidarity, liberation and so on, and stay outside Winnicott's implicit moral tone and conservative family values. *T-T S-O*, on the other hand, is different from both fetish and *TO*, also in the sense that it only calls for attention to the need for dialogically inclusive transformations of the amorphous relational context. Obviously, my pluralist position on *difference* (which is not necessarily a 'binary opposition', or is not only about 'the otherness') has different theoretical concerns, praxis priorities, and different implications for topics such as sexuation, dialogical ethics, the 'decentred and fragmented subject', 'identity politics' and 'neoliberalist market expansion' from those of the other positions which interiorize, essentialize and instrumentalize gender and any other 'identity'

category including religion and ethnicity within their predeterminis-
tically closed ideological discourses of fixed meanings, discussions of
which are beyond this essay.

Linking the intra/individual with the inter/soci(et)al

Unlike Lacanian discourse analysis, and even Kristeva's semiotics, and
just like the *excess* of the Real, I claim that there is still extra in
the (in/visible and un/sayable) Imaginary that is not deduced/abduced
to the Semiotic-Symbolic. Imaginary is an indeterminate, ahistorical
('timeless'), transversal ('placeless') and infinite pool of free-floating
('objectless') meaning potentials which are ontologically different in
kind and 'communicate' in a different mode from the other two
realms (e.g. Gülerce, 1987, 1992b). Neither is the unconscious structured
entirely ('like a language'), nor is it anything which relates to language.
This is similar to the Freudian view that *word-presentations* cannot belong
to the unconscious which strictly is the realm of *thing-presentations*
alone.

On the other hand, Freudian *Eros/Thanatos and Kleinian life drive/death
drive* are also metaphors of basic orientations towards 'oneness' and
'separateness', or *entropy* and *negentropy*. They point at relative and
joint meanings that are made in relation to each other, not to some
intrapsychic reifications, but to interpersonal/dialogical narratives. In
other words, the conflict arises not within the intrapsychic phantasy,
between the two falsely opposed ('personal') drives, but in the conjoint (inter)psychic ('interpersonal') imaginary sphere. Un/conscious
does not belong to the (intra of) the individual person, but to the
intermediate space of the (intra of) interpersonal interaction system.
One *triopus*' Imaginary 'communicate' with other *triopus*' Imaginary
even before the *speaking subject-object* emerges, begins to symbolize
and speak, or is 'subjugated' to the social discourse/language/Symbolic
(of the other). While other dialectical mechanisms are at work within
the Natural/historical-material Real and soci(et)al/discursive Symbolic
realms, it is *projectivication*[2] that is in operation within the polit-
ical/cultural Imaginary of *triopuses* in connection (Gülerce, 1992b,
2010a). (Inter)subjective imagination is a *continuous* 'by-product' of
the process of *projectivication*. Since the Imaginary is in a *transformationally trialectical interaction* at all times with the Symbolic and the
Real of the *triopus*, the (im)possibility of termination of this *oscilla-
tion* between the dialectical poles takes place as a function of *reflexive
consilience* (Gülerce, 2010a). Self-reflectivity always emerges as Freudian

Nachträglichkeit (deferred action, retrospective/retroactive insight) in a next point in time which is negotiated/determined by *trialectics* of different types of times of the three realms (Gülerce, 2010b).

Apparently, (re)productions of mythical-religious-traditional-post/modern authority over human history have been patriarchal and family-centred at all levels of sociocultural discourses and collective imaginary even in most 'avant-garde' forms. Thus, it might be useful to review the intra-/intersubjective family fantasy, discourse and relational dynamics that are repeatedly transferred between various 'levels of orders' and *triopuses* in our patriarchal global society.

The familial structure and the familiar fantasy in psychoanalysis

Totalization and wide dissemination of the Oedipal nuclear-family structure and fantasy of Freudian/Lacanian psychoanalysis are pervasive also 'outside the clinic'. For its high relevance to our discussion, I borrow a particular pattern from inside Slipp's (1984) clinic who developed a typology of 'symbiotic survival patterns' of *projective identification* in *object-relational family therapy*. Imagine, if you will, that the symptomatic daughter of this (let us call the T.s) family had formed an inanimate object attachment in (preverbal/pre-Oedipal) time *t-1*, much prior to her becoming an 'identified patient'. Now, let us listen to what the *speaking object t* gossips about the T. family's psychodynamics (in Slipp's voice, p. 105): Mr T. is an exploitative, demanding and narcissistic man with poor maternal internalization and self-differentiation. He feels entitled to dominate and use others to sustain his self-esteem. Thus he felt rejected whenever his wife refused to submit to his 'coercive measures', or in any way acted as separate. He then turned to, and accepted, the daughter T. on the condition of treating him as the 'constantly nurturing' *good maternal object*. The father's attempt to form a *seductive relationship* with his daughter is compensation for the poor relationship with his wife. Mrs T., on the other hand, 'although having sufficient autonomy to resist the submersion', remained in a 'masochistic, scapegoated position'. The daughter feels 'guilty for defeating the mother', but also justifies 'her own submission to her father's wishes on the basis of her magical control over the father' to prevent his leaving, to preserve her mother's self-esteem and the survival of the marriage/familial relationship.

Because the daughter *incorporated*, *acted out* her father's *good mother object*, and saw herself in the omnipotent role of 'go-between', she is diagnosed as *hysteric*. She could have possibly formed a *borderline condition*, however, for these diagnoses share the same family pattern. In the context of our earlier discussion, if the child (of any sex, in my transgender theorizing) 'opts' for the former, then the *object t* is a *fetish*, in the case of union with the mother, it is a *bodyself-object*, and of acting out mother's phantasy, it is *transitional object*. In the case of 'non-identity' (as 'post-Oedipal self-identity') that speaks a condition, which I call *inbetweenness* (not a compromise of 'both, and', but 'neither, nor'), rather than the *go-between*, then the object is *transformative-transformational object-subject* which potentially has many prospective meanings and transformative functions in/for the context.

Two additional points need to be made perhaps: First, there are many 'other ways of seducing the child, apart from the sexual', including indoctrination that regards the child as a 'possession for a particular goal' and 'violently interrupts the child's growth' (Miller, 1981, p. 75). Second, the 'psychoanalytic nature' of the object and/or the type of 'familial pattern' cannot be determined solely within the *triopus* of the family (as in *the closed and homeostatic nuclear/atomistic unit of survival* of the given typology). It has a transgenerational and historical location within the dynamic web of *triopuses* that plays a role in familial transformations. In brief, discourses like *family secrets* and *family myths* as in 'family trauma' reproduce a particular familial pattern in a particular historical time. Thus they work against the dynamics of what I call *family affect* (Gülerce, 1992a), and they only serve as 'closure' on the family (which actually is an open system), because they singularize and disguise the commonality of that particular family structure and pathologize family as if a self-contained 'unit of survival', just like the biologization, the interiorization and the (a)political psychologization of the autonomous individual in the hegemonic psy-model (Gülerce, 2007a).

On the other hand, Klein's concept of 'group feeling' (which has been further developed by Bion towards different ends) has been functional in the redefinition of democracy to include interpersonal relations. In his historical and contextual analysis of the role of Klein's work in the emergence of modern personal life, Zaretsky (1999) also stressed that she gave an account of 'the potentially democratic character to collective activity'. Together with the rise of industrial capitalism, the workplace was separated from the family where the individual's sense of identity was placed. Thus psychoanalysis developed as a knowledge-practice to 'liberate' the individual from parental phantasies for the project of personal(ident)ity. Since the family has been the primary mediating institution between the society and the individual, new production centres outside the family gave way to new forms of authority. Democratization no longer meant the protection of the individual within the private sphere, as in Freud, but was sought within collective activity, hence in the public sphere (Gülerce, 2005). Conservative masculinist and elementalist mentality that separates the private from the public, and the personal from the political, is questioned by modernist and postmodernist feminists. Notwithstanding, one can 'see' similar familial 'regimes of power' and 'mechanisms of control' in operation at other institutional/organizational levels 'outside the family', cross-sectioning the modern national/international and postmodern local/global divides that normalize/familiarize the same 'pattern of reproduction'. One can also 'hear' how super (Western phallic/capitalist) powers, for instance, patronize and 'enthuse' the Rest in the arena of international politics and neoliberalist glocal economy. What will be more useful, perhaps, is to comprehend not only the conditions of reproduction of the familiar, but also the emergence of resistent novelty.

Beyond the veil, or before our eyes?

A comparison of the 'archic' elements and the determining principles in three major (Judeo-Christian, Indian/Buddhist and Chinese) religious-philosophical traditions reveals that *progress* is a hallmark of Western enlightenment, modernity, scientism and technology. Watson (1993, p. 165) concluded that 'in no cultural tradition have reflexive principles been dominant', but his analysis excluded Islam. The earliest traces of philosophies of *process* or *becoming* and 'pluralism' are found in Buddhism, Taoism and Islamic Sufism. While some of these ideas are also evident in Freud (as in Bergson, Dewey, James, Mead, Whitehead and Pierce), they have been marginalized or 'lost in translation'. On the other hand, the Western end of Said's Orient, the Other, helped with the West's self-definition, its own 'Westernization', by its exoticization, sexualization, feminization, castration, inferiorization, barbarization and so on. Exploring Shahlins' dichotomy of 'the West and the Rest', Hall (1996, p. 221) also stated that the West 'would not be able to recognize and represent itself as the summit of human history' without referencing to the Rest (or to its own 'internal others'). At the end of the day, and unlike the prevailing presumption, neither Western thought (Gülerce, 1997, 2010b) nor psychoanalysis made a clear break from Judeo-Christianity, and are heavily nested in Biblical theology and Neoplatonic mysticism (Kirschner, 1996).

Western (post)modernism/psychoanalysis has 'fully identified' with its patriarchal Judeo-Christian *good parental object* as narcissistic 'saviour'.

There is absolutely no need to lay out some fundamental differences or similarities between the two/many religious discourses. It might be relevant and useful, however, to point at a classic text: In *Beyond the Veil*, Mernissi (1987) offered a fundamentalist Muslim account of female sexuality and women's place in the social order in contrast to the Western view in general, and Al-Ghazali's interpretations in comparison to Freud in particular. For instance, while gender inequality is striking and women are seen as detrimental to the social order in both religious traditions, ironically it was because they are passive in the former and active in the latter. Also, the tension between sexuality and religion is regulated in profoundly different ways in Western and Judeo-Christian social orders. In the former, 'sexuality itself was attacked, degraded as animality and condemned as anti-civilization'. The 'individual was split into two antithetical selves: the spirit and the flesh, the ego and the id. The triumph of civilization implied the triumph of soul over flesh, of ego over id, of the controlled over the uncontrolled, of spirit over sex.' Whereas in the latter, what is attacked was not sexuality, but women as the symbol of disorder, a '*fitna*, the epitome of the uncontrollable, a living representative of the dangers of sexuality and its rampant disruptive potential ... Sexuality *per se* is not danger' (p. 44). Put differently, the subject is not split, but (sexual) women and men are segregated in the public sphere. Because (active, powerful) women easily seduce (passive, weak) men, they are assigned to very specific roles of providing men with pleasure to release sexual tension, and offspring. In a similar vein, while, for Freud, civilization is a war against, and sublimation of, sexual energy, for Al-Ghazali sexual satisfaction is a necessary condition of civilization since 'work' is not the outcome of the frustration of sexual energy, but of a harmoniously lived sexual fulfilment.

Psychoanalysis and the veil

For contemporary Lacanians the 'Islamic veil' is 'a symptom of male phallic castration', a 'non-delivered meaning', as Miller (2000) defined the symptom. Ragland (2008), for instance, follows Riviere's 'strategy of masquerade' via Lacanian 'feminine strategy' that the veil excludes the social Other by making its wearer masquerade as it hides *jouissance*. Unlike 'the masculine strategy' that would hide the lack, the veiled woman accepts the inevitability of the lack of the Oedipal trauma. Thus she argues that the veil is an empty ('pure') signifier that covers over this meaninglessness (the lack), and yet, at the same time, it points at the battle between the sexes. Though for Lacan (who 'knew' about sexual segregation) rather than the signifier itself, the conditions of possibility for its becoming *a non-meaning site* were more 'meaningful'. Notwithstanding, to Lacanians 'the veil represents the woman as not a subject, but an object *a*, the signifier "Woman" represents her for the Other as absent. The veil says the woman has no place in the Symbolic order' (Ragland, 2008, p. 13).

Briefly, therefore, while the masculinist Freudian/phallic Lacanian views of sexuation and fe/male sexuality were already problematic, such an interpretation of the 'Islamic' veil of the twenty-first century 'from outside' as a regressive *fetish object* is not useful for radical politics, nor is it accurate. For the *veil* speaks 'from inside': This interpretation is nothing but a (psychological) sign of a 'cognitive/affective set', if not a (psychoanalytic) obsession that the paternal metaphor of Oedipus/History has created by totalizing (masculine/feminine) Western symbolic and imaginary spheres. It appears as mere projection of the 'phallic hysteric', including (Western/ized) 'feminism which is seduced by' (Gallop, 1982), *identified* with, the paternal 'aggressor', and 'uses' me as a displaced, distant, 'negative', 'male' *fetish object* to maintain its own 'positive' identity, narcissism, a false sense of 'liberated' self. Though there have been other Western voices that defined me as the 'female' object of self-expression, rather than male oppression (e.g. Charles, 2008; Krips, 2008), and some 'non-Western' ones that empathized with the destabilization which Western *progress* imposed upon the Muslim world causes (e.g. Göle, 2003; Mahmood, 2003), I will let you comment on those yourself (if not now, perhaps later).

International politics of the veil

Clearly, the veil is a practice which goes back much earlier than Islam. As it has gradually disappeared in the Judeo-Christian and Western(ized) world with modernity, the veil of the migrant Muslim women creates anxiety against 'regression' among other things. The religious and racial issues are closely intertwined with xenophobia/Islamophobia and 'identity politics'. Thus, on the one hand, the veil is frequently seen as a rejection of integration, resistance to assimilation and modernization, and even terrorism in the West after 9/11. On the other, however, it confronts whatever has been repressed, suppressed or denied in particular terms of modernity, capitalist social order and women's liberation. Western(ized) feminists, in general, view the issue within the discourse of *body politics* as an indication of patriarchal oppression, hence they deny any 'agency' to Muslim women. It is ironic, however, that, as I write these lines today, some of these women, who are (g/locally) denied intelligence, let alone agency, initiate and play active roles in the Jasmine Revolution in Tunisia and in Tahrir Square in Egypt against their autocratic administrators who have been enthused and supported by the West as was known for many years without needing Wikileaks.

To conclude, the issue of the veil brings closely together the discourses of Western Enlightenment, patriarchy, colonialism, imperialism, (multiple/alternative/non-Western) modernities, secularism, nationalism, capitalism, feminism, neoliberalism, politics of sexuality, Islamic ways of life and so on. The 'veil' is used as a blanket term with wide currency for all Islamic women's clothing in the West, but this usage does not only problematically homogenize diverse practices in many different societies with different social orders – such as *chador* in Iran, *hijab* in Britain, *burqa* in Afghanistan and so on – it also covers (up) many conflicts and potentially illuminating dynamics even between the subcommunities if it is not analysed from various (historical, economical, political, psychoanalytical, international, intergenerational, intersubjective, etc.) intermingling macro-micro perspectives in dynamic interaction. For a quick glance at them all in (inter)play in a particular setting, let us now turn to the Turkish context.

Psychic birth of a modern nation-state: Turkey

Postmodern and postcolonial studies on modernity and nationhood have already shown how the Eurocentric definitions of modernity, and of the nation as a homogeneous real entity with a distinct history, territory, culture, language, ethnicity and identity, have been constructed and normalized by Eurocentric historiographies. It was also presumed that the impact of (Weberian) 'Occidental rationalism', which is at the heart of modernity, would help with the 'transition' of the non-Western and traditional (premodern) societies. In fact, the case of Turkey's modernization set an example of Westernization that the two concepts have been used interchangeably in the modernity narratives of other non-Western societies.

An alternative psycho-political narrative of Turkey's modernization/ individuation as a hybrid child of European secular modernity/Western capitalism and the vast multireligious, multiethnic, multilingual Ottoman Empire and Islamic tradition was offered elsewhere (Gülerce, 2007b). There, I also provided an inter/intra-national *object-relational*

Liberalist *(Western Liberalism)*	Islamist *(Religious Conservatism)*
Nationalist *(Orientalist Modernism)*	Kemalist *(Anti-imperialist Secularism)*

Figure 12.2 Split (good/bad and self/other) collective imaginaries and sociopolitical discourses in the Turkish Republican nation's object-relational psychohistorical trajectories

account and described four partial communities, sociopolitical discourses and collective fantasies (good/bad self/other representations, etc.) in reference to such concepts as Anderson's 'imagined communities', Moscovici's 'social representations', Castoriadis' (1987) 'collective phantasy' and some of my own. So, I here offer a summative figure for these collective phantasies and split self/other (internal) discourses (see Figure 12.2).

Their sociohistorical dynamics were also discussed to set the background of the establishment of psychology as a modern discipline (Gülerce, 2006) as well as the curious journey of psychoanalysis in Turkey (Gülerce, 2008). A psychoanalytic (*object-relational*) interpretation of the psychic birth of this modern nation was also provided in order to shed light on the particular issues of modernization/secularization/Westernization/democratization (Gülerce, 2007b). Such a narration also gives one drastically different 'inter/intra-national familial/familiar relations' in the historical context – that is, multiple traumas, also in type, such as *war*, *birth* and *oedipal* – and rich phantasy – that is, multiple 'rapes' of the mother(land) by some 'neighbours' – that the War of 'Independence' was not only fought against those neighbours, but the father (Europe's 'sick/old man') as well, who could not protect the mother's 'body' and religious-nationalist/familial pride, and that both parents 'die' symbolically during, or soon after, the 'delivery'.[3]

The particular psychopolitical context and historical trajectories of this patriarchal familial structural discourse, but unfamiliar phantasy, point at the conjugal commitment of already split parental

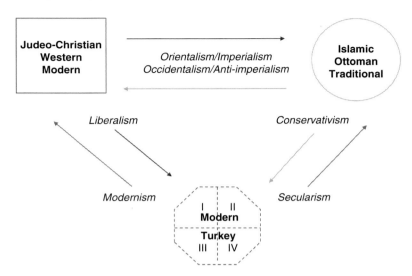

Figure 12.3 Early historical/developmental *projectivications* between the 'parental' (paternal/patronizing and maternal/nurturing) societies and 'infantile' Turkish Republican nation

utopian symbolic discourses and cultural political fantasies: Paternal (European/Judeo-Christian) modernity and maternal (Ottoman) Islam (see Figure 12.3).

On the one hand, the young secular father-state (*devlet baba*) that voluntarily adopted modernity and Westernization as the state policy, and idealized the 'sacred' motherland (*ana-vatan*) as the (*dead*) *public mother*. On the other, Islam, the 'maternal religion' of the great majority, was separated and repressed as the (*vivid*) *private mother*. For after all, in Islam, God is only an abstract notion (he can neither be called Father, nor have a divine Son) to be interpreted by each individual believer alone in private. That is how the projected phantasies differ between the parental discourses (Figure 12.3), and the internal collective discourses (Figure 12.2) are formed as continuous negotiations with those. Both the headscarf (traditional and maternal) and the national flag (modern and paternal) have been *triangulating* for almost a century in-between the 'motherless (paternal) state' and the 'fatherless (maternal) religion' as *T-T S-Os* of different split imaginary communities. They can be fetishized (as male-and-female collective objects) both from inside/outside by *acting out* parental phantasies, and through *overidentification* with the representational discourses.

The *türban*

I have discussed the role of the West (images of which also varied and which is split in time between the USA and the European Union)[4] in the revitalization of political Islam, and hence in the 'comeback' of women's headscarves and the emergence of the *türban* in the late 1980s (Gülerce, 2009b). Therefore, I here contour only small theoretical distinctions with large political implications in global praxis. Actually, for a short cut, let us decode the letter T of the 'T. family' as Turkey, and the *t* of *object t* as three different types of headscarves: *traditional headscarf, tülbent* and *türban*. The first one is very much like the extension of skin/*body-image/self* that does not even represent the symbolic maternal other (traditional Islam/rural way of living), for there is no separation, nor 'separation anxiety'. But a 'security blanket', perhaps, against 'stranger anxiety' of the unfamiliar and/or embarrassment before the gaze of intrusive paternal other (modernized/urbanized elite). The second one, which is used during religious practices, can be considered as a Winnicottian *transitional object*. It might signify a temporary and illusory (re)union with the imaginary (true) maternal other (God) when faced with uncertainty and need for protection and truth. As a matter of fact, Meissner (1987) instrumentalized the *transitional phenomena* towards religious ends. Notwithstanding, a sense of God, too, just as science, ideology or any religious/belief system, including psychoanalytic discourse itself, of course, can function as *fetish* or *transitional object*.

The *türban* emerged as a postmodern phenomenon primarily among the educated young women in large cities. Its appearance is synchronic to domestic migration, urbanization, upward socio-economic mobility and the inter/national politics of Western design of a 'mild Islam' model for the Middle East, to name only a few of the sociohistorical transformations (Gülerce, 2009c). In parallel with its visibility in public space, its political significance and 'use' increased dramatically through the *Kemalist/secularist* and the *political Islamist* discourses as the crack and the tension between them were amplified following its ban at the universities. It is *fetishized* and/or treated as *fetish* by the 'outsiders', including Kemalist/secularist feminists (the *go-between* with paternal identification), as well as the insiders, religious fundamentalists (the *go-between* with maternal identification). To conclude briefly in light of my quantitative-qualitative research with female (open/covered) university students and graduates, for the great majority the *türban* already appears as *an individual-collective and private-public transformative-transformational object-subject that triangulates in-between the two (split) parental other (equally detached and oppressive) discourses.*

The end of imagination?

One can argue that psychoanalytic practice as 'talking cure' has lost its significance since it completed its function, if not its mission, in early industrialized societies. Western 'narcissistic culture' (Lasch, 1978) and its capitalistic social order, which are already saturated with self-indulgence and individualism (Zaretsky, 2004), turned to pharmacology and neurobiology as it turned into a 'schizoculture' (by various means of the term) for the past several decades. However, the so-called collectivistic/communal/undifferentiated/totalitarian Rest has been importing/discovering 'unreflectedly' the Western model of the individual, and is enthused by all its 'freedom' and 'identity rights' discourses that further expand the market for a neoliberal economy, including a war industry, in our times of rapid glocalization. Thus, a politically responsible meta-reflection seems, to me at least, particularly timely. Deconstructive/reconstructive contextualizations of psychoanalysis need to include macro-historical and metaphilosophical reflections through *pluralist perspectival* lenses to further appreciate its blind spots. For instance, whatever might seem 'hidden' in one micro/macro culture of individual/collective discourse might be transparently 'visible' in another one, at another level of analysis. That is not quite the same as the Lacanian maxim, 'the unconscious is the discourse of the Other', though it might be related to the displacement in Freud's social thought.

In this essay, I hope to have drawn attention to several critical issues. Besides an integrally connected pluralist and transdisciplinary (metatheoretical) framework (Gülerce, 2009a), I pointed to *classical*, *ego*, *object-relations*, *self*, *discursive*, *interpersonal*, *relational* and *couple/family/group psychoanalytic* positions (by tackling the 'in/animate object use') as important (re)constructive resources of inspiration from within psychoanalysis itself for the multiplicity, political resistance and reparation needed. Postmodernists differ from modernists (who might be in 'paradigmatic transition') in that theory is practice, the individual is collective, the private is political and so on. Nonetheless, in both positions, intelligible uses of psychoanalysis as sociopolitical analysis demand some methodological and conceptual clarity as well as some educated inferences and cultivated imagination in order to make the necessary connections. For the first standpoint, I see family as a crucial *triopus* that is still unexplored as the agent of social change. It is important to master family psychodynamics in relation to power and to its sociopolitical (vertical-diagonal-horizontal) situatedness in the patriarchal and family-minded global society. Since that is also related to my humble suggestion for the latter, let me end this chapter with a remark which might be read perhaps as provocative (albeit not intended), and offer three parallel interpretations of the 'compulsively repeated' familial/familiar phantasy of psychoanalysis, including its reproductions by the critique:

Both the self-claimed 'son' (also read as Lacan, or 'phallic narcissistic' Western capitalism) and the 'daughter' (also read as Klein, or 'depressed narcissistic' Western feminism) have significant 'use value' for revitalizing current psychoanalytic theorizing including my own (e.g. Gülerce, 2003, 2005). Their partial identifications with the 'father' (also read as Freud, or psychoanalysis as a hybrid son of Western modernity and Judeo-Christianity) need to be comprehended in the context of the father's 'un/met needs' and 'transgenerational myths and desires'. As implicated earlier, a historical political psychoanalytic deconstructive reading of this 'open unit' of the 'extended family' cannot be 'complete', however, without the inclusion of other relatives (e.g. Jung, Adler, Ferenczi, Fairbairn, Horney, Rank, Reich, Fromm) and the siblings (e.g. Anna Freud, Thompson, Winnicott, Sullivan) and their dynamics of rivalry and envy as much as seduction and neglect, even if one stayed within the closed illusory boundaries of this 'cultish and introvert family'. Furthermore, and most crucially, not without the insertion of the omitted 'mother' (true Other) into our transgenerational analysis and without genuine understandings of the macro-historical and imaginary political dynamics and inter/exchanges of this tragicomic Shakespearean family drama. Hence, let us not only 'look for' the 'missing signifier' in the Symbolic or 'seek' the 'missing signified' in the Imaginary, but 'find' the missing (repressed, suppressed, scapegoated, silenced, invisible, submissive, passive, weak, depressed, irrational, masochistic, absent, and so on and so forth) 'woman' in the Real (not a formal one as in Lacan, but historically material), concealed in several places in (f)actual history:

(1) The repressed adult woman who is denied a symmetrical ('power'?) relationship, sexually or otherwise compatible and desireful equal partner that feminist critiques of patriarchy try to empower. That is not the 'immature' female as the infantile daughter in an asymmetrical position, not the devalued 'immoral' woman of seduction, not the idealized 'sacred' mother of the children as they appear in psychoanalysis.

(2) Female sexuality and *jouissance* in general as Freud's 'dark continent'.

(3) The 'dark continent' as in Khanna's (2003) postcolonialist critique.

(4) 'Mother nature' that Western scientism 'manipulates' and tries to exert 'control' over also by patronizing 'soft' knowledge and non-science with its false 'hardness', just like capitalism exploits with its technology (continuously penetrating and/or sucking the earth mother's vital energy sources for its own narcissistic survival).

(5) Mysterious (maternal) Islam; a giant 'dark hole', or a 'gap to mind', in Western history of philosophy and science.

Because there are various good accounts available on all these points, I just want to stress that the 'un/tying' of the *türban*, but also the appreciation of psychoanalysis today, might depend on the success of our collective ability to 'tie them together' (soul mates?) with those contextualized historical and non/discursive threads of premodernity-modernity-late/postmodernity from many meaning centres (including the invisible/the voiceless/the speechless) in 'a fresh' way of knitting of the reflexive philosophical, historical, symbolic and imaginary realities at once. In so doing, I ultimately hope to call for further possible ('dia-logically reflective' and 'mutually liberatory') transformations of both psychoanalytic and sociopolitical traditions if viewed from within a crit-ical perspective as *intermediate transformational-transformative knowledge-practice subject-object spheres* themselves in dialogue with each other and with their many (internal-external) 'others', and to advocate agnostic politics, and ethics of recognition and dialogical inclusion.

Notes

1. My fabulation of the term 'triopus' is a conflation of the words tripus (refer-ring to a kind of tiny unicellular organism with a simple structure which is being used in DNA research) and trio (sophisticated group activity), and is metaphorically intended to signify a three-legged ensemble in (intra–extra) communicative performance. Through such a neologism, that is 'neutral' to '*(not-)all*' biases without privileging *a priori* any known position or realm, I aim at integrally inclusive utility for all types and scales of subjects–objects of knowledge/practice at once, which are situated between many different contexts and levels within the intra-/inter-disciplinary discourses.

2. In my modification of *projective identification, projectivication* refers to the dialectical mechanism of *projection* and *subjectivication* that emphasizes *reci-procity, uncertainty* and *duration* of the communicative process. Imagine two metaphoric boomerangs of *projection*, if you will, which are 'interlocked', and they 'hang in the air' (unlike the single one that returns to its sender

in *projective identification*). It blurs the definitive tone in signification of the 'responsible self' as the source, of the other as the target, self-splitting prior to *projection*, and the 'termination of identity formation' in *projective identification*, by emphasizing the open-endedness and temporality of the ongoing process. Both parties mutually initiate *projection* onto the other from one's own position (i.e. infant/parent, native/colonizer, woman/man, other-centred/self-centred, inferior/superior, holistic/detailistic, etc.) in order to subjectivize/objectivize one's self (subject) and the other (object), without full *identification*, within the insecurities and vagueness of the novel relationship. *Projectivication* is a continuous imaginary process of both doubt (i.e. hate, devaluation) and trust (i.e. love, idealization) of both *self* and *non-self*.

3. The Turkish Republic was established in 1923; the Caliphate was ended in 1924.
4. Turkey became a NATO member in 1952, signed an association agreement with the EEC in 1963 and applied for full EU membership in 1987.

References

Bak, R. C. (1953). Fetishism. *Journal of the American Psychoanalytic Association*, 1, 285–98.
Bouveresse, J. (1995). *Wittgenstein Reads Freud: The Myth of the Unconscious*, trans. C. Cosman. Princeton University Press.
Brody, D. (1980). Transitional objects: Idealization of a phenomenon. *Psychoanalytic Quarterly*, 49, 561–605.
Campbell, C. (1987). *The Romantic Ethic and the Spirit of Modern Consumerism*. Oxford: Blackwell.
Castoriadis, C. (1987). *The Imaginary Institution of Society*. Cambridge, MA: MIT Press.
Charles, M. (2008). The masquerade, the veil, and the phallic mask: Commentary. *Psychoanalysis, Culture & Society*, 13, 24–34.
Davidson, D. (1992/2001). The second person. In *Subjective, Intersubjective, Objective*. Oxford: Clarendon Press, pp. 107–22.
Etzioni, A. (1986). Socio-economics: A proposal for a new interdisciplinary field. *Journal of Social Behavior and Personality*, 1, 475–82.
Freud, S. (1927). *Fetishism*, SE, vol. 21, pp. 1–182.
Freud, S. (1933). *New Introductory Lectures on Psycho-analysis*, SE, vol. 22, pp. 1–182.
Freud, S. (1937). *Analysis Terminable and Interminable*, SE, vol. 23, pp. 216–53.
Fromm, E. (1976). *To Have or to Be*. New York: Harper & Row.
Gallop, J. (1982). *The Daughter's Seductions: Feminism and Psychoanalysis*. London: Macmillan.
Gergen, K., Gülerce, A., Misra, G. and Lock, A. (1996). Psychological science in cultural context. *American Psychologist*, 51(5), 496–8.
Göle, N. (2003). The voluntary adoption of Islamic stigma symbols. *Social Research*, 70, 809–28.
Greenacre, P. (1953). Certain relationships between fetishism and faulty development of body image. *The Psychoanalytic Study of the Child*, 12, 47–72.
Greenacre, P. (1955). Further considerations regarding fetishism. *The Psychoanalytic Study of the Child*, 10, 187–94.

Greenacre, P. (1969). The fetish and the transitional object. *The Psychoanalytic Study of the Child*, 24, 144–64.

Gülerce, A. (1987). Transformational epistemology/ontology: A methodological synthesis of psychoanalysis and family systems thinking. Unpublished doctoral thesis, University of Denver.

Gülerce, A. (1990). Transitional object use in Turkey. *27ᵗʰ National Congress of Psychiatry*. Antalya, Turkey.

Gülerce, A. (1991a). How universal is the use of transitional objects? *International Association for Cross-cultural Psychology Congress*. Debrecen, Hungary.

Gülerce, A. (1991b). Reconsideration of the transitional phenomena. *International Association for Applied Psychology Congress*. Budapest, Hungary.

Gülerce, A. (1991c). Transitional objects: A reconsideration of the phenomenon. In F. R. Rudmin (ed.), *To Have Possessions: A Handbook on Ownership and Property*. New York: Random House.

Gülerce, A. (1992a). *AYDA: Aile Yapısını Değerlendirme Aracı El Kitabı ve Türkiye Normları*. (AYDA: Family Structure Assessment Device: The manual and the Turkish norms). Istanbul: Alphagraphics.

Gülerce, A. (1992b). Transformational epistemology. *First Socio-cultural Studies Conference*. Madrid, Spain.

Gülerce, A. (1992c). Mother–infant attachment and transitional object use. *Vth European Conference on Developmental Psychology*. Seville, Spain.

Gülerce, A. (1993). Parental notions of child development. *International Society for the Social and Behavioral Development Congress*. Recife, Brazil.

Gülerce, A. (1994a). An alternative parent training model. *International Association for Applied Psychology Congress*. Madrid, Spain.

Gülerce, A. (1994b). Parental expectancies, attitudes toward child rearing and children's competence. *International Society for the Social and Behavioral Development Congress*. Amsterdam, The Netherlands.

Gülerce, A. (1996). *Türkiye'de Ailelerin Psikolojik Örüntüleri* (Psychological Patterns of Families in Turkey). Istanbul: Boğaziçi Üniversitesi Yayınları.

Gülerce, A. (1997). Change in the process of change: Coping with indeterminism. In A. Fogel, M. A. Lyra and J. Valsiner (eds), *Process of Change and Indeterminism*. Hillsdale, NJ: Plenum.

Gülerce, A. (2003). Whatever you may say I am, you are another one: A critical reading of Lacan on subjectivity and identity. In N. Stephenson, L. Radtke, R. Torna and H. Stam (eds), *Theoretical Psychology: Critical Contributions*. Concord, ON: Captus.

Gülerce, A. (2005). Anxiety and phantasy as psychopolitical agents of resistance: Converging Klein and Lacan on theorizing individual and society. In A. Gülerce et al. (eds), *Contemporary Theorizing in Psychology: Global Perspectives*. Concord, ON: Captus.

Gülerce, A. (2006). History of psychology in Turkey as a sign of diverse modernization and global psychologization. In A. C. Brock (ed.), *Internationalizing the History of Psychology*. New York University Press, pp. 75–93.

Gülerce, A. (2007a). *Dönüşümsel Aile Kuramı ve Türkiye'de Ailelerin Psikolojik Örüntüleri* (Transformational Family Theory and Psychological Patterns of Families in Turkey). Istanbul: Boğaziçi Universitesi Yayınevi.

Gülerce, A. (2007b). An alternative narrative of modernization/Westernization/democratization/individuation: Agendas for multicultural discourse research. In Shi-xu (ed.), *Discourse as Cultural Struggle*. Hong Kong University Press, pp. 29–46.

Gülerce, A. (2008). On the absence of a presence/the presence of an absence: Psychoanalysis in the Turkish context. *Theory & Psychology*, 18(2), 237–51.

Gülerce, A. (2009a). Transdisciplinarity and transnationalization in theoretical psychology. In T. Teo (ed.), *Varieties of Theoretical Psychology*. Ontario: Captus Press, pp. 113–24.

Gülerce, A. (2009b). Headscarf: A civility test for the civic society. *International Conference of the Association of Moral Education*. Utrecht University.

Gülerce, A. (2009c). Headscarf as private-public individual-collective transitional-transformational object. *International Conference of Theoretical Psychology*. Nanjing Normal University.

Gülerce, A. (2010a). Self-reflective transformational-transformative co-ordinations of the psychological. *New Ideas in Psychology*, 28, 210–18.

Gülerce, A. (2010b). On the (im)possibilities of critically self-reflected transformational-transformative knowledge-practices. *International Symposium on Research Across Boundaries: Advances in Theory-building*. University of Luxembourg.

Hall, S. (1996). When was the postcolonial? Thinking at the limit. In I. Chambers and L. Curti (eds), *The Postcolonial: Common Skies, Divided Horizons*. London: Routledge.

Khanna, R. (2003). *Dark Continents: Postcolonialism and Psychoanalysis*. Durham, NC: Duke University Press.

Kirschner, S. R. (1996) *The Religious and Romantic Origins of Psychoanalysis: Individuation and Integration in Post-Freudian Theory*. Cambridge University Press.

Kohut, H. (1971). *The Analysis of the Self*. New York: International Universities Press.

Kohut, H. (1977). *The Restoration of the Self*. New York: International Universities Press.

Krips, H. (2008). The hijab, the veil, and sexuation. *Psychoanalysis, Culture & Society*, 13, 35–47.

Kristeva, J. (1984). Revolution in poetic language, trans. M. Waller. New York: Columbia University Press.

Lasch, C. (1978). *The Culture of Narcissism: American Life in an Age of Diminishing Expectations*. New York: W. W. Norton.

Mahler, M. S. (1972). On the first three subphases of the separation-individuation process. *International Journal of Psychoanalysis*, 53, 333–8.

Mahler, M. S., Pine, F. and Bergman, A. (1975). *The Psychological Birth of the Human Infant*. New York: Basic Books.

Mahmood, S. (2003). Ethical formation and the politics of individual autonomy in contemporary Egypt. *Social Research*, 70, 837–66.

Meissner, W. W. (1987). *Life and Faith: Psychological Perspectives on Religious Experience*. Washington, DC: Georgetown University Press.

Mernissi, F. (1987). *Beyond the Veil: Male–Female Dynamics in Modern Muslim Society*, rev. edn. Bloomington: Indiana University Press.

Miller, A. (1981). *The Drama of the Gifted Child*, trans. R. Ward. New York: Basic Books.

Miller, J. A. (2000). Paradigms of jouissance, trans. J. Jauregui. *Lacanian Ink*, 17, 8–48.

Ragland, E. (2008). The masquerade, the veil, and the phallic mask. *Psychoanalysis, Culture & Society*, 13, 8–23.

Ricoeur, P. (1965/1970). *Freud and Philosophy: An Essay on Interpretation*, trans. Denis Savage. New Haven: Yale University Press.

Rorty, R. (1989). *Contingency, Irony, and Solidarity*. Cambridge University Press.

Segal, H. (1952). Psychoanalytical approach to aesthetics. *International Journal of Psychoanalysis*, 33, 196–207.

Slipp, S. (1984). *Object Relations: A Dynamic Bridge between Individual and Family Treatment*. New York: Jason Aronson.

Sperling, M. (1963). Fetishism in children. *Psychoanalytic Quarterly*, 32, 374–92.

Tolpin, M. (1971). On the beginnings of a cohesive self: An application of the concept of transmuting internalization to the study of the transitional object and signal anxiety. *The Psychoanalytic Study of the Child*, 26, 316–52.

Watson, W. (1993). *The Architectonics of Meaning: Foundations of the New Pluralism*. University of Chicago Press.

Winnicott, D. W. (1953). Transitional objects and transitional phenomena. *International Journal of Psychoanalysis*, 34, 89–97.

Wulff, M. (1946). Fetishism and object choice in early childhood. *Psychoanalytic Quarterly*, 15, 450–71.

Zaretsky, E. (1999). *Psychoanalysis, Modernity and Personal Life*. London: Alfred J. Knopf.

Zaretsky, E. (2004). *Secrets of the Soul: A Social and Cultural History of Psychoanalysis*. New York: Vintage.

Way Out

Aydan Gülerce

> The way out is via the door.
> Why is it that no one
> uses this method?
>
> – Confucius

This book implicitly/explicitly suggests, through its diverse discussions, that psychoanalysis, if used 'properly', can serve to move out ('forward'?) of the *global double-binding paradox* that was described in the 'Entrance'. By 'proper' use I primarily intend to accentuate its *accurate* (both conceptually and ecologically valid) and *critical* (politically enabling) utilizations. However, to some, they might correspond exactly, or partially, to its 'wild' uses, which are what Freud was cautioning against in his 'Observations on "wild" psycho-analysis' as the *raison d'être* of the IPA. Nonetheless, one could argue that, particularly through some multidisciplinary, multidiscursive, multimodal, multidirectional, multilevel and perspectival lenses that some authors envisage here, the 'proper' in Freud's own sociohistorical and meaning context might be referring precisely to what we might find 'improper' today, exactly one hundred years after Freud's plea. Thus, we can perhaps comfortably conclude that *Re(con)figuring Psychoanalysis: Critical Juxtapositions of the Philosophical, the Sociohistorical and the Political* is against the preservation of human (read Freud's 'perverse') ingenuity and of post-Freudian psychoanalysis in any single predeterminist-static-teleological-closed discourse, or its imprisonment in a religious-masculinist-individualist-capitalist ideological practice, which has been historically and/or contextually de/valued.

We optimistically said that an urge to change has been voiced in Western philosophy and thought 'at last' in the waves of postmodernity towards what its 'old and silenced others' have been well aware, or 'conscious', of for centuries. Needless to mention, perhaps, this is neither being nostalgic about the Romanticist, conservative or religious critiques of Enlightenment and modernity, nor is it suggesting a longing for the grand narratives of modernity. Quite the contrary. Psychoanalysis can no longer remain detached from Western modernity's 'self-confrontations' with its own historical condition, or 'confessions' about its past works/acts, institutions and unreflected globalization, both of which are techniques of morality/salvation/change that itself promoted in secularized culture. Thus, radically transformative use of psychoanalysis to find an 'exit' from the 'no way out' situation of the current global paradox first demands some further transformations on the part of psychoanalysis towards serving as a *reflective transdisciplinary and transcultural metacommunication.* The authors discussed some of the numerous avenues, perils and potentials of psychoanalytic theory as social-political-cultural theory in that direction, which I will not repeat here.

Rather, I will end this 'exhibit' by leaving you with few general remarks. Psychoanalysis pursued different directions as the historical contexts and cultural/political/theoretical concerns changed. For instance, German idealism and conservatism, British empiricism and liberalism, American pragmatism and optimism, French revolutionary radicalism and structuralism, as well pessimistic war conditions, post-war/cold war international relations, unregulated growth of capitalism, globalization, and more, were reflected in different 'phases' and/or 'trajectories' of psychoanalysis. So that first of all, just like Bateson's use of Russell's *logical types* in *double-bind theory*, different meta/theoretical levels in psychoanalysis need to be carefully attended to in its responsible uses. It is equally important to deliberate the underlying principles (such as the dynamic, the economic, the genetic, the descriptive, the topographic, the functional, the structural, the systemic, the symbolic and the semiotic points of view in Freud) in different stages of its theory building, and to differentiate them from one another. It goes without saying that Freud's theories of clinical/therapeutic (counter/transference) analysis, clinical judgement, developmental pathology, psychodiagnostics, subjectivity, self, consciousness, unconscious determinism, crowd psychology, and so forth, deserve distinct attention, let alone other psychoanalysts' work and their diversifying presumptions, fantasies and intentions. Indeed, not only that a concern for object(ivity) to legitimize it as science, a need for determinate unconscious, a focus on self's treatment of external objects towards self-reliance and self-sufficiency, a preoccupation with the autonomous ego and the separate self, or the empty self, an enthusiasm in formal mathematics and language as determinative of human experience, and so on, that contoured most psychoanalysis until this day, have different implications for praxis (broadly understood as beyond individualistic psychotherapy), but also need to be intelligibly reconsidered and revised for our times. Dialogical engagements with other disciplinary discourses, diverse cultural experiences and with its own (good old notion of) dynamic unconscious are expected to creatively inspire psychoanalytic scholars towards radical imagination and social action.

Author Index

Subject Index

abject/abjection, 2, 168, 174, 233, 237
acting out, 70, 256, 262
adaptation, 6
affect, 6, 19, 22, 23, 29, 39, 55, 69, 99,
    104, 142, 150, 159, 160, 164–8,
    171, 175, 180–2, 204, 209, 222,
    228, 233, 252, 256
affective logic, 28, 164, 167, 178–80
Africa(n), 30, 153, 162, 164, 166,
    185–6, 191, 193–4, 196–7, 199,
    201
agency, 7, 22, 30, 200–1, 213, 246–7,
    253, 260
alienation, 5, 32, 55, 133, 149, 188,
    194–6
alterity, 20, 94, 97–8, 106–8, 138, 243
'an Englishman's home is his castle',
    206
anachronism, 224
ANC (African National Congress),
    192–3, 198–200
anecdotal theory, 227, 239
anti-Semitism, 61, 66, 72–5
anti-violence programmes, 208
anxiety, 2, 6, 29, 36–7, 104, 156, 166,
    167–73, 175, 177–8, 205, 207,
    216, 218–19, 229, 230, 247, 259,
    263, 268, 270
Aotearoa, *see* New Zealand/Aotearoa
apartheid/post-apartheid South Africa,
    184, 191–2, 195, 199
après coup, 224
asylum-seekers, 180, 205
autonomy, 3, 25, 36, 39, 55, 88,
    104–5, 203, 255, 269

babaylan/katalonan, 80, 91
bad object, 167, 205, 216
becoming, 151, 157, 226, 229, 233,
    238, 255
'Being in Berlin' group, 68–72, 74
Berlin, 60, 63, 67–73

biculturalism, 203, 210
Bill of Rights (US), 206
bio-power, 26
bipolarity
    of the language, 85, 88–9
    of the unconscious, 88–9
Black, 28, 41, 44, 82, 90, 150, 162,
    164–5, 169, 170, 172–3, 175–7,
    182–3, 186, 191–4, 199, 200
Black Skin, White Masks (Fanon), 28,
    164
Blackness, 165, 175, 183
borderline, 2, 3, 4, 255
breast, 204–5, 213, 214
breastfeeding, 204
Britain/British, 5, 6, 29, 32, 149,
    179–80, 202, 203, 207–8, 212,
    217, 260, 272

capitalism, 196, 198, 200–1, 222–3,
    225, 227–8, 232
Cartesian dualism, 81
cartography, 223
castration, 233
civil protection orders, 208
collective representations, 17
collective unconscious, 16
colonial desire/past/racism, 28, 29,
    169, 170, 179, 180, 212
colonialism, 28, 212, 215, 217, 224,
    227, 239, 260
colonization, 202, 212, 219
    Hispanic, 77
common law, 206, 208
community, 2, 33, 56, 67, 77, 79, 84,
    95, 100–2, 108, 129, 166, 168,
    175, 179, 183, 185, 187, 194–5,
    197, 214, 231
conflict, 214, 215, 216; *see also*
    violence
consumer/consumption, 186–7, 189,
    197

278